Social Networks and the Semantic Web

SEMANTIC WEB AND BEYOND
Computing for Human Experience

Series Editors:

Ramesh Jain
University of California, Irvine
http://ngs.ics.uci.edu/

Amit Sheth
University of Georgia
http://lsdis.cs.uga.edu/~amit

As computing becomes ubiquitous and pervasive, computing is increasingly becoming an extension of human, modifying or enhancing human experience. Today's car reacts to human perception of danger with a series of computers participating in how to handle the vehicle for human command and environmental conditions. Proliferating sensors help with observations, decision making as well as sensory modifications. The emergent semantic web will lead to machine understanding of data and help exploit heterogeneous, multi-source digital media. Emerging applications in situation monitoring and entertainment applications are resulting in development of experiential environments.

SEMANTIC WEB AND BEYOND
Computing for Human Experience
addresses the following goals:

➢ brings together forward looking research and technology that will shape our world more intimately than ever before as computing becomes an extension of human experience;
➢ covers all aspects of computing that is very closely tied to human perception, understanding and experience;
➢ brings together computing that deal with semantics, perception and experience;
➢ serves as the platform for exchange of both practical technologies and far reaching research.

Additional information about this series can be obtained from
http://www.springer.com

Social Networks and the Semantic Web

by

Peter Mika
Yahoo! Research Barcelona
Barcelona, Spain

 Springer

Peter Mika
Yahoo! Research Barcelona
Ocata 1, 1st floor
08003 Barcelona
Spain
pmika@yahoo-inc.com

ISBN-13: 978-0-387-71000-6   e-ISBN-13: 978-0-387-71001-3

Library of Congress Control Number: 2007926707

Social Networks and the Semantic Web by Peter Mika

Printed on acid-free paper.

9 8 7 6 5 4 3 2 1

springer.com

Foreword

Science is like a tree: contrary to popular belief, both trees and science grow at their edges, not at their core. For science, this means that most of the fruitful and exciting developments are not happening at the core of established fields, but are instead happening at the boundaries between such fields.

This has been particularly true for Computer Science. The most interesting database developments don't happen inside the Database community, but rather where databases hit Biology. Similarly, the most interesting developments in Artificial Intelligence in recent years have happened where AI met the Web.

The young field of Semantic Web research has been one of the results of a number of different subfields of Computer Science being exposed to the challenges of the Web: databases, computational linguistics, knowledge representation, knowledge-based systems and service-oriented computing are just some of the subfields that are all making contributions to the Semantic Web vision, namely a Web that consists not only of links between web-pages full of pictures and text, but of a Semantic Web that consists of links between computer-interpretable data. Such a Semantic Web would make it possible to query and reason over integrated data-sets consisting of separate pieces of information that were never intended to be linked together, but that can nevertheless be fruitfully combined and integrated, sometimes even by a third party who neither wrote nor owns any of the original pieces of data (just as is possible with web-pages on the current Web).

The current book on Social Networks and the Semantic Web is a fine example to illustrate that most exciting things in science do indeed happen on the overlapping boundaries of separate fields.

Peter Mika has taken the bold step of investigating the mutual benefit of these two fields in both directions. In one direction, the Web offers a fantastic observatory for scientists interested in social behaviour, since it combines both huge numbers of participants and electronic traceability of social relations between these participants. In the other direction, Semantic Web applications can greatly benefit by knowing in which social context certain pieces of information were generated or used, helping to provide much more socially aware information systems.

Besides investigating this bi-directional fertilisation of the two fields of Social Networking studies and Semantic Web, Peter Mika has done one more double-take, namely by using the Semantic Web community itself as the subject of some of the social networking studies which are themselves aided by the use of Semantic Web technology. Besides being an amusing double-take, this choice actually has some scientific justification, since it enabled Peter and his fellow researchers to evaluate the quality of the networking results they obtained, since the community was well known to themselves.

In this book, Peter certainly shows us that this meeting of Social Networking studies and Semantic Web research is a fruitful one. By deploying Semantic Web techniques, he manages to obtain social networking data-sets which are an order of magnitude larger than what is typical in such studies. And by using Social Networking techniques, he has developed an award winning Semantic Web use-case[1] of a kind that was not envisaged in any of the typical Semantic Web use-case catalogues, which mention search, personalisation, information-integration and service-discovery, but did not until Peter's work mention social network analysis.

Besides for its cross-disciplinary nature, the book is remarkable for another reason: the author is as much a thinker as he is a hacker (and I mean this as a compliment!). The book contains clear conceptual analyses, e.g. in the well-written introductions to both fields in the early chapter, and in quantitative analysis of its findings in the later chapters. But it also contains fine examples of solid software design and engineering, resulting in the systems Flink and openacademia.

Of course, a foreword should not end without a cautionary remark. It's well known that in every exploration of new fertile scientific ground, early progress is quick, and fruits are waiting to be found. This book certainly shows that the overlapping area of Semantic Web research and Social Networking studies is such a fertile area. I can only hope that other researchers will be inspired by this work to enter into this fertile area, and to show us that still other fruits grow in that place.

Frank van Harmelen,
Amsterdam,
April 2007.

---

[1] http://www.flink.org

Preface

Whether we changed the Web or the Web has changed us is difficult to distil even when equipped with the wisdom of hindsight.

While the process is a mystery, the changes are a fact. A recent large scale study on the Internet use of Americans have recorded the dramatic shift in the way that we approach the online world [BHWR06]. If we think of the Web as a giant billboard, the early days were spent with some affixing a note, but most merely passing by, carelessly surfing from one note to the next. These days we don't just 'surf' anymore: the Web has become an extension of our self that allows to reach others. We have learned to use the billboard to actively seek out others and made it a gathering place. Around the board we discuss matters, ask and give advice, share our tastes, experiences and ideas with friends and unknowns and build relationships in the process.

The end result is clear from the survey: we activate our new, online ties even in those situations that we used to solve exclusively with the help of our closest ties, our intimate friends and family. The Net has changed the size and composition of our social networks: in particular, our networks have grown with an array of weak ties – a common name for those familiar faces on our blog rolls, buddy lists, chat groups, fora, mailing lists and the myriad other forums of our interactions.

Needless to say, the billboard had to change to adapt to its new function. What we now call Web 2.0 is a collective name for these evolutionary changes. First, the Web has finally become the read/write Web that its inventor originally intended it to be: the popular 'places' of today are created by and for the people. The wisdom of the crowd is used to build and manage large repositories of knowledge such as Wikipedia, the online encyclopedia. But 'the crowd' is not only editing encyclopedias, but also sharing photos and music, hunting for books and news together, designing software, writing stories and much more.

Technologically, the Web needed to adapt as well. AJAX-based development has significantly improved the user experience while interacting with websites, while RSS feeds and other technologies improved the connectivity between users and the content of the Web. The intense popularity of scripting languages hints at the way programming is democratized and turned into a form of art, rather than engineering. Lastly, the sense of (collective) ownership continues to inspire creative experimentation with web content in the form of mash-ups, web applications that combine user generated content from multiple sources.

In contrast to Web 2.0, the Semantic Web is a more conscious effort on behalf of the World Wide Web Consortium (the standards organization behind the Web) to make the Web friendlier to machines. While at the moment most of the content in the online world is only accessible to human readers, the Semantic Web would provide additional layers of Web architecture for describing content using shared vocabularies called ontologies. This would allow computers to reason with the knowledge expressed in Web resources, e.g. to aggregate relevant information from multiple sources and come to conclusions in a manner that resembles human logic. While an infrastructure for machines, the knowledge that fills the Semantic Web and the rules of reasoning will in fact be provided by humans. In short, there is no semantics without humans and this makes the Semantic Web as much a social system as a technological one.

These developments are of interest to researchers in both the Social and Information Sciences, as well as to practitioners developing social-semantic software for the Web. On the one hand, the emergence of the Social Web opens up never foreseen opportunities for observing social behavior by tracing social interaction on the Web. On the other hand, user generated content and metadata in social software requires a different treatment than other content and metadata. In particular, user generated knowledge comes with additional information about the social context in which it is conceived and this information —in particular, the social networks of users— is also accessible for our machines to reason with. This provides unprecedented opportunities of building socially-aware information systems. For the Semantic Web in particular this means building intelligent applications that are aware of the social embeddedness of semantics.

In this book we provide two major case studies to demonstrate each of these opportunities. The first case study shows the possibilities of tracking a research community over the Web, combining the information obtained from the Web with other data sources (publications, emails). The results are analyzed and correlated with performance measures, trying to predict what kind of social networks help researchers succeed (Chapter 8). Social network mining from the Web plays an important role in this case study for obtaining large scale, dynamic network data beyond the possibilities of survey methods. In turn semantic technology is the key to the representation and aggregation of information from multiple heterogeneous information sources (Chapters 4 and 5).

As the methods we are proposing are more generally applicable than the context of our scientometric study, most of this volume is spent on describing our methods rather than discussing the results. We summarize the possibilities for (re)using electronic data for network analysis in Chapter 3 and evaluate two methods of social network mining from the Web in a separate study described in Chapter 7. We discuss semantic technology for social network data aggregation in Chapters 4 and 5. Lastly, we describe the implementation of our methods in the award-winning Flink system in Chapter 6. In fact these descriptions should not only allow the reader to reproduce our work, but to apply our methods in a wide range of settings. This includes adapting our methods to other social settings and other kinds of information sources, while preserving the advantages of a fully automated analysis process based on electronic data.

Our second study highlights the role of the social context in user-generated classifications of content, in particular in the tagging systems known as folksonomies (Chapter 9). Tagging is widely applied in organizing the content in many Web 2.0 services, including the social bookmarking application del.icio.us and the photo sharing site Flickr. We consider folksonomies as lightweight semantic structures where the semantics of tags emerges over time from the way tags are applied. We study tagging systems using the concepts and methodology of network analysis. We establish that folksonomies are indeed much richer in semantics than it might seem at first and we show the dependence of semantics on the social context of application. These results are particularly relevant for the development of the Semantic Web using bottom-up, collaborative approaches. Putting the available knowledge in a social context also opens the way to more personalized applications such as social search.

As the above descriptions show, both studies are characterized by an interdisciplinary approach where we combine the concepts and methods of Artificial Intelligence with those of Social Network Analysis. However, we will not assume any particularly knowledge of these fields on the part of the reader and provide the necessary introductions to both (Chapters 1 and 2). These introductions should allow access to our work for both social scientists with an interest in electronic data and for information scientists with an interest in social-semantic applications.

Our primary goal is not to teach any of these disciplines in detail but to provide an insight for both Social and Information Scientists into the concepts and methods from outside their respective fields. We show a glimpse of the benefits that this understanding could bring in addressing complex outstanding issues that are inherently interdisciplinary in nature. Our hope is then to inspire further creative experimentation toward a better understanding of both online social interaction and the nature of human knowledge. Such understanding will be indispensable in a world where the border between these once far-flung disciplines is expected to shrink rapidly through more and more socially immersive online environments such as the virtual worlds of Second Life. Only when equipped with the proper understanding will we succeed in designing systems that show true intelligence in both reasoning and social capabilities and are thus able to guide us through an ever more complex online universe.

The Author would like to acknowledge the support of the Vrije Universiteit Research School for Business Information Sciences (VUBIS) in conducting the research contained in this volume.

Contents

Part I

Introduction
to the Semantic Web and Social Networks

1

The Semantic Web

The Semantic Web is the application of advanced knowledge technologies to the Web and distributed systems in general.

But why would the Web need any extension or fixing? We will argue that the reason we do not often raise this question is that we got used to the limitations of accessing the vast information on the Web. We learned not to expect complete or correct answers and not to ask certain questions at all.

In the following, we will demonstrate this effect on the example of some specific queries (Section 1.1). What is common to these questions is that in all cases there is a knowledge gap between the user and the computer: we are asking questions that require a deeper understanding of the content of the Web on the part of our computers or assume the existence of some background knowledge. As our machines are lacking both our knowledge and our skills in interpreting content of all kinds (text, images, video), the computer falls short of our expectations when it comes to answering our queries.

Knowledge technologies from the field of Artificial Intelligence provide the necessary means to fill the knowledge gap. Information that is missing or hard to access for our machines can be made accessible using *ontologies*. As we will see in Section 4.1, ontologies are in part social, part technological solutions. On the one hand, ontologies are formal, which allows a computer to emulate human ways of reasoning with knowledge. On the other hand, ontologies carry a social commitment toward using a set of concepts and relationships in an agreed way.

As Tim Berners-Lee describes in his book on the origin of the Web, the success of the Web hinged on social adoption as much as technological issues [BLFD99]. The Semantic Web adds another layer on the Web architecture that requires agreements to ensure interoperability and thus social adoption of this new technology is also critical for an impact on the global scale of the Web. As the Semantic Web community is also the subject of this thesis we will describe the development of the Semantic Web from its recent beginnings in Section 1.3. We discuss the recent parallel and complementary development of Web technologies known as Web 2.0 in Section 1.4.

We will enter into the details of ontology-based representation, the core of Semantic Web technology in Chapter 4. In Chapter 5 we will show how to use Semantic

Web technology for the management of data sources in the social domain, which we later apply in our case study of the Semantic Web community in Chapter 8.

1.1 Limitations of the current Web

There is a general consent that the Web is one of the greatest inventions of the 20th century. But could it be better?

The reason that we do not often raise this question any more has to do with our unusual ability to adapt to the limitations of our information systems. In the case of the Web this means adaptation to our primary interface to the vast information that constitutes the Web: the search engine. In the following we list four questions that search engines cannot answer at the moment with satisfaction or not at all.

1.1.1 What's wrong with the Web?

The questions below are specific for the sake of example, but they represent very general categories of search tasks. As we will see later they also have in common that in each of these cases semantic technology would drastically improve the computer's ability to give more appropriate answers (Section 1.2).

1. **Who is Frank van Harmelen?**
   To answer such a question using the Web one would go to the search engine and enter the most logical keyword: *harmelen*. The results returned by Google are shown in Figure 1.1. (Note that the results are slightly different depending on whether one enters Google through the main site or a localized version.)
   If this question and answer would be parts of a conversation, the dialogue would sound like this:

   > Q: *Who is Frank van Harmelen?*
   > A: *I don't know but there are over a million documents with the word "harmelen" on them and I found them all really fast (0.31s). Further, you can buy Harmelen at Amazon. Free Delivery on Orders Over 15.*

   Not only the advertizement makes little sense, but from the top ten results only six are related to the Frank van Harmelen we are interested in. Upon closer inspection the problem becomes clear: the word Harmelen means a number of things. It's the name of a number of people, including the (unrelated) Frank van Harmelen and Mark van Harmelen. Six of the hits from the top ten are related to the first person, one to the latter. Harmelen is also a small town in the Netherlands (one hit) and the place for a tragic train accident (one hit).
   The problem is thus that the keyword *harmelen* (but even the term *Frank van Harmelen*) is polysemous. The reason of the variety of the returned results is that designers of search engines know that users are not likely to look at more than the top ten results. Search engines are thus programmed in such a way that the first page shows a diversity of the most relevant links related to the keyword.

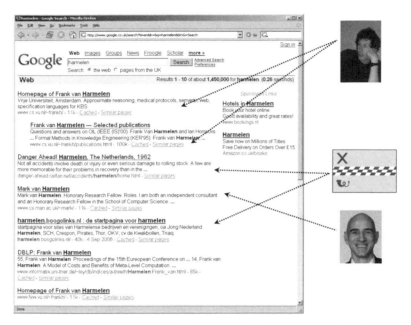

Figure 1.1. Search results for the keyword *harmelen* using Google.

This allows the user to quickly realize the ambiguity of the query and to make it more specific.

Studying the results and improving the query, however, is up to the user. This is a task we take for granted; in fact, most of us who are using search engines on a daily basis would expect this confusion to happen and would immediately start with a more specific query such as *Frank van Harmelen*. While this excludes pages related to the municipality of Harmelen, it is important to note that this would not solve our problem completely. If we browse further in the results we notice that the overwhelming majority of the results are related to prof. Frank van Harmelen of the Vrije Universiteit, but not all of them: there are other people named Frank van Harmelen. (In fact, finding them would be a lot more difficult: all of the high ranking pages are related to prof. Harmelen, who has a much larger representation on the Web due to his work related to Semantic Web technology.) Again, what we experience is an ambiguity of our query that we could solve by adding additional terms such as *Vrije Universiteit* or *research*. This leads to another problem: our request becomes overspecified. First, it is not guaranteed that every mentioning of Frank van Harmelen is accompanied by any or all of these words. Worse yet, pages about Frank van Harmelen may not even mention him by name. None of our queries would return pages about him where he is only mentioned by his first name for example or as *van Harmelen, F.* Not even if for the human reader it would be blatantly obvious that the Frank in question could only be Frank van Harmelen.

2. **Show me photos of Paris**

The most straightforward solution to this search task is typing in "paris photos" in the search bar of our favorite search engine. Most advanced search engines, however, have specific facilities for image search where we can drop the term photo from the query. Some of the results returned by Google Image Search are shown in Figure 1.2.

Figure 1.2. Search results for the keyword *paris* using Google Image Search.

Again, what we immediately notice is that the search engine fails to discriminate two categories of images: those related to the city of Paris and those showing Paris Hilton, the heiress to the Hilton fortune whose popularity on the Web could hardly be disputed.[1]

More striking is the quality of search results in general. While the search engine does a good job with retrieving documents, the results of image searches in general are disappointing. For the keyword *Paris* most of us would expect photos of places in Paris or maps of the city. In reality only about half of the photos on the first page, a quarter of the photos on the second page and a fifth on the third page are directly related to our concept of Paris. The rest are about clouds, people, signs, diagrams etc.

The problem is that associating photos with keywords is a much more difficult task than simply looking for keywords in the texts of documents. Automatic im-

---

[1] Although the most common search term of all times is "britney spears", see http://www.google.com/press/zeitgeist.html

age recognition is currently a largely unsolved research problem, which means that our computers cannot "see" what kind of object is on the photo. Search engines attempt to understand the meaning of the image solely from its context, e.g. based on the name of the file and the text that surrounds the image. Inevitably, this leads to rather poor results.

3. **Find new music that I (might) like**

This query is at an even higher level of difficulty so much so that most of us wouldn't even think of posing it to a search engine. First, from the perspective of automation, music retrieval is just as problematic as image search. As in the previous case, a search engine could avoid the problem of understanding the content of music and look at the filename and the text of the web page for clues about the performer or the genre. We suspect that such search engines do not exist for different reasons: most music on the internet is shared illegally through peer-to-peer systems that are completely out of reach for search engines. Music is also a fast moving good; search engines typically index the Web once a month and therefore too slow for the fast moving world of music releases. (Google News, the news search engine of Google addresses this problem by indexing well-known news sources at a higher frequency than the rest of the Web.)

But the reason we would not attempt to pose this query mostly has to do with formulating the music we like. Most likely we would search for the names of our favorite bands or music styles as a proxy, e.g. *"new release" ("Macy Gray" OR "Robbie Williams")*. This formulation is awkward on the one hand because it forces us to query by example. It will not make it possible to find music that is similar to the music that we like but from different artists. In other words it will not lead us to discover new music.

On the other hand, our musical taste might change in which case this query would need to change its form. A description of our musical taste is something that we might list on our homepage but it is not something that we would like to keep typing in again for accessing different music-related services on the internet. Ideally, we would like the search engine to take this information from our homepage or to grab it —with our permission— from some other service that is aware of our musical taste such as our online music store, internet radio stations we listen to or the music player of our own mp3 device.

4. **Tell me about music players with a capacity of at least 4GB.**

This is a typical e-commerce query: we are looking for a product with certain characteristics.

One of the immediate concerns is that translating this query from natural language to the boolean language of search engines is (almost) impossible. We could try the search *"music player" "4GB"* but it is clear that the search engine will not know that 4GB is the capacity of the music player and we are interested in all players with at least that much memory (not just those that have exactly 4GB). Such a query would return only pages where these terms occur as they are. Problem is that general purpose search engines do not know anything about music players or their properties and how to compare such properties. They are good at searching for specific information (e.g. the model number of an MP3 player), but not in searching for descriptions of items.

An even bigger problem is the one our machines face when trying to collect and aggregate product information from the Web. Again, a possibility would be to extract this information from the content of web pages. The information extraction methods used for this purpose have a very difficult task and it is easy to see why if we consider how a typical product description page looks like to the eyes of the computer. Even if an algorithm can determine that the page describes a music player, information about the product is very difficult to spot. We could teach the computer a heuristic that the price is the number that appears directly after the word "price". However, elements that appear close to each other on the page may not be close in the HTML source where text and styling instructions are mixed together. If we make the rules specific to a certain page our algorithm will not be able to locate the price on other pages or worse, extract the price of something else. (Price as a number is still among the easiest information to locate.)

Further, what one vendor calls "capacity" and another may call "memory". In order to compare music players from different shops we need to determine that these two properties are actually the same and we can directly compare their values.

In practice, information extraction is so unreliable that it is hardly used for product search. It appears in settings such as searching for publications on the Web. Google Scholar and CiteSeer are two of the most well-known examples. They suffer from the typical weaknesses of information extraction, e.g. when searching *York Sure*, the name of a Semantic Web researcher, Scholar returns also publications that are published in New York, but have otherwise nothing to do with the researcher in question. The cost of such errors is very low, however: most of us just ignore the incorrect results.

In the case of e-commerce search engines the cost of such mistakes is prohibitive. Comparison shopping sites as such Google's Froogle or Kelkoo either rely on data provided directly by shop owners or improve accuracy by implementing specific rules of extraction for each website and for each type of product. In the first case, the search is limited to the stores known by the system. On the other hand, the second method is limited by the human effort required for maintaining product categories as well as locating websites and implementing methods of information extraction. As a result, these comparison sites feature only a selected number of vendors, product types and attributes.

1.1.2 Diagnosis: A lack of knowledge

The questions above are arbitrary in their specificity but they illustrate a general problem in accessing the vast amounts of information on the Web. Namely, in all five cases we deal with a *knowledge gap*: what the computer understands and able to work with is much more limited than the knowledge of the user. The handicap of the computer is mostly due to technological difficulties in getting our computers to understand natural language or to "see" the content of images and other multimedia. Even if the information is there, and is blatantly obvious to a human reader, the computer may not be able to see anything else of it other than a string of characters. In that case it can still compare to the keywords provided by the user but without any understanding of what those keywords would mean.

This problem affects all of the above queries to some extent. A human can quickly skim the returned snippets (showing the context in which the keyword occurs) and realize that the different references to the word Harmelen do not all refer to persons and even the persons named Harmelen cannot all be the same. In the second query, it is also blatantly obvious for the human observer that not all pictures are of cities. However, even telling cities and celebrities apart is a difficult task when it comes to image recognition.

In most cases, however, the knowledge gap is due to the lack of some kind of *background knowledge* that only the human possesses. The background knowledge is often completely missing from the context of the Web page and thus our computers do not even stand a fair chance by working on the basis of the web page alone. In the case of the second query, an important piece of knowledge that the computer doesn't possess is the common knowledge that there is a city named Paris and there is a famous person named Paris Hilton (who is also different from the Hilton in Paris).

Answering the third query requires the kind of extensive background knowledge about musical styles, genres etc. that shop assistants and experts in music possess. This kind of knowledge is well beyond the information that is in the database of a typical music store. The third case is also interesting because there is also lacking background knowledge about the user. There has to be a way of providing this knowledge to the search engine in a way that it understands it.

The fourth query is noteworthy because it highlights the problem of aggregating information. The factual knowledge about particular products can be more or less extracted from the content of web pages, but if not, shop owners could be asked to provide it. It is unrealistic to expect, however, that all shops on the Web would agree to one unified product catalog (a listing of product types, properties, models etc) and provide information according to that schema. But if each shop provides information using its own classification we need additional knowledge in order to merge data from different catalogs. For example, we need to know that "mp3 players" and "mp3 capable mobile phones" both fit the category of digital music players, that "capacity" and "memory" are the same things and that 500 dollars is the equivalent of (about) 400 euros.

1.2 The semantic solution

The idea of the Semantic Web is to apply advanced knowledge technologies in order to fill the knowledge gap between human and machine. This means providing knowledge in forms that computers can readily process and reason with. This knowledge can either be information that is already described in the content of the Web pages but difficult to extract or additional background knowledge that can help to answer queries in some way. In the following we describe the improvement one could expect in case of our four queries based on examples of existing tools and applications that have been implemented for specific domains or organizational settings.

In the case of the first query the situation can be greatly improved by providing personal information in a semantic format. Although we will only cover the technological details in Chapter 4 and 5, an existing solution is to attach a semantic profile to personal web pages that describe the same information that appears in the text of the web page but in a machine processable format. The Friend-of-a-Friend (FOAF) project provides a widely accepted vocabulary for such descriptions. FOAF profiles listing attributes such as the name, address, interests of the user can be linked to the web page or even encoded in the text of the page. As we will see several profiles may also exist on the Web describing the same person. As all profiles are readable and comparable by machines, all knowledge about a person can be combined automatically.

For example, Frank van Harmelen has such a profile attached to his homepage on the Web. This allows a search engine to determine that the page in question is about a person with specific attributes. (Thus pages about persons and villages would not be confused.) Assuming that all other van Harmelens on the Web would provide similar information, the confusion among them could also be easily avoided. In particular, the search engine could alert us to the ambiguity of our question and ask for some extra information about the person we are looking for. The discussion with the search engine would be very different:

Q: *Who is Frank van Harmelen?*
A: *Your question is ambiguous: there is a great deal of information about a Frank van Harmelen who is a professor at the Vrije Universiteit. However, there are other persons named Harmelen and also a village in the municipality of Woerden. Which one did you mean?*

Note that from the perspective of search engines semantic technology is not only relevant for improving query results. A better understanding of the user profile, the search query and the content of the web pages makes it possible to more accurately select and customize the advertisements appearing alongside the queries. [2]

Similarly, the solution in the second case is to attach metadata to the images in question. For example, the online photo sharing site Flickr allows to annotate images using geographic coordinates. After uploading some photos users can add keywords to describe their images (e.g. "Paris, Eiffel-tower") and drag and drop the images on a geographic map to indicate the location where the photo was taken. In the background the system computes the latitude and longitude of the place where the user pointed and attaches this information to the image. Searching of photos of Paris

---

[2] Relevance is not the only criteria, though: the two main search engines, Google and Yahoo! take into account both the relevance of an ad and the outcome of the bidding for keywords when selecting and ordering the advertisements that are shown along search results. In other words, a less relevant ad may be placed above more relevant ads if the advertiser was willing to pay a high price.

becomes a breeze: we can look up Paris on the map and see what other photos have been put there by other users. Although in this case the system is not even aware that Paris is a city, a minimal additional information about photos (the geo-coordinates) enables a kind of visualization that makes the searching task much easier. And if over time the system notes that most images with the keyword "Paris" fall in a specific geographic area on the map, it can even conclude that Paris is a place on the map (see Figure 1.3).

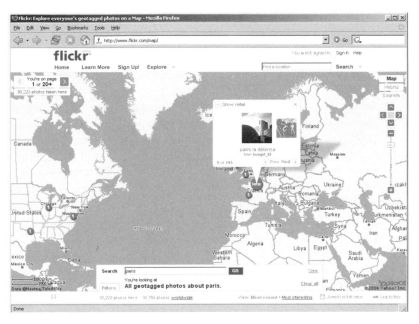

Figure 1.3. Searching for the keyword Paris using the geographic search of Flickr.

The same technique of annotating images with metadata is used in the Multi-MediaN research project to create a joint catalogue of artworks housed in different collections.[3] The knowledge provided extends to the content of images as well as other attributes such as the creator, style or material of the work. When these annotations are combined with existing background knowledge about the artists, art periods, styles etc., it becomes possible to aggregate information and to search all collections simultaneously while avoiding the pitfalls of keyword based search. For example, when searching for "Art Nouveau" the system not only returns images that are explicitly annotated as Art Nouveau in style, but also other works by painters who have been known to belong to the Art Nouveau movement. Further, it is aware that the term "palingstijl" is the Dutch equivalent of Art Nouveau and therefore works annotated with this term are also relevant to the query.

---

[3] http://e-culture.multimedian.nl/demo/search

The background knowledge required for recommending music is already at work behind the online radio called Pandora[4]. Pandora is based on the Music Genome Project, an attempt to create a vocabulary to describe characteristics of music from melody, harmony and rhythm, to instrumentation, orchestration, arrangement, lyrics, and the rich world of singing and vocal harmony. Over several years thousands of songs have been annotated by experts in music theory. This knowledge is now used by the system to recommend unknown music to users based on their existing favorites. The Foafing the Music project combines this idea with the retrieval of information about music releases and upcoming events related to our favorite artists.[5] A particularly interesting feature of this system is that it can reuse information about our musical tastes from other sources such as a personal profile on one's homepage or an online playlist of our recently played music. In order to track the fast-paced world of music, the system tracks newsfeeds updated by data providers on a daily basis.

Our fourth problem, the aggregation of product catalogs can also be directly addressed using semantic technology. As we have seen the problem in this case is the difficulty of maintaining a unified catalog in a way that does not require an exclusive commitment from the providers of product information. (In practice, information providers often have their own product databases with a proprietary classification system.) Further, we would like to keep the catalogue open to data providers adding new, emerging categories of products and their descriptions (e.g. *mp3 players* as a subclass of music players with specific attributes such as capacity, size, color etc.)

The Semantic Web solution is to create a minimal, shared, top-level schema in one of the ontology languages defined for the Semantic Web. The advantage compared to publishing a monolithic product catalogue in XML (such as RosettaNet[6]) is that semantic languages have been designed for extensibility in the distributed environment of the Web. This means that new characteristics and entire subcategories of products can be independently introduced by vendors. These vendor-specific extensions will be understood to the extent that they are described in terms of the existing elements of the shared schema. Further, mappings between entire schemas or parts of a schema can also be expressed using Semantic Web languages. For example, mappings between the product classifications of independent vendors allows the products classified by one classification to be retrieved according to an alternative classification. The mappings themselves can be developed and maintained by any of the two parties or even by an independent, third party.

This is the solution that Vodafone applied when putting together its Vodafone Live! portal, which is a catalog of content provided by partners of Vodafone [App05]. The approach was to capture the commonalities of mobile content in a single shared top-level schema that all partners follow, including the major categories of mobile content such as Games, Chat, Erotica etc. The advantage of the semantic solution is that partner's of the company have the flexibility to extend the general schema.

---

[4] http://www.pandora.com
[5] http://foafing-the-music.iua.upf.edu/
[6] http://www.rosettanet.org

Further, in case another operator (say, Vodafone's rival T-Mobile) would ask them to classify content according to a different schema, all that would be required is a mapping between the classifications used by the two companies. Using semantic technology page views per download decreased 50% at Vodafone while ringtone sales went up 20% in just two months.

In summary, in all the scenarios we have sketched above the the addition of knowledge in machine-processable languages has the potential to improve the access to information by clarifying the meaning of the content. Besides information retrieval, understanding the meaning of information is also an important step towards aggregating information from multiple heterogeneous sources (i.e. diverse sources of information each with their own schema.) Aggregation is in turn necessary for performing queries, analysis and reasoning across several information sources as if they would form a single uniform database.

Instead of going into further technical details, in the following we will look at the research and adoption of the Semantic Web from its recent beginnings. (We will return to technological issues in subsequent Chapters.) The history of the Semantic Web is interesting from a technological as well as a social perspective. First, the benefits of adopting semantic technology on a Web scale are dependent on a critical mass of users adopting the standards behind the Semantic Web. We will also return to the Semantic Web community as the object of our study in Chapter 8.

1.3 Development of the Semantic Web

1.3.1 Research, development and standardization

The vision of extending the current human-focused Web with machine processable descriptions of web content has been first formulated in 1996 by Tim Berners-Lee, the original inventor of the Web [BLFD99]. The Semantic Web has been actively promoted since by the World Wide Web Consortium (also led by Berners-Lee), the organization that is chiefly responsible for setting technical standards on the Web. As a result of this initial impetus and the expected benefits of a more intelligent Web, the Semantic Web has quickly attracted significant interest from funding agencies on both sides of the Atlantic, reshaping much of the AI research agenda in a relatively short period of time[7]. In particular, the field of Knowledge Representation and Reasoning took center stage, but outcomes from other fields of AI have also been put into to use to support the move towards the Semantic Web: for example, Natural Language Processing and Information Retrieval have been applied to acquiring knowledge from the World Wide Web.

---

[7] Examples of some of the more significant projects in the area include the US DAML program funded by DARPA and a number of large projects funded under the IST initiative of the EU Fifth Framework Programme (1998-2002) and the Strategic Objective 2.4.7 of the EU Sixth Framework Programme (2002-2006).

As the Semantic Web is a relatively new, dynamic field of investigation, it is difficult to precisely delineate the boundaries of this network.[8] For our research on the Semantic Web community we have defined the community by including those researchers who have submitted publications or held an organizing role at any of the past International Semantic Web Conferences (ISWC02, ISWC03, ISWC04) or the Semantic Web Working Symposium of 2001 (SWWS01), the most significant conference series devoted entirely to the Semantic Web.[9] We note that another commonly encountered way of defining the boundary of a scientific community is to look at the authorship of representative journals (see e.g. [HHvdB03]). However, the Semantic Web hasn't had a dedicated journal until 2004[10] and still most Semantic Web related publications appear in AI journals not entirely devoted to the Semantic Web.

The complete list of individuals in this community consists of 608 researchers mostly from academia (79%) and to a lesser degree from industry (21%). Geographically, the community covers much of the United States, Europe, with some activity in Japan and Australia (see Figure 1.4). As Figure 1.5 shows, the participation rate at the individual ISWC events have quickly reached the level typical of large, established conferences and remained at that level even for the last year of data (2004), when the conference was organized in Hiroshima, Japan. The number of publications written by the members of the community that contain the keyword "Semantic Web" has been sharply rising since the beginning.

The core technology of the Semantic Web, logic-based languages for knowledge representation and reasoning have been developed in the research field of Artificial Intelligence. As the potential for connecting information sources on a Web-scale emerged, the languages that have been used in the past to describe the content of the knowledge bases of stand-alone expert systems have been adapted to the open, distributed environment of the Web. Since the exchange of knowledge in standard languages is crucial for the interoperability of tools and services on the Semantic Web, these languages have been standardized by the W3C as a layered set of languages (see Chapter 4.

Tools for creating, storing and reasoning with ontologies have been primarily developed by university-affiliated technology startups (for example, Aduna[11], OntoText[12] and Ontoprise[13]) and at research labs of large corporations (see for example

---

[8] In fact, it is difficult to determine at what point does a new research concept become a separate field of investigation. With regard to Semantic Web, it is clear that many of the scientists involved have developed ties before their work on the Semantic Web, just as some of the research published in the Semantic Web area has been worked out before in different settings.

[9] Besides the international conferences, there have European Semantic Web Conferences (ESWC) held since 2004 and the first Asian Semantic Web Conference (ASWC) will be held in 2006.

[10] Journal of Web Semantics, Elsevier

[11] http://www.aduna-software.com

[12] http://www.ontotext.com

[13] http://www.ontoprise.com

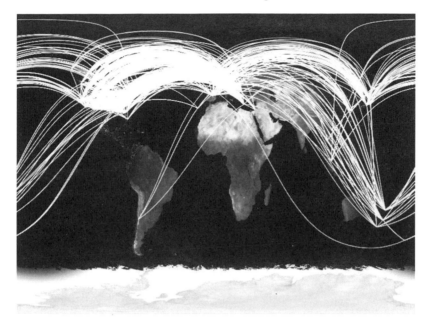

Figure 1.4. Semantic Web researchers and their network visualized according to geography.

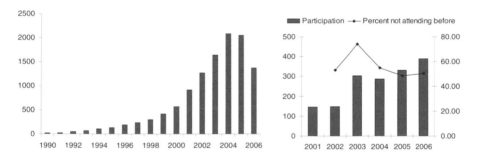

Figure 1.5. Semantic Web related publications per year (1990-2006) and participation at the yearly international Semantic Web events (2001-2006).

the work of the advanced technology groups at IBM[14] and Hewlett-Packard[15]. Most of these tools are available as open source as at the current stage vendors expect to make profit primarily by developing complete solutions and providing support for other developers.

The World Wide Web Consortium still plays a key role in standardization where the interoperability of tools necessitates mediation between various developer and user communities, as in the case of the development of a standard query language and protocol to access ontology stores across the Web (the SPARQL query language, see

---

[14] http://ibm-slrp.sourceforge.net/

[15] http://www.hpl.hp.com/semweb/

also Chapter 4). Further, realizing the importance of adoption the W3C is active in promoting Semantic Web technology, for example through the work of the Semantic Web Best Practices and Deployment Working Group[16] and vertical interest groups such as the Semantic Web Health Care and Life Sciences Interest Group[17].

1.3.2 Technology adoption

The Semantic Web was originally conceptualized as an extension of the current Web, i.e. as the application of metadata for describing Web content. In this vision, the content that is already on the Web (text, but also multimedia) would be enriched in a collaborative effort by the users of the Web. However, this vision was soon considered to be less realistic as their was a widespread belief that Semantic Web technologies would be too difficult to master for the average person contributing content to the Web. (Interesting to note that this was before the successes of Web 2.0 demonstrated that it is possible to engage collectives of users in collaborative annotation, see Section 1.4). The alternative view predicted that the Semantic Web will first break through behind the scenes and not with the ordinary users, but among large providers of data and services. The second vision predicts that the Semantic Web will be primarily a "web of data" operated by data and service providers largely unbeknown to the average user.

That the Semantic Web is formulated as a vision points to the problem of boot-strapping the Semantic Web. Part of the problem is that as a technology for developers, users of the Web never experience the Semantic Web directly, which makes it difficult to convey Semantic Web technology to stakeholders.[18] Further, most of the times the gains for developers are achieved over the long term, i.e. when data and services need to reused and re-purposed.

More significantly, as many other modern technologies, the Semantic Web suffers from what the economist Kevin Kelly calls the *fax-effect*[19]. Kelly notes that when the first fax machines were introduced, they came with a very hefty price tag. Yet they were almost useless: namely, the usefulness of a fax comes from being able to communicate with other fax users. In this sense every fax unit sold increases the value of all fax machines in use. While traditional goods such as the land or precious metals become more valuable the less is produced (called the law of scarcity), the fax machine network exhibits the opposite, which is called the law of plentitude.[20]

So is it with the Semantic Web: at the beginning the price of technological invest-ment is very high. One has to adapt the new technology which requires an investment

---

[16] http://www.w3.org/2001/sw/BestPractices/

[17] http://www.w3.org/2001/sw/hcls/

[18] All developers are faced with the typical user reaction to a Semantic Web enabled portal: "But this is just a website!"

[19] http://www.kk.org/newrules/newrules-3.html

[20] Metcalfe's law is an attempt to quantify utility in networked systems. It states that the value of a telecommunications network is proportional to the square of the number of users of the system (n^2). See http://en.wikipedia.org/wiki/Metcalfe's_law for the discussion.

in learning. Further, the technology needs time to become reliable. But most of all there need to be other adopters who also provide data in semantic formats and follow the basic protocols of interoperability such as the SPARQL query language and protocol for accessing remote data stores [PS06, Cla06]. The reader may note that this is nothing new: the first Web had to deal with the exact same effect. In fact, reading the account of Tim Berners-Lee one cannot help but wonder at the extent to which making the Web successful depended on Berners-Lee charisma in getting the first users on board among a general disbelief [BLFD99].

What makes the case of the Semantic Web more difficult, however, is an additional cost factor. Returning to the example of the fax network, we can say that it required a certain kind of agreement to get the system working on a global scale: all fax machines needed to adopt the same protocol for communicating over the telephone line. This is similar to the case of the Web where global interoperability is guaranteed by the standard protocol for communication (HTTP). However, in order to exchange meaning there has to be a minimal external agreement on the meaning of some primitive symbols, i.e. on what is communicated through the network. It is as if when installing the fax machine we would have to call our partners in advance to agree on the meaning of some of the symbols that we will use in our fax communications.

This agreement doesn't have to be complete as the meaning of unknown symbols can often be deduced from the context, in particular the meaning of related symbols and the meaning of relationships between symbols. Often a little semantics is enough to solve important tasks, hence the mantra "a little semantics goes a long way". Our machines can also help in this task to the extent that some of the meaning can be described in formal rules (e.g. if A is true, B should follow). But formal knowledge typically captures only the smaller part of the intended meaning and thus there needs to be a common grounding in an external reality that is shared by those at separate ends of the line.

While the research effort behind the Semantic Web is immense and growing dynamically, Semantic Web technology has yet to see mainstream use on the Web and in the enterprise. In the following, we will illustrate the growth of the Semantic Web by tracing its popularity on the Web. Although this method does not allow us to survey the use of Semantic Web technology in enterprise or governmental settings, we believe that internal applications of Semantic Web technology ("Semantic Webs" within organizations) are likely lagging behind due to the natural caution with which industry and the government treat any new technology.

To follow the popularity of Semantic Web related concepts and Semantic Web standards on the Web, we have executed a set of temporal queries using the search engine Altavista. The queries contained single terms plus a disambiguation term where it was necessary. Each query measured the number of documents with the given term(s) at the given point in time.

Figure 1.6 shows the number of documents with the terms *basketball*, *Computer Science*, and *XML*. We have divided all counts with the number of documents with the word *web* to account for the general growth of the Web. The flat curve for the term basketball validates this strategy: we could have expected the popularity of basketball to be roughly stable over this time period. Computer Science takes less and less share of the Web as the Web shifts from scientific use to everyday use. The share of XML, a popular pre-semantic web technology seems to grow and stabilize as it becomes a regular part of the toolkit of Web developers.

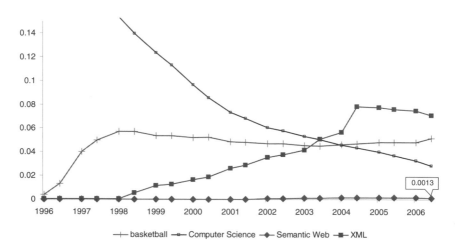

Figure 1.6. Number of webpages with the terms *basketball*, *Computer Science*, and *XML* over time and as a fraction of the number of pages with the term *web*.

Against this general backdrop we can also look at the share of Semantic Web related terms and formats, in particular the terms *RDF*, *OWL* and the number of ontologies (Semantic Web Documents) in RDF or OWL. As Figure 1.7 shows most of the curves have flattened out after January, 2004. It is not known at this point whether the dip in the share of Semantic Web is significant. While the use of RDF has settled at a relatively high level, OWL has yet to break out from a very low trajectory (only 4020 OWL documents were found by the search engine in June, 2006).

It is also interesting to look at the share of the mentioning of Semantic Web formats versus the actual number of Semantic Web documents using that format. The resulting *talking vs. doing* curve shows the phenomenon of technology hype in both the case of XML, RDF and OWL (see Figure 1.8). The hype reaches its maximum following the release of the corresponding W3C specifications: this is the point where the technology "makes the press" and after which its becoming increasingly used on the Web.[21] Interestingly, the XML and RDF hypes both settle at a fix value: there are roughly 15 pages mentioning XML for every XML document and 10 pages

---

[21] XML 1.0 was released as a W3C specification on February 10, 1998, see http://www.w3.org/TR/1998/REC-xml-19980210. RDF first became a W3C recommendation on February 22, 1999, see http://www.w3.org/TR/1999/REC-rdf-syntax-19990222/. OWL became a recommendation on February 10, 2004.

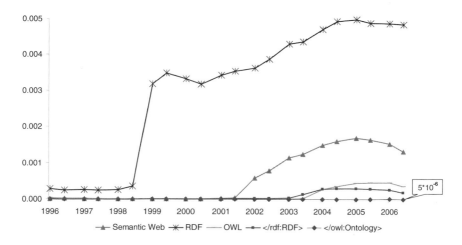

Figure 1.7. Number of webpages with the terms *RDF*, *OWL* and the number of ontologies (Semantic Web Documents) in RDF or OWL over time. Again, the number is relative to the number of pages with the term *web*.

mentioning RDF for every RDF document. OWL has not yet settled at such a value but seems to be approaching it.

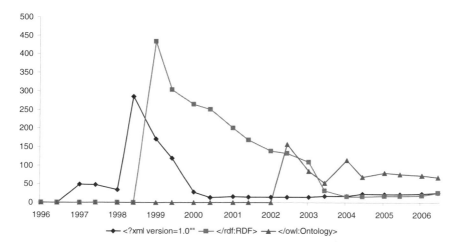

Figure 1.8. The hype cycle of Semantic Web related technologies as shown by the number of web pages about a given technology relative to its usage.

It is interesting to note that these curves are very similar in shape to the well known five-stage *hype cycle* of Gartner Research.[22] The hype cycle is defined by Gartner as follows:

> The first phase of a Hype Cycle is the "technology trigger" or breakthrough, product launch or other event that generates significant press and interest. In the next phase, a frenzy of publicity typically generates over-enthusiasm and unrealistic expectations. There may be some successful applications of a technology, but there are typically more failures. Technologies enter the "trough of disillusionment" because they fail to meet expectations and quickly become unfashionable. Consequently, the press usually abandons the topic and the technology. Although the press may have stopped covering the technology, some businesses continue through the "slope of enlighten-ment" and experiment to understand the benefits and practical application of the technology. A technology reaches the "plateau of productivity" as the benefits of it become widely demonstrated and accepted. The technology becomes increasingly stable and evolves in second and third generations. The final height of the plateau varies according to whether the technology is broadly applicable or benefits only a niche market.

Although the word hype has attracted some negative connotations, we note that hype is unavoidable for the adoption of network technologies such as the Semantic Web that exhibit the fax-effect described in Section 1.3.2. Namely creating technol-ogy visions is unavoidable in bootstrapping technology adoption as there are relative meager immediate benefits to early adopters compared to the value that a complete network could bring. The disillusionment that follows is also unavoidable partly be-cause the technology will need to mature but also because the technology will prove to be useful in different ways than originally predicted.

It is not surprising then that the adoption of the Semantic Web is also taking different paths than originally laid out in the often quoted vision of Tim Berners-Lee, which appeared on the pages of Scientific American in 2001 [BLHL01]. While standardization of the Semantic Web is mostly complete, Semantic Web technology is not reaching yet the mainstream user and developer community of the Web. In particular, the adoption of RDF is lagging behind XML, even though it provides a better alternative and thus many hoped it would replace XML over time. (Note that some of the benefits are in fact time-bound. Flexibility — a key benefit of a semantic infrastructure — is expected to show over time in easier adaptation of applications for serving different tasks based on different combinations of existing data and services.)

On the other hand, the recent support for Semantic Web standards by vendors such as Oracle[23] will certainly inspire even more confidence in the corporate world, leading to an adoption of semantic technologies for data and service integration within the enterprise. This could lead an earlier realization of the vision of the Se-

---

[22] http://www.gartner.com/pages/story.php.id.8795.s.8.jsp

[23] See   http://www.oracle.com/technology/tech/semantic_technologies/ index.html

mantic Web as a "web of data", which could ultimately result in a resurgence of general interest on the Web.

1.4 The emergence of the social web

Although Tim Berners-Lee envisioned a read/write Web (the very first browser also worked as an HTML editor), the Web was a read-only medium for a majority of users. The web of the 1990s was much like the combination of a phone book and the yellow pages (a mix of individual postings and corporate catalogs) and despite the connecting power of hyperlinks it instilled little sense of community among its users. This passive attitude toward the Web was broken by a series of changes in usage patterns and technology that are now referred to as Web 2.0, a buzzword coined by Tim O'Reilly.[24]

In the following, we summarize the history and the defining aspects of Web 2.0. The changes that led to the current level of social engagement online have not been radical or significant individually, which explains why the term Web 2.0 has been created largely after the fact. Nevertheless, these set of innovations in the architecture and usage patterns of the Web led to an entirely different role of the online world as a platform for intense communication and social interaction. The resulting increase in our capacity to obtain information and social support online can be quantified. A recent major survey based on interviews with 2200 adults shows that the internet significantly improves Americans' capacity to maintain their social networks despite early fears about the effects of diminishing real life contact. The survey confirms that not only networks are maintained and extended online, but they are also successfully activated for dealing with major life situations such as getting support in case of a major illness, looking for jobs, informing about major investments etc. [BHWR06]

The first wave of socialization on the Web was due to the appearance of *blogs*, *wikis* and other forms of web-based communication and collaboration. Blogs and wikis attracted mass popularity from around 2003 (see Figure 1.9). What they have in common is that they both significantly lower the requirements for adding content to the Web: editing blogs and wikis did not require any knowledge of HTML any more. Blogs and wikis allowed individuals and groups to claim their personal space on the Web and fill it with content at relative ease. Even more importantly, despite that weblogs have been first assessed as purely personal publishing (similar to diaries), nowadays the blogosphere is widely recognized as a densely interconnected social network through which news, ideas and influences travel rapidly as bloggers reference and reflect on each other's postings.

Although the example of Wikipedia, the online encyclopedia is outstanding, wikis large and small are used by groups of various sizes as an effective knowledge management tool for keeping records, describing best practices or jointly developing

---

[24] Tim O'Reilly is founder and CEO of O'Reilly Media, a technology publisher. Tim O'Reilly's original article on Web 2.0 can be found at http://www.oreillynet.com/pub/a/oreilly/tim/news/2005/09/30/what-is-web-20.html

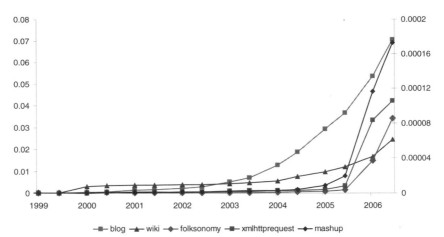

Figure 1.9. Development of the social web. The fraction of webpages with the terms *blogs*, *wiki* over time is measured on the left vertical axis. The fraction of webpages with the terms *folksonomy, XmlHttpRequest* and *mashup* is measured on the right hand vertical axis.

ideas. Regardless of the goal, the collective ownership of a Wiki enforces a sense of community (or at the worst reveals a lack of cohesion in social groups) through the necessary discussions over shared content. Similarly, the significance of instant messaging (ICQ) is also not just instant communication (phone is instantaneous, and email is almost instantaneous), but the ability to see who is online, a transparency that induces a sense of social responsibility.

The first *online social networks* (also referred to as social networking services) entered the field at the same time as blogging and wikis started to take off. In 2003, the first-mover Friendster[25] attracted over five million registered users in the span of a few months [Kah03], which was followed by Google and Microsoft starting or announcing similar services. Although these sites feature much of the same content that appear on personal web pages, they provide a central point of access and bring structure in the process of personal information sharing and online socialization. Following registration, these sites allow users to post a profile with basic information, to invite others to register and to link to the profiles of their friends. The system also makes it possible to visualize and browse the resulting network in order to discover friends in common, friends thought to be lost or potential new friendships based on shared interests. (Thematic sites cater to more specific goals such as establishing a business contact or finding a romantic relationship.)

These vastly popular systems allow users to maintain large networks of personal and business contacts. Members have soon discovered, however, that networking is only a means to an end in the cyberspace as well. The latest services are thus using user profiles and networks to stimulate different exchanges: photos are shared in Flickr, bookmarks are exchanged in del.icio.us, plans and goals unite members

---

[25] http://www.friendster.com

at 43Things. The idea of network based exchange is based on the sociological observation that social interaction creates similarity and vice versa, interaction creates similarity: friends are likely to have acquired or develop similar interests.

As we will see in Chapter 9 many of these systems build on collaborative annotation (*folksonomies*) to connect users to relevant content and other users interested in similar things. Much like Wikis, the new breed of websites achieve engagement by giving an active role to their community of users in creating and managing content, including the task of organizing it.

Explicit user profiles make it possible for these systems to introduce rating mechanism whereby either the users or their contributions are ranked according to usefulness or trustworthiness. Ratings are explicit forms of social capital that regulate exchanges in online communities in much the same way that reputation moderates exchanges in the real world. For example, in the technology news platform Digg, users give thumbs up or thumbs down to news items provided by other users. Further, Digg provides a way for users to see what other users are 'digging' real-time, catering to the creation of a similar sense of simultaneous social presence as in the case of instant messaging.

The design and implementation of Web applications have also evolved in order to make the user experience of interacting with the Web as smooth as possible. In terms of design, the new websites put the emphasis on a clean, accessible and attractive appearance that interferes the least possible with the functionality of the application. In terms of implementation, the new web sites are relying on new ways of applying some of the pre-existent technologies. (Asynchronous JavaScript and XML, or *AJAX*, which drives many of the latest websites is merely a mix of technologies that have been supported by browsers for years.)

In line with user friendliness, what can be also observed is a preference for formats, languages and protocols that are easy to use and develop with, in particular script languages, formats such as JSON, protocols such as REST. This is to support rapid development and prototyping (Flickr, for example, is known to adapt the user interface several times a day). Also, borrowing much of the ideology of the open source software movement, Web 2.0 applications open up their data and services for user experimentation: Google, Yahoo and countless smaller web sites expose key features of their systems through lightweight APIs while content providers do the same with information in the form of RSS feeds. The results of user experimentation with combinations of technologies are the so-called *mashups*, websites based on combinations of data and services provided by others. The best example of this development are the mashups based on Google's mapping service such as HousingMaps[26].

1.4.1 Web 2.0 + Semantic Web = Web 3.0?

Web 2.0 is often contrasted to the Semantic Web, which is a more conscious and carefully orchestrated effort on the side of the W3C to trigger a new stage of developments using semantic technologies. In practice the ideas of Web 2.0 and the Semantic Web are not exclusive alternatives: while Web 2.0 mostly effects how users

---

[26] See http://housingmaps.org

interact with the Web, while the Semantic Web opens new technological opportunities for web developers in combining data and services from different sources. In the following, we point out some of the opportunities that arise by the combination of ideas from these two developments.

Firstly, we note that the basic lesson of Web 2.0 is that *users are willing to provide content as well as metadata*. This may take the form articles and facts organized in tables and categories in Wikipedia, photos organized in sets and according to tags in Flickr or structured information embedded into homepages and blog postings using *microformats*.These latter are mini-vocabularies for encoding metadata of all kinds in HTML pages, for example information about the author or a blog item.[27])

While this observation may sound trivial, it addresses a primary concern of the Semantic Web community, namely whether users would be willing to provide metadata to bootstrap the Semantic Web. Interesting from a historical perspective is that the Semantic Web was originally also expected to be filled by users annotating Web resources, describing their home pages and multimedia content.[28] However, early implementations of embedding RDF into HTML (such as the SHOE project [HH01a]) have been abandoned as it was not conceived realistic to expect everyday users (who can barely write correct HTML) to master the intricacies of encoding metadata in RDF, or even to write correct XML.

Although it is still dubious whether everyday users could master Semantic Web languages such as RDF and OWL (see Chapter 4), from the lessons of Web 2.0 it seems clear that many are in fact willing to provide structured information, provided that they can do so in a task oriented way and through a user-friendly interface that hides the complexity of the underlying representation. Microformats, for example, proved to be more popular due to the easier authoring using existing HTML attributes. Further, web pages created automatically from a database (such as blog pages or personal profile pages) can encode metadata in microformats without the user necessarily being aware of it. At the same time, microformats retain all the advantages of RDF in terms of machine accessibility. For example, blog search engines are able to provide search on the properties of the author or the news item.

Noting this, the idea of providing ways to encode RDF into HTML pages has resurfaced (see microformats or RDF/A [AB06]). In a similar vein, there are also works under way to extend the MediaWiki software behind Wikipedia to allow users to encode facts in the text of articles while writing the text. This additional, machine-processable markup of facts would enable to easily extract, query and aggregate the knowledge of Wikipedia [VKV+06]. There are also similar works on entirely new Wiki systems that combine free-text authoring with the collaborative editing of structured information [ADR06].

Secondly, due to the extensive collaborations online many applications have *access to significantly more metadata about the users*. Information about the choices, preferences, tastes and social networks of users means that the new breed of applications are able to build on a much richer user profiles. Clearly, semantic technology

---

[27] See http://www.microformats.org

[28] Hence the name for RDF, the Resource Description Framework.

can help in matching users with similar interests as well as matching users with available content. Semantics, however, is not enough: as Golbeck shows, there are components of trust that are beyond of what can be inferred based on profile similarity alone [GH06]. Therefore social-semantic systems that can provide recommendations based on both the social network of users and their personal profiles are likely to outperform traditional recommender systems as well as purely network-based trust mechanisms.

Lastly, in terms of technology what the Semantic Web can offer to the Web 2.0 community is a standard infrastructure for the building creative combinations of data and services. Standard formats for exchanging data and schema information, support for data integration, along with standard query languages and protocols for querying remote data sources provide a platform for the easy development of mashups. San Francisco based startup MetaWeb is developing FreeBase[29], a kind of "data commons" that allows users to share, interlink, and jointly edit ontologies and structured data through a Web-based interface. A public API allows developers to build applications using the combined knowledge of FreeBase.

1.5 Discussion

The Semantic Web first appeared ten years ago as the ambitious vision of a future Web where all content is described in a way that computers can easily access, including the information that is currently only described in human language, captured by images, audio and video, or locked up in the many databases behind complex websites. Using such a web as an information source we would be able to automate complex tasks by automatically finding and pulling together the relevant pieces of information, adding the necessary background knowledge and applying human-like logic to decide complex questions, create plans, designs, find patterns and anomalies etc. In this Chapter we have only introduced the key idea behind the Semantic Web; technological details will follow in Chapters 4 and 5.

Although the Web has been already naturally evolving toward a separation of content and representation, the vision of the Semantic Web is rather revolutionary: not only major technological changes are required to realize this vision, but also a social adoption process had to be bootstrapped. In terms of technology, the past years have seen the formation of a substantial Semantic Web research community that delivers the innovative solutions required to realize the Semantic Web. (We will investigate this community in more detail in Chapter 8.) The World Wide Web Consortium (W3C) as the main body of standardization in the area of web technologies has also proceeded to issue official recommendations about the key languages and protocols that would guarantee interoperability on the Semantic Web.

The W3C is also the main propelling force behind the social adoption of the Semantic Web. We have tracked this process by looking at the mentioning and usage of certain key technological terms on the Web. We have noted that the social adoption

---

[29] http://www.freebase.com

of Semantic Web technology is lagging behind the scientific and standardization efforts, but it has the potential to take off in an exponential fashion due to the network effect. (The more data and services become available in Semantic Web compatible formats, the more attractive it becomes for others to switch to publish their data and services using the new technology.) The necessary push may come from the Web community, but also from large companies or governments where the complexity of data and service integration tasks could justify an investment in Semantic Web technologies based on internal benefits alone.

Contrary to the development of the Semantic Web, the notion of a Web 2.0 has emerged from the developer community of the Web as a characterization of incremental technological developments that have collective led to a distinct class of web applications. These applications focus on the social aspects of the Web and attempt to harness the power of a community of users in building up and organizing valuable information. The role of technology in this effort is relatively minor: the technological changes required focus on making attractive and efficient interfaces for manipulating content.

In many respects, Semantic Web and Web 2.0 are likely to benefit from a closer interaction in the future. Among others, the creation of mashups or combinations of diverse sources of data and services could greatly benefit from the shared representations and protocols proposed by the Semantic Web community. In Chapter 9, we will return to see how the Semantic Web itself could learn from the study of folksonomies, the bottom-up, user generated semantic structures that are used for organizing information in many Web 2.0 applications. We will find that folksonomies bring into play a so far unexplored dimension of knowledge representation, namely the social networks of the user community that creates annotations.

2

Social Network Analysis

How do we rank pages on the Web? How does HIV spread? How do we explain the success or failure of entrepreneurs in terms of their business contacts? What is the advantage of terrorist networks built from loosely coupled cells?

All these questions have in common that they can be rephrased using the vocabulary of network analysis, a branch of sociology and mathematics that is increasingly applied also to questions outside the social domain. In the following we give an introduction to the main theory and methods of Social Network Analysis, which will be applied later to the analysis of social networks (Section 8) as well as semantic networks (Section 9). By no means do we expect to provide a complete coverage of any topic involved. For a more encyclopedic treatment of network analysis we refer the reader to the social network analysis reference of Wasserman and Faust [WFIG94].

While Social Science is often looked upon by researchers from the exact sciences as vague and thus necessarily inconclusive, network analysis should appeal to all as one of the most formalized branches of Social Science. Most of these formalisms are based on the simple nodes and edges representations of social networks to which a large array of measures and statistics can be applied. While some of the more sophisticated of these methods require a deep mathematical understanding to be applied correctly, the simple concepts discussed in this Chapter should be easily understood by anyone with an advanced level of secondary-school mathematics.

2.1 What is network analysis?

Social Network Analysis (SNA) is the study of social relations among a set of actors. The key difference between network analysis and other approaches to social science is the focus on relationships between actors rather than the attributes of individual actors. Network analysis takes a global view on social structures based on the belief that types and patterns of relationships emerge from individual connectivity and that the presence (or absence) of such types and patterns have substantial effects on the network and its constituents. In particular, the network structure provides opportunities and imposes constraints on the individual actors by determining the transfer or flow of resources (material or immaterial) across the network.

The focus on relationships as opposed to actors can be easily understood by an example. When trying to predict the performance of individuals in a scientific community by some measure (say, number of publications), a traditional social science approach would dictate to look at the attributes of the researchers such as the amount of grants they attract, their age, the size of the team they belong to etc. A statistical analysis would then proceed by trying to relate these attributes to the outcome variable, i.e. the number of publications.

In the same context, a network analysis study would focus on the interdependencies within the research community. For example, one would look at the patterns of relationships that scientists have and the potential benefits or constraints such relationships may impose on their work. For example, one may hypothesize that certain kinds of relationships arranged in a certain pattern may be beneficial to performance compared to the case when that pattern is not present. The patterns of relationships may not only be used to explain individual performance but also to hypothesize their impact on the network itself (network evolution). Attributes typically play a secondary role in network studies as control variables.[1]

SNA is thus a different approach to social phenomena and therefore requires a new set of concepts and new methods for data collection and analysis. Network analysis provides a vocabulary for describing social structures, provides formal models that capture the common properties of all (social) networks and a set of methods applicable to the analysis of networks in general. The concepts and methods of network analysis are grounded in a formal description of networks as graphs. Methods of analysis primarily originate from graph theory as these are applied to the graph representation of social network data. (Network analysis also applies statistical and probabilistic methods and to a lesser extent algebraic techniques.)

It is interesting to note that the formalization of network analysis has brought much of the same advantages that the formalization of knowledge on the Web (the Semantic Web) is expected to bring to many application domains. Previously vaguely defined concepts such as *social role* or *social group* could now be defined on a formal model of networks, allowing to carry out more precise discussions in the literature and to compare results across studies.

The methods of data collection in network analysis are aimed at collecting relational data in a reliable manner. Data collection is typically carried out using standard questionnaires and observation techniques that aim to ensure the correctness and completeness of network data. Often records of social interaction (publication databases, meeting notes, newspaper articles, documents and databases of different sorts) are used to build a model of social networks. We return to the particular use of electronic data (data from the Internet and the Web) in Chapter 3.

---

[1] The role of control variables in statistical analysis is to exclude the effect of non-network variables on the outcome variable.

2.2 Development of Social Network Analysis

The field of Social Network Analysis today is the result of the convergence of several streams of applied research in sociology, social psychology and anthropology.

Many of the concepts of network analysis have been developed independently by various researchers often through empirical studies of various social settings. For example, many social psychologists of the 1940s found a formal description of social groups useful in depicting communication channels in the group when trying to explain processes of group communication. Already in the mid-1950s anthropologists have found network representations useful in generalizing actual field observations, for example when comparing the level of reciprocity in marriage and other social exchanges across different cultures.

Some of the concepts of network analysis have come naturally from social studies. In an influential early study at the Hawthorne works in Chicago, researchers from Harvard looked at the workgroup behavior (e.g. communication, friendships, helping, controversy) at a specific part of the factory, the bank wiring room [May33]. The investigators noticed that workers themselves used specific terms to describe who is in "our group". The researchers tried to understand how such terms arise by reproducing in a visual way the group structure of the organization as it emerged from the individual relationships of the factory workers (see Figure 2.1).[2] In another study of mixed-race city in the Southern US researchers looked at the network of overlapping "cliques" defined by race and age [WL41].[3] They also went further than the Hawthorne study in generating hypotheses about the possible connections between cliques. (For example, they noted that lower-class members of a clique are usually only able to connect to higher-class members of another clique through the higher-class members of their own clique.)

Despite the various efforts, each of the early studies used a different set of concepts and different methods of representation and analysis of social networks. However, from the 1950s network analysis began to converge around the unique world view that distinguishes network analysis from other approaches to sociological research. (The term "social network" has been introduced by Barnes in 1954.) This convergence was facilitated by the adoption of a graph representation of social networks usually credited to Moreno. What Moreno called a *sociogram* was a visual representation of social networks as a set of nodes connected by directed links. The nodes represented individuals in Moreno's work, while the edges stood for personal relations. However, similar representations can be used to depict a set of relationships

---

[2] The study became famous not so much of the network methods used but for what became known in management science as the *Hawthorne-effect*. In brief, managers at the Hawthorne factory were initially trying to understand what alterations in the work conditions affect productivity. To their surprise no matter what the change was it seemed to affect productivity in a positive way. Mayo and colleagues concluded that the mere participation in the research project itself was the key factor as workers were pleased with the management taking an interest in their conditions. Although it became widely known, the original study as well as the general existence of this effect is disputed [Gil93].

[3] Clique is a term that now has a precise definition in network analysis.

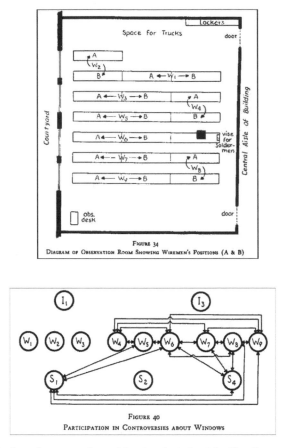

Figure 34
DIAGRAM OF OBSERVATION ROOM SHOWING WIREMEN'S POSITIONS (A & B)

FIGURE 40
PARTICIPATION IN CONTROVERSIES ABOUT WINDOWS

Figure 2.1. Illustrations from an early social network study at the Hawthorne works of Western Electric in Chicago. The upper part shows the location of the workers in the wiring room, while the lower part is a network image of fights about the windows between workers (W), solderers (S) and inspectors (I).

between any kind of social unit such as groups, organizations, nations etc. While 2D and 3D visual modelling is still an important technique of network analysis, the sociogram is honored mostly for opening the way to a formal treatment of network analysis based on graph theory.

The following decades have seen a tremendous increase in the capabilities of network analysis mostly through new applications. SNA gains its relevance from applications and these settings in turn provide the theories to be tested and greatly influence the development of the methods and the interpretation of the outcomes. For example, one of the relatively new areas of network analysis is the analysis of networks in entrepreneurship, an active area of research that builds and contributes to organization and management science.

The vocabulary, models and methods of network analysis also expand continuously through applications that require to handle ever more complex data sets. An example of this process are the advances in dealing with longitudinal data. New probabilistic models are capable of modelling the evolution of social networks and answering questions regarding the dynamics of communities. Formalizing an increasing set of concepts in terms of networks also contributes to both developing and testing theories in more theoretical branches of sociology.

The increasing variety of applications and related advances in methodology can be best observed at the yearly Sunbelt Social Networks Conference series, which started in 1980.[4] The field of Social Network Analysis also has a journal of the same name since 1978, dedicated largely to methodological issues.[5] However, articles describing various applications of social network analysis can be found in almost any field where networks and relational data play an important role.

While the field of network analysis has been growing steadily from the beginning, there have been two developments in the last two decades that led to an explosion in network literature. First, advances in information technology brought a wealth of electronic data and significantly increased analytical power. We examine the possibilities of using electronic data for network analysis in Chapter 3. Second, the methods of SNA are increasingly applied to networks other than social networks such as the hyperlink structure on the Web or the electric grid. This advancement —brought forward primarily by physicists and other natural scientists— is based on the discovery that many networks in nature share a number of commonalities with social networks. In the following, we will also talk about networks in general, but it should be clear from the text that many of the measures in network analysis can only be strictly interpreted in the context of social networks or have very different interpretation in networks of other kinds.

2.3 Key concepts and measures in network analysis

Social Network Analysis has developed a set of concepts and methods specific to the analysis of social networks. In the following, we introduce the most basic notions of network analysis and the methods we intend to use later in this book. We will proceed from the global structure of networks toward the measurement of *ego-networks* (personal networks), i.e. from the macro level to the micro level of network analysis. For a complete reference to the field of social network analysis, we refer the reader to the exhaustive network analysis "Bible" of Wasserman and Faust [WFIG94]. Scott provides a shorter, but more accessible introductory text on network analysis [Sco00].

---

[4] See http://www.insna.org/INSNA/sunbelt_inf.html
[5] See   http://www.elsevier.com/wps/find/journaldescription.cws_home/
505596/description#description

2.3.1 The global structure of networks

As discussed above, a (social) network can be represented as a graph $G = (V, E)$ where V denotes the finite set of vertices and E denotes a finite set of edges such that $E \subseteq V \times V$. Recall that each graph can be associated with its characteristic matrix $M := (m_{i,j})_{n*n}$ where $n = |V|, m_{i,j} = \left\{ \begin{array}{l} 1 \\ 0 \end{array} \middle| \begin{array}{l} (v_i, v_j) \in E \\ otherwise \end{array} \right\}$. Some network analysis methods are easier to understand when we conceptualize graphs as matrices (see Figure 2.2). Note that the matrix is symmetrical in case the edges are undirected. We will talk of a valued graph when we are also given a real valued weight function $w(e)$ defined on the set of edges, i.e. $w(e) := E \times \mathbb{R}$. In case of a valued graph, the matrix is naturally defined as $m_{i,j} = \left\{ \begin{array}{l} w(e) \\ 0 \end{array} \middle| \begin{array}{l} (v_i, v_j) \in E \\ otherwise \end{array} \right\}$

Loops are not excluded in the above definition, although they rarely in occur in practical social network data sets. (In other words, the main diagonal of the matrix is usually empty.) Typically, we also assume that the network is connected, i.e. there is a single *(weak) component* in the graph.[6] Otherwise we choose only one of the components for analysis.

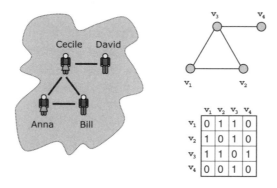

Figure 2.2. Most network analysis methods work on an abstract, graph based representation of real world networks.

At this point the question of what else can we say about the structure of social networks arises naturally. Are there any commonalities to real world (social) networks that we could impose on our graph models or any kind of graph is equally likely to occur in practice? These questions are relevant because having a general model of social networks would allow us to answer questions in general, i.e. in a way that the answer should hold for all networks exhibiting the common characteristics. In some cases we could verify theories solely on an abstract model instead of having

---

[6] A component is a maximal connected subgraph. Two vertices are in the same (strong) component if and only if there exists a (directed) path between them.

to collect network data. Further, understanding the global structure of networks can lead us to discover commonly occurring patterns of relationships or typical network positions worthy of formalizing in further detail.

An important clue about the structure of social networks came from a remarkable experiment by the American psychologist Stanley Milgram [Mil67]. Milgram went out to test the common observation that no matter where we live, the world around us seems to be *small*: we routinely encounter persons not known to us who turn out to be the friends of our friends. Milgram thus not only wanted to test whether we are in fact all connected but he was also interested in what is the average distance between any two individuals in the social network of the American society.

In order to find out he devised an experiment in which he gave letters to a few hundred randomly selected persons from Boston in Massachusetts and Omaha in the state of Nebraska. (The choice of these places was intentional: Milgram wanted to include a cross-section of the American society.) The participants were asked to send the letter to a single target person, namely a stockbroker in Sharon, Massachusetts. They were not allowed to send it directly to the target person, however. Instead every participant was asked to forward the letter to a person he or she knew on a first name basis. That person would then also need to follow the same instructions and send the letter to someone who was more likely to be acquainted with the stock broker. In the end, the letter would reach someone who knew the target person in question and would hand the letter to him. In other words, Milgram devised a chain-mail similar to the ones that now aimlessly circle the planet. However, these letters had a target and the chains stopped when they reached their final destination [Mil67].

Milgram calculated the average of the length of the chains and concluded that the experiment showed that on average Americans are no more than six steps apart from each other. While this is also the source of the expression *six degrees of separation* the actual number is rather dubious: not only was Milgram's sample too small, but even only 20% of the those letters have made it to their destination. Thus the number could be actually larger: those letters that did not make it would probably have resulted in longer paths. But the number could be also smaller as it is not guaranteed that the letters have travelled the shortest possible path from their source to the target. Still, Milgram's experiment had a tremendous impact on social network research and sociology as a whole as it showed that the number is orders of magnitude smaller than the size of the network.

Formally, what Milgram estimated is the size of the average shortest path of the network, which is also called *characteristic path length*. An open (simple) path in a graph is a sequence of vertices $v_{i_0}, v_{i_2}, \ldots, v_{i_n}$ such that $\forall j = 0 \ldots n - 1 (v_{i_j}, v_{i_{j+1}}) \in E$ and $\forall j, k = v_{i_j} \neq v_{i_k}$, in other words every vertex is connected to the next vertex and no vertex is repeated on the path.[7] The shortest path between two vertices v_s and v_t is a path that begins at the vertex v_s and ends in the vertex v_t and contains the least possible number of vertices. The shortest path between two vertices is also called a *geodesic*. The longest geodesic in the graph is called the diameter of the graph: this is the maximum number of steps that is required between

---

[7] We assume that Milgram checked whether this is true for the paths that he found.

any two nodes. The average shortest path is the average of the length of the geodesics between all pairs of vertices in the graph. (This value is not possible to calculate if the graph is not (strongly) connected, i.e. in case there exists a pair of vertices with no path between them.)

A practical impact of Milgram's finding is that we can exclude certain kind of structures as possible models for social networks. The two dimensional lattice model shown in Figure 2.3, for example, does not have the small world property: for a network of size n the characteristic path length is $2/3 * \sqrt{n}$, which is still too large a number to fit the empirical finding.

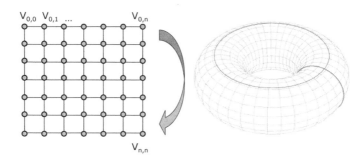

Figure 2.3. The 2D lattice model of networks (left). By connecting the nodes on the opposite borders of the lattice we get a toroidal lattice (right).

Another simple model could be the tree graph shown in Figure 2.4. However, a tree is unrealistic because it shows no *clustering*: we all know from practice that our friends are likely to know each other as well because we tend to socialize in groups. (If not for other reasons than other friends know each other because we introduced them to each other.) Clustering for a single vertex can be measured by the actual number of the edges between the neighbors of a vertex divided by the possible number of edges between the neighbors. When taken the average over all vertices we get to the measure known as *clustering coefficient*. The clustering coefficient of a tree is zero, which is easy to see if we consider that there are no triangles of edges (*triads*) in the graph. In a tree, it would never be the case that our friends are friends with each other.

The lattice and the tree also have the rather unappealing characteristic that every node has the same number of connections. We know from our everyday walks in life that some of us have much larger social circles than others. The *random graph* model proposed by the Hungarian mathematicians Erdős and Rényi offers an alternative. A random graph can be generated by taking a set of vertices with no edges connecting them. Subsequently, edges are added by picking pairs of nodes with equal probability. This way we create a graph where each pair of vertices will be connected with an equal probability. (This probability is a parameter of the process.)

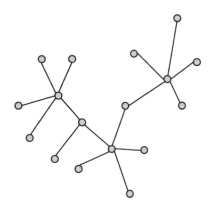

Figure 2.4. A tree is a connected graph where there are no loops and paths leading from a vertex to itself.

If we continue the process long enough —we choose a high enough probability— the resulting random graphs will have a small characteristic path length and most likely exhibit some clustering. (Needless to say if we go on we end up with a complete graph.) Still, we can raise significant concerns against the cold probabilistic logic of a random graph. Due to limitations of space —if not for other reasons— we are unlikely to make friends completely in random from anywhere in the world. Although we meet strangers occasionally by sitting next to them on an airplane, we mostly socialize in a given geographic area and even then in limited social environments such as our work and living space. Again, the friends of our friends are likely to be our friends as well. If that happens in a random graph, it happens by accident.

Nevertheless, the Erdős-Rényi random graphs are interesting in the sense that they are examples of generative models. That is, random graphs are not (only) defined by what they are but also *how* they arise, i.e. the process of growing such a graph. These kinds of processes are also at the centerpoint of interest for the field of complex networks in physics where researchers study the emergence of complex global structures from systems that are defined solely through elementary interactions between primitive elements.

It is not so surprising then that the next steps in the search for a more appropriate network model came from physicists and mathematicians. In a seminal paper published in 1999 the mathematicians Steven Strogatz and Duncan Watts presented their alpha-model of networks [Wat99]. In this model the network also grows, but not in a random fashion. In this model the number of mutual friends shared by any two nodes would determine the likelihood of a new tie forming. In the model of Watts and Strogatz a parameter alpha allows to fine-tune the exact influence of the number of friends on the probability of a tie. The alpha model was successful in generating graphs with small path lengths and relative large clustering coefficients.

The alpha-model was later simplified by the authors in the so-called beta-model, which achieves the same results although in a somewhat less intuitive process

[WS98]. The beta-model is also generative and it starts with a one-dimensional toroidal lattice where every node is connected not only to its neighbors but also to the neighbors of its neighbors. Consequently, a random edge is rewired by keeping one end of the edge fixed and reassigning the other end to another randomly selected node. We continue this process and rewire every link with a probability of beta, which is a parameter of the process. By choosing beta appropriately, the beta model allows to generate networks with small path lengths and relatively large clustering coefficients.

While the alpha and beta models could be considered perfect by these characteristics alone, they too fail to recreate an important feature of networks in nature: the scale-free characteristic of the degree distribution. The understanding of this phenomenon and the construction of a model that can reproduce it is due to another Hungarian, a physicist by the name of Albert-László Barabási [AR99].

To understand the scale-free phenomenon we have to look at the degree-distribution of networks. Such a diagram shows how many nodes in the network have a certain number of neighbors (degrees). In a toroidal lattice all nodes have an equal number of neighbors. In the alpha and beta models as well as the random graphs of Erdős and Rényi this distribution is a normal distribution: there is an average degree, which is also the most common one. Degrees deviating from this are increasingly less likely. In real social networks, however, this distribution shows a different picture: the number of nodes with a certain degree is highest for small degree and the number of nodes with a given degree rapidly decreases for higher degrees. In other words, the higher the degree the least likely it is to occur. What is also surprising is the steepness of the distribution: the vast majority of the nodes have much fewer connections than the few *hubs* of the network. The exact correlation is a *power law*, i.e. $p(d) = d^{-k}$ where $k > 0$ is a parameter of the distribution.

As an example, the upper part of Figure 2.5 shows the degree distribution for the co-authorship network of the Semantic Web research community. The chart is a histogram showing how many people have a certain degree, i.e. a certain number of co-authors. The chart shows that most people have only one or two co-authors while only very few researchers have more than twenty co-authors. (One co-author is slightly less likely than two because the data comes from publications and the average publication has about two authors.) The lower part of the Figure shows the degree distribution of a random network of similar size.

Barabási not only discovered that this is a fundamental characteristic of many networks that he studied, but also gave a generative model to reproduce it. In this model, we start with a single node and add nodes in every step. The trick of Barabási is that when adding new nodes we link the node to an already existing node with a probability that is determined by how many edges the node already has. In other words, the rich get richer in this model: a node that has already attracted more edges than others will have a larger probability to attract even more connections in subsequent rounds. Barabási showed that the resulting networks can have a short characteristic path lengths and a large clustering coefficient as well as a degree distribution that approaches a power law.

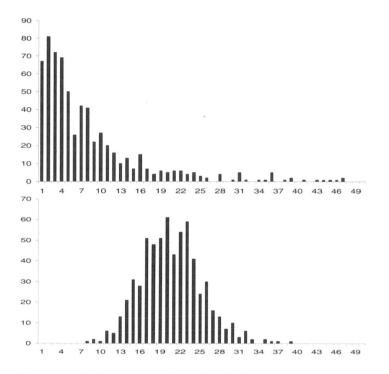

Figure 2.5. The degree distribution of a real world scale-free network (upper part) and the degree distribution of a random network of the same size (lower part).

The works of Watts, Strogatz, Barabási and his colleagues are largely responsible for bringing network research into the scientific forefront. We note here that their work would have had a much more limited impact if its applications were only sociological. However, the small world phenomenon and scale-free characteristics are still routinely identified in many networks in nature such as transport networks within the cell. Even technological networks such as the hyperlink structure of the World Wide Web or the electrical transport network exhibit scale-free characteristics: the rich get richer logic creates scale-free structures in these networks by rewarding nodes proportionally to their existing number of links. By analyzing the model instead of particular instances of it allows scientists to formulate precise and general claims about these networks, for example with respect to their vulnerability to specific kind of attacks or the possibility for the spread of viruses or failures across them. In technology this impacted the design of networks and resulted, for example, in more efficient structures for peer-to-peer networks.

2.3.2 The macro-structure of social networks

Based on the findings about the global characteristics of social networks we now have a good impression about what they might look like. In particular, the image that emerges is one of dense clusters or social groups sparsely connected to each other by a few ties as shown in Figure 2.6. (These weak ties have a special significance as we will see in the following Section.) For example, this is the image that appears if we investigate the co-authorship networks of a scientific community. Bounded by limitations of space and resources, scientists mostly co-operate with colleagues from the same institute. Occasional exchanges and projects with researchers from abroad, however, create the kind of shortcut ties that Watts explicitly incorporated within his model. These shortcuts make it possible for scientists to reach each other in a relatively short number of steps.

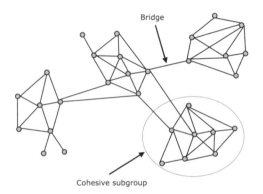

Figure 2.6. Most real world networks show a structure where densely connected subgroups are linked together by relatively few bridges

Particularly important are the hubs, the kind of individual such as Erdős was in the field of mathematics: he was one of the most prolific authors in the history of mathematics and co-authored with an unusual number of individuals. In fact, it is a common game in this field to calculate a researcher's Erdős-number, which is a measure of the number of steps in the co-authorship network from Erdős to the given researcher. Co-authors of Erdős are said to have an Erdős-number of one, their co-authors have a number of two etc.

Network visualizations based on topographic or physical principles can be helpful in understanding the group structure of social networks and pinpoint hubs that naturally tend to gravitate toward the center of the visualization. Unfortunately, computer generated network visualizations rarely show the kind of image seen in Figure 2.6. Displays based on multi-dimensional scaling, for example, attempt to optimize the visualization in a way that distances on the paper correlate with the distances between the nodes in the graph. However, with as few as four nodes it is easy to construct an example where there is no optimal solution to the placement problem. (Consider for example the 2D lattice shown in Figure 2.3.) In general, the more dense the graph and the fewer the dimensions of the visualization the more likely the graph will degenerate into a meaningless "spaghetti bowl" tangle of nodes and edges.[8]

Fortunately, visualizations are also not the only kind of tools in the network analysts' toolkit to uncover subgroup structure. Various clustering algorithms exist for creating disjunct or overlapping subsets of nodes based on different definitions of a what a subgroup is or how to find one.

Several definitions are based on the observations that subgroups are densely connected and their members are close to each other in the graph. For example, a *clique* in a graph is maximal complete subgraph of three or more nodes. As complete subgraphs are very rare, the definition of a clique is typically relaxed by allowing some missing connections. For example, a *k-plex* is a maximal subgraph in which each node is adjacent to no fewer than $g_s - k$ nodes in the subgraph, where g_s is the number of nodes in the subgraph. The larger we set the parameter k, the larger the k-plexes that we will find. Other definitions constrain subgroups by putting limits on the maximum path length between the members.

Yet another way of defining cohesiveness is to compare the density of ties within the group to the density of ties between members of the subgroup and the outside. The lambda-set analysis method we will use in our work is based on the definition of edge connectivity. Denoted with the symbol $\lambda(i, j)$, the edge connectivity of two vertices v_i and v_j is the minimum number of lines that need to be removed from a graph in order to leave no path between the two vertices. A lambda-set is then defined as a set of nodes where any pair of nodes from the set has a larger edge connectivity than any pair of nodes where one node is from within the set and the other node is from outside the set. Unlike the above mentioned k-plexes, lambda-sets also have the nice property that they are not overlapping.

The edge-betweenness clustering method of Mark Newman takes a different approach [GN02]. Instead of focusing on the density of subgroups, this algorithm targets the ties that connect them. The ties that are in between groups can be spotted by calculating their *betweenness*. The betweenness of an edge is calculated by taking the set of all shortest paths in the graph and looking at what fraction of them contains the given edge. An edge between clusters has a much higher betweenness than edges inside clusters because all shortest paths between nodes in the different clusters have to go through the given edge. By progressively removing the edges with the highest betweenness the graph falls apart in distinct clusters of nodes.

Clustering a graph into subgroups allows us to visualize the connectivity at a group level. In some cases we already have an idea of what this macro-structure might look like. A typical pattern that often emerges in social studies is that of a *Core-Periphery (C/P) structure*. A C/P structure is one where nodes can be divided in two distinct subgroups: nodes in the core are densely connected with each other and the nodes on the periphery, while peripheral nodes are not connected with each other, only nodes in the core (see Figure 2.7). The matrix form of a core periphery

---

[8] In fact, when used inappropriately, visualizations are among the most dangerous tools of a social network analyst: at worst they not only obscure important phenomena but also allow to argue false theories.

structure is a $\begin{pmatrix} 1 & . \\ . & 0 \end{pmatrix}$ matrix. Algorithms for identifying C/P structures and other *block models* (structural patterns) work by dividing the set of nodes in a way that the error the between the actual image and the "perfect" image is minimal. The result of the optimization is a classification of the nodes as core or periphery and a measure of the error of the solution.

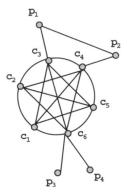

c_1	c_2	c_3	c_4	c_5	c_6	p_1	p_2	p_3	p_4
1	1	1	1	1	1	0	0	0	0
1	1	1	1	1	1	0	0	0	0
1	1	1	1	1	1	1	0	0	0
1	1	1	1	1	1	0	1	0	0
1	1	1	1	1	1	0	0	0	0
1	1	1	1	1	1	0	0	1	1
0	0	1	0	0	0	0	1	0	0
0	0	0	1	0	0	1	0	0	0
0	0	0	0	0	1	0	0	0	0
0	0	0	0	0	1	0	0	0	0

Figure 2.7. A Core-Periphery structure that would be perfect without the edge between nodes p_1 and p_2.

We will also encounter situations in our work where it is some additional information that allows us to group our nodes into categories. For example, in the case of a scientific community we might have data on the interests or affiliations of researchers. When we have such attribute data available we already have a division of our network into clusters based on shared interests or affiliations. These clusters are overlapping depending on whether a single person is allowed to have multiple interests or affiliations.

As it is fairly common to have attribute information on subjects besides the relational data, the study of *affiliation networks* is an important topic in network analysis. Affiliation networks contain information about the relationships between two sets of nodes: a set of subjects and a set of affiliations. An affiliation network can be formally represented as a *bipartite graph*, also known as a *two-mode network*. In general, an n-partite graph or n-mode network is a graph $G = \langle V, E \rangle$ where there exists a partitioning $V = \bigcup_{i=1}^{n} V_i$ such that $\bigcap_{i=1}^{n} V_i = 0$ and $(V_i \times V_i) \cap E = 0$. In other words, the set of vertices is divided into n disjoint sets and there are no edges between vertices belonging to the same set.

There are relative few methods of analysis that are specific to affiliation networks; when dealing with affiliation networks they are typically transformed directly to a regular, one-mode network. This transformation considers the overlaps between the affiliations as a measure of tie strength between the actors (see Figure 2.8). For example, we can generate a network among scientists by looking at how many interests they have in common. We would place an edge between two researchers if they have interests in common and would weight the edge according to the number of shared interests. The analysis of such a one-mode network would follow as usual.

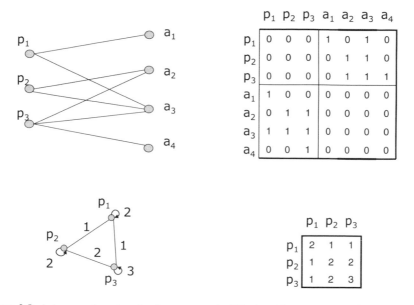

Figure 2.8. A two-mode network of persons and affiliation (shown as a graph and a matrix above) can be folded into a regular social network by considering the overlaps in affiliations (graph and matrix below).

Interestingly, we can also use this technique to map the relationship between the affiliations themselves. In this case, we create a network of the affiliations as the nodes and draw edges between the nodes based on the number of individuals who share that affiliations. This technique is commonly used, for example, to map *interlocking directorates*, overlaps in the board membership of companies. In such a setting the analysis starts with data on persons and their positions on the boards of various companies. Then a network of companies is drawn based on potential interactions through shared members on their boards. The website TheyRule[9] shows the potential conflicts of interests in the American business, political and media elite by charting the connectivity of individuals and institutions using this technique (see Figure 2.9).

2.3.3 Personal networks

In many cultures the term *networking* gained a negative connotation as a reference to nepotism, the unfair access to advantages through "friends of friends". However,

---
[9] http://www.theyrule.net

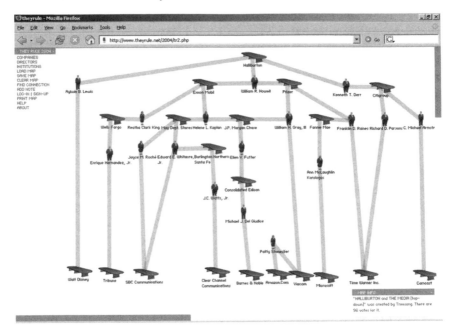

Figure 2.9. The site *theyrule.net* visualizes the interconnectedness of the American political, business and media elite by showing connections between executive boards of various institutions and their board members. Connections between individuals can be inferred by the boards in which they co-participate.

among others in the American society being a good "networker" has become to be seen as an important personal skill that every professional should master.

These terms reflect one of the basic intuitions behind network analysis: that social structure plays a key role in defining our opportunities and constraints with respect to access to key resources. In most settings network ties serve as important conduits for knowledge and other intangible resources such as social support. More often than not establishing social links to those who control tangible resources in a community provides competitive advantages to the individual, especially if those resources are scarce. In turn, a person with such access to key players will be increasingly sought after by other individuals. Conversely, the absence of such relations means the lack of access to the intangible resources "flowing" through social networks and to those tangible resources controlled by certain individuals or groups.

In the following we summarize different dimensions of *social capital* and some related concepts and measures based on the framework of Nahapiet and Ghoshal [NG98]. We choose this well-known framework as it describes social capital in relation to its function in the development of knowledge and knowing capability[10],

---

[10] The distinction references the long standing debate on the two forms of knowledge: objective, analytical and explicit knowledge versus subjective, experience-based and tacit.

which they call *intellectual capital*. In particular, they suggest that various aspects of social capital enable the creation of intellectual capital by allowing exchanges to take place that lead to the combination of knowledge (either incrementally or radically) possessed by individuals.

We hypothesize that social capital as a factor in building intellectual capital is key to the performance of individuals in research communities such as the Semantic Web that we investigate in Chapter 8. Note also that not only social capital can lead to intellectual capital but also the other way around, which is clearly visible in scientific communities. Consider that the very existence of a Semantic Web community is due to the accumulation of knowledge in the fields of Knowledge Representation and Web science and the understanding of the potential combination of the two. In effect, there is a complex feedback cycle where the intellectual capital brings researchers together leading to further socialization, which in turn leads to the creation of new intellectual capital.

Note that in the following we focus on the individual level of analysis. Although Nahapiet and Ghoshal extend intellectual capital to the collective level they note that there is significant discussion in the literature as to whether collectives can be attributed intellectual capital beyond the knowledge of their members and if yes, how the two levels of analysis are related.

Nahapiet and Goshal define social capital as the sum of actual and potential resources embedded within, available through, and derived from the network of relationships possessed by an individual or social unit [NG98]. They identify three main dimensions: the structural, relational and cognitive dimensions of social capital. Common to these dimensions is that they constitute some aspect of the social structure and that they facilitate actions of individuals.

The **structural dimension** of social capital refers to patterns of relationships or positions that provide benefits in terms of accessing large, important parts of the network. Common to structural measures of social capital is that they put a single node (the ego) in the center and provide a measure for the node based on his connectivity to other nodes (the alters).

A simple, but effective measure is the *degree centrality* of the node. Degree centrality equals the graph theoretic measure of degree, i.e. the number of (incoming, outgoing or all) links of a node. This measure is based on the idea that an actor with a large number of links has wider and more efficient access to the network, less reliant on single partners and because of his many ties often participates in deals as a third-party or broker. Degree centrality does not take into account the wider context of the ego, and nodes with a high degree may in fact be disconnected from large parts of the network. However, the degree measure features prominently in the scale-free model, which makes it an important measure to investigate.

A second, more intuitive measure of centrality is *closeness centrality*, which is obtained by calculating the average (geodesic) distance of a node to all other nodes in the network. Closeness centrality thus characterizes the reach of the ego to all other nodes of the network. In larger networks it makes sense to constrain the size of the neighborhood in which to measure closeness centrality. It makes little sense, for example, to talk about the most central node on the level of a society. The resulting measure is called *local closeness centrality*.

Two other measures of power and influence through networks are related to the similar advantages of *broker positions* and *weak ties*. A broker gains advantage by standing in between disconnected communities. As we have seen above ties spanning communities tend to be sparse compared to the dense networks of cohesive subgroups and as a result there are typically few *bridges* across communities. Brokers controlling these bridges are said to be in an advantageous position especially because of the value attributed to the information flowing across such ties.

The measure of *betweenness centrality* identifies broker positions by looking at the extent to which other parties have to go through a given actor to conduct their dealings. Consequently, betweenness is defined as the proportion of paths —among the geodesics between all pairs of nodes— that pass through a given actor. (Betweenness centrality is measured in a similar way as edge-betweenness, but it is a measure of a node, not of an edge.) As with closeness centrality it is often desirable to compute betweenness in a fixed neighborhood of the ego.

The more complex measure of Ronald Burt is related to the idea of *structural holes* [Bur95]. A structural hole occurs in the space that exists between closely clustered communities. According to Burt, a broker gains advantage by bridging such holes. Therefore this measure favors those nodes that connect a significant number of powerful, sparse linked actors with only minimal investment in tie strength. Burt suggests that structural holes show information benefits in three forms: access to large, disparate parts of the network (knowing where to turn for information, who can use some information), timing (receiving information sooner than others) and reputation through referrals.

In contrast to Burt, Coleman stresses the importance of a dense network with strong ties [Col88]. In such a network knowledge can be easily shared because of the high level of general trust and the presence of well-established norms. Density can be measured by computing the clustering coefficient measure introduced above on a neighborhood of the individual.

Researchers intending to reconcile these views emphasize that Burt and Coleman type network often serve different, complementary purposes in practice. Further, there is evidence that these are extreme views: overly dense networks can lead to *overembeddedness* [GB00]. On the other hand, structural embeddedness is necessarily present as through transitivity our friends are likely to develop ties of their own over time.

The aspect of tie strength is an example of the **relational dimension** of social capital, which concerns the kind of personal relationships that people have developed with each other through a history of interaction [Gra92]. The relationships of pairs of actors who occupy similar network positions in similar network configurations may significantly differ based on their past interactions and thus their possibilities for action might also differ.

The benefits of *weak ties* have been exposed by a renowned study in network analysis carried out by Mark Granovetter and described in his paper, *The Strength of Weak Ties* [Gra73]. In this first study, Granovetter looked at two Boston communities and their responses to the threat of urban development. He came to the conclusion that efficient response was not so much a function of a dense, strong tie network but it rather depended on occasional "weak" ties between individuals who only saw each other occasionally. In a second study he found the same effect when looking at how different individuals mobilize their social networks when finding a job. While it has been known long before that most jobs are found through personal connections, Granovetter showed that somewhat surprisingly close friends play a minor role in this process compared to casual acquaintances.

The discussion on the advantages of weak ties versus strong ties parallels the discussion on Burt and Coleman type networks: the connection between the two dimensions is that the bridge ties that we build to other social groups than our own tend to be weak ties as we invest much less of our energy in building and maintaining them. In particular, from the limited time available for social interaction we spend most in building strong ties to our immediate social circles of close colleagues, friends and family. It is a well-known adage in social science that social interaction creates similarity and similarity creates social interaction: we seek out those who are similar to us and in the process of interaction our peers become (even more) similar to us. As a result, our immediate contacts are likely to be "birds of a feather": individuals with similar resources, knowledge, ideas and social access and thus unlikely the provide the informational advantage required for successful job search. On the other hand, the personal trust, the accumulated experiences, the mutual lasting obligations that characterize strong ties reduce the cost (by reducing the risk) of many exchange transactions [Put93].

Less attention is devoted in the literature of social capital to the last, **cognitive dimension** of the Nahapiet-Goshal framework. The cognitive dimension of social capital refers to those resources providing shared representations, interpretations and systems of meaning [Cic73]. In particular, cognitive ties are based on the existence of shared languages, signs and narratives, which facilitate the exchange of knowledge. However, excessive cognitive similarity (associated with strong ties) is likely to lead to cognitive overembeddedness.

We investigate the distinct advantages of certain forms of cognitive embeddedness in our study of the Semantic Web community. In brief, we hypothesize that the access to a variety of cognitive contexts positively contributes to the performance of researchers beyond the well-known advantages of certain forms of structural embeddedness, i.e. that in fact the cognitive dimension is a separate and relevant dimension for assessing the ability of building intellectual capital. We will measure the impact of the cognitive dimension of social capital by comparing the performance of researchers with cognitively heterogeneous personal networks and cognitively homogeneous personal networks (see Chapter 8).

The reader might wonder at this point how these measures of various aspects of social capital are used in analysis. We have discussed in the beginning that the approach of network analysis is statistical and making claims about individual cases does not fit that approach. In fact, these measures are typically used in a "cases-by-variables" analysis where these network measures are correlated with some output variable using regression analysis. Besides network variables other attributes of the individuals are also entered into the model as control variables (see Figure 2.10).

case	var_1 var_2 ... var_n	var_o
Anna	0.92 0.23 ... 0.37	3.2
Bill	1.73 ...	...
Cecile	...	
David		

$$\lambda_1 var_1 + \cdots + \lambda_n var_n + c = var_o + \varepsilon$$

Figure 2.10. In a cases-by-variables analysis we fit a linear equation (below) to the model described by the table containing the values of the variables for each case.

For example, a typical study of this kind is the one carried out by Burt to verify that his structural holes measure can predict the creativity of supply chain managers at a large company. Burt's idea is that individual who have contacts spanning structural holes have better ideas due to their extended vision of the organization [Bur04]. Burt proves this idea by first mapping the organizational network and calculating the structural holes measure for every individual involved in the study. Subsequently he performs a study to measure the creativity of the supply chain managers by asking them to generate ideas about improving their work and then asking other, independent parties to rate those ideas. Lastly, he proves that the structural holes measure correlates with creativity by establishing a linear equation between the network measure and the individual characteristics on one side of the equation and creativity on the other side.

2.4 Discussion

In this Chapter we have introduced the development and key concepts of Social Network Analysis, which we will apply later in our case studies (Chapter 7,8 and 9. Social Network Analysis is a branch of sociology that is formalized to a great extent based on the mathematical notions of graph theory (and to a lesser degree matrix algebra and probability theory). This formal model captures the key observation of Social Network Analysis, namely that to a great extent social structure alone determines the opportunities and limitations of social units and ultimately effects the development of the network as well as substantial outputs of the community.

Social Network Analysis already enjoys many of the benefits of increasing formalization. Formerly vague theoretical concepts have been given a crisp, verifiable definition based on the network model of communities. This formality served network analysis to reduce the ambiguity in formulating and testing its theories and contributed to more coherence in the field by allowing researchers to reliably build on previous results.

In this book we will argue for further formalization in Network Analysis in order to capture more of the semantics of network data. We will argue that this is a necessary step to exploit the increasing availability of network data in electronic formats and to counter the need to combine such sources of information for analysis. In the next Chapter we will show some examples of the emerging possibilities in collecting social network data from the Internet. We will discuss the possibilities of semantic-based representations of electronic data in Chapters 4 and 5.

Part II

**Web data and semantics
in social network applications**

3

Electronic sources for network analysis

From the very beginning of the discipline collecting data on social networks required a certain kind of ingenuity from the researcher. First, social networks have been studied by observation. The disadvantage of this method is the close involvement of the researcher in the process of data collection. Standardized surveys minimize (but do not completely eradicate) the influence of the observer but they rely on an active engagement of the population to be studied. Unfortunately, as all of us are flooded these days by surveys of all kinds, achieving a high enough response rate for any survey becomes more and more problematic. In some settings such as within companies surveys can be forced on the participants, but this casts serious doubts on whether the responses will be spontaneous and genuine. Worse yet, observations and surveys need to be repeated multiple times if one would like to study network dynamics in any detail.

Data collection using these manual methods are extremely labor intensive and can take up to fifty per cent of the time and resources of a project in network analysis. Oftentimes the effort involved in data collection is so immense that network researchers are forced to reanalyze the same data sets over and over in order to be able to contribute to their field.

Network analysts looking for less costly empirical data are often forced to look for alternatives. A creative solution to the problem of data collection is to reuse existing electronic records of social interaction that were not created for the purposes of network analysis on the first place. Scientific communities, for example, have been studied by relying on publication or project databases showing collaborations among authors or institutes [BJN+02, GM02]. Official databases on corporate technology agreements allow us to study networks of innovation [Lem03], while newspaper archives are a source of analysis for studies on topics ranging from the role of social-cognitive networks in politics [vAKOS06] to the structure of terror organizations [Kre02]. These sources often support dynamic studies through historical analysis. Nevertheless, the convenience comes at a price: access to publication and patent databases, media archives, legal and financial records often carries a significant price tag.

However, there is one data source that is not only vast, diverse and dynamic but also free for all: the Internet. In the following, we look at a sample of works from the rapidly emerging field of *e-social science*. Common to these studies is that they rely entirely on data collected from electronic networks and online information sources, which allows a complete automation of the data collection process. None of these works rely on commercial databases and yet many of them are orders of magnitude larger than studies based on data collected through observation or surveys. They represent a diversity of social settings and a number of them also exploit the dynamics of electronic data to perform longitudinal analysis. We will spend more attention on methods of social network extraction from the Web that we use in our analysis of the Semantic Web community (Chapter 8).

There are limits of course to the potential of *e-social science*. Most trivially, what is not on the Web can not be extracted from the Web, which means that there are a number of social settings that can only be studied using offline methods. There also technological limits to the accuracy of any method that relies on Information Extraction. For these reasons it is natural to evaluate our methods before using them for network analysis. We return to this issue in Chapter 7.

3.1 Electronic discussion networks

One of the foremost studies to illustrate the versatility of electronic data is a series of works from the Information Dynamics Labs of Hewlett-Packard.

Tyler, Wilkinson and Huberman analyze communication among employees of their own lab by using the corporate email archive [TWH03]. They recreate the actual discussion networks in the organization by drawing a tie between two individuals if they had exchanged at least a minimum number of total emails in a given period, filtering out one-way relationships. Tyler et al. find the study of the email network useful in identifying leadership roles within the organization and finding formal as well as informal communities. (Formal communities are the ones dictated by the organizational structure of the organization, while informal communities are those that develop across organizational boundaries.) The authors verify this finding through a set of interviews where they feed back the results to the employees of the Lab.

Wu, Huberman, Adamic and Tyler use this data set to verify a formal model of information flow in social networks based on epidemic models [WHAT04]. In yet another study, Adamic and Adar revisits one of the oldest problems of network research, namely the question of *local search*: how do people find short paths in social networks based on only local information about their immediate contacts? Their findings support earlier results that additional knowledge on contacts such as their physical location and position in the organization allows employees to conduct their search much more efficiently than using the simple strategy of always passing the message to the most connected neighbor. Despite the versatility of such data, the studies of electronic communication networks based on email data are limited by privacy concerns. For example, in the HP case the content of messages had to be ignored by the researchers and the data set could not be shared with the community.

Public forums and mailing lists can be analyzed without similar concerns. Starting from the mid-nineties, Marc Smith and colleagues have published a series of papers on the visualization and analysis of USENET newsgroups, which predate Web-based discussion forums (see the author's homepage or the book [Smi99]). In the work of Peter Gloor and colleagues, the source of these data for analysis is the archive of the mailing lists of a standard setting organization, the World Wide Web Consortium (W3C) [GLDZ03]. The W3C —which is also the organization responsible for the standardization of Semantic Web technologies— is unique among standardization bodies in its commitment to transparency toward the general public of the Internet and part of this commitment is the openness of the discussions within the working groups. (These discussion are largely in email and to a smaller part on the phone and in face-to-face meetings.)

Group communication and collective decision taking in various settings are traditionally studied using much more limited written information such as transcripts and records of attendance and voting, see e.g. As in the case with emails Gloor uses the headers of messages to automatically re-create the discussion networks of the working group.[1] The main technical contribution of Gloor is a dynamic visualization of the discussion network that allows to quickly identify the moments when key discussions take place that activate the entire group and not just a few select members. Gloor also performs a comparative study across the various groups based on the structures that emerge over time.

Although it has not been part of this work, it would be even possible to extend such studies with an analysis of the role of networks in the decision making process as voting records that are also available in electronic formats. Further, by applying emotion mining techniques from AI to the contents of the email messages one could recover agreements and disagreements among committee members. Marking up the data set manually with this kind of information is almost impossible: a single working group produces over ten thousand emails during the course of its work.

3.2 Blogs and online communities

Content analysis has also been the most commonly used tool in the computer-aided analysis of blogs (web logs), primarily with the intention of trend analysis for the purposes of marketing.[2] While blogs are often considered as "personal publishing" or a "digital diary", bloggers themselves know that blogs are much more than that: modern blogging tools allow to easily comment and react to the comments of other

---

[1] A slight difference is that unlike with personal emails messages to a mailing list are read by everyone on the list. Nevertheless individuals interactions can be partly recovered by looking at To: and CC: fields of email headers as well as the Reply-To field.

[2] See for example the works presented at the 2006 AAAI Spring Symposium on Computational Approaches to Analyzing Weblogs at http://www.umbriacom.com/aaai2006_weblog_symposium/ or the Workshop on the Weblogging Ecosystem at http://wwe2005.blogspot.com/

bloggers, resulting in webs of communication among bloggers. These discussion networks also lead to the establishment of dynamic communities, which often manifest themselves through syndicated blogs (aggregated blogs that collect posts from a set of authors blogging on similar topics), blog rolls (lists of discussion partners on a personal blog) and even result in real world meetings such as the Blog Walk series of meetings[3]. Figure 3.1 shows some of the features of blogs that have been used in various studies to establish the networks of bloggers.

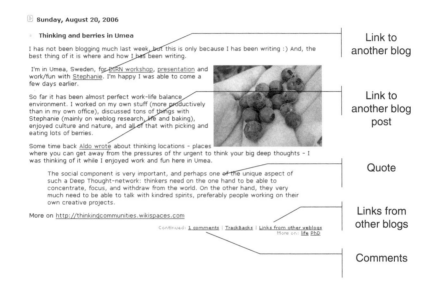

Figure 3.1. Features of blogs that can be used for social network extraction. Note also that —unlike web pages in general— blog entries are timestamped, which allows to study network dynamics, e.g. the spread of information in online communities.

Blogs make a particularly appealing research target due to the availability of structured electronic data in the form of RSS (Rich Site Summary) feeds. RSS feeds contain the text of the blog posts as well as valuable metadata such as the timestamp of posts, which is the basis of dynamic analysis. For example, Kumar et al. and Gruhl et al. study information diffusion in blogs based on this information [KNRT03, GGLNT04]. The early work of Efimova and Anjewierden also stands out in that they were among the first to study blogs from a communication perspective [AE06]. Adar and Adamic offer a visualization of such communication in blogs in [AA05b].

The 2004 US election campaign represented a turning point in blog research as it has been the first major electoral contest where blogs have been exploited as a method of building networks among individual activists and supporters (see for example [AG05]). Blog analysis has suddenly shed its image as relevant only to

---

[3] http://blogwalk.interdependent.biz/wikka.php?wakka=HomePage

marketers interested in understanding product choices of young demographics; following this campaign there has been explosion in research on the capacity of web logs for creating and maintaining stable, long distance social networks of different kinds. Since 2004, blog networks have been the object of study for a number of papers in the blog research track of the yearly Sunbelt social networks conference.

Online community spaces and social networking services such as MySpace, LiveJournal cater to socialization even more directly than blogs with features such as social networking (maintaining lists of friends, joining groups), messaging and photo sharing.[4] As they are typically used by a much younger demographic they offer an excellent opportunity for studying changes in youth culture. Paolillo, Mercure and Wright offer a characterization of the LiveJournal community based on the electronic data that the website exposes about the interests and social networks of its users [PMW05]. Backstrom et al. also study the LiveJournal data in order to answer questions regarding the influence of certain structural properties on community formation and community growth, while also examining how changes in the membership of communities relates to (changes in) the underlying discussion topics [BHKL06]. These studies are good examples of how directly available electronic data enables the longitudinal analysis of large communities (more than 10,000 users). Similar to our work in Chapter 8 these studies also go beyond investigating purely structural network properties: in posing their questions they build on the possibility to access additional information about user interests.

LiveJournal exposes data for research purposes in a semantic format, but unfortunately this is the exception rather than the norm. Most online social networking services (Friendster, Orkut, LinkedIn and their sakes) closely guard their data even from their own users. (Unless otherwise stated these data provided to an online service belongs to the user. However, most of these services impose terms of use that limit the rights of their users.) A technological alternative to these centralized services is the FOAF network (see also Chapter 5). FOAF profiles are stored on the web site of the users and linked together using hyperlinks. The drawback of FOAF is that at the moment there is a lack of tools for creating and maintaining profiles as well as useful services for exploiting this network. Nevertheless, a few preliminary studies have already established that the FOAF network exhibits similar characteristics to other online social networks [PW04, DZFJ05].

3.3 Web-based networks

The content of Web pages is the most inexhaustible source of information for social network analysis. This content is not only vast, diverse and free to access but also in many cases more up to date than any specialized database. On the downside, the quality of information varies significantly and reusing it for network analysis poses

---

[4] In July, 2006 MySpace has passed Google and Yahoo! as the most popular website on the Web, see http://www.techcrunch.com/2006/07/11/myspace-hit-1-us-destination-last-week-hitwise/

significant technical challenges. Further, while web content is freely accessible in principle, in practice web mining requires efficient search that at the moment only commercial search engines provide.[5]

There are two features of web pages that are considered as the basis of extracting social relations: links and co-occurrences (see Figure 3.2). The linking structure of the Web is considered as proxy for real world relationships as links are chosen by the author of the page and connect to other information sources that are considered authoritative and relevant enough to be mentioned. The biggest drawback of this approach is that such direct links between personal pages are very sparse: due to the increasing size of the Web searching has taken over browsing as the primary mode of navigation on the Web. As a result, most individuals put little effort in creating new links and updating link targets or have given up linking to other personal pages altogether.

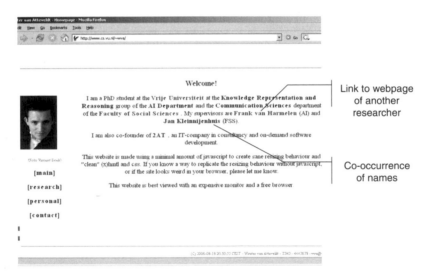

Figure 3.2. Features in web pages that can be used for social network extraction.

For this reason most social studies based on the linking structure of the web are looking at relationships at higher levels of aggregation. For example, members of the EICSTES project investigate the web connectivity of entire scientific institutions for the purposes of *webometrics* or web-based scientometrics in the EICSTES project[6]. For example, Heimeriks, Hörlesberger and Van den Besselaar compare communication and collaboration networks across different fields of research using a

---

[5] Unfortunately, search engines such as Google or Yahoo! typically limit the number of queries that can be issued a day. There has been work on an open source search engine since 2003, see http://lucene.apache.org/nutch/. However, to this day this effort did not result in an alternative to commercial search engines

[6] http://www.eicstes.org/

multi-layered approach [HHvdB03]. The data for this analysis comes from biblio-graphic records, project databases and hyperlink networks. The connections for the latter are collected by crawling the websites of the institutions involved. In principle it could be possible to extract more fine-grained networks from the homepages of the individual researchers. However, links between homepages are too sparse to be analyzed on their own and automating this task would also require solving what is known as the home page search problem: locating the homepage of individuals given their name and description.

Co-occurrences of names in web pages can also be taken as evidence of rela-tionships and are a more frequent phenomenon. On the other hand, extracting rela-tionships based on co-occurrence of the names of individuals or institutions requires web mining as names are typically embedded in the natural text of web pages. (Web mining is the application of text mining to the content of web pages.) The techniques employed here are statistical methods possibly combined with an analysis of the contents of web pages.

Web mining has been first tested for social network extraction from the Web in the work of Kautz el al. on the ReferralWeb project in the mid-90s [KSS97]. The goal of Kautz et al. was not to perform sociological experiments but to build a tool for automating what he calls *referral chaining*: looking for experts with a given expertise who are close to the user of the system, i.e. experts who can be accessed through a chain of referrals. An example of a question that could be asked to the system is "show me all experts on simulated annealing who are at most three steps away from me in the network."

As the authors were researchers themselves, they were primarily interested in solving the referral chaining problem in the scientific domain where finding experts on a given topic is a common problem in organizing peer-reviews. (Kautz also ap-plied his system later toward recommending experts in a corporate setting at AT&T.) The ReferralWeb system was bootstrapped with the names of famous AI researchers. The system extracted connections between them through co-occurrence analysis. Us-ing the search engine Altavista the system collected page counts for the individual names as well as the number of pages where the names co-occurred. Note that this corresponds to a very shallow parsing of the web page as indirect references are not counted this way (e.g. the term "the president of the United States" will not be asso-ciated with George Bush even if he was mentioned as the president elsewhere in the text.)

Tie strength was calculated by dividing the number of co-occurrences with the number of pages returned for the two names individually (see Figure 3.3). Also known as the *Jaccard-coefficient*, this is basically the ratio of the sizes of two sets: the intersection of the sets of pages and their union [Sal89]. The resulting value of tie strength is a number between zero (no co-occurrences) and one (no separate men-tioning, only co-occurrences). If this number has exceeded a certain fixed threshold it was taken as evidence for the existence of a tie.

Although Kautz makes no mention of it we can assume that he also filtered ties also based on support, i.e. the number of pages that can be found for the given indi-viduals or combination of individuals. The reason is that the Jaccard-coefficient is a

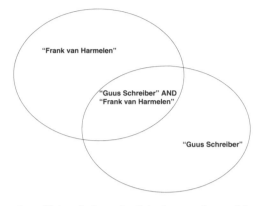

Figure 3.3. The Jaccard-coefficient is the ratio of the intersection and the union of two sets. In the case of co-occurrence analysis the two sets contain the pages where the individual names occur. The intersection is formed by the pages where both names appear.

relative measure of co-occurrence and it does not take into account the absolute sizes of the sets. In case the absolute sizes are very low we can easily get spurious results: for example, if two names only occur once on the Web and they occur on the same page, their co-efficient will be one. However, in this case the absolute sizes are too low to take this as an evidence for a tie.

The expertise of individuals was extracted by looking for capitalized phrases that appeared in documents returned by the search engine that were not proper names. The network in the system has grown two ways. Firstly, the documents from the Web were searched for new names using *proper name extraction*, a fairly reliable NLP technique. These names were then used to extract new names, a process that was repeated two or three times. (Note that this is similar to the *snowballing technique* of network analysis where the network under investigation is growing through new names generated by participants in the study.) Second, users of the system were also allowed to register themselves.

Kautz never evaluated his system in the sense of asking whether the networks he extracted are an accurate reflection of real world networks. He notes that the system as a recommender system performed well on both the research domain and in the corporate setting, although "the recommendations made by (any) recommender system tend to be either astonishingly accurate, or absolutely ridiculous [, which is] true for any AI-complete problem". However, he suggest that the system is able to keep the trust of the user provided that it is made transparent. For example, the system can show the evidence on which the recommendation is based and indicate the level of confidence in its decisions. With respect to the corporate setting Kautz also notes that the results in principle can be better than using the official corporate records for locating experts as personal pages are often more up-to-date. In the scientific setting such records are non-existent and even if there existed a central system where experts can describe their social networks and expertise it would be just as likely to become obsolete on the long term as corporate yellow pages are.

In our work we use the basic method of Kautz in a slightly different way. Since our goal is the extraction of social networks we are given a list of names to begin with. We consult the search engine for investigating the possible tie between all pairs of names. Note that the number of queries required grows quadratically with the number of names, which is not only costly in terms of time but is limited by the number of queries that search engines allow. While this is not a problem in our case study, optimizations are required for larger scale analysis. A solution is proposed by Matsuo et al. who recreate the original method of Kautz by first extracting possible contacts from the results returned by the search engine for the individual names [MHT+06]. This significantly reduces the number of queries that need to be made to the search engine at a minimal loss.

We also experiment with different measures of co-occurrence. A disadvantage of the Jaccard-coefficient is that it penalizes ties between an individual whose name often occurs on the Web and less popular individuals (see Figure 3.4). In the science domain this makes it hard to detect, for example, the ties between famous professors and their PhD students. In this case while the name of the professor is likely to occur on a large percentage of the pages of where the name of the PhD student occurs but not vice versa. For this reason we use an asymmetric variant of the coefficient. In particular, we divide the number of pages for the individual with the number of pages for both names and take it as evidence of a directed tie if this number reaches a certain threshold. We experiment with choosing an appropriate value for this threshold and the threshold for tie strength in Chapter 7.

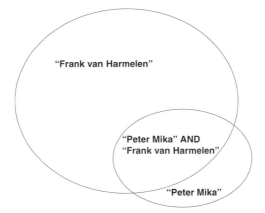

Figure 3.4. The Jaccard-coefficient does not show a correlation in cases where there is a significant difference in the sizes of the two sets such as in the case of a student and a professor.

Second, we associate researchers with topics in a slightly different way. In our study of the Semantic Web community, the task is to associate scientists with research topics that have been collected manually from the proceedings of ISWC conference series. The system calculates the strength of association between the name of a given person and a certain topic. This strength is determined by taking the number of the pages where the name of an interest and the name of a person co-occur divided by the total number of pages about the person. We assign the expertise to an individual if this value is at least one standard deviation higher than the mean of the values obtained for the same concept.[7] We also borrow from the work of Mutschke and Quan Haase, who perform network analysis based on bibliographic records that contain keywords of publications. Before applying an analysis of the social-cognitive network of co-authors, the authors cluster keywords into themes based on the co-occurrences of keywords on publications, assign documents to themes and subsequently determine which themes are relevant for a person based on his or her publications [MH01]. We also perform a simple clustering of keywords based on their co-occurrences among the interests of researchers (see 6.6).

Kautz already notes that the biggest technical challenge in social network mining is the disambiguation of person names. Persons names exhibit the same problems of polysemy and synonymy that we have seen in the general case of web search. Queries for researchers who commonly use different variations of their name (e.g. *Jim Hendler* vs. *James Hendler*) or whose names contain international characters (e.g. *Jérôme Euzenat*) may return only a partial set of all relevant documents known to the search engine. Queries for persons with common names such as *Martin Frank* or *Li Ding* return pages about all persons with the same name. Another problem is that the coverage of the Web can be very skewed: for example, *George Bush* the president is over-represented compared to *George Bush* the beer brewer. Not only statistical methods suffer, but also content analysis as in this case the top pages returned by the search engine may not even mention the beer brewer (web pages are largely ranked by popularity). This is a typical web scale problem: such name collisions are rare in even the largest of corporate settings but a common phenomenon on the Web.

There have been several approaches to deal with name ambiguity. Bekkerman and McCallum deal with this problem by using limited background knowledge: instead of a single name they assume to have a list of names related to each other [BM05]. They disambiguate the appearances by clustering the combined results returned by the search engine for the individual names. The clustering can be based on various networks between the returned webpages, e.g. based on hyperlinks between the pages, common links or similarity in content. Bollegala, Matsuo and Ishizuka also apply clustering based on the content similarity but go a step further in mining the resulting clusters for key phrases [BMI06]. The idea is that such key phrases can be added to the search query to reduce the set of results to those related to the given target individual. For example, when searching for *George Bush* the beer brewer one would add the term *beer* to the query.

---

[7] Note that we do not factor in the number of pages related to the concept, since we are only interested in the expertise of the individual relative to himself. By normalizing with the page count of the interest the measure would assign a relatively high score —and an overly large number of interests— to individuals with many pages on the Web. We only have to be careful in that we cannot compare the association strength across interests. However, this is not necessary for our purposes.

In our work in extracting information about the Semantic Web community we also add a disambiguation term our queries. We use a fixed disambiguation term (*Semantic Web OR ontology*) instead of a different disambiguation term for every name. This is a safe (and even desirable) limitation of the query as we are only interested in relations in the Semantic Web context. The method of Bollegala et al. would likely suggest more specific key phrases for every individual and that would increase the precision of our queries, but likely result in much lower recall. (As the co-occurrences we are looking for are relatively rare we cannot afford to lower recall by adding too many or too specific terms.)

We also experiment with a second method based on the concept of *average precision*. When computing the weight of a directed link between two persons we consider an ordered list of pages for the first person and a set of pages for the second (the relevant set) as shown in Figure 3.5. In practice, we ask the search engine for the top N pages for both persons but in the case of the second person the order is irrelevant for the computation. Let's define $rel(n)$ as the relevance at position n, where $rel(n)$ is 1 if the document at position n is the relevant set and zero otherwise ($1 \leq n \leq N$). Let $P(n)$ denote the precision at position n (also known as $p@n$):

$$P(n) = \frac{\sum_{r=1}^{n} rel(r)}{n}$$

Average precision is defined as the average of the precision at all relevant positions:

$$P_{ave} = \frac{\sum_{r=1}^{N} P(r) * rel(r)}{N}$$

The average precision method is more sophisticated in that it takes into account the order in which the search engine returns document for a person: it assumes that names of other persons that occur closer to the top of the list represent more important contacts than names that occur in pages at the bottom of the list. The method is also more scalable as it requires only to download the list of top ranking pages once for each author. (This makes it linear in the number of queries that need to be made instead of quadratic.) The drawback of this method is that most search engines limit the number of pages returned to at most a thousand. In case a person and his contacts have significantly more pages than that it is likely that some of the pages for some the alters will not occur among the top ranking pages.

Lastly, we would note that one may reasonably argue against the above methods on the basis that a single link or co-occurrence is hardly evidence for any relationship. In fact, not all links are equally important nor every co-occurrence is intended. For example, it may very well happen that two names co-occur on a web page without much meaning to it (for example, they are on the same page of the corporate phone book or appear in a list of citations). What is important to realize about these methods is that they are statistical and assume that the effects of uneven weights and spurious occurrences disappear by means of large numbers. We will evaluate the robustness of both the simple co-occurrence and the average precision based methods in Chapter 7.

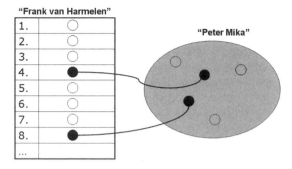

Figure 3.5. The average precision method considers also the position of the pages related to a second person in the list of results for the first person.

3.4 Discussion

The term e-social science covers the new movement in Social Sciences toward the (re)use of electronic data for social studies. The basis of this new opportunity for the Social Sciences is the through and through digitalization of modern life, including a transition of much of our communication and social interaction into the online world. The electronic records of online social activity offer a tremendous possibility for social scientist to observe communicative and social patterns at much larger scales than before. (Parallel advances in computer technology make it also possible to deal with the exploding amounts of data at hand.) Further, as the unscalable human element is removed from the data collection process it becomes possible to sample data at arbitrary frequencies and to observe dynamics in a much more reliable fashion. Longitudinal studies built on observation or survey data typically rely on looking at the state of the network at just two distinct time points; the human effort involved in collecting more data points is usually prohibitive.

The expansion of the online universe also means a growing variety of social settings that can be studied online. We have shown above a cross-section of studies in e-social science that represent the diversity of topics in this emerging field. These studies rely on very different data sources, each with its own method of extraction and limitations as to what extent it can be used as a proxy for observing social phenomena.

The method we will use in our work is social network extraction from the content of Web pages. These Information Retrieval based methods have the advantage of generality: they can be used to extract networks of a variety of social units (individuals, institutes etc.) but can also be limited to particular settings by focusing the extraction to certain parts of the Web. The only requirement is that the network to be studied should have a significant coverage on the Web so that the extraction can produce reliable results even if the face of noise e.g. spurious co-occurrences of names on web pages. In Chapter 7 we will evaluate this method and show that it is robust to such noise and suited for network analysis.

The most important technical hurdle to overcome when applying such methods is the problem of person name disambiguation, i.e. the matching of references to actual persons they represent. Person names are neither unique nor single: a person may have different ways of writing his name and two persons may have the same name. Interestingly this is exactly the kind of problem the Semantic Web is designed to solve. Websites such as LiveJournal that already export data in a semantic format do not suffer from this problem. In their case, a machine processable description is attached to every web page, containing the same information that appears on the web page but in a way that individuals are uniquely identified. We will show how such semantic descriptions work in the following Chapter. In Chapter 5 we will apply this technology to a related problem: the merging of multiple electronic data sources for analysis.

4

Knowledge Representation on the Semantic Web

The key idea of the Semantic Web is to represent information on and about the current Web using formal languages that computers can process and reason with. Recapturing the information on the current Web and adding additional descriptions of Web resources (metadata) would allow our machines to support us in performing intelligent tasks such as providing analysis by combining information from multiple sources.

Representing and reasoning with knowledge are core issues for the Semantic Web, but not all of the challenges are new. Questions of knowledge representation and reasoning have been extensively studied in Artificial Intelligence for several decades, in particular with respect to building expert systems, where for example the idea of separating domain knowledge from task knowledge (the process of solving a problem) has already emerged [SAA+99, Ste95]. Through this separation a system for diagnosis, for example, could be reused in different domains by replacing the underlying knowledge base. (The process of reasoning toward a solution is the same regardless whether we are performing medical diagnosis or trying to find the source of a break-down in a car.) Conversely, medical knowledge about the location of body parts in the human body that is used in one diagnostic system could be exported to another system, possibly serving a different task, but using some of the same general knowledge about the human body.

The field of expert systems has developed a number of logic-based knowledge representation languages for describing both the domain knowledge and task knowledge of such systems (see for example KIF[1] and OCML[2]). Arriving to standard or at least widely accepted languages for knowledge representation enabled the exchange of knowledge between systems, reducing the effort that went into developing knowledge bases by increasing reusability. While task knowledge is more general, domain knowledge is typically derived from experts using various knowledge-elicitation techniques and formalized by knowledge engineers into logic-based representations. Domain models that captured the agreement of a group of experts and were

---

[1] http://logic.stanford.edu/kif/kif.html
[2] http://kmi.open.ac.uk/projects/ocml/

represented using formal languages for reusability came to be referred to by the term *ontology*[3].

However, AI is not the only field in Computer Science where formal modelling plays a key role. Domain modelling is also an important step in the requirement specification and design phases of software engineering. Software specification methodologies such as UML and the E/R models of database design allow software developers to model expert knowledge about the application domain in a semi-formal, visual way. These serve the dual purpose of reaching an agreement with domain experts and serving as an input toward the design of an object-oriented software or relational database schema, respectively. In both cases the standardization of languages has been crucial in at least two respects. One, having standard languages ensured that engineers interpret the models unambiguously. Second, standard languages were required to achieve interoperability among various software applications (e.g. modelling applications, code generators). [4]

Although the goal of modelling is similar —adding domain knowledge to an information system—, the context of the Semantic Web is different from these use cases. In particular, the Semantic Web is envisioned to connect knowledge bases on a web-wide scale. The particular challenges related to this situation necessitated the design of new languages. This section gives a brief, non-exhaustive introduction to knowledge representation (modelling) using Semantic Web languages such as RDF and OWL. We explain the RDF/OWL ontology languages by comparing them to related, well-known information modelling techniques familiar to Computer Scientists and practitioners: the above mentioned E/R and relational models, UML class models and XML, which is currently widely used in exchanging structured information across the Web. (With respect to XML and related standards, we will see that their interoperability with the Semantic Web stack of languages and protocols is limited, despite popular belief.)

Software engineers and web developers often find RDF and OWL difficult to learn, which has to do with the grounding of these languages in formal logic, which is not well covered in most Computer Science curricula. However, we would like to show that RDF and OWL can also be quickly understood when explained using the more familiar concepts of software and database design. In effect, all these models are based on simple statements about objects, properties and their values. Some basic understanding of logic will only be required when we discuss the notion of semantics in Section 4.2.1.

For authoritative information on RDF and OWL, we refer the reader to the appropriate W3C specifications and the more easily readable, non-normative RDF Primer

---

[3] The term ontology originates from Philosophy. Ontology (with a capital O) is the most fundamental branch of metaphysics. It studies being or existence as well as the basic categories thereof –trying to find out what entities and what types of entities exist. See http://en.wikipedia.org/wiki/Ontology

[4] That domain models need to be readable by human experts as well as computers is also the case for ontology languages. Human experts need to be able to read the models in order to be able to check if they agree to what is being modeled.

and OWL Guide documents [MM04, SWM04][5]. In the past few years a number
of academic books have also appeared, based on research and teaching experience
at leading Semantic Web research institutes and universities, for example the recommended Semantic Web Primer by Antoniou and Harmelen [AvH04]. Lastly, practical
programming guides are also starting to appear as technology becomes more widely
adopted [Pow03].

4.1 Ontologies and their role in the Semantic Web

In the following two Sections, we introduce the concept of ontologies and their role
in the architecture of the Semantic Web. It is important to separate the two: while
ontologies and ontology languages have existed long before the Semantic Web, the
unique requirements of the Semantic Web necessitated the development of a new set
of languages. We introduce these languages in the remaining parts of this Chapter.

4.1.1 Ontology-based Knowledge Representation

As already discussed in Chapter 1, the idea of the Semantic Web is to extend unstruc-
tured information with machine processable descriptions of the meaning (semantics)
of information and to provide missing background knowledge where required.

The key challenge of the Semantic Web is to ensure a shared interpretation of information. Related information sources should use the same concepts to reference the
same real world entities or at least there should be a way to determine if two sources
refer to the same entities, but possibly using different vocabularies. Ontologies and
ontology languages are the key enabling technology in this respect. An ontology, by
its most cited definition in AI, is a shared, formal conceptualization of a domain,
i.e. a description of concepts and their relationships [Gru93, BAT97]. Ontologies are
domain models with two special characteristics, which lead to the notion of shared
meaning or semantics:

1. Ontologies are expressed in formal languages with a well-defined semantics.
2. Ontologies build upon a shared understanding within a *community*. This understanding represents an agreement among members of the community over the
   concepts and relationships that are present in a domain and their usage.

The first point underlines that an ontology needs to be modelled using languages
with a formal semantics. RDF [MM04] and OWL [MvH04]), the ontology languages
that we introduce later in this Chapter, have standardized syntaxes and logic-based
formal semantics. RDF and OWL are the languages most commonly used on the
Semantic Web, and in fact when using the term ontology many practitioners refer to
domain models described in one of these two languages. The second point reminds

---

[5] The home page http://www.w3.org/2001/sw/ of the W3C Semantic Web Activity
gives access to a wealth of information, including presentations, articles as well as the
technical specifications we reference in this Chapter.

as that there is no such thing as a "personal ontology". For example, the schema of a database or a UML class diagram that we have created for the design of our own application is not an ontology. It is a conceptual model of a domain, but it is not shared: there is no commitment toward this schema from anyone else but us.

Note that the definition does not define the level of detail at which ontologies need to be modeled nor does it specify the minimal expressivity required from an ontology language.[6] In practice, ontologies differ greatly in complexity. In Figure 4.1, adapted from the work of Smith and Welty [SW01], we loosely organize the most common ontological structures according to the their complexity.

The most simple structures are glossaries or controlled vocabularies, in essence an agreement on the meaning of a set of terms. (Note that a mere bag of words doesn't meet the criteria of shared meaning.) An example would be a controlled vocabulary used inside a support center for describing incidents reported. Such a controlled vocabulary facilitates the communication among the helpdesk and the technical staff of a support center as it enables a uniform description of the reported problems.

Semantic networks are essentially graphs that show also how terms are related to each other. Thesauri are richer structures in that they describe a hierarchy between concepts and typically also allow to describe related terms and aliases. Thesauri are also the simplest structures where logic-based reasoning can be applied: the broader-narrower relationships of these hierarchies are transitive, in that an item that belongs to a narrower category also belongs to its direct parent and all of its ancestors.

In the context of the Semantic Web research, it is often assumed that an ontology at least contains a hierarchy between the concepts (subclass relationships). Weaker models with no explicit hierarchies, such as the folksonomies we describe in Chapter 9 are often excluded from the definition. However, we will argue in time that it is possible to extract hierarchies as well as relationships between the tags in folksonomies. Further, folksonomies contain additional information about the social context of tags, i.e. the set of users who have been using them.

The term *lightweight ontology* is typically applied to ontologies that make a distinction between classes, instances and properties, but contain minimal descriptions of them. On the other hand, *heavyweight ontologies* allow to describe more precisely how classes are composed of other classes, and provide a richer set of constructs to constrain how properties can be applied to classes. At the far end of the spectrum are complex knowledge bases that use the full expressivity of first order logic (FOL) to define to a great detail the kind of instances a concept may have and in which cases two instances may be related using a certain relationship. The more constrained the descriptions of concepts are, the less likely that their meaning will be misinterpreted by human readers. Further, the closer to the far end of the spectrum, the larger the role that computers can play in reasoning with ontologies. Typical reasoning tasks

---

[6] These are not the same: the expressivity of the language determines the level of detail at which concepts and relations can be characterized using the constructs of the language. Expressivity is an upper-limit, however, and most models do not use all the features of a given modeling language. For example, in UML many things can be said about a class, but only the name is minimally required.

include checking the consistency of the usage of terms, classifying concepts (finding subclass relations among concepts) and checking for equivalent terms.

An ontology is a...

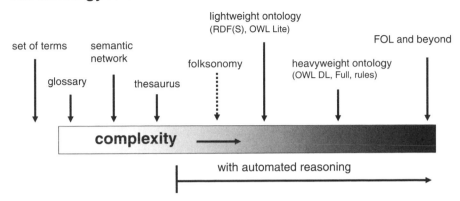

Figure 4.1. Ontologies can be organized according to complexity (informally, the level of semantics).

Roughly speaking, the models that can be captured using less expressive languages can also be expressed using more expressive languages, e.g. a modeling language capable of describing a semantic network (a graph structure) is typically also capable to describe a classification hierarchy (a tree structure). One may thus wonder why a single, most expressive language is not enough to satisfy all modeling needs. The answer is partly that a language that is too expressive (offers features that are not used) can be in the way of modeling. Just like in the case of programming languages, every ontology language offers a slightly different (and not entirely overlapping) set of features that precisely matches the representation needs of a specific task or domain. We will also see that less expressive modelling languages have lower guaranteed computational complexity when it comes to reasoning.

In practice, the most common Web ontologies are all lightweight ontologies due to the need of serving the needs of many applications with divergent goals. Widely shared Web ontologies also tend to be small as they contain only the terms that are agreed on by a broad user base. Large, heavyweight ontologies are more commonly found in targeted expert systems used in focused domains with a tradition of formalized processes and vocabularies such as the area of life sciences and engineering. We have argued elsewhere that the trade-off between the formality and sharing scope of knowledge is unavoidable: models that need to be shared among many applications will end up to be shallow, while a limited scope allows to create more detailed models of the world [MA04].

4.1.2 Ontologies and ontology languages for the Semantic Web

Although the notion of ontologies is independent of the Web, ontologies play a special role in the architecture of the Semantic Web. We show a schematic view of this architecture in Figure 4.2. This architecture provides the main motivation for the design of ontology languages for the Semantic Web: RDF and OWL are both prepared for the distributed and open environment of the Web.

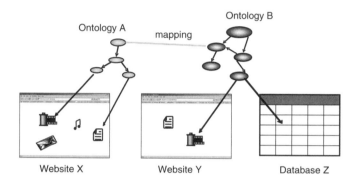

Figure 4.2. The Semantic Web in envisioned as a network of ontologies that adds machine-processable semantics to existing web content, including Web resources and databases.

As we have discussed in Chapter 1, the Semantic Web will be realized by annotating existing Web resources with ontology-based metadata and by exposing the content of databases by publishing the data and the schema in one of the standard ontology languages.

Ontology languages designed for the Semantic Web provide the means to identify concepts in ontologies using globally unique identifiers (URIs). These identifiers can be used in data sources to point to a concept or relationship from an external, public ontology. Similar to creating HTML pages and linking them to existing ones, anyone can create and publish an ontology, which may reference the concepts in remote ontologies. Much like the hyperlinks among web pages, it is expected that these references will form a contiguous web linking all knowledge sources across the Web. As URLs are also URIs, ontologies can also reference existing Web resources and describe their characteristics. [7]

The (meta)data and its schema can be made public either by publishing an RDF or OWL document online (which may be dynamically generated from a database or through a Web service invocation) or by providing access to a data source through implementing the standard query language and protocol[8] of the Semantic Web. The

---

[7] The metadata may be embedded inside the content, in which case there is obviously no need to reference the resource that is being described. An example of this is the proposed RDF/a standard, which provides a way of embedding RDF data in HTML [AB06]. Metadata in RDF is also embedded inside files in a PDF format.

[8] We introduce the SPARQL query language and protocol in Section 4.2.1

schema and the data itself can be published as separate documents or query end-points, but as we will see, ontology languages for the Semantic Web allow to mix information about the schema of a data source and the instances (the records, in database terms).

Semantic Web applications collect or query such data sources, aggregate and reason with the results. Information described according to a single schema that is known by the application developer can be directly consumed: by committing to an ontology the parties involved have already implicitly agreed on the meaning of the information. In this case, the interesting task left is the aggregation of instance data, i.e. finding equivalent instances across the data sources, if they exist. Formal semantics plays an important role in this task, as we will see in Chapter 5.

When annotating Web content or exposing the content of a database, one may choose to create an ontology from scratch, or reuse an existing ontology while possibly extending it. However, as their is no coordination of any kind in reusing ontologies, it may happen that two communities develop ontologies that cover the same or overlapping domains. (For example, there are several known ontologies that describe types of scientific publications and their properties (e.g. scientific articles that have a title, a set of authors, a journal and a publication date.) In this case, we need to determine how the classes in one ontology are related to the classes in another ontology. (For example, that the Article class in one ontology is the same as the JournalPublication class in another ontology.) Finding equivalences and other relations among terms in different ontologies is the task of *ontology mapping*, a problem we do not address in this volume.

What we would like to emphasize is the role of machine-processable semantics in both the mapping of classes and instances. The more formal and detailed an ontology is, the more accurately it can capture the intended meaning of concepts and relationships. This is particularly relevant in the context of the Web, where ontologies are shared in a wide scope. In particular, precise definitions prevent that someone trying to understand a previously unseen ontology will interpret the terms of the ontology in unintended ways. This is important for humans but crucial for machines: while a human may be able to read the labels of concepts and textual comments about what a concept means, a machine can only rely on the formal semantics to "understand" a term, e.g. to be able to determine whether a newly discovered term is the same as a previously seen term in order to map the two concepts automatically. The finding of mappings between classes and instances is a difficult task to automate, but such automation is indispensable at the scale of Web data.

4.2 Ontology languages for the Semantic Web

In the following, we introduce the ontology languages RDF and OWL, which have been standardized in recent years by the World Wide Web Consortium.

4.2.1 The Resource Description Framework (RDF) and RDF Schema

The Resource Description Framework (RDF) was originally created to describe resources on the World Wide Web (in particular web pages and other content), hence the name. In reality, RDF is domain-independent and can be used to model both real world objects and information resources. RDF itself is a very primitive modelling language, but it is the basis of more complex languages such as OWL.

There are two kinds of primitives in RDF: resources and literals (character sequences). The definition of a resource is intentionally vague; in general everything is modelled as a resource that can be (potentially) identified and described. Resources are either identified by a URI or left blank. URIs are identifiers with a special syntax defined in [BLFM98].[9] Blank resources (*blank nodes*) are the existential quantifiers of the language: they are resources with an identity, but whose identifier is not known or irrelevant. (These is no way in the RDF model itself to assign an identifier to a blank node.) Literals are strings (character literals) with optional language and datatype identifiers.

Expressions are formed by making statements (*triples*) of the form (subject, predicate, object). The subject of a statement must be a resource (blank or with a URI), the predicate must be a URI and the object can be either kind of resource or a literal. Literals are thus only allowed at the end of a statement.[10]

RDF is very easy to understand in practice. The following brief RDF document describes a person named Rembrandt (see Figure 4.3). The six statements are also shown as a directed, labelled graph in Figure 4.4. In this visualization the nodes are the subjects and objects of statements, labelled with the URI or literal or left blank, and the edges connect the subjects and objects of statements and are labelled with the URI of the property.[11] As we can see the statements of the RDF model form a graph because the object of one statement can be the subject of another statement. (As noted literals cannot be the subjects of statements, i.e. there are no arrows going from literals.)

This fragment is written in the Turtle syntax, one of the many notations of RDF graphs . We will later also encounter the RDF/XML syntax, an XML-based notation defined by the World Wide Web Consortium (see Section 4.2.5). RDF/XML has been

---

[9] URLs used on the Web (such as the ones starting with http:) are also a form of URIs. The registration of new URI schemes is regulated in [PK99]. In practice, it is most common to use http: URIs as identifiers even if the resources modelled are not Web resources.

[10] There has been some discussions in the RDF community to allow statements about literals, which would be useful, for example, to define inverses of properties with literal values. For example, in the context of the example in Figure 4.3 this would allow to make statements such as "Rembrandt" *ex:firstNameOf ex:Rembrandt*. However, it would also encourage poor modelling, in particular confusing resources with their labels (e.g. "Rembrandt" *foaf:gender* "male" instead of *ex:Rembrandt foaf:gender* "male").

[11] This visualization follows the conventions of the RDF Primer document [MM04]. Unlike in the case of visual modelling languages such as UML, visualization plays a minor role in RDF modelling. In fact, there is no standard visual modelling language for ontologies; the kind of generic graph visualization shown here results in a very complex image for any real ontology.

the first and up to date the most widely used syntax. As an XML based syntax, it also has the advantage of being processable by XML tools. However, other notations such as Turtle are often preferred for their readability by human authors.

Turtle as well as RDF/XML allow to abbreviate URIs using namespaces. Namespaces are not a feature of RDF, but rather syntactic sugar in many RDF notations. The resources from the FOAF namespace that we use are defined separately in the so called Friend-of-a-Friend (FOAF) ontology, which resides at `http://xmlns.com/foaf/0.1/index.rdf`. We discuss FOAF in more detail in Section 5.2. For now it is enough to know that it is another RDF document on the Web defining some of the terms that we are using in the example.

```
@prefix rdf: <http://www.w3.org/1999/02/22-rdf-syntax-ns> .
@prefix rdfs: <http://www.w3.org/2000/01/rdf-schema#label> .
@prefix foaf: <http://xmlns.com/foaf/0.1/> .
@prefix example: <http://www.example.org/> .

example:Rembrandt rdf:type foaf:Person .
example:Saskia    rdf:type foaf:Person .
example:Rembrandt foaf:name "Rembrandt" .
example:Rembrandt foaf:mbox <mailto:rembrandt@example.org> .
example:Rembrandt foaf:knows example:Saskia .
example:Saskia    foaf:name "Saskia" .
```

Figure 4.3. A set of triples describing two persons represented in the Turtle language.

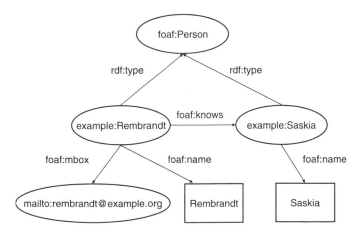

Figure 4.4. A graph visualization of the RDF document shown in Figure 4.3.

The RDF language provides the basic term to assign a type to a resource (*rdf:type*) and to declare a resource as a property (see 4.1). It also provides features to describe collections of instances[12] and to make statements about statements (*reification*)[13]. The descriptive power of RDF is minimal that in practice it is always used in combination with RDF Schema. RDF Schema is a simple extension of RDF defining a modelling vocabulary with notions of classes and subclasses (see Table 4.2). Classes and properties can be connected by specifying the domain and range of properties.

Note that the division of terms between the RDF and RDF Schema namespaces is very unnatural: for example, *rdf:type* property appears in the RDF namespace, even though there are no classes in RDF. On the other hand, the *rdfs:Literal* class is in the RDF(S) namespace even though literals are a feature of RDF. For this reason and for the limited use of RDF on its own, most people refer to an RDF Schema ontology when talking about an 'RDF ontology' or 'RDF data'. In the following, we will also use the term RDF in this sense and apply the term RDF Schema when we specifically intend to speak about the RDF Schema vocabulary.

Basic constructs	*rdf:type*
	rdf:Property
	rdf:XMLLiteral
Collections	*rdf:List*
	rdf:Seq
	rdf:Bag
	rdf:Alt
	rdf:first
	rdf:rest
	rdf:nil
	rdf:_n
	rdf:value
Reification	*rdf:Statement*
	rdf:subject
	rdf:predicate
	rdf:object

Table 4.1. The RDF vocabulary.

Figure 4.5 shows some of the statements from the FOAF ontology. The first group of statements describe the class Person. The type of the resource is specified as *owl:Class*, we give a label, name a superclass and state that this class is disjoint from the class of documents. (We return to these terms from the OWL vocabulary in Section 4.2.2). We then describe the *foaf:knows* and *foaf:name* properties we have

---

[12] The RDF vocabulary contains four collection types and two ways of describing their contents: by creating linked lists using *rdf:first*, *rdf:rest* and *rdf:nil*, or by enumerating the elements. Unfortunately, making this latter possible required the introduction of an infinite number of properties of the form *rdf:_n* where $n = 1, 2 \ldots n$. In theory, this makes the RDF vocabulary infinitely large, but causes little problems in practice.

[13] We will return to the use of reification in Chapter 5.

Basic constructs	*rdfs:domain*
	rdfs:range
	rdfs:Resource
	rdfs:Literal
	rdfs:Datatype
	rdfs:Class
	rdfs:subClassOf
	rdfs:subPropertyOf
Collections	*rdfs:member*
	rdfs:Container
	rdfs:ContainerMembershipProperty
Documentation & reference	*rdfs:comment*
	rdfs:seeAlso
	rdfs:isDefinedBy
	rdfs:label

Table 4.2. The RDF Schema vocabulary.

used above, specifying their type label, domain, range and a superproperty in the case of *foaf:name*.

What is likely to be surprising here is that in comparison to most other modelling frameworks we use the same model of subject/predicate/object to describe instances as well as classes. The statements describing a set of instances (Figure 4.3) and the statements describing the higher level of classes (Figure 4.5) are typically stored in separate documents on the Web, but this is not a requirement: when put together they form a single graph like the one showed in Figure 4.4.

In fact it is not always trivial to separate the description of the instances from the description of classes. We may want to store instance data and the ontology together for practical reasons. But also, for example, we may want to describe a class using typical instances such as when describing the concept of a Weekday, which is a class of five days. In this case drawing a clear line between instance data (metadata) and class data (schema) is problematic even from a conceptual point of view. This is reflected in the rather ambiguous usage of the term ontology, which is sometimes used to refer to the classes only, and sometimes to a set of instances and classes bundled together.

The example also reveals some of the impressive flexibility of RDF. The constructs of language itself form a vocabulary just like the terms of any domain ontology. In other words, terms like *rdfs:Class* are not treated any different from user-defined classes.[14] This means that it is very well possible to form statements about the elements of the language itself. This is used sometimes to establish relationship between elements of a domain and the RDF Schema vocabulary, for example to state that a domain specific labelling property (such as a property providing the name for a person) is a subproperty of the more general *rdfs:label* property. We have done that when declaring the *foaf:name* property as a subproperty of the *rdfs:label* property.

---

[14] The class *rdfs:Class* is the class of classes, i.e. all classes are instances of this class.

```
@prefix foaf: <http://xmlns.com/foaf/0.1/> .

foaf:Person rdf:type owl:Class .
foaf:Person rdfs:label "Person" .
foaf:Person rdfs:subClassOf foaf:Agent
foaf:Person owl:disjointWith foaf:Document .

foaf:knows rdf:type owl:ObjectProperty .
foaf:knows rdfs:label "knows" .
foaf:knows rdfs:domain foaf:Person .
foaf:knows rdfs:range foaf:Person .

foaf:name rdf:type owl:DatatypeProperty .
foaf:name rdfs:label "name" .
foaf:name rdfs:subPropertyOf rdfs:label .
foaf:name rdfs:domain owl:Thing .
foaf:name rdfs:range rdfs:Literal
```

Figure 4.5. Some statements from the FOAF ontology about the terms used in the previous example.

Although it makes little sense, one might even state for example that *rdfs:Resource* is an *rdfs:subClassOf rdfs:Class*, effectively claiming that all resources are classes in the model.

Further, RDF makes no clear separation between classes, instances and properties. One can create classes of instances (metamodeling), which is often required in modelling practical knowledge. (The classical example is modelling the notion of species as a class of classes of animals.) Metamodeling is also present in the example, as we have seen that the *rdf:type* is used on both an instance (Rembrandt, whose class is Person), and a class (Person, whose class is the class of all classes) and we used the *rdfs:label* property on both instances, classes and properties. Classes of properties are also often used to characterize properties. For example, in the case of the OWL language the resource *owl:DataTypeProperty* is the class of properties that have Literal values.

Lastly, part of the flexibility of RDF is that language constructs are not interpreted as strictly as we might expect. For example, even though the range of the *foaf:knows* property is defined to be *foaf:Person* we can still add the statement that *example:Rembrandt foaf:knows mailto:saskia@example.org*. While one would might expect that this leads to a logical contradiction as we are confusing people and their email addresses, this RDF statement is merely interpreted as a hint that the resource *mailto:saskia@example.org* is both an email address *and* a Person.[15] This

---

[15] There is no way of expressing in RDF(S) that such an intersection of classes is empty, but it is possible in OWL, see Section 4.2.2.

example points to the importance of understanding the precise meaning of RDF(S) constructs, which is the subject of the following Section.

RDF and the notion of semantics

In the above we have been largely concerned with the syntax of the language: the kind of symbols (resources and literals) we have and the way to form statements from them. Further, we introduced some special resources that are part of the RDF and RDF Schema languages (e.g. *rdfs:subClassOf*) and gave their meaning in a colloquial style. However, if we want to use RDF(S) for conveying knowledge across the Web, we need to be able to define the meaning of our language (and thus the meaning of ontologies) in a much more reliable fashion. This is important from the perspective of machine reasoning: for example, we are often interested to check whether a certain statement necessarily follows from a set of existing statements or whether there is contradiction among a set of statements. What we then need is an agreement on a method to unambiguously answer such questions independently of our interpretation of the natural language description of the RDF(S) constructs.

The meaning of RDF(S) constructs is anchored in a model-theoretic semantics, one of the most common ways to provide semantics [Hay04]. Using model-theoretic semantics meaning is defined by establishing a mapping from one model to a meta-model where the truth of propositions is already uniquely determined. In the context of RDF such a mapping is called an *interpretation*.

Although a meta-model can be defined in another formal system, it is convenient to think of the meta model as some independently existing reality that the ontology is intended to describe. Thus an interpretation can be thought of as a mapping between symbols and the objects or relations they intended to describe (see Figure 4.6).

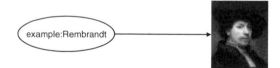

Figure 4.6. An interpretation is a mapping between the terms of an ontology and an interpretation domain.

The constructs of RDF are used to put constraints on possible interpretations and to exclude thereby some of the unintended interpretations. For example, we only want to allow interpretations where symbols for the two persons are mapped to different objects. In other words, we want to exclude interpretations where the two instances are mapped to the same object. In order to achieve this we can specify that the instance Rembrandt is *owl:differentFrom* the second instance Saskia. This excludes the interpretation shown in Figure 4.7.

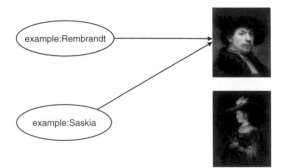

Figure 4.7. An unintended model where symbols for different persons are mapped to the same object. We can exclude this interpretation by adding a statement to the ontology claiming that the two individuals are different from each other. (*owl:differentFrom*)

The model theory of RDF(S) provides some axiomatic triples that are true in every RDF(S) interpretation (for example, *rdf:Property rdf:type rdfs:Class*) and defines the constraints that language elements put on possible interpretations of RDF(S) models. In practice, these semantic conditions can be expressed as a set of rules: for example, the semantics of *rdfs:subPropertyOf* is given by the following rules:[16]

$$(aaa, rdfs{:}subPropertyOf, bbb) \wedge (bbb, rdfs{:}subPropertyOf, ccc)$$
$$\rightarrow (aaa, rdfs{:}subPropertyOf, ccc)$$
$$(aaa, rdfs{:}subPropertyOf, bbb) \rightarrow (aaa, rdf{:}type, rdf{:}Property)$$
$$(aaa, rdfs{:}subPropertyOf, bbb) \rightarrow (bbb, rdf{:}type, rdf{:}Property)$$
$$(xxx, aaa, yyy) \wedge (aaa, rdfs{:}subPropertyOf, bbb) \rightarrow (xxx, bbb, yyy)$$

The most noteworthy feature of RDF semantics is that the interpretation of the language is based on an open world assumption and is kept monotonic. An open world assumption means that based on a single document we cannot assume that we have a complete description of the world or even the resources explicitly described therein. Monotonicity means additional knowledge added to an RDF knowledge base cannot make previous inferences invalid.[17] For example, if we specify that the range of the foaf:knows property is Person and then state that Rembrandt knows an instance of another class such as Pluto the dog (or even a literal value) we do not cause a (logical) contradiction; it is assumed that there could exist a statement defining that some other class (e.g. Dog) is also in the range of *foaf:knows*.

---

[16] Strictly speaking, the semantics of the property is of course related to the semantics of the *rdf:type* property and the *rdf:Property* class which occur in these rules. In general, the semantics of symbols is often given using the semantics of other primitive symbols.

[17] It is altogether impossible to create logical inconsistencies in RDF with the exception of a datatype clash.

A consequence of monotonicity is that it makes no sense of talking about RDF validation: RDF Schema statements about an RDF resource only add additional information about the resource and cannot invalidate or contradict statements previously inferred about that resource. In fact, RDF Schema semantics is specified as a set of inference rules; in the example, these rules would allow to infer that the resource provided as the object of the *foaf:knows* property is (also) a Person besides possibly being other things (a Dog).[18]

SPARQL: querying RDF sources across the Web

Through the years several ontology databases (triple stores) have been developed, each featuring their own query language. As all of these query languages operate on the same data model (an RDF graph), these query languages have in common that they allow to select retrieve parts of an RDF graph by matching a graph pattern provided by the query and return the possible values of variables in the query pattern.[19] There are, however, differences in syntax and the exact set of features.

At the time of writing, the World Wide Web Consortium is working on creating a recommendation called SPARQL, establishing a standard query language and a protocol for interacting with RDF sources. The query language captures the common set of features of the existing RDF query languages [PS06]. The protocol prescribes the way a software application would query a remote ontology store across the Internet, i.e. the way to submit a SPARQL query to a server and the expected format of the results (and eventual error messages) [Cla06]. The SPARQL specifications are expected to significantly increase the interoperability of Semantic Web applications. Also, the content of non-RDF databases may also be exposed using a SPARQL interface, opening up their content to the Semantic Web world. (The process of wrapping a relational database in a SPARQL interface can be partially automated.[20]

4.2.2 The Web Ontology Language (OWL)

The Web Ontology Language (OWL) was designed to add the constructs of Description Logics (DL) to RDF, significantly extending the expressiveness of RDF Schema both in characterizing classes and properties. Description Logics are a set of Knowledge Representation languages with formal semantics based on their mapping to First Order Logic (FOL). Description Logics have been extensively studied since the 1980s including studies on the tradeoffs between the expressivity of the chosen

---

[18] There is no such thing as a name clash in RDF due to the unique identification of resources and thus it is not possible to conclude that there are two different knows properties or Person classes involved.

[19] The analogy to querying relational databases is that an SQL query defines a pattern of tuples and the variables to be selected. The query is evaluated by finding matching tuples in the joined relations and projecting them to the variable space.

[20] See for example, the D2R Server project at http://sites.wiwiss.fu-berlin.de/suhl/bizer/d2r-server/

language and the efficiency of reasoning. OWL has been designed in a way that it maps to a well-known Description Logic with tractable reasoning algorithms.

The Web Ontology Language is in fact a set of three languages with increasing expressiveness: OWL Lite, OWL DL and OWL Full. These languages are extensions of each other ($OWL_{Lite} \subseteq OWL_{DL} \subseteq OWL_{Full}$) both syntactically and semantically. For example, every OWL Lite document is a valid OWL DL document and has the same semantics when considered as an OWL DL document, e.g. it leads to the same logical conclusions. The vocabularies of these languages extend each other and languages further up in the hierarchy only relax the constraints on the use of the vocabulary. Although it is generally believed that languages of the OWL family would be an extension of RDF(S) in the same sense, this is only true for OWL Full, the most expressive of the family ($RDF(S) \subseteq OWL_{Full}$).

The middle language, OWL DL was the original target of standardization and it is a direct mapping to an expressive Description Logic. This has the advantage that OWL DL documents can be directly consumed by most DL reasoners to perform inference and consistency checking. The constructs of OWL DL are also familiar, although some of the semantics can be surprising mostly due to the open world assumption [RDH+04]. (Table 4.2 shows the OWL DL vocabulary, which is the same as the vocabulary of OWL Full.) Description Logics do not allow much of the representation flexibility introduced above (e.g. treating classes as instances or defining classes of properties) and therefore not all RDF documents are valid OWL DL documents and even the usage of OWL terms is limited.

For example, in OWL DL it is not allowed to extend constructs of the language, i.e. the concepts in the RDF, RDF Schema and OWL namespaces. In the case of the notion of a Class, OWL also introduces a separate *owl:Class* concept as a subclass of *rdfs:Class* in order to clearly distinguish its more limited notion of a class. Similarly, OWL introduces the disjoint classes of object properties and datatype properties. The first refers to properties that take resources as values (such as *foaf:knows*) and the latter is for properties ranging on literals such as *foaf:name*.

OWL Full is a "limitless" OWL DL: every RDF ontology is also a valid OWL Full ontology and has the same semantics when considered as an OWL Full document. However, OWL Full is undecidable, which means that in the worst case OWL Full reasoners will run infinitely. OWL Lite is a lightweight sub-language of OWL DL, which maps to a less expressive but even more efficient DL language. OWL Lite has the same limitations on the use of RDF as OWL DL and does not contain some of the terms of OWL DL.

In summary, RDF documents are not necessarily valid OWL Lite or OWL DL ontologies despite the common conviction (see also Figure 4.11). In fact, "downgrading" a typical RDF or OWL Full ontology to OWL DL is a tedious engineering task. It typically includes many simple steps such as declaring whether properties are object properties or datatype properties and importing the external ontologies used in the document, which is mandatory in OWL but not in RDF. However, the process often involves more fundamental modelling decisions when it comes to finding alternate representations.[21]

Most existing web ontologies make little use of OWL due to their limited needs, but also because general rule-based knowledge cannot be expressed in OWL. The additional expressivity of OWL, however, is required for modelling complex domains such as medicine or engineering, especially in supporting classification tasks where we need to determine the place of a class in the class hierarchy based on its description.

Note that there is currently no standard query language for OWL, although there is such a proposal by Fikes, Hayes and Horrocks [FHH04].

4.2.3 Comparison to the Unified Modelling Language (UML)

UML is most commonly used in the requirements specification and design of object-oriented software in the middle tier of enterprise applications [Fow03]. The chief difference between UML and RDF(S)/OWL is their modelling scope: UML contains modelling primitives specific for a special kind of information resource, namely objects in an information system characterized by their static attributes and associations, but also their dynamic behavior. Many of the modelling primitives of UML are thus specific to objects and their role in OO systems; interfaces, functions etc. are examples of such constructs.[22] Nevertheless, if we ignore these constructs of the languages and the difference in scope, there is still a significant overlap in the expressiveness of object-oriented models of a domain and ontological models.

Figure 4.8 shows our example modelled in UML. It is natural to model properties that take primitive values as datatypes and model all other properties as associations. (However, attributes can also take model classes as types.) UML is primary a schema definition language and thus the modelling of instances is limited.

Based on the comparison of OWL Full and UML 2.0 we can note that there is a significant overlap as well as differences in the modelling capabilities of OWL and UML [HEC+04]. In the following we summarize the more specific differences by looking at the unique features of these frameworks.

- **Unique features of RDF/OWL**
  - In general, the modelling of RDF is less constrained than that of UML, which means that many RDF models have no equivalent in UML. OWL DL also provides more primitives than UML such as the disjointness, union, intersection and equivalence of classes.

---

[21] The author has carried out this process both with the OWL-S and FOAF ontologies and reported his experiences on the appropriate mailing lists.

[22] The distinction between modelling information resources and real world objects is not explicit in UML. Some models of UML such as activity diagrams are primarily used for modelling used real world concepts, e.g. business processes. Other diagrams such as use case diagrams indicate how real world actors interact with the system, i.e. they contain real world objects and information resources in the same diagram.

Boolean class combinations	*owl:unionOf*
	owl:complementOf
	owl:intersectionOf
(In)equality of classes and instances	*owl:equivalentClass*
	owl:disjointWith
	owl:equivalentProperty
	owl:sameAs
	owl:differentFrom
	owl:AllDifferent
	owl:distinctMembers
Enumerated types	*owl:oneOf*
	owl:DataRange
Property characteristics	*owl:ObjectProperty*
	owl:DatatypeProperty
	owl:inverseOf
	owl:TransitiveProperty
	owl:SymmetricProperty
	owl:FunctionalProperty
	owl:InverseFunctionalProperty
Property restrictions	*owl:Restriction*
	owl:onProperty
	owl:allValuesFrom
	owl:someValuesFrom
	owl:hasValue
	owl:minCardinality
	owl:maxCardinality
	owl:cardinality
Ontology versioning	*owl:versionInfo*
	owl:priorVersion
	owl:backwardCompatibleWith
	owl:incompatibleWith
	owl:DeprecatedClass
	owl:DeprecatedProperty
Ontology metadata	*owl:Ontology*
	owl:imports
	owl:AnnotationProperty
	owl:OntologyProperty

Table 4.3. The OWL Full vocabulary.

– OWL allows to describe defined classes, i.e. definitions that give necessary and sufficient conditions for an instance to be considered as a member of the class.
– RDF/OWL both treat properties as first class citizens of the language. Properties are global: they do not belong to any class, while UML attributes and associations are defined as part of the description of a certain class. In other words, the same property can be used with multiple classes. Further, RDF

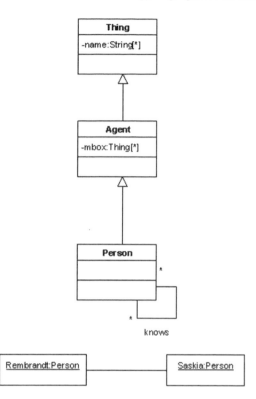

Figure 4.8. A UML model of our example.

properties, just as any other resource can be supplied as values of properties etc.

− Properties can be defined as subproperties of other properties. This is possible, but much less straightforward in UML.
− Classes can be treated as instances, allowing for meta-modelling.
− RDF reification is more flexible than the association class mechanism of UML. For example, statements concerning literal values can also be reified in RDF. These would be modelled as attributes in UML and association classes cannot be attached to attributes.
− All non-blank RDF resources are identified with a URI, UML classes, instances, attributes etc. do not have such an ID.
− Instances can and usually have multiple types. (This is not to be confused with multiple inheritance, which is supported by both UML and RDF/OWL.)
• **Unique features of UML**
− UML has the notion of relationship roles, which is not present in RDF/OWL.

- UML allows n-ary relations, which are not part of RDF, although they can be re-represented in a number of ways.[23]
- Two common types of part-whole relations are available in UML (aggregation and composition). These can be remodelled in OWL to some extent[24]
- UML makes a distinction between attributes and associations. This is also different from the distinction between datatype and object-properties in OWL. On the one hand, attributes can have instances as values, while datatype properties can only have literal values. On the other hand, cardinality constraints, for example, can be applied to both datatype and object properties in OWL, reification can be applied to statements involving datatype properties etc.

A direct comparison of the semantics of UML class models and RDF/OWL models is difficult. The semantics of UML is given by its meta-language (the Meta Object Facility or MOF) and there is no direct mapping between RDF/OWL and the MOF. One obvious difference is that the MOF is built on a closed world assumption while RDF/OWL assumes an open world (see Section 4.2.1).

As most enterprise software is specified according to OO methodologies and implemented in object oriented languages the relationship of UML and OWL is important to consider. Especially in cases where a Semantic Web application is to be written in an object-oriented framework, it is a natural idea to generate the object model from an existing ontological model or vice versa. There are code generators for creating object models in Java and other languages directly from RDF(S) and OWL ontologies.[25]. Further, there are also tools for the more straightforward conversion from UML class models to OWL ontologies. Lastly, there have been significant work on the creation of a UML profile (presentation syntax) for OWL ontologies called the Ontology Definition Metamodel (ODM)[26]. The ODM will be in effect a visual modelling language for OWL based on UML and the necessary extensions.

4.2.4 Comparison to the Entity/Relationship (E/R) model and the relational model

The Entity/Relationship (E/R) model is commonly used in information modelling for the data storage layer of applications, because it maps easily to the relational model used for defining data structures in database management systems (RDBMS). It is much simpler than UML, see the original description in [Che76].

The E/R language contains the constructs that are necessary for modelling information on the basis of relationships. Relationships are characterized in terms of the arity of the relationship and the participating entity sets, their cardinalities and

---

[23] See the W3C note on n-ary relations at http://www.w3.org/TR/swbp-n-aryRelations/

[24] See the W3C note on simple part-whole relations at http://www.w3.org/2001/sw/BestPractices/OEP/SimplePartWhole/

[25] See for example Jastor, http://jastor.sourceforge.net

[26] http://codip.grci.com/odm/draft/submission_text/ODMPrelimSubAug04R1.pdf

dependency on the relationship. Similar to the reification features in RDF and UML, the E/R model also allows attaching attributes to a relationship and including relationships in other relationships.

Entity sets roughly correspond to classes in UML. (There is no way to represent individual entities.) The modelling of entity sets is less of a concern to the E/R model, the only predefined relationship type between entity sets being generalization. The semantics of this construct is limited to attribute inheritance, i.e. it simply means that the lower level entity sets have all the attributes of the higher level entity sets. (Unlike in UML and RDF, generalization between relationships (*rdfs:subPropertyOf*) is not allowed.)

A special feature of the E/R model is the notion of keys of entity sets, i.e. sets of attributes whose values together uniquely identify a given entity. E/R also has a notion of weak entities: entities that are identified not only by a set of attributes but also some of their relations to other entities. (For example the unique identification of a room depends on the identification of the building.) As we will see, keys of single attributes can be modelled in RDF by making the given property functional (max cardinality 1) and inverse functional. Complex keys, however, cannot be accurately modelled in RDF/OWL.

Figure 4.9 shows an E/R representation of our previous example and the corresponding relational model. Notice that the E/R diagram does not allow to represent instances, only the schema of our model. Further, when trying to fill the relational tables with the instances of our example we run into the problem that instance Saskia is missing the primary key mbox and thus cannot be identified. RDF naturally solves this problem as every resource has an inherent identifier (a URI or bNode ID), which allows to uniquely identify the instance even if the description is partial. (We could have recreated this by introducing a new primary key for the Person entity. This is the equivalent to the practical solution of creating a new column for the Person table with some unique identifier.)

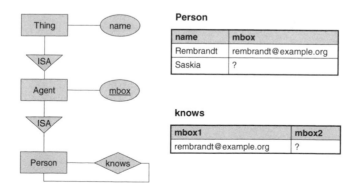

Figure 4.9. An entity/relationship model of our example, showing also a straightforward mapping to relations, which would be the tables in a database.

Although conceptually the data storage layer of applications is the furthest from their Web interface, the relationship between E/R models and ontologies in an important one to consider. While there are specific storage facilities based on the RDF model (just as there are object databases and relational databases with object extensions), the firm legacy of relational databases means that companies with significant investment in relational databases will most likely to keep their data in an RDBMS and expose it through a web interface in the form of RDF. In such case it makes sense to establish a close mapping between the relational database schema and an ontology that can be published along with the data (http://www.w3.org/DesignIssues/RDB-RDF.html). Unfortunately, the automated mapping of relational schemas to ontologies is difficult in practice. When implementing databases the E/R diagrams may be mapped in multiple ways to the much simpler relational model, which are then often "tweaked" to produce optimal performance. As a result, relational models extracted from existing databases typically require significant post-processing and enrichment to arrive at an accurate model of the domain (see [VOSS03]).

4.2.5 Comparison to the Extensible Markup Language (XML) and XML Schema

Up to date XML is the most commonly used technology for the exchange of structured information between systems and services. From all languages discussed the role of XML is thus the most similar to RDF in its purpose.

The most commonly observed similarity between XML and RDF is a similarity between the data models: a directed graph for RDF, and a directed, ordered tree for XML. In XML, the tree is defined by the nesting of elements starting with a single root node. This model originates from the predecessor of XML called SGML which was primarily used for marking up large text documents. Text documents follow the tree structure themselves as paragraphs are nested in subsections, subsections are nested in sections, sections are nested chapters etc. The ordering of the children of an element matters, which is again inherited from the text processing tradition. On the other hand, RDF proposes a more relaxed data model based on arbitrary directed graphs built from single edges between the nodes representing classes or instances. This structure is better suited for creating conceptual domain models, which are often so rich in cross-taxonomical relationships that a hierarchical representation would prove to be difficult. Noting that every tree is a graph (and ignoring the ordering of children for a moment) one would expect that it is trivial to represent XML models in RDF, although as we will see this is not the case.

Much like RDF, XML itself is merely a common conceptual model and syntax for domain specific languages each with their own vocabulary (hence the name extensible). Examples of these languages include XHTML, but also specialized languages such as the GraphML language for descriptions of graphs or the SVG image format for vector graphic images. XML has a number of schema languages such as XML Schema and Relax NG to define such languages. The use of these schema languages, however, is radically different. Namely, schemas written in XML schema languages not only define the types of elements and their attributes but also prescribe syntax i.e.

the way elements are allowed to be nested in the tree. XML documents can be validated against a schema on a purely syntactic level. Schema languages for RDF (RDF Schema and OWL) do not impose constraints directly on the graph model but effect the possible interpretations of metadata. Consistency of an RDF/OWL model is checked by searching for possible interpretations. (If there are no possible interpretations of a model than it is inconsistent.) As we have already seen, RDF and OWL also transcend the relatively vague notions of XML (such as elements, attributes, nesting etc.) and provide a more refined set of constructs (classes, instances and properties).

To illustrate the difference in the focus of XML and RDF, let us consider how we would represent the same information captured in Figure 4.3 in XML. Figure 4.10 shows three possible XML representations. While the intended meaning (semantics) of these documents is the same, the syntax and thus the resulting XML tree is different. (The order of the branches matters in XML, which is the only difference between the second and third examples.) This means that applications working on the basis of different representations would be incompatible: XML queries and XSL transformations performed on these different representations would produce different results. Thus there needs to be an agreement on both syntax and semantics when using XML. For web-based data interchange RDF has a clear advantage here in that agreement on a shared XML format would require a much stronger commitment than the agreement of using RDF. The kind of agreement that is needed to exchange RDF documents concerns only the representation of individual statements (the simple subject/predicate/object model) as we have seen on the example of the Turtle language.

As an aside, we also see the difficulty of XML in dealing with graph-like structures: choosing the top node is an arbitrary decision when dealing with such information. This is particularly obvious in representing social networks (Person entities linked with knows relationships), it is generally true that real world domain models can be rarely forged into a single, unique tree structure.[27]

XML is highly appreciated for the variety of complementary tools and technologies such as XML databases, standard schema, query and transformation languages (XQuery and XSLT), a range of editors, parsers, processors etc. The legacy of XML compelled also the W3C to adopt it also as a notation for RDF and OWL. This kind of contingency is popularized by the famous Semantic Web layer cake diagram in Figure 4.11[28] This picture shows the vision of the Semantic Web as a set of languages building upon existing standards such as XML, URIs and Unicode. Despite the good intentions, however, this diagram obfuscates the true relationship between XML and ontology languages from the W3C such as RDF and OWL. (We have already seen that the relationship between RDF and OWL is also more complicated than simple

---

[27] As a fix, XML offers two mechanisms for modelling links between individual elements or branches of the XML tree. One is the simple ID/IDREF mechanism provided by the XML specification, the other is the more sophisticated XLink language for XML.

[28] The diagram has appeared in presentations of the W3C such as http://www.w3.org/2001/09/06-ecdl/slide17-0.html.

```
<Person name="Rembrandt">
    <mbox>mailto:rembrandt@example.org</mbox>
    <knows>
        <Person name="Saskia" />
    </knows>
</Person>

<Person name="Rembrandt">
    <mbox>mailto:rembrandt@example.org</mbox>
    <knows>
        <Person ID="1"/>
    </knows>
</Person>
<Person name="Saskia" ID="1" />

<Person name="Saskia" ID="1" />
<Person name="Rembrandt">
    <mbox>mailto:rembrandt@example.org</mbox>
    <knows>
        <Person ID="1"/>
    </knows>
</Person>
```

Figure 4.10. Three different XML representations of the same information.

extension.) By doing so it has done more damage to the argument for ontology languages over XML than any other conceptualization of the next generation Web.

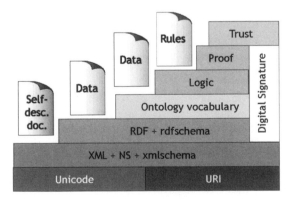

Figure 4.11. The Semantic Web layer cake.

What the layer cake suggests, namely that RDF builds on XML is true only to the extent that RDF models can be exchanged using an XML format named

RDF/OWL have been specifically engineered for knowledge representation in distributed settings such as the Web.

	Origin	Application domain	Primitive	Expressivity	Distributed representation	Formal semantics
E/R	1976	Relational databases	Relation	●	no	no
UML	1995	OO software	Object	●●	no	yes[33]
XML	1998	Text markup and data exchange	Entity	●●	yes	no
RDF/OWL	2004	Resource markup and data exchange	Resource	● - ● ● ●	yes	yes

Table 4.4. Comparison of the E/R, UML, XML and RDF/OWL languages.

Firstly, RDF/OWL provides the way to distribute data and schema information across the Web and discover such information by traversing the Web of RDF documents. As in the case of XML, RDF documents can reside anywhere on the Web and reference any other RDF vocabulary using globally unique identifiers (URIs). Following the much debated decision of W3C, the use of URIs also connects RDF resources to the Web: URIs with an http: protocol can be looked up on the Web and the response of the Web server can provide a clue whether the resource is an information resource or not.[34] By using redirection, the web server can also provide the authoritative description of the resource. Further, the RDF Schema and OWL vocabularies contain specific terms (*rdfs:seeAlso*, *rdfs:definedBy* and *owl:import*) that can be used to point to other RDF documents to the Web. Using these mechanisms, RDF/OWL documents can be woven into a Web just like HTML documents form a web through the links among the documents.[35]

The second key feature of RDF/OWL is the existence of formal semantics. Formal semantics ascertains that the language is interpreted unambiguously, which is critical to sharing information across the Web. The meaning of the language constructs is defined by the constraints they put on possible mappings to a domain of

---

[33] From UML 2.0

[34] See the discussion over the issue named httpRange-14

[35] XML Schema has similar features although they are much less intuitive to use and therefore mostly ignored. instance data can reference the location of a web-based schema through the xsi:schemaLocation attribute, while schemas can reference, import or extend the elements of other web-based schemas. Section 4.3 of the XML Schema specification defines the relationship between XML Schema documents and the Web infrastructure. The use of these advanced schema extension features is not widespread nor recognized as a precursor to Semantic Web techniques.

interpretation (model-theoretic semantics). Informally, the domain of interpretation is convenient to be thought of as some independently existing reality. In this sense the language can be used to exclude unwanted interpretations, i.e. possible mappings to real world objects and relations that we would like to exclude.

A clear difference between OWL and RDF is the non-monotonicity of the logic of OWL and the possibility to create inconsistencies. As negation is part of the language it is trivial to create situations where new knowledge contradicts previous assertions. As a result, OWL behaves more like a constraint language, where contradictions in the schema itself (for example, unsatisfiable classes) or the violation of the constraints by the instances (for example, a violation of cardinalities) can be detected as logical inconsistence. OWL reasoners can help to localize the source of inconsistencies, but the automation of removing inconsistencies is still a research problem.

In summary, RDF/OWL are a set of languages of varying expressivity specifically designed for information sharing across the Web. RDF/OWL are different in their purpose from other well-known knowledge representation formalisms used in Computer Science but share many primitives with E/R, UML and XML models. (Table 4.4 summarizes some of our observations.) In particular, accurately representing and sharing the meaning of information (formal semantics) is critical to information sharing in heterogeneous setting where one cannot rely on other mechanisms of creating a shared understanding. A semantic-based representation of knowledge is also an important first step toward data integration in cases where data is distributed and resides under diverse ownership and control. This is the topic of the following Section.

5

Modelling and aggregating social network data

In this Chapter we apply the ontology-based Knowledge Representation techniques introduced in Chapter 4 to the representation and aggregation social network data. There are two fundamental reasons for developing semantic-based representations of social networks.

Firstly, as we will demonstrate, maintaining the semantics of social network data is crucial for aggregating social network information, especially in heterogeneous environments where the individual sources of data are under diverse control. The benefits are easiest to realize in cases where the data are already available in an electronic format, which is typically the case in the network analysis of online communities but also in the intelligence community.[1]

Secondly, semantical representations can facilitate the exchange and reuse of case study data in the academic field of Social Network Analysis. The possibilities for electronic data exchange has already revolutionized a number of sciences with the most well-known examples of bio-informatics and genetics. With the current state-of-the art in network analysis, however, the network data collected in various studies is stored and published either in data formats not primarily intended for network analysis (such as Excel sheets, SPSS tables) or in the rather proprietary graph description languages of network analysis packages that ignore the semantics of data, e.g. the types of instances, the meaning of the attributes etc. Hence, it is difficult —if not impossible— to verify results independently, to carry out secondary analysis (to reuse data) and to compare results across different studies. This last effect is particularly hurtful because single studies in network analysis are always focused on relatively small communities while the field as a whole tries to explain commonalities across all social networks.

In the following, we first sketch the state-of-the-art in network data representation and motivate the case for semantics. We discuss separately the possibilities for semantic-based representations of social individuals (Section 5.2) and social relationships (Section 5.3). While the representation of social individuals is relatively

---

[1] Little is known in this respect, but it is widely speculated that U.S. intelligence agencies are major users of both network analysis and data consolidation/data mining technologies.

straightforward, the representation of social relations is a much more challenging problem. Our main contribution is thus a first step towards an ontology of social relations.

While reasoning with social relations is still future work, we discuss the aggregation of social individuals, which can be well automated based on the current representations and their formal semantics (Section 5.4). This is also a key technical component of our end-to-end system for collecting, aggregating and presenting social network data. In the following we discuss the design options for implementing semantics-based data aggregation and return to our particular implementation in the following Chapter.

5.1 State-of-the-art in network data representation

In the chapters before we have seen that the most common kind of social network data can be modelled by a graph where the nodes represent individuals and the edges represent binary social relationships. (Less commonly, higher-arity relationships may be represented using hyper-edges, i.e. edges connecting multiple nodes.) Additionally, social network studies build on attributes of nodes and edges, which can be formalized as functions operating on nodes or edges.

A number of different, proprietary formats exist for serializing such graphs and attribute data in machine-processable electronic documents. The most commonly encountered formats are those used by the popular network analysis packages Pajek and UCINET. These are text-based formats which have been designed in a way so that they can be easily edited using simple text editors. Figure 5.1 shows a simple example of these formats.

Unfortunately, the two formats are incompatible. (UCINET has the ability to read and write the .net format of Pajek, but not vice versa.) Further, researchers in the social sciences often represent their data initially using Microsoft Excel spreadsheets, which can be exported in the simple CSV (Comma Separated Values) format. As this format is not specific to graph structures (it is merely a way to export a table of data), additional constraints need to be put on the content before such a file can processed by graph packages. To further complicate matters for the researcher, visualization software packages also have their own proprietary formats such as the dot format used by the open source GraphViz package developed at AT&T Research.[2]

The GraphML format represents an advancement over the previously mentioned formats in terms of both interoperability and extensibility [BEL04, BEH+01]. GraphML originates from the information visualization community where a shared format greatly increases the usability of new visualization methods. GraphML is therefore based on XML with a schema defined in XML Schema. This has the advantage that GraphML files can be edited, stored, queried, transformed etc. using generic XML tools.

Common to all these generic graph representations is that they focus on the graph structure, which is the primary input to network analysis and visualization. Attribute

---

[2] http://www.graphviz.org/

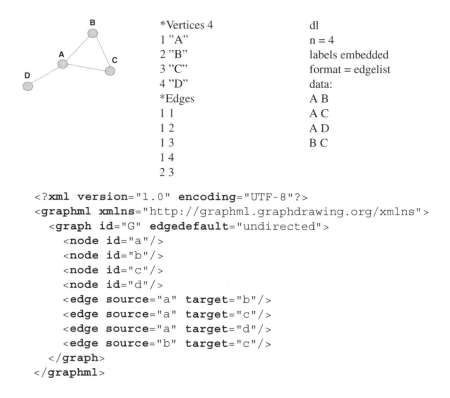

```
<?xml version="1.0" encoding="UTF-8"?>
<graphml xmlns="http://graphml.graphdrawing.org/xmlns">
  <graph id="G" edgedefault="undirected">
    <node id="a"/>
    <node id="b"/>
    <node id="c"/>
    <node id="d"/>
    <edge source="a" target="b"/>
    <edge source="a" target="c"/>
    <edge source="a" target="d"/>
    <edge source="b" target="c"/>
  </graph>
</graphml>
```

Figure 5.1. A simple graph (upper left) described in Pajek .NET, UCINET DL and GraphML formats.

data when entered electronic form is typically stored separately from network data in Excel sheets, databases or SPSS tables.[3]

However, none of these formats support the aggregation and reuse of electronic data, which is our primary concern. To motivate our case for data aggregation, consider the typical scenario in Figure 5.2 where we would like to implement a network study by reusing a number of data sources describing the same set of individuals and their relationships (for example, email archives and publication databases holding information about researchers). One of the common reasons to use multiple data sources is to perform *triangulation* i.e. to use a variety of data sources and/or methods of analysis to verify the same conclusion [Rob02]. Often the data sources to be used contain complementary information: for example, in *multi-layer studies* such

---

[3] GraphML goes in this direction by using the extension features of XML Schema. For example, the GraphML node element can be redefined to attach extra attributes to nodes. (These attributes may be defined in other existing schemas.) However, GraphML gives no standard way to define the types of nodes or edges. More precisely: these elements have a type and XML does not allow providing multiple types to an element.

as the one performed by Besselaar et al. [HHvdB03] a multiplex network is studied using data sources that contain evidence about different kinds of relationships in a community. This allows to look at, for example, how these networks differ and how relationships of one type might effect the building of relationships of another type.

In both cases we need to be able to recognize matching instances in the different data sources and merge the records before we can proceed with the analysis. In fact, the graph representations discussed above strip social network data of exactly those characteristics that one needs to consider when aggregating data or sharing it for reuse: namely, these graph formats reduce social individuals and their relationships to nodes and edges, which is the only information required for the purposes of analyzing single networks.

What we need to support aggregation and reuse is a representation that allows to capture and compare the identity of instances and relationships. (The instances we deal with are primarily persons, but it might be for example that we need to aggregate multiple databases containing patents or publications, which is then used to build a network of individuals or institutions.) Maintaining the identity of individuals and relationships is also crucial for preserving our data sets in a way that best enables their reuse and secondary analysis of data.

Solving these problems requires a very different kind of representation from the graph based formats shown above. Our proposed solution is a rich, semantic-based representation of the primary objects in social networks data, namely social individuals and their relationships. A semantic-based representation will allow us to wield the power of ontology languages and tools in aggregating data sets through domain-specific knowledge about identity, i.e. what it requires for two instances to be considered the same. As we will see, a semantic-based format has the additional advantage that at the same time we can easily enrich our data set with specific domain knowledge such as the relatively simple fact that if two people send emails to each other, they know each other, or that a certain kind of relationship implies (or refutes) the existence of another kind of relationship.

The two key problems in aggregating social network data are the identification and disambiguation of social individuals and the aggregation of information about social relationships. We treat these problems separately in the following Sections.

5.2 Ontological representation of social individuals

The Friend-of-a-Friend (FOAF) ontology that we use in our work is an OWL-based format for representing personal information and an individual's social network. FOAF greatly surpasses graph description languages in expressivity by using the powerful OWL vocabulary to characterize individuals. More importantly, however, using FOAF one can rely on the extendibility of the RDF/OWL representation framework for enhancing the basic ontology with domain-specific knowledge about identity.

The classes and properties in the current version of the FOAF vocabulary are shown in Figure 5.1. We have seen an example of a FOAF profile in Figure 4.3.

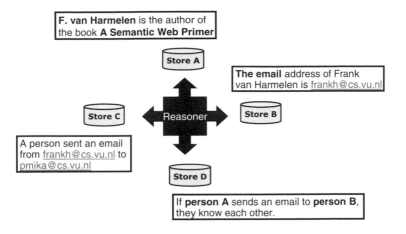

Figure 5.2. Example of a case of identity reasoning. Based on a semantic representation, a reasoner would be able to conclude, for example, that Peter Mika knows the author of the book *A Semantic Web Primer* [AvH04]

In terms of deployment, two studies give an insight of how much the individual terms of the FOAF are used on the Web [PW04, DZFJ05]. Both studies note that the majority of FOAF profiles on the Web are auto-generated by community sites such as LiveJournal[4], Opera Communities[5] and Tribe.net[6]. As FOAF profiles are scattered across the Web it is difficult to estimate their number, but even the number of manually maintained profiles is likely to be in the tens of thousands.

FOAF started as an experimentation with Semantic Web technology. The idea of FOAF was to provide a machine processable format for representing the kind of information that made the original Web successful, namely the kind of personal information described in homepages of individuals. Thus FOAF has a vocabulary for describing personal attribute information typically found on homepages such as name and email address of the individual, projects, interests, links to work and school homepage etc. FOAF profiles, however, can also contain a description of the individual's friends using the same vocabulary that is used to describe the individual himself. Even more importantly, FOAF profiles can be linked together to form networks of web-based profiles.

FOAF became the center point of interest in 2003 with the spread of Social Networking Services such Friendster, Orkut, LinkedIn etc. Despite their early popularity, users have later discovered a number of drawbacks to centralized social networking services. First, the information is under the control of the database owner who has an interest in keeping the information bound to the site and is willing to protect the data through technical and legal means. The profiles stored in these systems typically

---

[4] http://www.livejournal.com
[5] http://my.opera.com/community/
[6] http://tribe.net

cannot be exported in machine processable formats (or cannot be exported legally) and therefore the data cannot be transferred from one system to the next. (As a result, the data needs to be maintained separately at different services.) Second, centralized systems do not allow users to control the information they provide on their own terms. Although Friendster follow-ups offer several levels of sharing (e.g. public information vs. only for friends), users often still find out the hard way that their information was used in ways that were not intended.

These problems have been addressed with the use of Semantic Web technology. Unlike in the case of Friendster and similar sites, FOAF profiles are created and controlled by the individual user and shared in a distributed fashion. FOAF profiles are typically posted on the personal website of the user and linked from the user's homepage with the HTML META tag. The distributed nature of FOAF networks means that FOAF requires a mechanism to link individual profiles and thus allow the discovery of related profiles. For this purpose, FOAF uses the *rdfs:seeAlso* mechanism described above. Related profiles can be thus discovered by crawling the FOAF network along these links. This is the way the so-called scutters (RDF crawlers) operate.[7] Note that FOAF profiles generated from user profiles at online communities only contain links to members of the same website. For example, the FOAF representation of a LiveJournal profile only links to other LiveJournal members. This means that such sites are 'black holes' in terms of crawling: there are only links leading to them, but no links leading out of them.

The distributed nature of FOAF data also means that the designers of the ontology had to address the issues of identification and aggregation early on.[8]. It was very clear from the beginning that again centralized solutions such as a registry for the URIs of individuals would not be feasible. When making a list of friends how would one find out their URIs?

The answer is to identify persons using their characteristic properties such as their email address, homepage etc. When describing a friend one would create a blank node with enough detail to uniquely identify that particular person. Recall that blank nodes in RDF are unidentified resources which can be thought of as the existential quantifier of the language. For example, the statements in the example of Figure 4.3 can be read as *There exists a Person named Peter with email ... who knows a person named Dirk.*.

With the introduction of OWL it has become possible to describe these identifying properties of the *foaf:Person* class as inverse-functional properties (IFP). IFPs are properties whose value uniquely identifies a single object.[9] In other words, if two

---

[7] Needless to say search engines such as Google that have the capacity of crawling the HTML web will also discover profiles that are linked to individual homepages by either a meta tag or a regular HTML anchor tag. Google is thus also a source of FOAF profiles. The easiest way to locate such profiles is by restricting the search by file type and searching for foaf:Person as a keyword.

[8] In fact, FOAF is the first major ontology where this issue surfaced, see http://rdfweb.org/mt/foaflog/archives/2003/07/10/12.05.33/index.html

[9] Mathematically, IFPs are inverses of functional properties and hence the name. For example the inverse of the IFP *foaf:mbox* would be a functional property ("mailboxOf").

resources have the same value for an inverse-functional property than they must denote the same object. For example, email address is an inverse-functional as every email address belongs to a single person.[10] Name, however is not inverse-functional: the same name can belong to multiple persons. (Nevertheless, the probability of name clashes might be negligibly small depending on the size of the community we consider). We return to the issue of reasoning with this kind of knowledge in Section 5.4.

An advantage of FOAF in terms of sharing FOAF data is the relative stability of the ontology. The number of FOAF users means that the maintainers of the ontology are obliged to keep the vocabulary and its semantics stable. Interestingly, contingency requires that even inconsistencies in the naming of terms are left uncorrected: while most terms follow the Java convention[11], in some cases an underscore is used to separate words (mbox_sha1sum, family_name). When the meaning of terms does change, the evolution is toward generalization so as not to break existing applications.[12] For example, various sub-properties of the *foaf:knows* (*foaf:knowsWell* and *foaf:friend*) term have been removed due to their overlap in meaning. The description of the *foaf:schoolHomepage* has been extended to sanction its use for describing university homepages.[13]

To facilitate adoption, terms are not added to the vocabulary any more, rather authors are encouraged to create extensions using the mechanisms of RDF, e.g. creating subclasses and subproperties and adding new properties to existing classes. The terms of the FOAF vocabulary and *foaf:Person* in particular are also often referenced in other ontologies where there is a need for describing individuals. For example, the SIOC (Semantically Enabled Online Communities) project aims at connecting discussions across various types of fora (Usenet, discussion boards, blogs, mailing lists etc.) by exposing the postings according to a shared ontology.[14] The key concepts of this ontology are the *sioc:User* account that is used to create a *sioc:Post*, which is part of a *sioc:Forum* at a certain *sioc:Site*. A *sioc:User* is not a subclass of *foaf:Person* (as a person may have multiple accounts), but related to the description of a person using the *sioc:account_of* property. Other examples using FOAF include the DOAP (Description of a Project) ontology for describing open source software projects[15] and the BuRST format used for describing publications in openacademia (see Section 6.3.2). In both cases, terms of the FOAF vocabulary are adopted for describing the maintainers and authors of projects and publications, respectively.

---

[10] With the exception of generic email addresses such as *support@microsoft.com*, which belongs to multiple persons. Such email addresses should not be used as values for this property.

[11] http://java.sun.com/docs/codeconv/html/CodeConventions.doc8.html

[12] A primary concern in the change management (versioning) of ontologies is the effect of changes on applications. See the thesis of Klein on the issues regarding change management in distributed ontologies [Kle04].

[13] The term school has this broader meaning in the US, while the original authors of the vocabulary are from the UK.

[14] http://sioc-project.org/

[15] http://usefulinc.com/doap/

FOAF Basics	Personal Information	Online Accounts / IM
Agent	weblog	OnlineAccount
Person	knows	OnlineChatAccount
name	interest	OnlineEcommerceAccount
nick	currentProject	OnlineGamingAccount
title	pastProject	holdsAccount
homepage	plan	accountServiceHomepage
mbox	based_near	accountName
mbox_sha1sum	workplaceHomepage	icqChatID
img	workInfoHomepage	msnChatID
depiction (depicts)	schoolHomepage	aimChatID
surname	topic_interest	jabberID
family_name	publications	yahooChatID
givenname	geekcode	
firstName	myersBriggs	
	dnaChecksum	

Projects and Groups	Documents and Images
Project	Document
Organization	Image
Group	PersonalProfileDocument
member	topic (page)
membershipClass	primaryTopic
fundedBy	tipjar
theme	sha1
	made (maker)
	thumbnail
	logo

Table 5.1. Classes and properties of the FOAF ontology.

While FOAF has a rich ontology for characterizing individuals —especially with respect to their online presence—, but it is rather poor as a vocabulary for describing relationships. There is a single *foaf:knows* relationship defined between Persons and this relationship has no ontological restrictions on its use and is broadly defined in text on the basis of what is not required (e.g. that the relationship is reciprocated or an actual meeting has taken place). This is intentional on behalf of the creators of the vocabulary who wanted FOAF to be applicable in the widest scope possible. However, the consequence is that the meaning of the knows term is now significantly diluted through usage.

The makers of the vocabulary expected, however, that others would use the extensibility of the RDF/OWL language to define more precise notions of relationships. For example, one may define in RDF a relationship called *example:supervises* between a *example:Teacher* and a *example:Student*, where supervises is a subPropertyOf "knows" and Teacher and Student are subclasses of *foaf:Person*. OWL would allow to put additional constraints on the use of this relationship, for example to say

that every Student is supervised by at least one Teacher. Nevertheless, to characterize relationships beyond the two participants it is desirable to have a representation
where relationships themselves are the object of the ontology. This is the subject of
the following section.

5.3 Ontological representation of social relationships

Ontological representations of social networks such as FOAF need to be extended
with a framework for modelling and characterizing social relationships for two principle reasons: (1) to support the automated integration of social information on a
semantical basis and (2) to capture established concepts in Social Network Analysis.

In this section we approach this task using the engineering method of decom-
position. The key idea is that the representation of social relationships needs to be
fine-grained enough so that we can capture all the detail from the individual sources
of information in a way that these can be later recombined and taken as an evidence
of a certain relationship.

Network analysis itself can be a help in that it has a rich vocabulary of characterizing social relationships. As these are the terms that are used by social scientists,
they are prime candidates to be included in any ontology. For illustration, we list
below some of the most commonly discussed characteristics of social relationships.
(We specifically focus on interpersonal-relations, ignoring social relationships at different level of analysis, such as institutional relationships or institutional trust.)

- Sign: (*valence*) A relationship can represent both positive and negative attitudes
  such as like or hate. The positive or negative charge of relationships is important
  on its own for the study of balance within social networks, which is the subject
  of balance theory.
- Strength: The notion of tie strength was first introduced by Granovetter in his
  groundbreaking work on the benefits of weak ties [Gra73]. Tie strength itself is
  a complex construct of several characteristics of social relations. In her survey,
  Hite lists the following aspects of tie strength discussed in the literature: Affec-
  t/philos/passions , Frequency/frequent contact , Reciprocity, Trust/enforceable
  trust , Complementarity, Accommodation/adaptation, Indebtedness/imbalance,
  Collaboration, Transaction investments, Strong history, Fungible skills, Expectations, Social capital, Bounded solidarity, Lower opportunistic behavior, Density, Maximize relationship over org., Fine-grained information transfer, Problem
  solving, Duration, Multiplexity, Diffusion, Facilitation, Personal involvement,
  Low formality (few contracts), Connectedness [Hit03].
  As this list shows, the conceptualization of tie strength is rather fuzzy. There is
  little agreement in the field as to the importance of these individual aspects of tie
  strength [MC84]. In practice researchers tend to ignore aspects that are irrelevant
  to their actual study. More unfortunate is the fact that no agreed upon method
  has emerged yet for measuring them, which means that researchers in the field
  use different elicitation methods and questions when it comes to measuring any

of these aspects. As a result data about tie strength as a numerical value or as a binary distinction between weak and strong ties is hardly comparable across studies. Nevertheless, there is a need for representing measured tie strength, for example, for purposes of secondary analysis.

- Provenance: A social relationship may be viewed differently by the individual participants of the relationship, sometimes even to the degree that the tie is unreciprocated, i.e. perceived by only one member of the dyad. Similarly, outsiders may provide different accounts of the relationship, which is a well-known bias in SNA.

- Relationship history: Social relationships come into existence by some event (in the most generic, philosophical sense) involving two individuals. (Such an event may not require personal contact (e.g. online friendships), but it has to involve social interaction.[16] From this event, social relationships begin a lifecycle of their own during which the characteristics of the relationship may change through interaction or the lack of (see e.g. Hite and Hesterly [HH01b]).

- Relationship roles: A social relationship may have a number of social roles associated with it, which we call relationship roles. For example, in a student/professor relationship within a university setting there is one individual playing the role of professor, while another individual is playing the role of a student. Both the relationship and the roles may be limited in their interpretation and use to a certain social context (see below). Social roles, social contexts and their formalization are discussed in Masolo et al. [MVB+04]

In the case of Web-based social networking services we also see a variety of ways of capturing relationship types and other attributes of relationships. For example, Orkut allows to describe the strength of friendship relations on a 5-point scale from "haven't met" to "best friend", while other sites may choose other scales or terms. Further, various sites focus on very different kind of relationships and exchanges, e.g. LinkedIn differs from Orkut in focusing on professional exchanges.

Ideally, all users of all these services would agree to a single shared typology of social relations and shared characterizations of relations. However, this is neither feasible nor necessary. What is required from such a representation is that it is minimal in order to facilitate adoption and that it should preserve key identifying characteristics such as the case of identifying properties for social individuals. Consider that two FOAF-aware software systems can determine if two person objects reference the same individual even if they define different subtypes of the *foaf:Person* class.

In summary, a rich ontological characterization of social relationships is needed for the aggregation of social network information that comes from multiple sources and possibly different contexts, which is the typical scenario of the Web but is also the case for network data aggregation in the social sciences. We propose a representation of relationships on the basis of patterns (descriptions) that can be mapped to or

---

[16] Note that the "knows" notion of FOAF is somewhat misleading in this sense, e.g. I know (cognitively recognize) George Bush, but I certainly never had any social interaction with him.

extracted from observations about the environment. In other words, we consider relationships as higher-order concepts that capture a set of constraints on the interaction of the individuals.

5.3.1 Conceptual model

The importance of social relationships alone suggests that they should be treated as first-class citizens. (In other words, we would like to discuss social relations as objects, not only as relations between objects.) Alternatively, social relations could be represented as n-ary predicates; however, n-ary relations are not supported directly by the RDF/OWL languages. There are several alternatives to n-ary relations in RDF/OWL described in a document created by the Semantic Web Best Practices and Deployment Working Group of the W3C.[17]

In all cases dealing with n-ary relations we employ the technique that is known as *reification*: we represent the relation as a class, whose instances are concrete relations of that type. One may recall that RDF itself has a reified representation of statements: the *rdf:Statement* object represents the class of statements. This class has three properties that correspond to the components of a statement, namely *rdf:subject*, *rdf:predicate*, *rdf:object*. These properties are used to link the statement instance to the resources involved in the statement.

Thus the trivial way to enrich the representation of relations in FOAF is to use the reification feature of the RDF language. We propose two alternative RDF(S) representation of relationships, both using the reification mechanisms of RDF(S) to reify the original triple asserting the existence of the relationship (for example, a *foaf:knows* statement). In other words relationships become subclasses of the *rdf:Statement* class (see Figures 5.3 and 5.4). Common also to both representations is that the new Relationship class is related to a general Parameter class by the hasParameter relationship. Relationship types such as Friendship are subclasses of the Relationship class, while their parameters (such as strength or frequency) are subtypes of the Parameter class. Note that the hasParameter metaproperty cannot be defined in OWL DL (its domain is *rdf:Statement* while its range is *owl:Class* or some subclass of it).

The two alternatives differ in the representation of parameters. The first scheme borrows from the design of OWL-S for representing service parameters, as used in the specification of the profile of a Web Service [MOGS04]. Here, parameters are related by the valued-by metaproperty to their range (*owl:Thing* or a datatype, depending on whether the parameter takes objects or datatypes as values). For example in an application Strength may be a subclass of Parameter valued-by integers. The disadvantage of this solution is that specifying values requires two statements or the introduction of a constructed property (the necessary axiom is not expressible in OWL).

The second alternative differs in that the "native" method of RDF is used for representing parameters: the generic Parameter class is defined as a subclass of

---

[17] http://www.w3.org/TR/swbp-n-aryRelations/

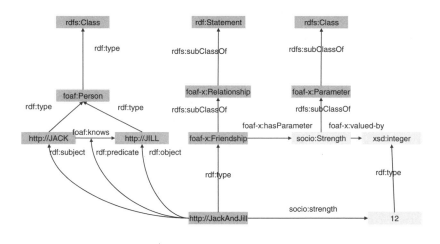

Figure 5.3. An RDF representation of social relationships.

rdf:Property. This model has the advantage that it becomes more natural to represent parameter values and restrictions on them. The disadvantage is that this solution is not compliant with OWL DL: declaring properties ranging on properties and creating subclasses *rdf:Property* are not allowed in this species of OWL.

The advantage of describing relations using statement reification is that this form of reification is directly supported by RDF and can be efficiently stored and queried in quad-based triple stores (see Chapter 6).

Some caution is also due when using RDF reification. Unlike the reader might expect, reification has no formal semantics in RDF or OWL[18]. In particular, the existence of the reified version of a statement does not imply the existence of the ground statement or vice versa. Further, many would expect reification to be a form of quotation, i.e. the representation of a certain stating of a particular statement that can be attributed to someone. This is not the case due to the interaction with the semantics of OWL.[19] The opposite view, i.e. that two *rdf:Statement* instances with the same subject, predicate and object are necessarily identical, does not hold either [Hay04].

The simple reification based representation is also not powerful enough to capture social relationships with an arity higher than two. For example, brokering is a relationship between two people and a broker. Such relationships cannot be directly represented in RDF and therefore they cannot be reified either.

---

[18] The use of the reification vocabulary is allowed in OWL, i.e. it is not considered an extension of the otherwise protected rdf namespace.

[19] See http://lists.w3.org/Archives/Public/semantic-web/2006Mar/0194.html

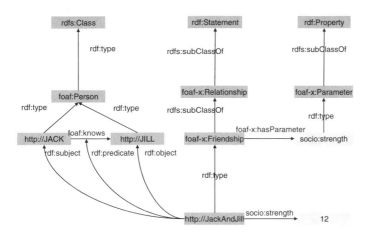

Figure 5.4. An alternative RDF representation of social relationships.

Further, there are two related characteristics of social relations that we would like to capture in a more advanced representation. The first characteristic is the context dependence of social relations and the second is the separation between an observable situation and its interpretation as a social relation between two individuals.

Social relations are socially constructed objects: they are constructed in social environments by assigning a label to a common pattern of interaction between individuals. Much like social roles discussed in the work of Masolo et al. [MVB+04], social relationships have a strong contextual dependence in that they own their definition (the ability to identify them) to the social context in which they are interpretable. Only within this social context are we able to identify and interpret a certain interaction-pattern among individuals as a certain kind of relationship. This process, which is known as cognitive structuring, works by applying the generic pattern we associate with such a relationship to the actual state-of-affairs we observe. However, the same observed state-of-affairs may be interpreted according to another pattern as a different kind of relationship. For example, a student/professor relationship at the Free University of Amsterdam (and the attached role of student and professor) is defined by the social context of the university and this kind of relationship may not be recognizable outside of the university. (In another sense, we may talk about student as the entire class of roles of students at learning institutions around the world.)

The individual relationships and their generic description are thus clearly separate. The generic pattern of the relationship comprises those and only those aspects that are shared among particular occurrences of the relationship (for example, there are always two distinct roles in the case of a student/professor relationship with

certain requirements for playing those roles). The description is partial in the sense
that it allows variation in the particular relations between individuals.

The representation of context and the separation of the level of state-of-affairs
(observations of objects and sequences of events) from the higher level of descriptions (contexts) that can be used to interpret those state-of-affairs turns out to be a
common problem in the representation of much of human knowledge. A solution
proposed by [GM03] is the Descriptions and Situations ontology design pattern that
provides a model of context and allows to clearly delineate these two layers of representation (Figure 5.5).

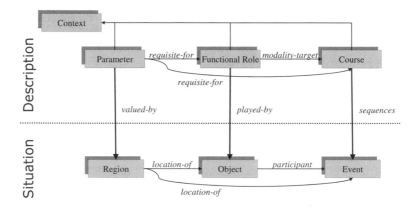

Figure 5.5. The Descriptions and Situations ontology design pattern.

D&S is a generic pattern for modelling non-physical objects whose intended
meaning results from statements, i.e. it emerges in combination with other entities.
For example, a norm, a plan, or a social role is usually represented as a set of statements and not as a concept. On the other hand, non-physical objects may change
and be manipulated similar to physical entities, and are often treated as first-order
objects. That means that an ontology should account for such objects by modelling
the context or frame of reference on which they depend.

D&S is an ontology-design pattern in the sense that it is used as a template for
creating domain ontologies in complex areas. D & S has been successfully applied
in a wide range of real-life ontology engineering projects from representing Service
Level Agreements (SLAs) to the descriptions of Web Services [MOGS04].

D&S builds on some basic categories from the DOLCE foundational ontology, namely the notions of Objects, Events and Regions. (These concepts represent the top level ontological choice in almost all Foundational Ontologies.) As depicted in the Figure, the notion of Context in D & S is composed of a set of Parameters, Functional Roles and Courses of Events. Axioms enforce that each descriptive category acts as a selector on a certain basic category of DOLCE: Parameters are valued-by Regions, Functional Roles are played-by Objects (endurants) and Courses of Events sequence Events (perdurants). The elements of the context thus mirror the elements of the state-of-affairs (a set of objects, events and their locations), but add additional semantics to them. Note also that these levels of description and situation are clearly separate in that the same state-of-affairs may be interpreted according to another theory by mapping the elements of that other theory to the same set of objects and events. D & S captures the intuition that multiple overlapping (or alternative) contexts may match the same world or model, and that such contexts can have systematic relations among their elements.

D&S has been already used by Masolo et al. for the representation of social contexts and social roles. Their arguments about the context dependence of social roles equally hold for social relations and we follow their approach in using D&S for the design of our conceptual model for the representation of social relationships. In particular, we model a Social Relationship as a subclass of Context and particular social relationships such as Friendship a subclass of this generic concept. As contexts, Social Relationships can have a number of Parameters, Roles and single Course as components.

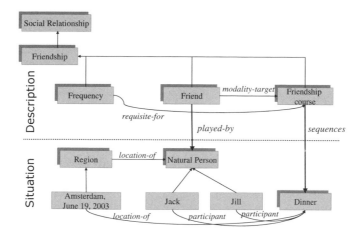

Figure 5.6. An instantiation of the Descriptions and Situations pattern for social relationships.

A typical Role is the Relationship Role, a subclass of the Social Role concept introduced by [MVB$^+$04]. An example of a relationship role is (the trivial) Friend role in a friendship relation, the Student and Professor roles in a student/advisor relationship and the Uncle/Nephew roles of kinship. Relationship Roles are restricted to be played by Natural Persons.

The course of the relationship captures the generic characteristics for the course of a certain relationship, i.e. the kinds of event and their possible sequences that characterize a certain kind of relationship. The course is related to the actual events in a particular relationship by the sequences relationship.

Characteristics of relationships such as the ones mentioned above are conceptualized as parameters, mostly a requisite for the course of the relationship. For example, frequency may be axiomatized as the average number of events in the course of the relationship within a given time unit. We recognize that softer qualities of relationships (such as the emotional content of the relationship) may be harder to capture precisely, but the engineer should strive in any case to relate it to other components of the relationship. (If the semantics cannot be captured precisely, at least the elicitation question(s) that were used to determine the quality should be documented.)

Figure 5.6 shows the representation of the friendship relation (some property instances are not shown for visualization purposes). Friendship in general is a social relationship with a single role called Friend, played by actual persons such as Jack and Jill. Friendship also has a typical course; an event such as a dinner where both Jack and Jill have participated may be related to this course, which would indicate at least that it has a significance to the development of a friendship between Jack and Jill. (Friendship is difficult to capture more precisely in this respect in that there is hardly a typical course for a friendship. Nevertheless, one may discern typical events, such as the point that the participants consider as the "beginning" of their friendship.)

In summary, we propose an advanced representation of social relationships as higher order concepts (patterns) that map to a concrete state-of-affairs representing observations about the environment. This view of relationships fits very well with the increasing availability of fine-grained electronic data (such as emails) about the history of social interactions between individuals. We expect this trend to continue in the future as we will be surrounded with more and more mobile and ubiquitous devices that collect data on our whereabouts and interactions with other people. While this may sound like a doomsday scenario, technology for tracking and observing social relationships based on sensor data is accepted in cases where it occurs with the agreement of the participants and where it serves a well-defined purpose. For example, Matsuo et al. describe a ubiquitous system for supporting the networking of conference participants [MHT+06]. Through infrared sensors and later, RFID cards the system observes social networks based on the participants physical presence in the conference space and through their explicit actions: conference participants may touch their badges to readers to indicate that they have met and the system reacts by displaying information related to their meeting (e.g. shared interests). The technology has been already applied for three consecutive years at the yearly meetings of AI researchers in Japan (JSAI 2003-2005) and at the UbiComp conference in 2005.

5.4 Aggregating and reasoning with social network data

Supposing that we have started out with some data sets in traditional formats (relational databases, Excel sheets, XML files etc.) our first step is to convert them into an RDF-based syntax, which allows to store the data in an ontology store and manipulate it with ontology-based tools. In this process we need to assign identifiers to resources (an issue that we deal with in Section 5.4.1) and re-represent our data in terms of a shared ontology such as FOAF.

In case our data sets come from external sources it is often more natural to preserve their original schema. For example, in case of converting data from a relational database or Excel sheet it is natural to preserve the schema of the database or spreadsheet as represented by the table definitions or table headings. We can then apply *ontology mapping* to unify our data on the schema level by mapping classes (types) and properties from different schemas to a shared ontology such as FOAF. In effect, ontology mapping allows us to treat the data set as if it had a single shared schema. Note that research on automated methods for ontology mapping is an active research area within the Semantic Web community. It is not our primary concern as the number of ontologies involved and their size does not make it necessary to automate ontology mapping in our typical case.

The task of aggregation, however, is not complete yet: we need to find identical resources across the data sets. This is a two step process. First, it requires capturing the domain-specific knowledge of when to consider two instances to be the same. As we will see the FOAF ontology itself also prescribes ways to infer the equality of two instances, for example based on their email address. However, beyond these properties it is likely that we need to introduce some domain-specific criteria based on domain-specific properties. In order to do this, we need to consider the general meaning of equality in RDF/OWL (Section 5.4.2). In practice, only a limited part of the knowledge regarding instance equality can be captured in RDF or OWL. For example, determining equality is often considered as applying a threshold value to a similarity measure, which is a weighted combination of the similarity of certain properties. (The threshold is determined by experimentation or through machine learning.) In this and many other practical cases that involve computation we need a procedural representation of knowledge.

Once we determined the rules or procedures that determine equality in our domain, we need to carry out the actual instance unification or *smushing* (see Section 5.4.4). Unlike much of the related work on instance unification, we consider smushing as a reasoning task, where we iteratively execute the rules or procedures that determine equality until no more equivalent instances can be found. The advantage of this approach (compared to a one-step computation of a similarity measure) is that we can take into account the learned equalities in subsequent rounds of reasoning.

We will discuss the advantages and disadvantages of using rule-based reasoners and Description Logic reasoners for this task and the trade-off between forward- and backward chaining reasoning. We will also outline the approach in case we need to combine procedural and rule based reasoning.

5.4.1 Representing identity

One of the main advantages of RDF over other representation formalisms such as UML is the possibility to uniquely identify resources (instances, classes, as well as properties). The primary mechanism for this is the assignment of URIs to resources. Every resource, except blank nodes is identified by a URI.

However, in practice it is often the case that there are a number of candidates for identifiers. For example, in the publishing world a number of identifier schemes are in use. Standard schemes such as ISBN and ISSN numbers for books and periodicals as well as DOIs (Digital Object Identifiers) are widely adopted, while each publisher and online repository also maintains its own identifier scheme. Further, publications that are accessible online can be represented by their URL. All of these identifiers are unique (an identifier identifies a single resource), but mostly not single (a resource may be identified by multiple identifiers). This is the case with URLs (the same publication may be posted at multiple URLs), but it happens even with DOIs whose registration is centralized that the same publication is assigned two or more identifiers.

Multiple identifiers can be represented in RDF in two separate ways. First, one can introduce a separate resource and use the identifiers as URIs for these resources. Once separate resources are introduced for the same object, the equality of these resources can be expressed using the *owl:sameAs* property (see the following section). The other alternative is to chose one of the identifiers and use it as a URI.

Note that in all cases resource identifiers need to conform to the URI specification and good practice. Many modern identifier schemes such as DOIs have been designed to conform to the URI specification. Other identifier schemes can be recoded as URIs with the new[20] info: prefix (protocol), which is regulated in [dSHNW06]. It is also a common practice to create URIs within a web domain owned or controlled by the creator of the metadata description. For example, if the registered domain name of a public organization is http://www.example.org then a resource with the identifier 123 could be represented as http://www.example.org/id/123. This satisfies the guidelines for good URIs, in particular that good URIs should be unique and stable.[21] The first criterion means that good URIs should be unambiguous or at least should be chosen such that it is unlikely that someone else would use the same URI for something different. This is important because resources with the same URI but different intended meanings are likely to result in inconsistencies (a *URI clash*). The second criterium is also important because there is no way to rename resources (to reassign URIs). Once a URI changes the only solution is to introduce a new resource and assert its equivalence with the old resource. However, in large scale systems such as the web there is no way to notify remote systems of the new identifier and they are likely to continue referencing the resource by its old identifier. Thus it is bad idea for example to encode unstable property values in identifiers as done in [PP06], where publications are assigned identifiers based on e.g. the journal,

---

[20] April 2006
[21] See   http://www.w3.org/Addressing/   and   http://esw.w3.org/topic/
GoodURIs

the volume and the page number. If there turns out to be a data entry mistake in one of the values, the identifier becomes obsolete and is potentially ambiguous.

The use of http:// URIs has been somewhat complicated by the long outstanding issue of whether such URIs could be used for only web resources or also for abstract concepts (which has been the practice), and if yes, what should web servers respond to HTTP requests related to such URIs.[22] The resolution of this issue is that the response code of the web server should indicate whether the URI denotes a web resource (HTML page, image about a person, publication etc.) or some abstract concept (such as a person, a publication etc.) The response code used by web servers to indicate success should be used only for web resources.

A practical consequence is that for abstract concepts one should not choose URIs that are recognized by a server, e.g. the location of an existing HTML page, as this would be a case of URI clash. While the decision also opens the road to look up metadata about abstracts concepts using the HTTP protocol there are currently very few web servers configured to support this.

5.4.2 On the notion of equality

RDF and OWL (starting with OWL Lite) allow us to identify resources and to represent their (in)equality using the *owl:sameAs* and *owl:differentFrom* properties. However, these are only the basic building blocks for defining equality. In particular, the meaning of equality with respect to the objects of the domain depends on the domain itself and the goals of the modelling. For example, it is part of the domain knowledge what it takes for two persons or publications to be considered the same, i.e. what are the characteristics that we take into account. Further, depending on the level of modelling we may distinguish, for example, individual persons or instead consider groups of persons (e.g. based on roles) and consider each individual within the group to be equivalent (role equivalence).

Nevertheless, it is interesting to take a short de-tour to the domain of philosophy, where a number of attempts have been made over the centuries to capture the general characteristics of the notions of identity and equality (indiscernibility). The most well-known formulation of equality was given by Wilhelm Gottfried Leibniz in his *Discourse on Metaphysics*. The Identity of Indiscernibles or Leibniz-law can be loosely phrased as the principle of all things being identical unless we are able to distinguish (discern) them or put it differently: no two distinct objects have exactly the same properties.[23] The Leibniz-law is formalized using the logical formula given in Formula 5.1. The converse of the Leibniz-law is called Indiscernibility of Identicals and written as Formula 5.2. The two laws taken together (often also called Leibniz-law) are the basis of the definition of equality in a number of systems.

---

[22] The issue has been codenamed httprange-14 by the Technical Architecture Group (TAG) of the W3C and has been on the agenda for four years, see http://www.w3.org/2001/tag/issues.html#httpRange-14

[23] http://plato.stanford.edu/entries/identity-indiscernible/

$$\forall P : P(x) \leftrightarrow P(y) \to x = y \qquad (5.1)$$
$$\forall P : P(x) \leftrightarrow P(y) \leftarrow x = y \qquad (5.2)$$

The reflexive, symmetric and transitive properties of equality follow from these definitions. Notice that both formulas are second-degree due to the quantification on properties. This quantification is also interesting because it provides the Leibniz-law different interpretations in open and closed worlds. Namely, in an open world the number of properties is unknown and thus the Leibniz-law is not useful in practice: we can never conclude that two resources are equal since we can never be certain whether there is another property out there that could allow us to distinguish them. In a closed world we can possibly iterate over all properties to check if two resources are equal; if we can distinguish them by some property we can assume they are equal.

In practice, a closed world assumption can be equally undesirable as an open one. In most cases we have almost complete information about our resources, but still we may not want two resources to be considered identical just because of a lack of information. For example, if we have two resources and we only know that they are the same gender, we may not want to assume they are identical (which would be the consequence in a closed world).

Philosophical ontologists have also argued against the Leibniz-law in the original form because it is stronger than our natural notion of equality. Consider for example a perfectly symmetrical space with two perfect spheres at some distance d to each other. Our natural intuition would consider the two spheres indistinguishable. However, they can be distinguished as the first sphere is distance d from the second sphere, which is not true for the second sphere (it is zero distance to itself). The solution to this problem is to limit the kind of properties to be considered, in particular to exclude impure, extrinsic properties such as distance to other instances.

The same strategy can be followed in closed worlds to introduce weaker notions of equality at will. For example, one might specify the set of properties to be checked and exclude such properties as *foaf:based_near*, which gives the geo-location of the individual or transient properties such as *foaf:gender*, which may change during the lifetime of an individual.

Lastly, let's consider the relationship of the Leibniz-law to OWL and the semantics of the *owl:sameAs* relationship. First, we should note that the properties we are interested in are the statements that are made about a resource. We could always distinguish two resources for example by their URIs. However, we do not want to consider the URI a property of the resource, since this would be too strong of a notion of equality. (Resources could never be equal, only bNodes.)

The semantics of OWL is built on an open world assumption, which means that the Leibniz-law cannot be used to infer identity, not even if we reduce the property space even further. However, we can still infer the equality of instances by necessity (see the following Section).

On the other hand, the semantics of *owl:sameAs* conforms to Formula 5.2. Namely, *owl:sameAs* restricts the interpretation of the theory to those models where the two symbols denote the same object and thus they must be indiscernible in the sense that they are interchangeable in statements:

$$(s_1, owl{:}sameAs, s_2) \wedge (s_1, p, o) \rightarrow (s_2, p, o)$$
$$(p_1, owl{:}sameAs, p_2) \wedge (s, p_1, o) \rightarrow (s, p_2, o)$$
$$(o_1, owl{:}sameAs, o_2) \wedge (s, p, o_1) \rightarrow (s, p, o_2) \tag{5.3}$$

The reflexive, symmetric and transitive properties of sameAs also follow:

$$\forall s : (s, owl{:}sameAs, s)$$
$$(s_1, owl{:}sameAs, s_2) \rightarrow (s_2, owl{:}sameAs, s_1)$$
$$(s_1, owl{:}sameAs, s_2) \wedge (s_2, owl{:}sameAs, s_3) \rightarrow (s_1, owl{:}sameAs, s_3) \tag{5.4}$$

Note that it is not inconsistent to have resources that are *owl:sameAs* but have different stated properties, e.g. Formula 5.5 is not an inconsistent ontology. The explanation lies again in the open world assumption: we can assume that the missing statements (that s_1 has the *foaf:name* Paul and s_2 has the *foaf:name* John) exist somewhere. In a closed world this ontology would be inconsistent.

$$(s_1, owl{:}sameAs, s_2)$$
$$(s_1, foaf{:}name, "John")$$
$$(s_2, foaf{:}name, "Paul") \tag{5.5}$$

5.4.3 Determining equality

In our case, we are interested in capturing knowledge about the identity of resources that can lead to conclude the (in)equality of resources.

In OWL there are a limited set of constructs that can lead to (in)equality statements. Functional and inverse functional properties (IFPs) and maximum cardinality restrictions in general can lead to conclude that two symbols must denote the same resource when otherwise the cardinality restriction could not be fulfilled. For example, the *foaf:mbox* property denoting the email address of a person is inverse-functional as a mailbox can only belong to a single person. As another example, consider a hypothetical *ex:hasParent* property, which has a maximum cardinality of two. If we state that a single person has three parents (which we are allowed to state) an OWL reasoner should conclude that at least two of them has to be the same. Once inferred, the equality of instances can be stated by using the *owl:sameAs* property.[24] There are more ways to conclude that two symbols do not denote the same object, which is expressed by the *owl:differentFrom* property. For example, instances of disjoint classes must be different from each other.

---

[24] Note that the *owl:sameAs* property can be used to state the equivalence of classes and properties, but only in OWL Full. (This requires classes and properties to be treated as individuals.)

Often, the knowledge that we need to capture cannot be expressed in OWL, only in more expressive rule languages. A typical example is the case of complex keys: for example, we may want to equate two persons only if both their names and their birth dates match. This is not possible to express in OWL but can be captured in Horn logic[25], a typical target for rule languages for the Semantic Web (see e.g. [HPSB+04]).

However, there are even situations when the expressivity of rule languages is not sufficient either. In our early work on one of the first ontology-based Knowledge Management systems we have already noted that several elementary reasoning steps could not be expressed in declarative, logic based formalisms [Mik02]. Functions for simple data type manipulation such as the concatenation of literals is not part of either DL or rule languages. A an example of this is the matching of person names.

In our applications, person names are matched by separating the first and the last name in the first step. We apply a simple heuristic for determining the cutting point. (It is not possible to completely automate the separation of first names and last names in a language-independent way.[26]) Then the last names are compared in a case unsensitive manner. If they match, the first names are compared using fuzzy string matching. In both cases we have to deal with abbreviations, e.g. to match *F.v. Harmelen* against *Frank van Harmelen*.

This algorithm is easy to describe in a programming language or more power-ful transformation languages such as XSLT, which contains the necessary datatypes, data manipulation functions and the three basic constructs of procedural program-ming (the sequence operator, the if statement and the for loop). Rule languages in a Semantic Web context, however, lack this expressive power.

The solution is to combine declarative and procedural reasoning as described in [Mik02] or as proposed by Korotkiy [KT06]. Similar to procedural attachments, the main idea is to compute certain relationships with components/services that conform to a particular interface. Reasoning is a combination of calling these services and executing a regular Description Logic or rule-based reasoner.

5.4.4 Reasoning with instance equality

Reasoning is the inference of new statements (facts) that *necessarily* follow from the set of known statements. As discussed in the previous Chapter, what follows from a set of statements is determined by the semantics of the language. Every fact we add to our knowledge base has a meaning in the sense that it represents some constraint on the mapping between the symbols of our representation and some domain of

---

[25] In logic, a Horn clause is a disjunction of literals with at most one positive literal, i.e. Horn clauses are formulas of the form $p \wedge q \wedge \cdots \wedge t \rightarrow u$

[26] It is easy to see that the separation of first name and last name is a very complex natural language problem. For example, encountering the Dutch name *Mirjam Huis in 't Veld* most foreigners assume that the word *Huis* belongs to the first name. However, it belongs to the last name, which means "House in the Field". As another example consider languages such as Hungarian, where first name is written last and last name is written first, as in the name of the author of this book: *Mika Péter*.

interpretation. In other words, every piece of additional knowledge excludes some unintended interpretation of our knowledge base.

In most sufficiently complex languages, an infinite number of new statements could be inferred from any non-trivial knowledge base. In practice, however, we are not interested in all statements that might be deduced from a knowledge base, but only those that are relevant to some task. In other words, we would like to complete our knowledge base to contain all the important knowledge relevant to that task.

There are a number of choices one has to consider when implementing reasoning, which mostly concern trade-offs between efficiency and scalability. In the following, we review some of the options and choices to be made.

Description Logic versus rule-based reasoners

Our task is instance equality reasoning, i.e. the inference of *owl:sameAs* and *owl:differentFrom* statements. In general, OWL (DL) reasoners are of limited use in performing this kind of reasoning. As mentioned in the previous Chapter, our representation needs are also slightly different from the OWL language: we use a limited set of OWL constructs (corresponding to the unofficial OWL Tiny variant), while some of our knowledge can only be captured by rules.

Nevertheless, we can use OWL reasoners to reason with the part of the knowledge that can be expressed in OWL. As many other practical applications, however, we do not benefit from the theoretical results about the efficiency (complexity) of OWL DL reasoning, which were the original motivation behind the design of the OWL language. In particular, OWL DL was designed with the idea that the language should be as expressive as possible with the limitation that it should be also *decidable* and that it should be possible to create *efficient* reasoners for it.

In many practical cases OWL is more expressive than necessary. Decidability (the guarantee to find an answer in finite time) or completeness (the guarantee to find all the complete answers) are also not an issue in cases where the time or memory available for the reasoning is limited. Lastly, results about the complexity of OWL DL are theoretical, because they concern worst-case complexity. In practice, only the average case matters as the worst cases may be extremely rare. Further, when resources are limited we are not interested in the asymptotic behavior of the algorithm; on a short scale an approximate anytime algorithm with exponential complexity may be faster than a linear one.

Description Logic reasoners are designed to support primary tasks of classification[27] and the consistency checking of ontologies. Other reasoning tasks are usually reformulated as consistency checking. In the case of equality reasoning this means that if we want to check whether two instances are necessarily the same, we add the opposite to the ontology and check for inconsistency. If the reasoner signals inconsistency, we can be certain that the instances are the same and add that to our knowledge base. (As discussed before the lack of inconsistency would not mean that

---

[27] Determining the complete subclass hierarchy of the ontology, i.e. finding implicit *rdfs:subClassOf* relations.

the instances are necessarily different, we might simply lack enough information.) Unfortunately, this kind of reasoning is very inefficient in practice as we need to perform a consistency check for every pair of instances in the ontology.

A better alternative is to consider rule-based reasoning and this is the method we explored in our work in combination with procedural attachments. The semantics of RDF(S) can be completely expressed using a set of inference rules, which are given in [Hay04]. Further, a significant part of the OWL semantics can be captured using rules and this contains the part that is relevant to our task. Horst shows a partial rule-based axiomatization of OWL in [tH05]. These rules are implemented among others by the OWLIM reasoner[28], but can also be used with any sufficiently expressive rule-based reasoner such as the query language or the custom-rule based reasoner of Sesame[29].

Forward versus backward chaining

Rules can be used either in a forward-chaining or backward-chaining manner with different trade-offs. Forward chaining means that all consequences of the rules are computed to obtain what is called a *complete materialization* of the knowledge base. Typically this is done by repeatedly checking the prerequisites of the rules and adding their conclusions until no new statements can be inferred. The advantage of this method is that queries are fast to execute since all true statements are readily available. (The reasoning is performed before queries are answered, typically right after adding some new knowledge.) The disadvantage is that storing the complete materialization often takes exorbitant amounts of space as even the simplest RDF(S) ontologies result in a large amount of inferred statements (typically several times the size of the original repository)[30], where most of the inferred statements are not required for the task at hand. Also, the knowledge base needs to be updated if a statement is removed, since in that case all other statements that have been inferred from the removed statements also need to be removed (if they cannot be inferred in some other way).

With backward-chaining, rules are executed "backwards" and on demand, i.e. when a query needs to be answered. While with forward chaining we check the prerequisites of rules and add all their conclusions, here we are given a conclusion and check whether it is explicitly stated or whether it could inferred from some rule, either because the prerequisites of the rule are explicitly stated to be true or again because they too could be inferred from some other rule(s). The drawback of backward-chaining is longer query execution times.

The advantage of a rule-based axiomatization is that the expressivity of the reasoning can be fine-tuned by removing rules that would only infer knowledge that is irrelevant to our reasoning task. For example, the general RDF(S) inference rule

---

[28] http://www.ontotext.com/owlim/
[29] http://www.openrdf.org
[30] In fact, the number of RDF statements that follow from any RDF(S) model is infinite: there is an infinite number of axiomatic triples due to container-membership properties [Hay04].

which says that all entities that occur as subjects of a statement are instances of the *rdfs:Resource* class can be ignored if it is irrelevant for our reasoning what the members are of this class. Especially in the case of forward-chaining we can save significant amounts of space by not having to store this irrelevant (and rather trivial) knowledge about every resource. (In the backward chaining case we do not gain anything if we would not ask any queries anyway about the membership of this class.)

In the Flink system (see Section 6.2), we first used the built-in inference engine of the ontology store. However, some of the rules required cannot be expressed declaratively and thus we implemented our own identity reasoner in the Java language. The reasoning is performed using a combination of forward- and backward chaining in order to balance efficiency and scalability. The rules that are used to infer the equality of instances are executed iteratively in a forward chaining manner by querying the repository for the premise(s) and adding the consequents of the rules. The semantics of the resulting *owl:sameAs* statements is partly inferred in a backward-chaining manner.

In particular, the rules expressed in Formulae 5.4 are added in a forward-chaining manner, while those in Formulae 5.3 are dealt with at query time by rewriting queries. For example, consider the following SeRQL query which asks for the email address of the instance Peter:

```
SELECT email FROM
{example:Peter} foaf:mbox {email}
USING NAMESPACE
foaf = <http://xmlns.com/foaf/0.1/>,
example = <http://www.example.org/>
```

This query is rewritten in a way to also return all email addresses of other instances that are *owl:sameAs* this instance:

```
SELECT email FROM
{example:Peter} owl:sameAs {other},
{other} foaf:mbox {email}
USING NAMESPACE
foaf = <http://xmlns.com/foaf/0.1/>,
example = <http://www.example.org/>
```

Note that this will also return the email attached to the instance *example:Peter*, because of the reflexivity of the *owl:sameAs* property. At this point we already added for all instances that they are sameAs themselves. This query rewriting is implemented in the Elmo API introduced in Chapter 6.1.3.

The timing of reasoning and the method of representation

There are three basic variations on what point the identity reasoning is performed. Also, there is the related choice of whether to represent equivalence using the *owl:sameAs* relationship or to directly merge the descriptions of the equivalent instances.

In the first variation, smushing is carried out while adding data into a repository. This is the method chosen by Ingenta when implementing a large-scale publication metadata repository: when a new instance is added to the repository, it is checked whether an equivalent instance already exists in the repository [PP06].

In the Ingenta case, the descriptions are merged: only one of the identifiers is kept and all information about the resource is consolidated under that identifier. This method has the advantage that the repository size is reduced, since there are no redundant instances connected to each other with *owl:sameAs* relations. There is a serious potential drawback, however: if it turns out later that the two instances merged are not the same (for example, because the data were erroneous, the criteria for equality changed or an identifying property of the resource changed) it is impossible to unmerge the descriptions. Using the *owl:sameAs* relationship it is very easy to revise the results of equality reasoning by removing the appropriate statements.

The second variation is when the reasoning is performed after the repository has been filled with data containing potential duplicates. This is the choice we take in the Flink system (see Section 6.2). In this case again there is also a choice between representing the results by merging identifiers or by *owl:sameAs* relationships. However, the benefits of the first are not as obvious, because removing statements is an expensive operation with most triple stores.[31]

Lastly, reasoning can be performed at query time. This is often the only choice such as when querying several repositories and aggregating data dynamically in an AJAX interface such as the with the openacademia application described in Section 6.3. In this case the solution is to query each repository for instances that match the query, perform the duplicate detection on the combined set and present only the purged list to the end-user.

5.4.5 Evaluating smushing

Smushing can be considered as either a retrieval problem or a clustering problem. In terms of retrieval, we try to achieve a maximum precision and recall of the theoretically correct set of mappings. Note that unlike in ontology mapping where there is typically a one-to-one mapping between elements of two ontologies, in the instance unification problem a single resource may be mapped to a number of other resources. Thus we can also conceptualize this task as clustering and evaluate our clusters against the ideal clustering.

---

[31] The reason is that the triple store needs to make sure that all other statements that can be inferred *only* from the statement that is being removed are also removed.

Instance unification or smushing can be considered as an optimization task where we try to optimize an information retrieval or clustering-based measure. Note that instance unification is "easier" than ontology mapping where one-to-one mappings are enforced. In particular, in ontology mapping a local choice to map two instances may limit our future choices and thus we run the risk of ending up in a local minimum. In case of smushing, we only have to be aware that in cases where we have both positive and negative rules (entailing *owl:sameAs* and *owl:differentFrom*) there is a possibility that we end in an inconsistent state (where two resources are the same as well as different). This would point to the inconsistency of our rules, e.g. that we did not consider certain kind of input data.

While there are a number of measures in the literature for measuring the success of retrieval or clustering, it depends ultimately on our application what are the costs of certain types of mistakes (false positives and false negatives) and how that measures up against the costs of reducing them.

5.5 Discussion

As shown in the previous Chapter, ontology languages offer a more flexible, distributed way of representing knowledge, which is particularly appealing in scenarios where knowledge sources under independent control need to be combined. This is the typical case of the Web, but occurs in much smaller scale scenarios all the way to integrating application data on a single computer.

In this Chapter, we have seen how to use ontology-based Knowledge Representation for modelling social individuals and social relationships. We have also noted that unlike more traditional representation mechanisms, ontology languages directly support the task of data integration on both the schema and instance levels by providing the necessary constructs to represent mappings. On the schema level, this task is called ontology mapping, which is a vibrant area of research within the Semantic Web community. Our main concern, however, has been integration on the instance level, which is also called smushing. The OWL ontology language supports this task by rigorous identification, declarative means to describe what it requires for two instances to be the same or different (e.g. using cardinality restrictions or disjointness) and to represent (in)equality using the *owl:sameAs* and *owl:differentFrom* properties.

However, a great deal of the knowledge we wanted to capture could not be expressed in the OWL language. We discuss these limitations in the next Section.

5.5.1 Advanced representations

As we have seen, some of the knowledge we wanted to express could not be captured in OWL DL. Some of the missing features that do not significantly change the complexity of the language such as the conspicuously absent *owl:ReflexiveProperty* are likely to appear in future revisions of OWL.[32] However, OWL will remain limited by

---

[32] At the time of writing there is already a proposal for OWL 1.1, see http://www-db. research.bell-labs.com/user/pfps/owl/overview.html.

the original complexity concerns, most of which do not apply to practical scenarios as explained in Section 5.4.4. More expressive power in representation is expected from the Rule Interchange Format (RIF) currently under development by the W3C. Although its development is primarily driven by requirements from use cases, RIF will most likely include first-order logic (FOL).

Additional expressive power can be brought to bear by using logics that go beyond predicate calculus. For example, *temporal logic* extends assertions with a temporal dimension: using temporal logic we can express that a statement holds true at a certain time or for a time interval. Temporal logic is required to formalize ontology versioning, which is also called change management [Kle04]. With respect to our information integration task, changes may effect either the properties of the instances or the description of the classes, including the rules of equivalence, i.e. what it means for two instances of a class to be equivalent. In most practical cases, however, the conceptualization of classes in the ontology should be more stable than the data and the rules of equivalence should not include dynamic properties. Nevertheless, it is sometimes still desirable to match on such properties. For example, when merging person descriptions we might consider the color of a person's hair. Such a property can change its value over time, which means we have to consider the time when the assertions were true[33].

Extending logic with *probabilities* is also a natural step in representing our problem more accurately. As we have already discussed, the matching of properties often result in probabilistic statements. For example, when we match person names using a string matching algorithm we get a measure of the similarity of the two strings. This can be taken on its own or combined with similarity measures for other properties to form a probability for two persons to be the same.[34] When combining similarities we can use weights to express the relevance of certain properties. Such weights can be determined ad hoc or can be learned from training data using machine learning. The resulting probability could be represented in a probabilistic logic. In our work we apply a threshold to such probabilities in order to return to binary logic where two instances are either the same or not.

---

[33] Or will be true: temporal logic can be used of course to represent statements about the future true

[34] This is different from fuzziness: in fuzzy logic the equivalence of the two instances would be expressed on a scale of [0,1]. In our case, two instances are still either the same or not the same. It is merely that we have some uncertainty of which one is true.

6

Developing social-semantic applications

Most of the current data-driven applications populating the Web have been developed using relational databases as a back-end, for example in the most common LAMP framework, using Linux, Apache, MySQL and PHP. How does a Semantic Web application differ from such a prototypical web application? In short, the difference lies in the kind of data dealt with (ontologies with formal semantics) and the emphasis on the distributed nature of applications.

The characteristics that define a Semantic Web application are most succinctly captured by the definition used for the Semantic Web Challenge, a yearly competition of Semantic Web applications.[1] In order to be considered a Semantic Web application with respect to the Challenge, an application has to meet the following criteria:

1. The meaning of data has to play a central role.
   - Meaning must be represented using formal descriptions.
   - Data must be manipulated/processed in interesting ways to derive useful information and
   - this semantic information processing has to play a central role in achieving goals that alternative technologies cannot do as well, or at all;
2. The information sources used
   - should be under diverse ownership or control
   - should be heterogeneous (syntactically, structurally, and semantically), and
   - should contain substantial quantities of real world data (i.e. not toy examples).
3. It is required that all applications assume an open world, i.e. that the information is never complete.

The novelty of Semantic Web development has to do with the unusual setting of building applications on distributed, heterogeneous information sources. As we have discussed in Chapter 4, exchanging data across domains of ownership and interest necessitates new kind of formats, namely representations that are able to capture to meaning of the data. Consider that in a typical Web application (we can think of

---

[1] See http://challenge.semanticweb.org

the prototypical online book store), the data comes from a single source (typically a relational database), which is solely under the control of the application. In this case, the meaning of the data is known in advance and its consistency is assured. All possible reasoning with the data can be thus hard-coded in the application. By contrast, in building Semantic Web applications one has to deal with distributed data sources of varying quality, formatted according to different, but possibly overlapping schemas and containing possibly overlapping sets of instances.

However, those delving into Semantic Web development are often stopped short even before getting to deal the with substantial issues of data integration and reasoning. Developers new to Semantic Web development need to get familiar with the slate of technologies related to ontology-based knowledge representation such as standard ontology languages (RDF/OWL), representations (RDF/XML) and query languages (SPARQL) as discussed previously. Although developers can still use their preferred operating systems and programming languages, they need to familiarize themselves with a new set of tools for processing semantic data.

In the past, this has meant that engineering Semantic Web applications required a very steep learning curve. This has long hindered the adoption of Semantic Web technology. Many developers left dissatisfied especially when applying these "heavyweight" technologies to trivial problems such our online bookstore, where the price for dealing with semantic data is paid in terms of performance, but the immediate returns are minimal. (The advantages of semantic-based application development often manifest themselves on the long run as applications need to be combined with external data sources or data from the application need to be re-purposed to be used in other applications.) Lastly, there is also the chicken and egg problem of lacking applications due to a lack of data in RDF format and lacking data due to a lack of applications. As in the early days of the Web itself, 'joining' the Semantic Web by adopting its standards had no immediate benefits for application developers.

Some of these problems have been resolved, for example the scalability of ontology databases (the so-called triple stores) has reached the point when switching to RDF as a native data format of an application does not lead to a significant loss in performance. Developers are more motivated to go the semantic way as the number of ontologies available and the number of data sources to connect to increases. However, the key problem of development overhead has not been addressed so far. In order to further lower the threshold for developing Semantic Web applications in general and social network applications in particular, we have developed a set of programming tools. We introduce them in this Chapter by describing their features and exemplifying their use in real-world applications.

Our main contribution is a developer's toolkit named Elmo[2], which enables software engineers to create semantic applications that manipulate RDF/OWL data at the level of domain concepts (persons, publications etc.) instead of working at the lower level of the ontology language (resources, literals and statements). Acting as a middle layer between the RDF ontology store and the application, Elmo hides much of the complexity of application development so that the developer can focus on imple-

---

[2] Elmo has been co-developed by James Leigh and the present author.

menting application logic. In addition, Elmo contains a number of tools for dealing with RDF data, including tools for working with FOAF data and performing instance unification as discussed previously. Elmo also helps the programming to deal with incorrect data by providing a validation framework. We also introduce a simple utility named GraphUtil maps the FOAF representation of network data to the graph model of the JUNG (Java Universal Network Graph) API, allowing the developer to deal with network data in FOAF at the level of network concepts such vertices, edges etc. and to compute network statistics such as various measures of centrality (see Chapter 2).

In the following, we first describe the general design of Semantic Web applications so that we can pinpoint the place of these components. Subsequently, we briefly introduce Sesame, Elmo, the GraphUtil utility. As examples we describe two applications using these core components. These typical Semantic Web applications with social networking aspects highlight the features of our tools and the advantages of semantic technology in building intelligent applications on top of heterogeneous, distributed information sources.

6.1 Building Semantic Web applications with social network features

In the following we first sketch the shared design of most current Semantic Web application. This will help us to pinpoint the focus of Semantic Web application development, and the role of triple stores and ontology APIs.

Next, we introduce Sesame[3], a general database for the storing and querying RDF data. Along with Jena[4], Redland[5] and the commercial offerings of Oracle[6], Sesame is one of the most popular triple stores among developers, appreciated in particular for its performance. Sesame has been developed by Aduna (formerly Aidministrator), but available as open source (currently under LGPL license).

Next, we describe the Elmo API, a general purpose ontology API for Sesame. Elmo allows to manipulate RDF/OWL data at the level of domain concepts, with specific tools for collecting and aggregating RDF data from distributed, heterogeneous information sources. Elmo has been developed in part by the author and is available under the same conditions as Sesame, using the same website.

Lastly, we introduce a simple utility called GraphUtil which facilitates reading FOAF data into the graph object model of the Java Universal Network Graph (JUNG) API. GraphUtil is open source and available as part of Flink (see Section 6.2).

---

[3] http://www.openrdf.org

[4] http://jena.sourceforge.net/

[5] http://librdf.org/

[6] http://www.oracle.com/technology/tech/semantic_technologies/index.html

6.1.1 The generic architecture of Semantic Web applications

As the history of submissions to the Semantic Web challenge attest, Semantic Web applications have been developed in the past years in a wide range of domains from cultural heritage to medicine, from music retrieval to e-science. Yet, almost all share a generic architecture as shown in Figure 6.1. By the definition above, all Semantic Web applications are mashups in that they build on a number of heterogeneous data sources and services under diverse ownership or control.

Before external, heterogeneous data sources can be reused, they need to be normalized syntactically as well as semantically. The first refers to transforming data into an RDF syntax such as RDF/XML, while the latter means that the ontologies (schemas and instances) of the data sources need to be reconciled. Needless to say, the first step can be skipped if the data is exposed as an RDF or OWL document, or can be queried dynamically using the SPARQL query language and protocol.

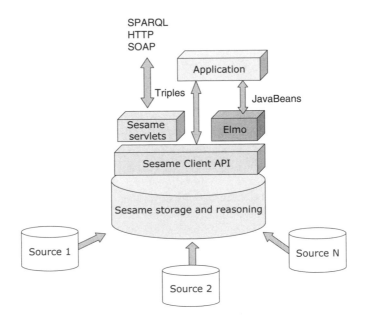

Figure 6.1. The generic design of Semantic Web applications using Sesame and Elmo. Developing with other triple stores results in similar architectures, but in general application code is not portable among triple stores due to proprietary APIs.

Most current Semantic Web applications are based on a fixed, small number of data sources selected by the application developer. In this case, the schemas of the data sources are known in advance and their mapping can be performed manually. In the future, it is expected that Semantic Web applications will be able to discover and select new data sources and map them automatically.[7]

Semantic Web applications persist information in ontology stores (also known as triple stores), databases specifically designed for the storage, manipulation and querying of RDF/OWL data. Ontology stores are almost always equipped with a reasoner or can be connected to an external reasoning service. Reasoning is used to infer new information based on the asserted facts or to check the existing information for consistency. Some triple stores also allow to define custom rules that are evaluated by the reasoner along with the rules prescribed by the ontology language itself. As we have discussed in Chapter 5, the task of instance unification can also be partly solved by OWL DL or rule-based reasoning. Reasoning can take place either when the data is added to a repository (forward-chaining) or at query time (backward-chaining).

Most Semantic Web applications have a web interface for querying and visualization and thus considered by all as web applications. However, this is not a requirement: Semantic Web applications may have a rich client interface (desktop applications) or other forms of access. More importantly, Semantic Web applications are expected to expose data in the same way they expect to consume the data of other applications: using the standard languages and protocols of the Semantic Web, and conforming to the architectural style of the Web in general[8] In order to facilitate this, most triple stores implement the SPARQL query language and protocol (see Section 4.2.1) and some also implement REST[9] style interfaces. A SPARQL service allows other applications to query the triple store, but it provides no data manipulation features such as adding or removing data. Therefore most triple stores also provide custom web interfaces for data manipulation. A Semantic Web application may also expose data or services at higher levels of abstraction than the level of triples, i.e. on the level of domain objects and operations that can be executed on them.

As one would assume, the application logic of Semantic Web applications is placed between the triple store and the eventual web interface(s). The application normally accesses the triple store through its client API. When working with the API of the triple store, the programmer manipulates the data at the level of RDF triples,

---

[7] Regrettably, one of the missing pieces of the Semantic Web infrastructure is an agreed way of publishing ontologies and metadata online. Finding ontologies and RDF/OWL data sets requires one to either search using a traditional search engine or to query a search engine targeted at indexing ontologies, such as Swoogle[DFJ+04]. However, neither of these methods provide adequate meta-information about the ontologies, for example by whom they have been developed, for what purpose and what web applications are using them. Another stumbling block in the way of automatically integrating new data sources is the difficulty of automating schema mapping. Automated ontology (schema) mapping is among the hardest research problems and the methods that exist are certainly not on par with the performance of humans carrying out these tasks. Nevertheless, automated methods for ontology mapping are crucial for this future scenario, where only computers will be able to cope with the amount of schema information to be processed.

[8] By respecting, for example, the guidelines for linking data, see http://www.w3.org/DesignIssues/LinkedData.html.

[9] Representational State Transfer

i.e. the basic operations are adding and removing triples. (Updates are handled by removing the given triple and then adding a new one.) Queries are given as a combination of triple patterns and return a table (a set of variable bindings) as a result. This is similar to accessing a relational database. Its notable, however, that at the current stage of developments applications can only access triple stores through proprietary APIs or the above mentioned SPARQL protocol, which provides limited, read-only access and is only suitable for accessing remote data sources. (With most web applications, the database and the application are co-hosted on the computer. In such a situation communicating over HTTP adds unnecessary overhead.) In other words, what is lacking is an equivalent of the ODBC and JDBC protocols for relational databases. This means that without additional abstraction layers (such as the one provided by Elmo), all application code is specific to a particular triple store.

Further, in most cases it is desirable to access a triple store on an ontological level, i.e. at the level of classes, instances and their properties. This is also the natural level of manipulating data in object-oriented frameworks. The Elmo library to be introduced facilitates this by providing access to the data in the triple store through Java classes that map the ontological data in the triple store. Setting and reading attributes on the instances of these classes result in adding and removing the corresponding triples in the data store.

Elmo is a set of interfaces that have been implemented for the specific case of working with data in Sesame triple stores. Sesame is one of the most popular RDF triple stores and it is to be introduced next. We note that the Elmo interfaces can be implemented for other, Java-based triples stores such as Jena. Interfacing with non-Java triple stores would require an agreement on standard protocols similar to JDBC.

6.1.2 Sesame

Sesame is a triple store implemented using Java technology. Much like a database for RDF data, Sesame allows creating repositories and specifying access privileges, storing RDF data in a repository and querying the data using any of the supported query languages. In the case of Sesame, these include Sesame's own SeRQL language and SPARQL. (While SPARQL has the advantage in terms of standardization, it is also minimal by design; SeRQL is a more expressive query language with many useful features.) The data in the repository can be manipulated on the level of triples: individual statements can be added and removed from the repository. (There is no direct update operation. Updates can be carried out by removing and then adding a statement.) RDF data can be added or extracted in any of the supported RDF representations including the RDF/XML and Turtle languages introduced in Chapter 4. Sesame can persistently store and retrieve the data from a variety of back-ends: data can persist in memory, on the disk or in a relational database.

As most RDF repositories, Sesame is not only a data store but also integrates reasoning. Sesame has a built-in inferencer for applying the RDF(S) inference rules (see Section 4.2.1). While Sesame does not support OWL semantics, it does have a rule language that allows to capture most of the semantics of OWL, including the notion of inverse-functional properties and the semantics of the *owl:sameAs* relationship (see Section 5.4.2). Reasoning can be enabled or disabled for specific repositories. When enabled, reasoning is performed at the time when data is added to the repository or when it is removed[10]

An important, recently added feature of Sesame is the ability to store and retrieve context information. In distributed scenarios, it is often necessary to capture metadata about statements. For example, in the case of collecting FOAF profiles from the Web, we might want to keep track of where the information came from (the URL of the profile) and the time it was last crawled. Context information is important even for centralized sites with user contributed content. In previous versions of Sesame, the only possibility to store context information was to represent it using the reification mechanism of RDF (see Section 4.2.1), which is very inefficient. Starting from Sesame 2.0, the repository natively supports the storage and querying of context information. In effect, every triple becomes a *quad*, with the last attribute identifying the context. Contexts are identified by resources, which can be used in statements as all other resources. Contexts (named graphs) can also be directly queried using the SPARQL query language supported by this version of Sesame.

The above mentioned functionalities of Sesame can be accessed in three ways. First, Sesame provides an HTML interface that can be accessed through a browser. Second, a set of servlets exposes functionality for remote access through HTTP, SOAP and RMI. Lastly, Sesame provides a Java client library for developers which exposes all the above mentioned functionality of a Sesame repository using method calls on a Java object called *SesameRepository*. This object can provide access to both local Sesame servers (running in the same Java Virtual Machine as the application) or and remote servers (running in a different JVM as the application or on a remote machine.

Working with the Sesame client API is relatively straightforward. Queries, for example, can be executed by calling the *evaluateTableQuery* method of this class, passing on the query itself and the identifier of the query language. The result is another object (*QueryResultsTable*) which contains the result set in the form of a table much like the one shown in the web interface (see Figures 6.2 and 6.3). Every row is a result and every column contains the value for a given variable. The values in the table are objects of type *URI*, *BNode* or *Literal*, the object representations of the same notions in RDF. For example, one may call the *getValue*, *getDatatype* and *getLanguage* methods of *Literal* to get the String representation of the literal, its datatype and its language.

Sesame's client library is appropriate for manipulating RDF data at the level of individual triples. Object-oriented applications, however, manipulate data at the level of objects and their attributes; and while objects are characterized by a set of attributes and their values, individual triples capture only a single value for a single property. Updating an attribute of an object may translate to updating several triples. Similarly, removing an object, results in the removal of a number of triples. There

---

[10] When a statement is removed, one also needs to remove in addition all those statements that were inferred from the removed statement (and from that statement only).

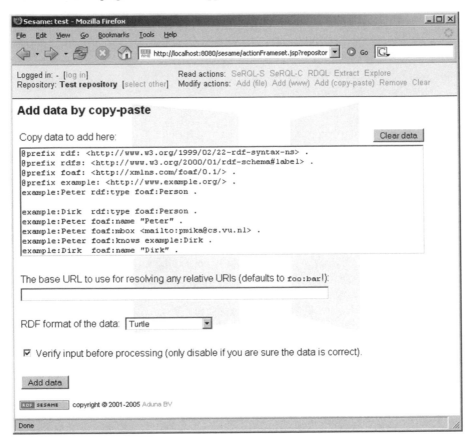

Figure 6.2. Adding data to a Sesame repository using the web interface. Here we add the data used in the examples of Chapter 4.

is thus a need for an API that can translate between operations on objects and the underlying triple representation. This is one of the main concerns of the Elmo API.

6.1.3 Elmo

Elmo is a development toolkit consisting of two main components. The first one is the Elmo API, providing the above mentioned interface between a set of JavaBeans representing ontological classes and the underlying triple store containing the data that is manipulated through the JavaBeans. The API also includes the tool for generating JavaBeans from ontologies and vice versa. The second main component consists of a set of tools for working with RDF data, including an RDF crawler and a framework of smushers (instance unification methods).

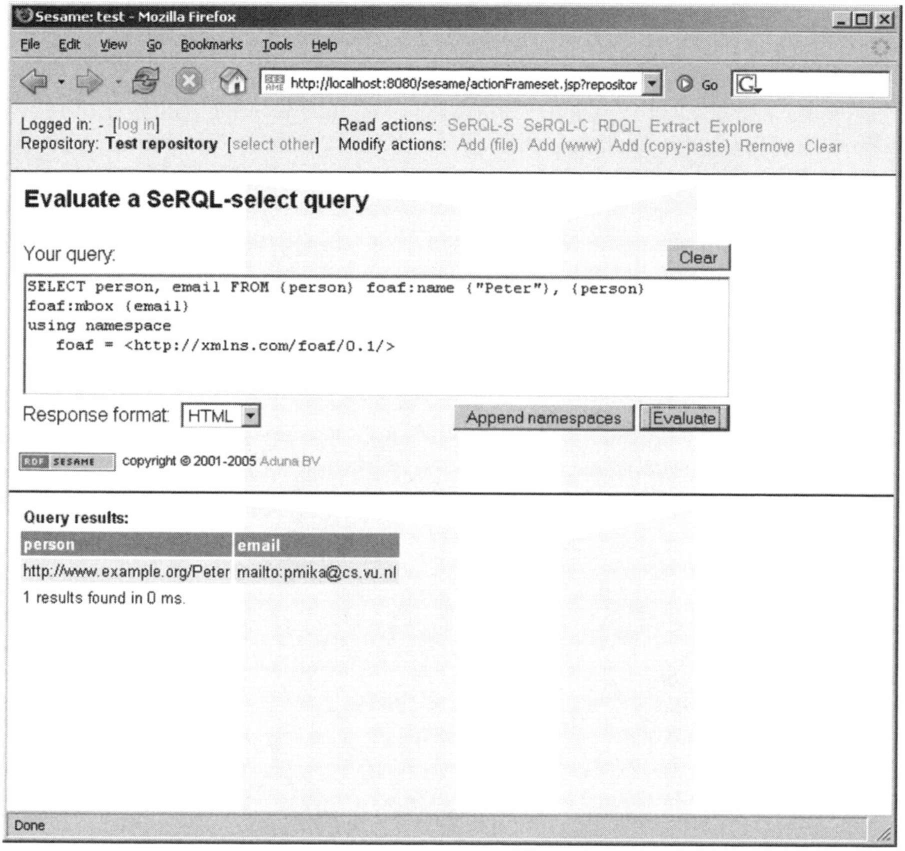

Figure 6.3. Querying data through the web interface of Sesame. The results are displayed below in a table.

The Elmo API

The core of the Elmo API is the *ElmoManager* a JavaBean pool implementation that is responsible for creating, loading, renaming and removing ElmoBeans. ElmoBeans are a composition of *concepts* and *behaviors*. Concepts are Java interfaces that correspond one-to-one to a particular ontological class and provide getter and setter methods corresponding to the properties of the ontological class. (The mapping is maintained using annotations on the interface.) The inheritance hierarchy of the ontological classes is mapped directly to the inheritance hierarchy of concepts. Elmo concepts are typically generated using a code-generator.

Instances of ElmoBeans corresponds to instances of the data set. As resources in an ontology may have multiple types, ElmoBeans themselves need to be composed of multiple concepts. ElmoBeans implement particular combinations of concept interfaces. Note that it is necessary to generate separate classes for every particular combination of types that are occurring in the data set, because its not possible in

Java for an instance to belong to multiple classes. ElmoBeans can be generated run-time as the types of resources may change during the run-time of the application.

ElmoBeans may also implement behaviors. Behaviors are concrete or abstract classes that can be used to give particular implementations of the methods of a con-cept (in case the behavior should differ from the default behavior), but can also be used to add additional functionality. Behaviours can be mixed-in to ElmoBeans the same way that additional types can be added runtime.

The separation of concepts and behaviors, and the ability to compose them at will supports the distributed application development, which is the typical scenario in case of Web applications.

As a separate package, Elmo also provides ElmoBean representations for the most popular Web ontologies, including FOAF, RSS 1.0 and Dublin Core. For exam-ple, in the FOAF model there is *Person* JavaBean with the properties of *foaf:Person*. Getting and setting these properties manipulates the underlying RDF data. This higher level of representation significantly simplifies development. For example, a simple FOAF profile can be created in ten lines of Java code (see Figure 6.4).

```
Repository repository = new SailRepository(new MemoryStore());
repository.initialize();

SesameManagerFactory factory =
    new SesameManagerFactory(repository);
ElmoManager manager = factory.createElmoManager();

QName jackID = new QName("http://www.example.org#","jack");
Person jack = manager.createBean(jackID, Person.class);

jack.getFoafFirstName().add("Jack");

System.out.println(jack.getFoafFirstNames());
```

Figure 6.4. Creating and writing out a FOAF profile in Elmo.

As we see in this example, after creating the repository all the interaction with the contents of the repository is encapsulated by the *ElmoManager* class, which is used to load and instantiate the JavaBean. After setting some of the properties of the *Person* instance, we write it out as an RDF/XML document.

An additional module of the Elmo API, the AugurRepository, can be used to improve the performance of applications through (predictive) caching. Information read from the repository is cached for further queries. (Similarly, writes are also cached until the transaction is committed. The default, however, is automatic com-mit.) Caching also involves predicting the kind of queries the user is likely to ask and pre-loading the information accordingly. Already when a resource is first accessed all the properties of that resource are preloaded. Another strategy requires keeping track of the queries from which resources have been retrieved. If later a property is read on such a resource, the same property is retrieved for all the resources originating from the same query. Optionally, the query re-writing introduced in Section 5.4.4 can also be performed by Elmo: for example, when executing the *getName* method on a Person instance not only the names of current instance is returned, but also all the names of all instances that are *owl:sameAs* the current instance.

Lastly, Elmo helps developers to design applications that are robust against incorrect data, which is a common problem when designing for the Web. In general, Semantic Web applications processing external data typically have few guarantees for the correctness of the input. In particular, many of the RDF documents on the Web —especially documents written by hand—, are either syntactically incorrect, semantically inconsistent or violate some of the assumptions about the usage of the vocabularies involved. Most of these problems result from human error. For example, many users of FOAF mistakenly assume that the value of the *foaf:mbox* property should be a Literal. In reality, the ontology expects a URI that encodes the email address using the mailto protocol, e.g. *mailto:pmika@cs.vu.nl*.

Syntax can be easily checked by syntax validators such as the online RDF validation service of the W3C[11][12] Inconsistency can be checked by OWL DL reasoners. [13] Elmo provides solutions for performing checks that can only be carried out programmatically, for example checking if the value of the *foaf:mbox* property begins with the mailto: prefix (protocol identifier). (The mistake of using a Literal would also be found by an OWL DL reasoner, because the *foaf:mbox* property is declared to be an *owl:ObjectProperty*.)

Using aspect-oriented programming, interceptors can be added to setter methods of JavaBeans in order to validate information that is being inserted to the repository. On the other hand, *validators* can be written for checking existing data for correctness. It is the choice of the programmer whether to stop processing when such check fail, or rather try to recover, for example by removing or correcting erroneous data.

Elmo tools

Elmo also contains a number of tools to work with RDF data. The Elmo *scutter* is a generic RDF crawler that follows *rdfs:seeAlso* links in RDF documents, which typically point to other relevant RDF sources on the web.[14] RDF(S) seeAlso links are also the mechanism used to connect FOAF profiles and thus (given a starting location) the scutter allows to collect FOAF profiles from the Web.

Several advanced features are provided to support this scenario:

---

[11] http://www.w3.org/RDF/Validator/

[12] Another possible strategy to deal with invalid data would be to create "forgiving parsers" that correct common user mistakes on the fly and without requiring the involvement of the user. This is the way web browsers work when tolerating many of the mistakes authors make when creating HTML pages.

[13] Recall that RDF ontologies can not be inconsistent, except for the rare case of datatype inconsistency.

[14] The Elmo scutter is based on original code by Matt Biddulph for Jena.

- Blacklisting: sites that produce FOAF profiles in large quantities are automatically placed on a blacklist. This is to avoid collecting large amounts of uninteresting FOAF data produced by social networking and blogging services or other dynamic sources.
- Whitelisting: the crawler can be limited to a domain (defined by a URL pattern).
- Metadata: the crawler can optionally store metadata about the collected statements. This metadata currently includes provenance (what URL was the information coming from) and timestamp (time of collection)
- Filtering: incoming statements can be filtered individually. This is useful to remove unnecessary information, such as statements from unknown namespaces.
- Persistence: when the scutter is stopped, it saves its state to the disk. This allows to continue scuttering from the point where it left off. Also, when starting the scutter it tries to load back the list of visited URLs from the repository (this requires the saving of metadata to be turned on).
- Preloading from Google: the scutter queue can be preloaded by searching for FOAF files using Google
- Logging: The Scutter uses Simple Logging Facade for Java (SLF4J) to provide a detailed logging of the crawler.

The task of the Elmo *smusher* is to find equivalent instances in large sets of data, which is the problem we discussed in Section 5.4. This is a particularly common problem when processing collections of FOAF profiles as several sources on the Web may describe the same individual using different identifiers or blank nodes.

Elmo provides two kinds of smushers that implement strategies to smushing. The first kind of smusher uses class-specific comparators for comparing instances. Implementations are given for comparing *foaf:Person* objects based on name, email addresses and other identifying properties. There is also a comparator for comparing publications based on a combination of properties.

The second kind of smusher compares instances in a repository based on a certain property, i.e. in this case smushing proceeds property-by-property instead of instance-by-instance. For example, inferring equality based on inverse functional properties can be done with a single query for all such properties:

```
CONSTRUCT {x} owl:sameAs {y} FROM
{prop} rdf:type {owl:InverseFunctionalProperty},
{x} prop {v}, {y} prop {v}
USING NAMESPACE
foaf = <http://xmlns.com/foaf/0.1/>,
example = <http://www.example.org/>,
owl = <http://www.w3.org/2002/07/owl#>
```

When resolving such a CONSTRUCT query first the graph pattern described after the FROM keyword is matched against the repository and for every occurrence the variables are bound to actual values.[15] With these bindings a set of new graphs is constructed by filling the variables in the pattern described in front of the FROM keyword. These graphs are merged and returned in a single RDF document. Notice that the query will also infer *owl:sameAs* relations where $x = y$, although only for instances that do have at least one value specified for at least one inverse functional property. This can be prevented by adding an additional WHERE clause.

The smushers report the results (the matching instances) by calling methods on registered listeners. We provide several implementations of the listener interface, for example to write out the results in HTML, or to represent matches using the *owl:sameAs* relationship and upload such statements to a Sesame repository.

Smushers can also be used as a *wrapper*. The difference between a wrapper and a smusher is that a smusher finds equivalent instances in a single repository, while a wrapper compares instances in a source repository to instances in a target repository. If a match is found, the results are lifted (copied) from the source repository to the target repository. This component is typically useful when importing information into a specific repository about a certain set of instances from a much larger, general store.

6.1.4 GraphUtil

GraphUtil is a simple utility that facilitates reading FOAF data into the graph object model of the Java Universal Network Graph (JUNG) API. GraphUtil can be configured by providing two different queries that define the nodes and edges in the RDF data. These queries thus specify how to read a graph from the data. For FOAF data, the first query is typically one that returns the *foaf:Person* instances in the repository, while the second one returns *foaf:knows* relations between them. However, any other graph structure that can be defined through queries (views on the data) can be read into a graph.

JUNG[16] is a Java library (API) that provides an object-oriented representation of different types of graphs (sparse, dense, directed, undirected, k-partite etc.) JUNG also contains implementations for the most well known graph algorithms such as Dijkstra's shortest path. Various implementations of the *Ranker* interface allow to compute various social network measures such as the different variations of centrality described in Section 2.3.3. We extended this framework with a new type of ranker called *PermanentNodeRanker* which makes it possible to store and retrieve node rankings in an RDF store.

---

[15] From a practical perspective, it is also worth noting that the order of the graph expressions in the query does matter with respect to performance. Queries are evaluated from left to right by most engines and there it is reasonable to put in from the pattern that produces the least matches. In our case the first triple pattern contains only one variable (property) and that can only be bound to a small number of values (the number of inverse functional properties). The other two triple patterns contain three variables and thus match all statements in the repository. Putting them in front would result in a very inefficient query resolution.

[16] http://jung.sourceforge.net

Lastly, JUNG provides a customizable visualization framework for displaying graphs. Most importantly, the framework let's the developer choose the kind of layout algorithm to be used and allows for defining interaction with the graph visualization (clicking nodes and edges, drag-and-drop etc.) The visualization component can be used also in applets as is the case in Flink and openacademia.

6.2 Flink: the social networks of the Semantic Web community

Flink has been the first system that exploits semantic technologies for the purposes of network analysis based on heterogeneous knowledge sources and has been the winner of the Semantic Web Challenge of 2004. Flink, developed by the present author, is a general system that can be instantiated for any community for which substantial electronic data is available.

The current, public instantiation of Flink[17] is a presentation of the professional work and social connectivity of Semantic Web researchers.[18] For the purposes of this website we have defined this community as those researchers who have submitted publications or held an organizing role at any of the past International Semantic Web Conferences (ISWC) or the Semantic Web Working Symposium of 2001. At the moment this is a community of 744 researchers from both academia and industry, covering much of the United States, Europe and to a lesser degree Japan and Australia (see Figure 1.4).

The information sources are largely the natural byproducts of the daily work of a community: HTML pages on the Web about people and events, emails and publications. From these sources Flink extracts knowledge about the social networks of the community and consolidates what is learned using a common semantic representation, namely the FOAF ontology.

The *raison d'être* of Flink can be summarized in three points. First, Flink is a demonstration of the latest Semantic Web technology. In this respect, Flink is interesting to all those who are planning to develop systems using Semantic Web technology for similar or different purposes. Second, Flink is intended as a portal for anyone who is interested to learn about the work of the Semantic Web community, as represented by the profiles, emails, publications and statistics. Hopefully Flink will also contribute to bootstrapping the nascent FOAF-web by allowing the export of the knowledge in FOAF format. This can be taken by the researchers as a starting point in setting up their own profiles, thereby contributing to the portal as well. Lastly, but perhaps most importantly, the data collected by Flink is used for the purposes of social network analysis, in particular learning about the nature of power and innovativeness in scientific communities (see Chapter 8).

---

[17] http://flink.semanticweb.org
[18] We plan to introduce a version of Flink open to external researchers who would like to experiment with data about different communities.

6.2.1 The features of Flink

Flink takes a network perspective on the Semantic Web community, which means that the navigation of the website is organized around the social network of researchers. Once the user has selected a starting point for the navigation, the system returns a summary page of the selected researcher, which includes profile information as well as links to other researchers that the given person might know. The immediate neighborhood of the social network (the ego-network of the researcher) is also visualized in a graphical form (see Figure 6.5).

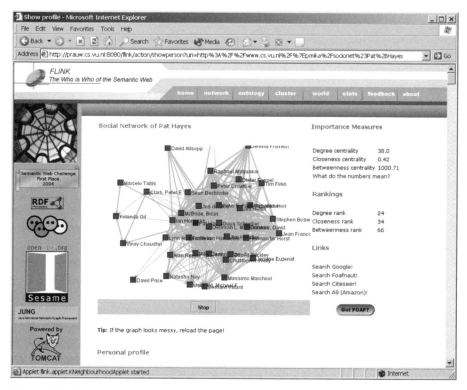

Figure 6.5. The profile of a researcher in Flink. Individual statistics (rankings) are shown on the right.

The profile information and the social network is based on the analysis of webpages, emails, publications and self-created profiles. (See the following Section for the technical details.) The displayed information includes the name, email, homepage, image, affiliation and geographic location of the researcher, as well as his interests, participation at Semantic Web related conferences, emails sent to public mailing lists and publications written on the topic of the Semantic Web. The full text of emails and publications can be accessed by following external links. At the time of writing, the system contained information about 7269 publications authored by members of the community and 10178 messages sent via Semantic Web-related mailing lists.

The navigation from a profile can also proceed by clicking on the names of co-authors, addressees or others listed as known by this researcher. In this case, a separate page shows a summary of the relationship between the two researchers, in particular the evidence that the system has collected about the existence of this relationship. This includes the weight of the link, the physical distance, friends, interests and depictions in common as well as emails sent between the researchers and publications written together. The information about the interests of researchers is also used to generate a lightweight ontology of the Semantic Web community. The concepts of this ontology are research topics, while the associations between the topics are based on the number of researchers who have an interest in the given pair of topics (see Figure 6.6).

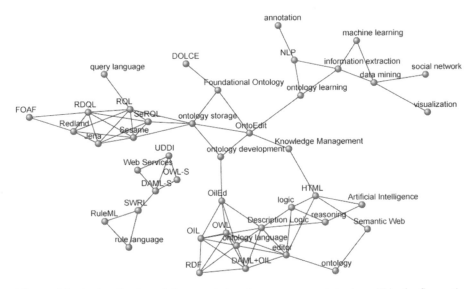

Figure 6.6. A visualization of the associations between research topics within the Semantic Web community.

An interesting feature of this ontology is that the associations created are specific to the community of researchers whose names are used in the experiment. This means that unlike similar lightweight ontologies created from a statistical analysis of generic web content, this ontology reflects the specific conceptualizations of the community that was used in the extraction process (see the following Section). Also, the ontology naturally evolves as the relationships between research topics changes (e.g. as certain fields of research move closer to each other). For a further discussion on the relation between sociability and semantics, we refer the reader to Chapter 9.

The visitor of the website can also view some basic statistics of the social network. Degree, closeness and betweenness are common measures of importance or influence in Social Network Analysis, while the degree distribution attests to a general characteristic of the network itself (see Figure 6.7).

Indegree centrality		Closeness Centrality		Betweenness Centrality	
1 Steffen Staab	130.0	1 Steffen Staab	0.4995	1 Steffen Staab	16864.4403
2 Dieter Fensel	125.0	2 Dieter Fensel	0.4967	2 Ian Horrocks	14098.6831
3 Ian Horrocks	120.0	3 Ian Horrocks	0.4953	3 Dieter Fensel	13544.063
4 Frank van Harmelen	118.0	4 Frank van Harmelen	0.4948	4 Frank van Harmelen	12537.5246
5 Stefan Decker	102.0	5 Stefan Decker	0.4844	5 Stefan Decker	10238.5444
6 Rudi Studer	95.0	6 Rudi Studer	0.4668	6 Tim Finin	6547.5342
7 Guus Schreiber	82.0	7 Guus Schreiber	0.4563	7 Chen Li	6506.0598
8 Raphael Volz	74.0	8 Peter F. Patel-Schneider	0.4508	8 Guus Schreiber	5372.3001
9 York Sure	67.0	9 Enrico Motta	0.4489	9 Katia Sycara	4826.9771
10 Enrico Motta	62.0	10 Jim Hendler	0.4447	10 Rudi Studer	4178.6547
11 Tim Finin	57.0	11 Jeremy Frumkin	0.4414	11 Carole Goble	3882.1959
12 Peter F. Patel-Schneider	55.0	12 Raphael Malyankar	0.4406	12 Roger King	3686.1388
13 Katia Sycara	52.0	13 Masahiro Hori	0.4337	13 Dimitris Plexousakis	3337.4544
14 Jim Hendler	51.0	14 Raphael Volz	0.4327	14 Enrico Motta	3107.1791
15 Sean Bechhofer	49.0	15 York Sure	0.4327	15 Luke McDowell	2950.3047
16 Daniel Brickley	46.0	16 Aseem Das	0.4323	16 Jeremy Frumkin	2792.4088
17 Ora Lassila	46.0	17 Ora Lassila	0.4299	17 Daniel Brickley	2780.8619
18 Jeen Broekstra	45.0	18 Trastour, David	0.4278	18 Sean Bechhofer	2714.4584
19 Jeremy Carroll	44.0	19 Roger King	0.4278	19 Jim Hendler	2625.8347
20 Heiner Stuckenschmidt	43.0	20 Carole Goble	0.4257	20 Yang Li	2608.5416

Figure 6.7. A visualization of the degree distribution of the network. The inset shows the rankings of researchers according to various network measures.

Geographic visualizations of the Semantic Web offer another overview of the network by showing the places where researchers are located and the connections between them (see Figure 1.4).

6.2.2 System design

Similarly to the design of most data-driven applications, the architecture of Flink can be divided in three layers concerned with metadata acquisition, storage and presentation, respectively. Figure 6.8 shows an overview of the system architecture with the three layers arranged from top to bottom. In the following, we describe the layers in the same order.

Information collection

This layer of the system concerns the acquisition of metadata. Flink uses four different types of knowledge sources: HTML pages from the web, FOAF profiles from the Semantic Web, public collections of emails and bibliographic data. Information

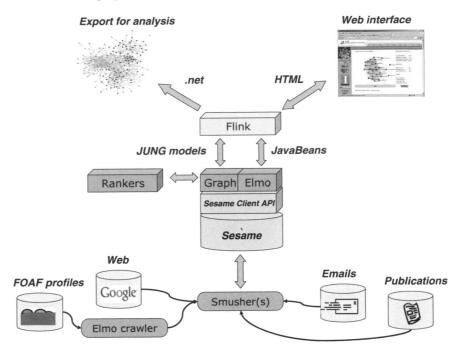

Figure 6.8. The architecture of Flink.

from the different sources is collected in different ways but all the knowledge that is learned is represented according to the same ontology (see the following Section). This ontology includes FOAF and minimal extensions required to represent additional information.

The web mining component of Flink employs a co-occurrence analysis technique described in Chapter 3. The web mining component also performs the additional task of finding topic interests, i.e. associating researchers with certain areas of research. The network ties, the interest associations and other metadata are represented in RDF using terms from the FOAF vocabulary such as *foaf:knows* for relationships and *foaf:topic_interest* for research interests. A reification-based extension of the FOAF model is necessary to represent association weights. (See Section 5.3.)

FOAF is the native format of profiles that we collect from the Web. FOAF profiles are gathered using the Elmo scutter, starting from the profile of the author. Our scutter is focused in that it only collects profiles related to one of the community members and it is also limited to potentially relevant statements, i.e. those triples where the predicate is in the RDF, RDF-S, FOAF or WGS-84 namespace. These restrictions are necessary to limit the amount of data collected, which can easily reach millions of triples after running the scutter for only an hour. The context features of Elmo are used to record the provenance of the statements collected. Provenance in our system consists of the source of a statement and the time it was collected.[19]

Information from emails is processed in two steps. The first step requires that the emails are downloaded from a POP3 or IMAP store and the relevant header information is captured in an RDF format, where FOAF is used for representing information about senders and receivers of emails, in particular their name (as appears in the header) and email address. (There is no common ontology for representing emails, so the rest of the header information is represented using a custom ontology.) The second step is smushing: matching the Person instances found in the email collection with the instances describing our target community.

Lastly, bibliographic information is collected in a single step by querying Google Scholar with the names of individuals (plus the disambiguation term). From the results we learn the title and URL of publications as well as the year of publication and the number of citations where available.

Publication metadata is represented using the "Semantic Web Research Community" (SWRC) ontology[20] The SWRC ontology maps the types and fields of the BibTeX bibliographic description format in the most straightforward manner to RDF classes and properties. For example, the BibTeX item type InBook has the equivalent class of *swrc:InBook* in the ontology, with common properties such as *swrc:year* for the year of publication.

An alternative source of bibliographic information (used in previous versions of the system) is the Bibster peer-to-peer network [HSB+05], from which metadata can be exported directly in the SWRC ontology format.

Storage and aggregation

This is the middle layer of our system with the primary role of storing and aggregating metadata. Aggregation requires mapping the ontologies used and performing the instance reasoning described in Section 5.4.

In our case ontology mapping is a straightforward task: the schemas used are small, stable, lightweight web ontologies (SWRC and FOAF). Their mapping cause little problem: such mappings are static and can be manually inserted into the knowledge base. An example of such a mapping is the subclass relationship between the *swrc:Person* and *foaf:Person* classes or the subproperty relationship between *swrc:name* and *foaf:name*. Note that at the moment we throw away all the data we find through crawling that is not in one of the two ontologies. Incorporating knowledge in unknown schemas would require automated ontology mapping.

The aggregated collection of RDF data is stored in a Sesame server. Note that since the model is a compatible extension of FOAF, from this point the knowledge can be further processed by any FOAF-compatible tool, e.g the FOAF explorer[21]. Another example is the generic component we implemented for finding

---

[19] This information is not used, only displayed at the moment. In the future it would allow to introduce features such as the ranking of information based on recency or trustworthiness.

[20] See http://ontoware.org/projects/swrc/ .

[21] http://xml.mfd-consult.dk/foaf/explorer/

the geographical locations (latitude, longitude coordinates) of place names found in the FOAF profiles. This component invokes the ESRI Place Finder Sample Web Service[22], which provides geographic locations of over three-million place names worldwide.[23]

From a scalability perspective, we are glad to note that the Sesame server offers very high performance in storing data on the scale of millions of triples, especially using native repositories or in memory storage. Speed of upload is particularly important for the RDF crawler, which itself has a very high throughput. Unfortunately, the speed of upload drops significantly when custom rules need to be evaluated.

While the speed of uploads is important to keep up with other components that are producing data, the time required for resolving queries determines the responsiveness of the user interface. At the moment query optimization is still a significant challenge for the server. Our experience is that in many cases, the developer himself can improve the performance of a query by rewriting it manually, e.g. by reordering the terms. The trade-off between executing many small queries versus executing a single large query also requires the careful judgement of the developer. The trade-off is in terms of memory footprint vs. communication overhead: small, targeted queries are inefficient due to the communication and parsing involved, while large queries produce large result sets that need to be further processed on the client side.

Besides aggregation, we also use reasoning to enrich the data. For example, we infer *foaf:knows* relations between the senders and recipients of emails and the co-authors of publications.

Lastly, at this stage we pre-compute and store the kind of network statistics displayed in the interface. Computing these statistics takes time and therefore it cannot be done on the fly. Instead, we store the statistics in an RDF repository and read it when required. In practice, statistics are stored separately from the data because they are kept longer than the data itself: the interface also displays changes in statistics, i.e. the difference between the last two values measured for a given node using a given measure.

User interface

The user interface of Flink is a pure Java web application based on the Model-View-Controller (MVC) paradigm. The key idea behind the MVC pattern is a separation of concerns among the components responsible for the data (the model), the application logic (controller) and the web interface (view). The Apache Struts Framework used by Flink helps programmers in writing web applications that respect the MVC pattern by providing abstract application components and logic for the pattern. The role of the programmer is to extend this skeletal application with domain and task specific objects.

---

[22] http://www.esri.com/software/arcwebservices/

[23] Web Service invocation is facilitated by the Apache Web Service Invocation Framework, which uses the WSDL profile of a web service to generate the code required to interact with the service.

The model objects of Flink are Elmo beans representing persons, publications, emails etc. When requests reach the controller, all the beans that are necessary to generate the page are retrieved from the store and passed on to the view layer. The GraphUtil utility is used again to read the social network from the repository, which is also handed over to the visualization. (Much like the Elmo beans the network is also kept in memory to improve performance.)

In the view layer, servlets, JavaServer Pages (JSP) and the Java Standard Tag Library (JSTL) are used to generate a front-end that hides much of the code from the designer of the front-end. This means that the design of the web interface may be easily changed without affecting the application and vice versa.

In the current interface, Java applets are also used on parts of the site for interactive visualization of social networks. These applets communicate with a servlet that retrieves the part of the network to be visualized from the repository and sends back a serialized form to the applet, which then computes the layout. The user can pan and zoom the image as required.

We consider the flexibility of the interface to be important because there are many possibilities to present social networks to the user and the best way of presentation may depend on the size of the community as well as other factors. The possibilities range from "text only" profiles (such as in Orkut[24]) to fully graphical browsing based on network visualization (as in the FOAFnaut[25] browser). The uniqueness of presenting social networks is also the primary reason that we cannot benefit from using Semantic Web portal generators such as HayStack [QK04], which are primarily targeted for browsing more traditional object collections.

The user interface also provides mechanisms for exporting the data. For more advanced analysis and visualization options, the data can be downloaded in the format used by Pajek, a popular network analysis package [BM98]. Users can also download profiles for individuals in RDF/XML format. Lastly, we provide marker files for XPlanet, an application that visualizes geographic coordinates and geodesics by mapping them onto surface images of the Earth (see Figure 1.4).

6.3 openacademia: distributed, semantic-based publication management

Information about scientific publications is often maintained by individual researchers. Reference management software such as EndNote and BibTeX help researchers to maintain a personal collection of bibliographic references. (These are typically references to one's own publications and also those that have been read and cited by the researcher in his own work.) Most researchers and research groups also have to maintain a web page about publications for interested peers from other institutes. Typically, personal reference management and the maintenance of web pages is a separate effort: the author of a new publication adds the reference to his own

---

[24] http://www.orkut.com
[25] http://www.foafnaut.org/

collection, updates his web page and possible that of his research group. From then on it is waiting for other researchers to discover the newly added publication.

The openacademia system removes the unnecessary duplication of effort involved in maintaining personal references and webpages. It also solves the problem of creating joined publication lists for webpages at the group or institutional level. At the same time it gives a new way of instantly notifying interested peers of new works instead of waiting for them to visit the web page of the researcher or the institute.

openacademia is a distributed system on its own. A public openacademia website is available on the Web for general use, i.e. anyone can submit his own publications to this service.[26] openacademia can also be installed at research groups locally in order to collect and manage the shared publication metadata of the group.

6.3.1 The features of openacademia

The most immediate service of openacademia is the possibility to generate an HTML representation of one's personal collection of publications and publish it on the Web. This requires filling out a single form on the openacademia website, which generates the code (one line of JavaScript!) that needs to be inserted into the body of the home-page. The code inserts the publication list in the page dynamically and thus there is no need to update the page separately if the underlying collection changes (see Figure 6.9). The appearance of the publication list can be customized by choosing from a variety of stylesheets.

More interestingly, one can also generate an RSS feed from the collection. Adding such an RSS feed to a homepage allows visitors to subscribe to the publication list using any RSS news reader. Whenever a new publication is added, the subscribers of the feed will be notified of this change through their reader (*information push*).

A number of generic tools are available for reading and aggregating RSS information, including browser extensions, online aggregators, news clients and desktop readers for a variety of platforms. Mozilla Firefox also natively supports RSS feeds as the basis for creating dynamic bookmark folders (see Figure 6.10). These folders refresh their contents from an RSS feed whenever the user opens them.

The RSS feeds of openacademia are RDF-based and can also be consumed by any RDF aware software such as Piggy Bank browser extension.[27] Piggy Bank allows users to collect RDF statements linked to Web pages while browsing through the Web and to save them for later use.

Research groups can install their own openacademia server. Members of the research group can submit their publications by creating a FOAF profile pointing to the location of their publication collection. What the system provides is the possibility to create a unified group publication list and post it to a website similarly to personal lists. (Needless to say, groups can have RSS feeds as well.)

---

[26] http://www.openacademia.org
[27] simile.mit.edu/piggy-bank/

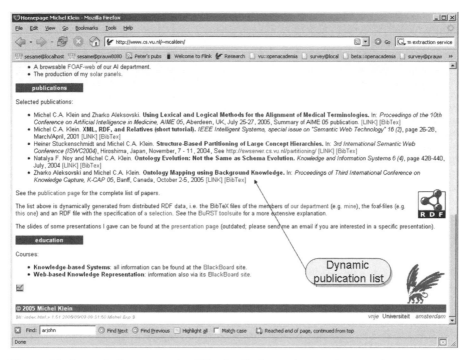

Figure 6.9. Dynamically generated publication list inserted to a web page using remote syndication.

There is also an AJAX based interface for browsing and searching the publication collection (see Figure 6.11). This interface offers a number of visualizations. For example, the important keywords in the titles of publication matching the current query can be viewed as a *tagcloud*[28], where the size of the tags shows the importance of the keyword. It is also possible to browse the co-authorship networks of researchers using the same interactive applet used by Flink. Another interactive visualization shows publication along a timeline that can be scrolled using the mouse (see Figure 6.12).[29]

Keywords or tags can be added to publications using the features of BibTeX or EndNote. The system also extracts keywords automatically from titles of publications. Lastly, openacademia connects to blog search engines in order to import blog comments about publications.

6.3.2 System design

The architecture of openacademia follows the same design as Flink: in the middle of the architecture is an RDF repository that is filled with a variety of information sources and queried by a number of services (see Figure 6.13).

---

[28] http://en.wikipedia.org/wiki/Tag_cloud
[29] This time-based visualization uses the Timeline widget developed by the SIMILE project.
See http://simile.mit.edu/timeline/

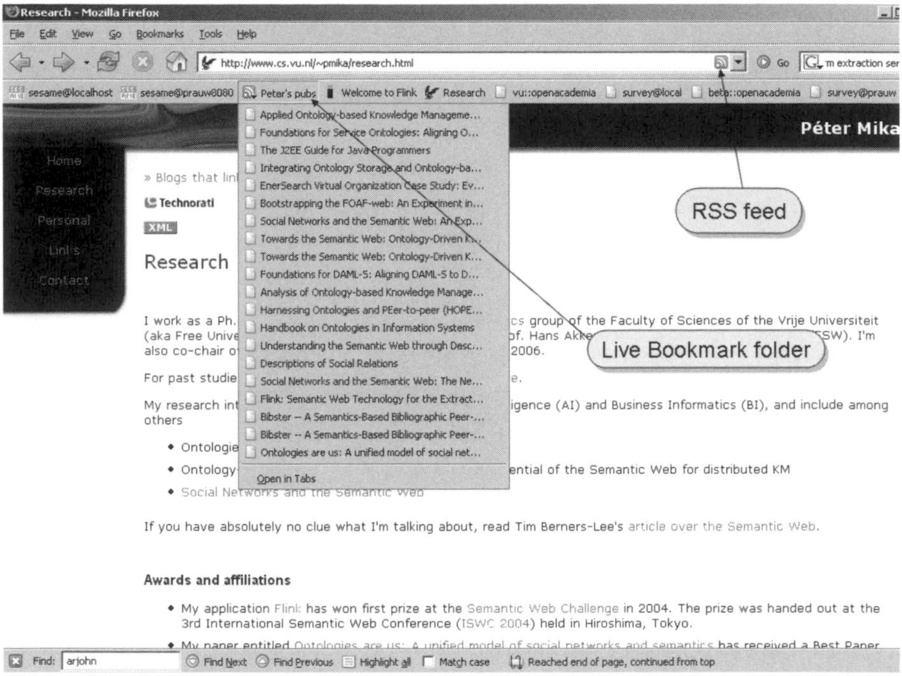

Figure 6.10. Modern browsers such as Mozilla Firefox have built in RSS feeders that allow to subscribe to RSS feeds attached to webpages. Using the Live Bookmark feature of Firefox it is also possible to save a publication list as a bookmark folder that automatically refreshes itself.

The difference lies in the dynamics of the two systems. Flink is filled with data every two or three months in a semi-automated fashion. openacademia repositories refresh their content every day automatically.[30] In case a publication feed is generated from a single BibTeX or EndNote file the entire process of filling and querying the repository is carried out on the fly. In this case we use an in-memory repository that is discarded after the answer has been served.

Information collection

For obtaining metadata about publications, we rely on the BibTeX and EndNote formats commonly in use in academia worldwide. We ask authors to include a BibTeX file with their own publications on a publicly accessible part of their website. For most authors in the sciences this does not require additional work, as they typically maintain their own web space and have such a file at hand. Further, researchers fill

---

[30] The frequency of updates can be configured. The advantage of a daily update is that a change in any of the sources propagates to the triple store within 24 hours. The disadvantage is that updates take computing resources and time during which the repository is unavailable.

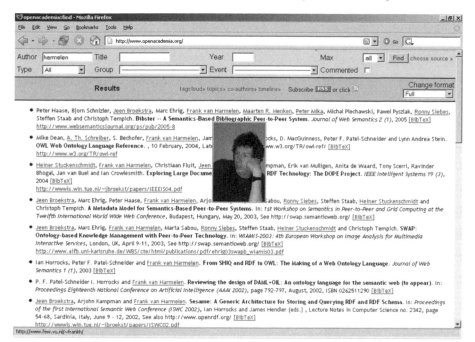

Figure 6.11. The AJAX-based query interface of openacademia builds queries and displays the results. If the underlying data source includes FOAF data even the researchers' photos are shown (with links to their homepage).

out a form to create a basic FOAF profile, which contains at least their name and the location of their references. Needless to say, this step can be skipped in case the researcher already has a FOAF profile.

We use the Elmo crawler to collect such profiles. As mentioned before, the crawler can be restricted to a domain, which is useful for limiting the data collection to the domain of an institute. The BibTeX files are translated to RDF using the BibTeX-2-RDF service,[31] which creates instance data for the "Semantic Web Research Community" (SWRC) ontology. A simple extension of the SWRC ontology was necessary to preserve the sequence of authors of publications. To this end we defined the *swrc-ext:authorList* and *swrc-ext:editorList* properties, which have *rdf:Seq* as range, comprising an ordered list of authors.

At the Vrije Universiteit, Amsterdam we have also implemented a service that dynamically queries the local LDAP database and represents the contents as FOAF profiles. Most importantly, the LDAP database contains information about group membership, but it also contains real names and email addresses. We do not reveal the email addresses of employees, but use a hash of the email address as identifier. By relying on the LDAP database for this information we delegate the task of

---

[31] See http://www.cs.vu.nl/~mcaklein/bib2rdf/.

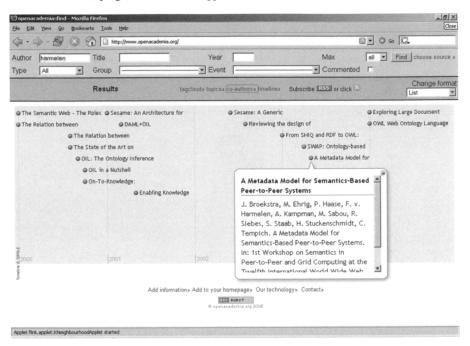

Figure 6.12. Interactive time based visualization using the Timeline widget.

maintaining user data to the existing infrastructure in the department i.e. the user account administration.

Storage and aggregation

As our system is designed to reuse information in a distributed, web-based environment, we have to deal with the arising semantic heterogeneity of our information sources. Heterogeneity effects both the schema and instance levels.

Similarly to Flink, the schemas used are stable, lightweight web ontologies (SWRC and FOAF) and their mapping causes no problems. Heterogeneity on the instance level arises from using different identifiers in the sources for denoting the same real world objects. This certainly effects FOAF data collected from the Web (where typically each personal profile also contains partial descriptions of the friends of the individual), but also publication information, as the same author or publication may be referenced in a number of BibTeX sources.

We use the Elmo smusher framework to match *foaf:Person* instances based on name and inverse-functional properties. Publications are matched on a combination of properties. In the current system, we look for an exact match of the date of the publication and a tight fuzzy match of the title. Matching publications based on authors is among the future work.

The instance matches that we find are recorded in the RDF store using the *owl:sameAs* property. Since Sesame does not natively support OWL semantics at the

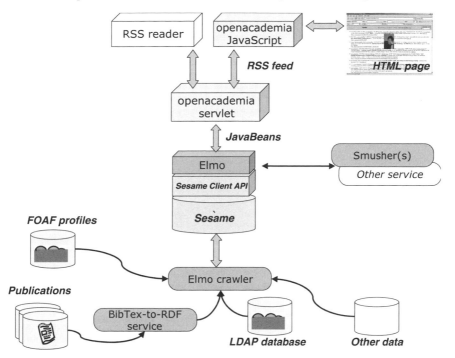

Figure 6.13. The architecture of openacademia.

moment, in earlier versions of the system we expanded the semantics of this single property using Sesame's custom rule language. These rules expressed the reflexive, symmetric and transitive nature of the property as well as the intended meaning, namely the equality of property values. The disadvantage was that these rules added a large number of statements by assigning all the equivalent resources the same the set of properties. On the upside these rules are executed by the custom inferencer during uploads, which means that queries are fast to execute. In the current solution we apply the approach outlined in Section 5.4.4, i.e. a combination of forward chaining and backward chaining.

As in the case of Flink, semantic technology allows us to infer additional knowledge from the data. For example, we can add a rule to our knowledge base which states that the co-authors of publications are persons who know each other. The generated information can be used to enrich the personal profiles of individuals, but also to further disambiguate individuals based on their friends.

Presentation

After all information has been merged, the triple store can be queried to produce publications lists according to a variety of criteria, including personal, group or publication facets. The online interfaces helps users to build such queries against the publication repository. The queries are processed by another web-based component, the publication web service.

In order to appreciate the power of a semantics-based approach, it is illustrative to look at an example query. The query in Figure 6.14, formulated in the SeRQL language, returns all publications authored by the members of the Artificial Intelligence department in 2005. This department is uniquely identified by its homepage. (The *foaf:homepage* property is inverse functional according to the FOAF vocabulary, i.e. a certain URL uniquely identifies a given group.)

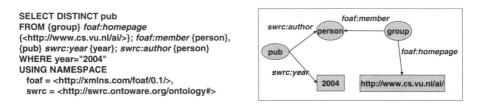

Figure 6.14. Sample SeRQL query and its graphical representation.

Note first that the successful resolution of this query relies on the schema and instance matching described in the previous section. The query answering requires publication data as well as information on department membership and personal data from either the LDAP database or the self-maintained profile of the researcher. This points to a clear advantage of the Semantic Web approach: a separation of concerns. Researchers can change their personal profiles and update their publication lists without the need to consult or notify anyone. Similarly, the maintainer of the departmental LDAP database can add and remove individuals as before. All this information will be connected and merged automatically.

The publications that match this query necessarily come from different sources, i.e. from the collections of personal publications of individual researchers. Publications that have been co-authored by members of the department will appear in a number of BibTeX sources, possibly with different spellings of the author names and providing a different set of metadata (e.g. one source may describe only the authors and the title, while another may mention the title and year, but not the authors). Identifying matching publications is the task of the publication smusher introduced before, which is thus also essential to correctly answering this query.[32]

The publish service takes a query like the one shown above, the location of the repository, the properties of the resulting RSS channel and optional style instructions as parameters. In a single step, it queries the repository, performs the post-processing and generates an RSS channel with the publications matching the query.

---

[32] The query still requires some post processing as we might encounter duplicate publications that have different URIs; SeRQL is an RDF query language with no support for OWL equivalence. The *DISTINCT* keyword guarantees only that the URIs returned are unique.

The resulting channel appears as an RSS 1.0 channel for compatible tools while preserving RDF metadata. The method of mixing publication metadata into an RSS channel is described in the BuRST specification[33]. The BuRST format —illustrated in Figure 6.15— is based on an explicit rule of RSS processing, namely that RSS parsers (many of them working on the XML tree of data) should ignore all information that they do not understand. This means that if the general structure of the RSS document is preserved (i.e. all mandatory elements are present and written in the correct order) existing parsers will turn a blind eye to the additional metadata attached to RSS items. In our case, we attach publication metadata to RSS items using the *burst:publication* property. This is the only property defined by the BuRST specification.

```
<rdf:RDF
  xmlns:rdf="http://www.w3.org/1999/02/22-rdf-syntax-ns#"
  xmlns:rdfs="http://www.w3.org/2000/01/rdf-schema#"
  xmlns:swrc="http://swrc.ontoware.org/ontology/ontoware#"
  xmlns:foaf="http://xmlns.com/foaf/0.1/"
  xmlns:dc="http://purl.org/dc/elements/1.1/"
  xmlns:burst="http://xmlns.com/burst/0.1/">

<rss:channel rdf:about="http://www.cs.vu.nl/~pmika/burst.rdf">
  <rss:title>Peter Mika's publications</rss:title>
  <rss:link>http://www.cs.vu.nl/~pmika/research/pub.rdf</rss:link>
  <rss:description>
   Semantic Web related publications authored by Peter Mika.
  </rss:description>
  <rss:items>
    <rdf:Seq>
      <rdf:li rdf:resource="http://www.cs.vu.nl/~pmika/burst#1" />
      <rdf:li rdf:resource="http://www.cs.vu.nl/~pmika/burst#2" />
    </rdf:Seq>
  </rss:items>
  <rdfs:seeAlso rdf:resource="http://www.cs.vu.nl/~mcaklein/pub.rdf" />
</rss:channel>

<rss:item rdf:about="http://www.cs.vu.nl/~pmika/burst#1">
  <rss:title>Bootstrapping the FOAF-Web: An Experiment
         in Social Network Mining
  </rss:title>
  <rss:link>http://www.w3.org/2001/sw/Europe/events/foaf-galway/papers/fp/bootstrapping_the_foaf_web/</rss:link>
  <rss:description>
   Bootstrapping is a problem that affects all applications of the
   Semantic Web, including the network of interlinked Friend-of-a-Friend (FOAF)
   profiles known as the FOAF-web. In this paper we introduce a hybrid system ...
  </rss:description>
  <dc:subject>Semantic Web</dc:subject>
  <burst:publication>
    <swrc:InProceedings>
      <swrc:title>Bootstrapping the FOAF-Web: An Experiment in Social Network Mining</swrc:title>
      <swrc:author>
        <foaf:Person rdf:ID="PeterMika">
          <foaf:name>Peter Mika</foaf:name>
          <foaf:mbox_sha1sum>ffe33bbe8be2a2123f0adb793e61a6d84ae9a739</foaf:mbox_sha1sum>
          <rdfs:seeAlso rdf:resource="http://www.cs.vu.nl/~pmika/foaf.rdf" />
        </foaf:Person>
      </swrc:author>
      <swrc:year>2004</swrc:year>
    </swrc:InProceedings>
  </burst:publication>
</rss:item>
...
```

Figure 6.15. Example of a BuRST channel.

[33] http://www.cs.vu.nl/~pmika/research/burst/BuRST.html

The presentation service can also add XSL stylesheet information to the RSS feed, which allows to generate different HTML layouts (tables, short citation lists or longer descriptions with metadata). The HTML output can be viewed with any XSLT capable browser and it can be tailored even further by adding a custom CSS stylesheet (for changing colors, font styles etc.)

Stylesheets are also used to generate the XML input of the Timeline widget. One can even reproduce a BibTeX or EndNote representation of the publication feed by applying the appropriate stylesheets.

6.4 Discussion

It is just a few years ago that the development of a Semantic Web application still required the kind of effort represented by European projects such as On-To-Knowledge, which combined the best minds in academia with the development prowess of industry [DFvH03]. Only a few select developers (the *übergeeks* of the community) possessed the kind of technical skills to do the same independently.

However, the effort required to develop applications for the Semantic Web has significantly dropped in the past years. The W3C opened the way to stable software development by finishing the standardization of the RDF and OWL ontology languages (2004) and the SPARQL query language and protocol (2006), which together provide for the interoperability of semantic applications and services. Open source tools such as the Sesame storage facility have also significantly matured both in terms of robustness and scalability.

Programming tools such as the Elmo API contribute to this development by reducing the learning and adaptation required from the average Java developer. Elmo shields the developer from the low level details of representation by offering static object models for working with common web ontologies such as FOAF, RSS and Dublin Core. It integrates with Sesame to provide additional services such as caching.

Elmo also provides the common components required by most Semantic Web applications. As we have seen on the example of Flink and openacademia one of these common tasks is the crawling (scuttering) of RDF data from the data sources. In both cases, these data included RDF documents from the Web as well as structured data from the sources that were not originally intended for these applications (email archives, publication databases). The dynamic collection of data from a variety of sources is a typical characteristic of Semantic Web applications as this is the scenario where semantic technology brings the greatest benefits. Crawling data from interconnected data sources is the task of the Elmo scutter used both by Flink and openacademia.

Another common task in working with heterogeneous data sources is the aggregation of instance data, which can be automated by using the extensible smusher framework of Elmo. As we have discussed in the Chapter on data aggregation, instance reasoning often requires procedural components as the kind of knowledge required cannot be fully represented in ontology languages (and thus this task cannot be solved by reasoners alone).

Flink and openacademia are examples of Semantic Web applications that address very different problems: data collection for network analysis and publication metadata management. Nevertheless, they re-use many of their components by building on Elmo, which allows the developer to focus on the specific task of these applications (the so called *business logic*) and reduce the complexity of the code to a minimum.

As a demonstration of how to apply this technology for e-science, and in particular network analysis, we will use the Flink system as our tool for data collection and management in our study on the Semantic Web research community (see Chapter 8. But first, in order to justify our use of electronic data, we will take a closer look at the relationship between real-world networks and online networks in a scientific setting.

Part III

Case studies

Evaluation of web-based social network extraction

The Internet and computer communication networks in general have been extensively studied as indicators for social networks from as early as 1996. Several internet studies suggest that internet interaction replaces the traditional role of social networks [OR02, WSD⁺96]. Taking this observation to the extreme, network researchers with a background in physics or computer science study online networks as the equivalents of real world networks. On the other hand, network analysts with a social science background apply an extreme caution and most often still treat electronic communication networks and online communities as a separate field of investigation where different theories and methods apply than in the study of real world networks.

Nevertheless, surprisingly little is known about the exact relationship between real world networks and their online reflections. In particular, the question is: to what extent electronic data obtained from the Web reveal social structures such as those mentioned by actors when questioned by specific network questionnaires?

In the following we limit our attention to data generated by methods of social network mining from the Web as introduced in Chapter 3 and discussed in [Mik05a, MHT⁺06]. It is likely that different forms of electronic data could serve as a source for obtaining information about different types of social relations. For electronic data such as email traffic that represent message exchanges between individuals a higher degree of correspondence with social network data is plausible while for others such as web logs a more distant perspective seems to be warranted. Social network mining from the Web based on co-occurrence is an interesting method as it is likely to produce evidence of ties of different strengths based on the variety of the underlying data.

Further, email and online collaboration is likely to be used in different ways in different social settings. Bearing in mind the limitations of this method, we have chosen members of a research organization[1] as the subjects of our study. Scientific communities are particularly well-suited to be studied based on their online presence

---

[1] We will use the more specific term research organization to denote scientific groups (communities) active in a formal organization.

due to the amount and variety of information that is present online, including personal homepages, information on research collaborations in the form of projects and publications, descriptions of events (conferences and workshops) etc.

We choose to evaluate electronic data extraction against the results of a survey method, which is the dominant approach to data collection for network analysis. Standard questionnaires are preferred in theory testing for their fixed structure, which guarantees the comparability of results among test subjects and across studies. Various forms of asking for one's social relations have been tested through the years for reliability. The fixed structure of questionnaires also allows to directly extract relational data and attributes for processing with network analysis tools and statistical packages. Questionnaires are also minimally invasive and can be easily mailed, emailed or administered online.

In the following we compare the results of our social network mining methods with the outcomes of a study we have conducted using a common type of network questionnaire. Note that we will call the results of our survey the golden standard, reflecting the viewpoint of network analysis. However, we can already project one of the most important limitations of our analysis: with any discrepancy we may find between the results of online and off-line analysis the difference could be attributed to limitations of either of the two. While network questionnaires are dominant, they are hardly infallible and by treating them as a benchmark we may try to match their imperfection. (And vice versa: if we were to treat online data as a benchmark for evaluating survey methods we would try to reproduce their errors.)

Our study is unique as we have no knowledge of any evaluation of network extraction methods using real world data. Thus our main contribution is the description of how such an evaluation can be carried out and the questions it raises.[2] Second, we will use this evaluation to compare different network mining methods, fine tune their parameters and measure the effect of disambiguation techniques. Lastly, we will give a sense of how good the results of these extraction methods are by comparing network measures computed on our web-based networks with the same measures calculated on the graphs from our survey.

We expect this evaluation to be relevant for anyone who is considering to use data extracted from the Web as a proxy for real world data. Web-based extraction requires significantly less effort to execute than data collection using surveys or observation. Further, the results can be scaled to any number of participants and the data collection can be repeated at any number of times, even retrospectively, provided that the community to be investigated had a significant web presence at the time. As more and more communities move more of their activities online, we expect that web mining will become a preferred source of data for many network experiments in the future.

---

[2] Unfortunately, we cannot make our data set public due to privacy restrictions. This limitation holds for most real world experiments in network analysis. In fact, we have no knowledge of any publicly available data sets that we could have used for our evaluation. Nevertheless, it would be highly desirable to have such a data set as a benchmark for evaluating network analysis methods in a completely transparent way.

7.1 Differences between survey methods and electronic data extraction

In the above we have already mentioned some of the key advantages of electronic data extraction, which mostly have to do with the differences in how data are collected. In the following we focus on the outcomes and summarize the potential sources of disagreement between the results we obtain from a typical network survey compared to the results of our method of mining the Web for social network data.

This list will serve as a guideline when looking for possible explanations for the discrepancies in the results. We will explicitly test for some of these differences as potential sources of disagreements and leave some for future work.

Note that some of these points are specific to our method of network extraction or the specific research setting.[3] Nevertheless, this list can also serve as a checklist for anyone considering similar comparisons, possibly in different settings using different methods of network data extraction.

- Differences in what is measured
  - What is not on the Web cannot be extracted from the Web, which limits the scope of extraction. Also, these data can be biased in case part of the community to be studied is better represented on the Web than other parts. This is similar to the sampling problem of survey methods: one needs to take care that the data collected allows to build a balanced representation of the underlying social structure.
  - Our network extraction method is likely to find evidence for different kinds of relationships resulting in what is called a multiplex network. These relationships are not easily entangled although some progress can be made by applying machine learning to disambiguate relationships. Matsuo et al. demonstrate this method by learning typical features of Web pages that characterize certain relationships in the research domain [MHT⁺06]. They report good results in distinguishing between co-authors, colleagues and co-participation relationships.
    We address this problem differently: we measure a number of relationships in our survey and use these data to understand the composition of relationships we find on the Web (see Section 7.6).
  - The equivalent problem in survey methods is the difficulty of precisely formulating those questions that address the relationship the researcher actually wants to study. This is a hard, if not the hardest problem as shown by the attention that is paid to this question in most network studies. For example, the key network question in the General Social Survey (GSS) of the United States was originally formulated to ask respondents about the persons with whom they discuss *personal matters* [MSLB06]. This was later changed to the same question asking about *important matters* because in a separate study it was

---

[3] We have discussed the potential sources of errors in network extraction in Chapter 3, but we repeat these points here for the sake of completeness.

found that respondents varied greatly in their understanding of personal matters and sometimes interpreted this term in very narrow ways [Rua98]. Even such a minor change, however, complicates the comparison between results obtained using the original question and the new formulation [MSLB06].

- Errors introduced by the extraction method
  - There are errors that affect the extraction of particular cases. Homonymy affects common names (e.g. *J. Smith* or *Xi Li*), but can be reduced somewhat by adding disambiguation terms to queries. Synonymy presents a problem whenever a person uses different variations of his or her name. Different variations of first names (e.g. *James Hendler* vs *Jim Hendler*), different listing of first and middle names, foreign accentuation, different alphabets (e.g. Latin vs. Chinese) etc. can all lead to different name forms denoting the same person.
    In the following, we will address this problem by experimenting with various measures that could predict if a particular name is likely to be problematic in terms of extraction. We can test such measures by detecting whether the personal network of such persons is in fact more difficult to extract than the networks of other persons.
  - Another class of errors is likely to affect all names with equal probability. An example of such a systemic error is the accidental co-occurrence of two names on a web page. Further, even if intended not all co-occurrences carry equal weight e.g. many co-occurrences are likely to be duplicates.
    Such systemic errors or noise are likely to be reduced by means of large numbers and are altogether less threatening as they affect all cases with equal probability.
- Errors introduced by survey data collection
  - Unlike network mining from the Web, surveys almost never cover a network completely. Although a response rate lower than 100% is not necessarily an error, it does require some proof that either the non-respondents are not significantly different from the respondents with respect to the survey or that the collected results are so robust that the response from the non-respondents could not have affected it significantly.
  - The respondents are not likely to be equally co-operative either. There are most likely differences in the level of cooperativeness and fatigue. Some of these factors can be measured and checked in order to make sure that the responses by the less cooperative or more fatigued population are not significantly different from the rest [MSLB06]. In small scale studies the situation is even more problematic as the non-respondents and the respondents are likely to be clustered as the subjects discuss the matter of the survey and influence each other in responding to it or not.
  - The mere fact of observation can introduce a bias. At best this bias affects all subjects in an equal manner.
  - Not only the type of relationship that is considered by the respondent but also the recall of contacts is affected by the way a question is formulated (see Section 7.3) and how it is placed in the sequence of questions [MSLB06].

7.2 Context of the empirical study

We have collected network data on the social networks of the 123 researchers working at the Department of Computer Science of the Vrije Universiteit, Amsterdam in September 2006. We have received contact information about the researchers and an approval for our study from the head of the Department.

The Department is organized is six Sections of various sizes, which are in decreasing order of size: Computer Systems (38), Artificial Intelligence (33), Information Management and Software Engineering (22), Business Informatics (17), Theoretical Computer Science (9) and Bioinformatics (4).[4] The Sections are further divided internally into groups[5], each led by a professor. Researchers in each section include part- or full-time PhD students, postdocs, associate and full professors, but the study excluded master students, support staff (scientific programmers) and administrative support.

Note that this research organization is by nature different from a research community such as the Semantic Web community introduced earlier in that is not primarily bound by a broad research interest but rather a shared affiliation with an institution. Nevertheless, this affiliation is rather loose as most within the organization consider the level of the department as a purely administrative level. Thus the overall image is close to that of a research community: in both cases relationships between individuals are largely driven by specific research interests or affiliation with a smaller group[6] rather than their common relationship with the organization or research community. (As it turns out, the network of the organization is even less centralized than the research community of the Semantic Web.)

We have chosen this community as a subject of our study because the author is a member of the Business Informatics group of the Department. This position allowed us to directly address the participants of the study and most likely resulted in a higher response rate than it would have been possible otherwise. On the downside, some participants felt that this study should not have been carried out by "one of their own" as they did not feel comfortable with providing personal information to a colleague, even with the assurance that only statistics would be computed from the data and that the data would not be used for management purposes.[7] In effect, nine people have voted out of the study. From the remaining 114 researchers we have collected 79 responses (a response rate of 64%), with above average response rates in the BI group (88%) and the closely interlinked AI (79%) group.

---

[4] For more information on the research of the department, please visit `http://www.cs.vu.nl`

[5] These are the *leerstoelgroepen* in Dutch.

[6] Members of the same group are typically also co-located in the same parts of the building.

[7] No doubt most of the participants did not realize how much information about their networks is available online.

7.3 Data collection

We collected personal and social information using a custom-built online survey system. An online survey offers several advantages compared to a paper questionnaire:

- Easy accessibility for the participants. The participants did not need to be physically present. They were sent a user name and a password in email and could log on anytime.
- Greater flexibility in design, allowing for a better survey experience. Using an electronic survey it is possible to adapt questions presented to the user based on the answers to previous questions. This reduces the time to complete the survey and thus diminishes non-response.
- Easier processing for the survey administrator. Our system recorded electronic data directly in RDF using the FOAF-based semantic representations discussed in Chapter 5. As we already had the components for reading FOAF data and exporting it in the formats supporting by SNA packages, the data required no post-processing. Also, the system did part of the error checking as the participants were filling out the survey (e.g. checking that all mandatory fields were filled out).

There are a number of electronic survey tools available on the Web either for free or against a small payment. Unfortunately, these solutions allow very little customization for either error checking or for implementing survey logic. Further, as these off-the-shelf tools are not specifically designed for network surveys, they would have produced data in formats that are difficult to post-process (typically Excel sheets).

The survey is divided over several pages. The first page asks the participant to enter basic personal information: his or her full-time or part-time status, age, years at the organization, name of the direct supervisor and research interests. The second and third pages contain standard questions for determining the level of self-monitoring and the extent someone identifies with the different levels of the organization. These control variables were not used in the current evaluation.

The fourth page asks the participant the select the persons he or she knows from a complete list of Department members. This question is included to pre-select those persons the participant might have any relationship with. The next page asks the participant to specify the nature of the relationship with the persons selected. In particular, the participant is suggested to consider six types of relationships and asked to specify for each person which type of relationship applies to that person.

The six types of relations we surveyed were advice seeking, advice giving, future cooperation, similarity perceptions, friendship, and adversarial ties. The first three questions assessed instrumental ties, whereas the last three questions represented affective ties and general perceptions of similarity.

The advice network was operationalized following [Kra90] and [IA93]. The respondents were asked to look through an alphabetical list of all employees and check the names of the people "who you regularly approach if you have a work-related problem or when you want advice on a decision you have to make". Advice giving was operationalized analogously with a formulation "who regularly approaches you...". Future cooperation inquired about preferences for future work by asking "who would you like to work with in the future".

As for the similarity perceptions and affective ties, we followed the operationalization of [MKB98] for the identity network asking the respondents to check the names of the people "who you consider especially similar to yourself". In assessing friendship, we asked to mark those people "whom you consider a personal friend, e.g., a person you like to spend breaks with or engage in social activities". This question was found to reliably distinguish a "friendly relationship" from a "friend" in a validation study, conducted at a dialysis and nursing department of a Dutch hospital [vdB99]. Moreover, the question assessing the friendship network in the study of Mehra, Kilduff, & Brass was formulated in a similar vein [MKB01]. Following Baldwin, Bedell, & Johnson [BBJ97] and van de Bunt [vdB99] we assessed the negative relations asking respondents to check names of the people "with whom you have a difficult relation, e.g., you cannot get along with this person".

We used the roster method instead of a free recall to collect social network data (cf. [WFIG94]). The alternative survey method of name generators carries the risk that participants forget to mention some of their contacts. (They name those that first come to mind.) In order to limit the measurement error, respondents were not restricted to a fixed number of nominations [HL73].

We believe that the two step process of pruning the list of participants before presenting relationship choices was beneficial because it put much less strain on the participant than the traditional questionnaire method where the participant fills out a fixed-size matrix. Such a matrix would be very large and sparse in our case, which increases the likelihood of errors, the time to fill out the survey and consequently the risk of abandonment. In fact, most of our survey users informally reported that the survey in the current form was very smooth and easy to "click through", costing about 15 minutes of their time.

Upon completion of the last page, the survey software stored the results in a Sesame RDF store [BKvH02], saved the data on backup and notified the survey administrator in email.

7.4 Preparing the data

The networks we have collected each contained 123 nodes corresponding to the equal number of survey participants. In a first step, we have removed all non-respondents from these networks, reducing the number of nodes to the 79 respondents. The number of nodes with edges in each of the networks is lower, since not all respondents provided information about all of their networks. Note also that this step also reduced the number of edges in the networks since respondents may have mentioned non-respondents and these edges were removed. Non-respondents were also removed from the graph obtained from web mining: this graph contained edges also for those who did not respond to our survey.

Next, we removed directionality from our survey networks and our web-based network. It is unlikely that the directionality measured by our social network extraction method would correspond directly to any of the measured dimensions. Further, the network measures we generally compute do not take directionality into account. Table 7.1 shows the basic statistics about our collected data before and after the pre-processing.

Graph	Advice seeking	Advice giving	Friend-ship	Troubled relation	Similar-ity	Future work
Nodes after non-respondent removal	79	79	79	79	79	79
Nodes w/edges	74	58	70	18	60	74
Edges	363	290	447	40	323	546
Edges after non-respondent removal	226	194	298	21	221	361
Edges after direction removal	197	161	229	20	193	282

Table 7.1. Statistics of our networks from the survey.

7.5 Optimizing goodness of fit

In order to prepare the comparison with our web-based networks, we had to filter the nodes and edges of this network and remove the directionality in this case as well.

Filtering of the web-based network requires to specify cut-off values for two parameters: the minimal number of pages one must have on the Web to be included (pagecount) and the minimal strength of the relationships (strength). Recall that the first parameter is used to exclude individuals with too few pages to apply web mining, while the second parameter is used to filter out ties with too little support (thus one is a criterium on the nodes to be included and the other is a criterium on the edges to be included, see Chapter 3).

Figures 7.1 and 7.2 show the distribution of these values. Note that while the strength values show a smooth power law distribution, there are two different scaling regimes for the page counts. Typically PhD students have less than 1000 pages on the Web, while post-docs and more senior department members have over 10000 pages. Note also that unlike in the case of the Semantic Web community, we do not use any disambiguation term, which results in some outliers due to famous namesakes (e.g. Michel Klein).

We mention that filtering is either carried out before removing directionality or one needs to aggregate the weights of the edges going in different directions before the edges can be filtered. Some alternatives are taking the sum, average, maximum or minimum of the values.

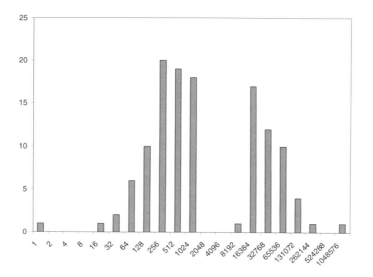

Figure 7.1. Histogram for the number of web pages per individual. Note that the x-axis is on a logarithmic scale.

Finding the appropriate parameters for filtering can be considered as an optimization task where we would like to maximize the similarity between our survey networks and the extracted network. For this optimization we need to choose a similarity measure.

We can consider relationship extraction as an information retrieval task and apply well-known measures from the field of information retrieval. Let's denote our graphs to be compared as $G_1(V_1, E_1)$ and $G_2(V_2, E_2)$. Some of the measures to be considered are listed in Table 7.2. Precision, recall and the F-measure are common measures in information retrieval (see e.g. [vR79]), while the Jaccard-coefficient is also used for example in UCINET [BEF02].

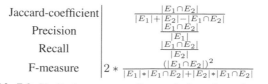

Jaccard-coefficient	$\frac{\|E_1 \cap E_2\|}{\|E_1\| + \|E_2\| - \|E_1 \cap E_2\|}$
Precision	$\frac{\|E_1 \cap E_2\|}{\|E_1\|}$
Recall	$\frac{\|E_1 \cap E_2\|}{\|E_2\|}$
F-measure	$2 * \frac{(\|E_1 \cap E_2\|)^2}{\|E_1\| * \|E_1 \cap E_2\| + \|E_2\| * \|E_1 \cap E_2\|}$

Table 7.2. Similarity measures for graphs based on edge sets

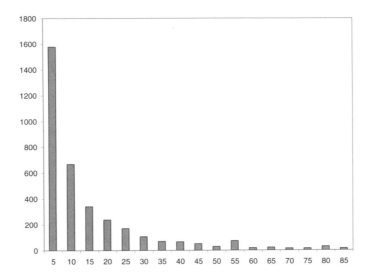

Figure 7.2. Histogram for the strength of relationships based on the web extraction method.

Once we have chosen a measure, we can visualize the effect of the parameters on the similarity using surface plots such as the one shown in Figures 7.3. These figures show the changes in the similarity between the advice seeking network and the network obtained from web mining as we change the pagecount and strength thresholds (the two horizontal axes show the parameter settings and the vertical axis shows the resulting similarity). As expected, for symmetric measures such as the F-measure this is a convex surface: extremes along both axis result in zero similarity. Figures 7.4 and 7.5 show the asymmetric precision and recall measures, which help us understand why this is the case. Setting the thresholds to zero results in high recall (82%) but low precision (21%). Conversely, setting the thresholds high results in high precision (approximating 100%) but low recall (reaching 0%) corresponding to the extreme case where all nodes and edges have been filtered out up to the last edge.

The F-measure, which is the harmonic mean of precision and recall, has a single highest peak (optimum) and a second peak representing a different trade-off between precision and recall. As it is the case that the mining graph at this second peak contains more nodes and edges (higher recall, lower precision), it might be preferable over the optimum depending on the goal of the application. To accommodate differences in the importance of precision and recall, it is also possible to apply a weighted version of the F-measure.

In general, we note that it seems easier to achieve high recall than high precision. This suggests the possibility of a two-stage acquisition process where we first collect a social network using web mining and then apply a survey in which we ask respondents to remove the incorrect relations and add the few missing ones. Such a pre-selection approach can be particularly useful in large networks where listing all names in a survey would result in an overly large table. Further, subjects are more easily motivated to correct lists than to provide lists themselves.

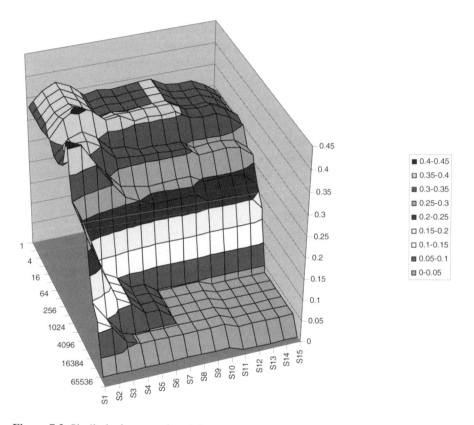

Figure 7.3. Similarity between the advice seeking network and the network obtained from the Web using the F-measure. The similarity (plotted on the vertical, z axis) depends on the value of the two parameters of the algorithm.

7.6 Comparison across methods and networks

Our benchmark survey data also allows a direct comparison of methods for social network mining. In this case we compare the best possible results obtainable by two

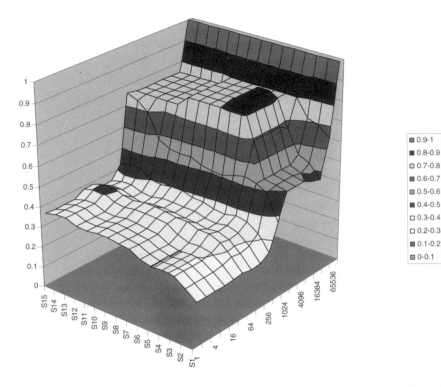

Figure 7.4. Similarity between the advice seeking network and the network obtained from the Web using the precision measure. The precision (plotted on the vertical, z axis) depends on the value of the two parameters of the algorithm.

(or more) methods, i.e. we choose the parameters for each method separately such that some similarity measure is optimized.

We have subjected to this test our benchmark method of co-occurrence analysis and the method based on average precision (see Chapter 3). Figure 7.6 shows a comparison of these two methods in terms of the lowest precision, highest recall and highest F-measure they can achieve on any of our six networks.

The results confirm our intuition that the average precision method produces higher precision, but lower recall resulting in only slightly higher F-measure values. By looking at the numbers across networks, we can see that the easiest to predict are the advice seeking, advice giving and future work networks. This is true for both methods, i.e. it seems to be a feature of the data, rather than the method of extraction. The possibility to predict future work relations might be a bit surprising considering that the question behind it is about the future. However, respondents were not specifically instructed to exclude current work relations.

In fact, it is likely that the relationships we extract from the Web reflect a number of underlying relationships, including those we asked in our survey and possibly others we did not. To measure to what extent each of our surveyed relationships is

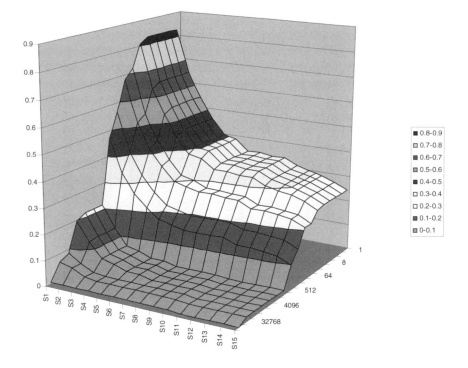

Figure 7.5. Similarity between the advice seeking network and the network obtained from the Web using the recall measure. The recall (plotted on the vertical, z axis) depends on the value of the two parameters of the algorithm.

present on the Web it would be possible to perform a p* analysis, where we assume that the Web-based network is a linear combination of our survey networks (see Equation 7.1).

$$\lambda_1 S_1 + \lambda_2 S_2 + \lambda_3 S_3 + \lambda_4 S_4 + \lambda_4 S_4 + \lambda_5 S_5 = W \qquad (7.1)$$

The analysis would then return the coefficients of this linear equation, i.e. the weights with which the individual survey networks contribute to the Web-based network. Notice that for this we need to fix the parameters of the Web-based network. In fact, we can consider this as an optimization task where we try to maximize the fit between the survey networks and the Web-based network by adjusting the weights of the survey networks instead of changing the parameters of the Web-based network as we have done previously. This kind of analysis is among the future work.

7.7 Predicting the goodness of fit

In Chapter 3 we have suggested the influence of a number of factors on the success of extracting social networks from the Web. Many of these factors are personal. For

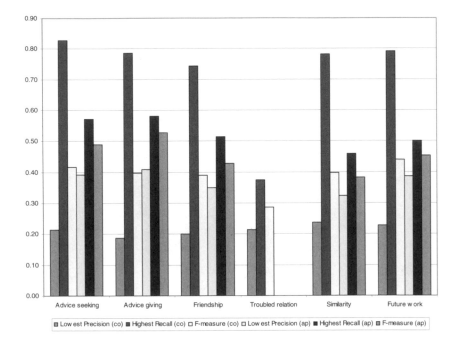

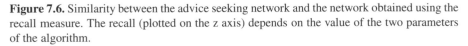

Figure 7.6. Similarity between the advice seeking network and the network obtained using the recall measure. The recall (plotted on the z axis) depends on the value of the two parameters of the algorithm.

example, the amount of information available about a person or the commonality of someone's name on the Web. In our current study, we also find that the number of pages on the Web mentioning someone varies widely in the community, partly affected in fact by the problem of namesakes (either many namesakes or a single famous namesake).

Based on the attribute data we have collected from our survey (and other attributes we can compute) it is interesting to investigate whether some of these factors can indeed be linked to the success of obtaining the person's social network from the Web. Trying to predict a-priori the goodness of fit between an individual's real social network and its Web-based image has important practical significance: if we find measures that help us to predict when the extraction is likely to fail we can exclude those individuals from the Web-based extraction and try other methods or data sources for obtaining information about their relations.

To carry out this kind of analysis, we have to measure the similarity between personal networks from the survey and the Web and correlate it with attributes of the subjects. (Thus, in contrast to the previous section, we compute similarity measures on ego-networks.) In this kind of study, we work with a single network from our survey and a mining network with fixed parameters. (As described previously, we fix the parameters of extraction such that the overall fit between the survey and the network from the Web is maximized.)

The attributes we consider are those from our survey, e.g. the number of relations mentioned (*surveydegree*), the age of the individual and the number of years spent at the VU (variables *age* and *entry*). We also look at Web-based indicators such as the number of relations extracted (*miningdegree*) and the number of pages for someone's name, which we recode based on its distribution by taking the logarithm of the values (*pagecount*). Last, we experimented with measures for name ambiguity based on the existing literature on name disambiguation [BM05, BMI06]. Both of these works apply clustering methods on the results returned by the search engine in order to predict how many persons or personalities[8] are found in the result set and which pages belong to which individual. These measures try to estimate the web presence of the particular individual we are looking for:

- NC1: Jaccard-coefficient between the first name and the last name. The idea behind this measure is to predict how much a first name and a last name belong together. The expectation is that the larger this quotient, the least common the name is.
- NC2: The ratio of the number of pages for a query that includes the full name and the term *Vrije Universiteit* divided by the number of pages for the full name only. This is a measure of the number of pages that are certainly about the correct individual versus the total number of pages. It is expected that the higher this value, the easier it is to retrieve the correct individual.

In general, we find that the more respondents are mentioned by someone, the higher the precision of the extraction. There can be two alternative explanations to this. First, it is possible that some respondents are mentioning more of their social network than others and the more relations they name the higher the precision goes. Second, it is possible that respondents with larger social networks have a correspondingly larger web presence, which makes it easier to extract their correct relations. We also trivially find that the more relations are extracted from the Web for any individual, the lower the precision and the higher the recall.

Interestingly, none of the survey attributes has a direct influence on the result, even though age and entry are correlated with the number of web pages as expected. The NC1 measure has no significant effect. On closer inspection, a problem with this measure is that it assigns high scores also to persons who have a common first name and last name, but whose combination of first and last name is rare. The measure is also unable to distinguish between name commonality (e.g. Li Ding) and famous namesakes (e.g. George Bush). Somewhat surprisingly, the NC2 measure has a negative effect on the F-measure. The explanation could be that respondents who have a

---

[8] A person may have multiple contexts of activity, even if we consider the professional activities alone. For example, Noam Chomsky is known both as a linguist and a prolific political writer. In an application where we want to distinguish his networks in these different contexts, we would prefer a disambiguation module that is able to separate the pages related to these two activities even if they belong to the same person.

		surveydeg	miningdeg	age	entry	na_1	na_vu	pc_recode	fmeasure	precision	recall
surveydeg	Pearson	1	0.667	-0.035	-0.004	-0.058	-0.038	0.361	0.390	0.355	0.148
	Sig. (2-tailed)		0.000	0.764	0.975	0.617	0.737	0.003	0.023	0.034	0.357
	N	79	79	77	77	77	79	65	34	36	41
miningdeg	Pearson		1	-0.090	-0.022	-0.072	0.128	0.152	-0.206	-0.370	0.798
	Sig. (2-tailed)			0.434	0.848	0.534	0.260	0.227	0.241	0.026	0.000
	N		79	77	77	77	79	65	34	36	41
age	Pearson			1	0.671	0.169	-0.001	0.325	0.015	-0.133	-0.136
	Sig. (2-tailed)				0.000	0.146	0.994	0.009	0.933	0.448	0.404
	N			77	77	75	77	63	34	35	40
entry	Pearson				1	0.072	0.029	0.332	-0.003	-0.189	-0.057
	Sig. (2-tailed)					0.540	0.799	0.008	0.985	0.276	0.729
	N				77	75	77	63	34	35	40
na_1	Pearson					1	-0.140	0.250	0.155	0.089	0.025
	Sig. (2-tailed)						0.223	0.048	0.390	0.611	0.880
	N					77	77	63	33	35	40
na_vu	Pearson						1	-0.114	-0.498	-0.277	0.226
	Sig. (2-tailed)							0.367	0.003	0.103	0.155
	N						79	65	34	36	41
pc_recode	Pearson							1	0.019	-0.030	-0.159
	Sig. (2-tailed)								0.920	0.872	0.354
	N							65	30	32	36
fmeasure	Pearson								1	0.694	0.128
	Sig. (2-tailed)									0.000	0.471
	N								34	34	34
precision	Pearson									1	-0.111
	Sig. (2-tailed)										0.520
	N									36	36
recall	Pearson										1
	Sig. (2-tailed)										
	N										41

**. Correlation is significant at the 0.01 level (2-tailed).
*. Correlation is significant at the 0.05 level (2-tailed).

Figure 7.7. Correlations between personal attributes and the similarity between the personal networks from the survey and the Web.

high percentage of their mentioning linked to the Vrije Universiteit produce a higher recall which results in lower precision (at an already high level of recall).

7.8 Evaluation through analysis

Typically, networks from surveys or the Web are used as raw data for computing complex measures of Network Analysis. What we are really interested in is thus the extent to which a Web-based network can replace a survey when used in analysis. It is likely that if the network extraction is optimized to match the results of the survey it will give similar results in analysis. However, we will see that a 100% percent match is not required for obtaining relevant results in applications: most network measures are statistical aggregates and thus relatively robust to missing or incorrect information.

Group-level analysis, for example, is typically insensitive to errors in the extraction of specific cases. Figures 7.9 and 7.8 show the structure of our advice seeking network and the optimized mining network, including the group affiliation of individuals. (Names have been replaced with numbers for privacy reasons.) The macro-level social structure of our department can be retrieved by collapsing this network to show the relationships between groups using the affiliations or by clustering the network. (These functions are available for example in Pajek.) By applying these procedures to the two networks they reveal the same underlying organization: two of the groups (the AI and BI sections) built close relationships with each other and with the similarly densely linked Computer Systems group. The explanation for the first observation is that several members of the two groups are involved in similar research on the topic of the Semantic Web. (This mismatch between the informal and formal organization is also very well recognized by the researchers themselves.) The remaining groups are either very small (Theoretical Informatics, Bioinformatics) or very loosely connected both internally and to the other groups (IMSE).

Our experiments also show the robustness of centrality measures such as degree, closeness and betweenness. For example, if we compute the list of the top 20 nodes by degree, closeness and betweenness we find an overlap of 55%, 65% and 50%, respectively. While this is not very high, it signifies a higher agreement than would have been expected: the correlation between the values is 0.67, 0.49, 0.22, respectively. The higher correlation of degrees can be explained by the fact that we optimize on degree when we calibrate our networks on precision/recall.[9]

In general, we argue that the level of similarity between our survey and Web-based networks is high enough that it is unlike that we find a network effect based on the Web data that would not hold if we were to use the survey network. The rationale is similar to arguing for sampling in social sciences. When working with a sample instead of the entire population we might obfuscate some significant effects. However, if the sampling is done in a uniform manner it is unlikely that we introduce a significant effect just through the process of sampling.

7.9 Discussion

The Web is rapidly becoming one of the most important sources of data for network analysis. Not only the adoption of the Web is taking off, but also the Web itself has been turning into a place of active socialization through technologies such as social networking, blogging, instant messaging, and platforms collaborative work on software and content. The availability of electronic data presents an unprecedented opportunity for network science in conducting large scale studies using dynamic (time-bound) data. Further, these data can be either collected as is or it can be easily extracted through well-known methods of web mining. The resulting data set can be directly manipulated by machines, which further lowers the costs of network studies.

Before Web data can be subject to analysis, however, network analysis needs to investigate the extent to which Web-based data can replace the input from traditional survey and observation methods of data collection. In this Chapter we have addressed this question by providing methodological guidance for evaluation and argued that in

---

[9] One might play with the idea of optimizing fit based on these network measures, e.g. selecting the parameters of network mining such that the correlation between centrality measures is maximized.

Figure 7.8. The network from Web mining (after optimizing for maximum similarity with the advice seeking network). Colors indicate different Sections within the Department.

the particular domain of scientific communities electronic data that can be collected on the Web is a close enough reflection of real world networks to use it in place of survey data as the input of network analysis.

We have noted that the disagreement between our alternate methods could be explained by either differences in what is being measured or imperfections in either the survey or the web extraction method of data collection. Although it is the dominant method of data collection, one should in fact be cautious in considering survey data as a golden standard as it can lead to reproduce the imperfections of the survey method. We have tested for some of the explanations that could explain existing differences and proposed some as future work.

Evaluations similar to ours could be (and should be) carried out with a variety of network data in order to prove the robustness of our methods across domains. For example, network mining methods could be applied to the extraction of corporate networks, which could be more easily tested against existing databases on joint ventures and other forms co-operation as used in [Lem03].

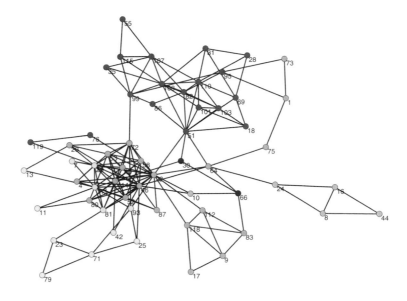

Figure 7.9. The advice seeking network of researchers. Colors indicate different Sections within the Department.

8

Semantic-based Social Network Analysis in the sciences

In social studies of science, research fields have been considered as self-organized communities, also referred to as invisible colleges [Cra71]. Recently smaller groups with shared research interests have been addressed as virtual teams [AC99, AGC03]).

Both notions relate to the observation that social connectivity is relevant to many key aspects of research. Conceptualizing research fields as either self-organized communities or virtual teams also allows us to study them using network analysis methods of social science. In past works, various features of the social networks of researchers have proved useful in explaining scientific performance on the individual and organizational level.[1]

The informal nature of scientific communities, however, has also made it difficult to obtain network data for analysis. Traditionally, information about the informal social structure of scientific communities is gathered through labor-intensive methods of data collection, e.g. through interviews or network questionnaires. Alternatively, researchers from deSolla Price [dP65] to Barabási and Newman [BJN+02, New01]) have relied on more tangible evidence of formal work relations such as co-authoring and co-citation of scientific publications or investigated co-participation in research projects [HHvdB03, GM02]. For obtaining much of these data and for measuring scientific performance, most authors have relied on commercially available databases of journal articles, patent- and project grants.

More recently, the use of electronic data extraction is gaining ground in the study of networks. While traditional survey or interview methods are limited in the size of networks and the number of measurements (time-points), electronic data enable large scale, longitudinal studies of networks. In many cases, electronic data also break the reliance on commercial providers of information, lowering the costs of access. This process is visible, for example, in the unfolding clash between freely consultable

---

[1] Studies at the intersection of network analysis and scientometrics appear either in the journal Scientometrics (Akadémiai Kiadó, co-published with Springer Science+Business Media B.V.) or in the Social Network Analysis literature (see Chapter 2).

online publication databases based on Information Extraction technology (such as Citeseer[2] and Google Scholar[3]) and those maintained by the publishers themselves.

Scientific communities in high technology domains such as Artificial Intelligence or Bioinformatics are among the ones that lend themselves most naturally to be studied through their online presence, due the openness of the (academic) research environment and their use of advanced communication technology for knowledge sharing in emails, forums and on the Web. For example, email communication in research and standardization settings are the source of social networks in [GLDZ03] and [AA05a], while other studies extract social networks from the content of web pages [KSS97, MMIF04] or —somewhat less successfully— by analyzing the linking structure of the Web [HHvdB03]. As the first to publish such a study, Paolillo and Wright offer a rough characterization of the FOAF[4] network in [PW04].

The availability of a multitude of information sources provides the opportunity to obtain a more complete view of the social network of a scientific community, thereby it increases the robustness and reliability of research designs. In particular, by decreasing our reliance on the single sources of information our findings become less prone to the errors in the individual sources of information. However, the availability of a number of data sources also poses a previously unmet challenge, namely the aggregation of information originating from heterogeneous information sources not primarily created for the purposes of network analysis.

We meet this challenge by offering methodological contributions that also allow us to carry out novel theoretical investigations into network effects on scientific performance. Note that theoretical contributions to scientometrics go beyond much of the related work advanced by physicists such as Barabási and Newman. Their main interest lies in discovering the intrinsic properties of large scale networks in general, i.e. they are looking for the commonalities across networks in nature. (Their interest stems from the field of complex networks and dynamics in physics, where the focus is on explaining large scale phenomenon that is emerging from elementary interactions.) Their works are not in the domain of sociology, where the interest is in explaining substantial external outcomes (such as the performance of actors in a network) through the constraints and opportunities that network connectivity provides.

Our first contribution is the use of semantic technology in the management of social network data, in particular the semantics-based aggregation of information from heterogeneous information sources. As described in Section 6.2, our system extracts information from web pages, emails and online collections of publications. Our method of social network extraction from the Web deserves particular attention as it allows to scale network studies considerably and enrich it with network ties that can only be observed through the Web (see Chapter 7 for more details). Semantic technology allows us to uniquely identify references across these sources and merge our sources to form a single data set. Thereby we automate much of the effort

---

[2] http://citeseer.ist.psu.edu/
[3] http://scholar.google.com
[4] see Section 5.2

involved in building network studies on a combination of data sources, such as in [New01].

Second, we advance the theory of network effects on scientific performance by going beyond a structural analysis of our networks and incorporating the effects of cognitive diversity in ego networks. Our analysis of the potential content of relationships is enabled by our method of extracting the research interests of scientists from electronic sources. In particular, we will look at the content of relations and the effects of cognitive (dis)similarity. We hypothesize that cognitive diversity in the ego network of researchers will be positively related to their performance, especially for newcomers, juniors researchers entering the field.

In the following, we begin by introducing the context of our study, the Semantic Web research community. In Section 8.2 we introduce our first contribution, our system for extracting and aggregating social network information from various electronic information sources. In Section 8.3, we formalize our hypotheses concerning the effects of social and cognitive networks on scientific performance and test these hypotheses using the data collected. We summarize our work in Section 8.4.

8.1 Context

The context of our study is the community of researchers working towards the development of the Semantic Web, an extension of the current Web infrastructure with advanced knowledge technologies that have been originally developed in the Artificial Intelligence (AI) community. The idea of the Semantic Web is to enable computers to process and reason with the knowledge available on the World Wide Web. The method of extending the current human-focused Web with machine processable descriptions of web content has been first formulated in 1996 by Tim Berners-Lee, the original inventor of the Web [BLFD99]. See Chapter 1 for more details on the Semantic Web and its development up to the present.

As the Semantic Web is a relatively new, dynamic field of investigation, it is difficult to precisely delineate the boundaries of this network.[5] For our purposes we have defined the community by including those researchers who have submitted publications or held an organizing role at any of the past International Semantic Web Conferences (ISWC02, ISWC03, ISWC04) or the Semantic Web Working Symposium of 2001 (SWWS01), the most significant conference series devoted entirely to the Semantic Web. We note that another commonly encountered way of defining the boundary of a scientific community is to look at the authorship of representative journals (see e.g. [HHvdB03]). However, the Semantic Web has not had a dedicated journal until 2004 and still most Semantic Web related publications appear in AI journals not entirely devoted to the Semantic Web.

---

[5] In fact, it is difficult to determine at what point does a new research concept become a separate field of investigation. With regard to Semantic Web, it is clear that many of the scientists involved have developed ties before their work on the Semantic Web, just as some of the research published in the Semantic Web area has been worked out before in different settings.

The complete list of individuals in this community consists of 608 researchers mostly from academia (79%) and to a lesser degree from industry (21%). Geographically, the community covers much of the United States, Europe, with some activity in Japan and Australia (see Figure 1.4). As Figure 1.5 shows, the participation rate at the individual ISWC events have quickly reached the level typical of large, established conferences and remained at that level even for the last year of data (2004), when the conference was organized in Hiroshima, Japan. The number of publications written by the members of the community that contain the keyword "Semantic Web" has been sharply rising since the beginning.

8.2 Methodology

Our methodology combines existing methods of web mining and extraction from publication and email sources, with semantic-based techniques for storing, aggregating and reasoning with social network data. Flink, our self-implemented semantic software supports the complete process of data collection, storage and visualization of social networks based on heterogeneous sources of electronic data (see Section 6.2).

While semantic technology has been quickly adopted by online communities, it has been left largely unnoticed in the social sciences, despite important benefits for the management of social network data. As Flink demonstrates, semantic technology allows us to map the schema of our information sources and to find correspondences among the instances. The use of standard semantic languages for the representation of social science data makes it possible to use generic Semantic Web tools and infrastructure for editing, storing, querying and reasoning with our data. Lastly, the semantic data store is the basis for a web-based user interface for browsing the data set, computing social network statistics and exporting the networks and the results of the computations.

We have discussed Flink in Chapter 6, so we restrict ourselves here to a summary of how various layers of the system -concerned with data acquisition, representation and visualization-, are used in the current study.

8.2.1 Data acquisition

The first layer of the Flink system is concerned with data acquisition. Flink makes use of four different types of knowledge sources: text-based HTML pages from the web, FOAF profiles, public collections of emails and bibliographic data. Information from the different sources is extracted in different ways as described below. In the final step, however, all the data gathered by the system is represented in a semantic format (RDF), which allows us to store heterogeneous data in a single knowledge base and apply reasoning (see the following Section).

The web mining component of Flink extracts social networks from web pages using a co-occurrence analysis technique introduced in Chapter 3. Although the technique has also been applied before in the AI literature to extract social networks for the automation of referrals (see [KSS97]), to our knowledge this is the first time that the output of the method is subjected to network analysis.

Given a set of names as input, the system uses the search engine Google to obtain the number of co-occurrences for all pairs of names from the membership list of the ISWC community. (The term "(Semantic Web OR ontology)" is added to the queries for disambiguation.) We filter out individuals whose names occurs less then a certain threshold, because in their case the extracted relationships would have very low support.

The absolute strength of association between individuals is then calculated by dividing with the page count of a single individual. In other words, we calculate the fraction of pages where both names are mentioned compared to all pages where an individual is mentioned.[6] The resulting associations are directed and weighted. We consider such an association as evidence of a tie if it reaches a certain predefined threshold. In our experiments this minimum is set at one standard deviation higher than the mean of the values, following a "rule of thumb" in network analysis practice.

The web mining component of Flink also performs the additional task of associating individuals with domain concepts. In our study of the Semantic Web community, the task is to associate scientists with research interests. (The list of terms characterizing research interests has been collected manually from the proceedings of ISWC conferences.) To this end, the system calculates the strength of association between the name of a given person and a certain concept. This strength is determined by taking the number of the pages where the name of an interest and the name of a person co-occur divided by the total number of pages about the person. We assign the expertise to an individual if this value is at least one standard deviation higher than the mean of the values obtained for the same concept.[7] This is different from the more intricate method of Mutschke and Quan Haase, who first cluster keywords into themes, assign documents to themes and subsequently determine which themes are relevant for a person based on his or her publications [MH01].

We can map the cognitive structure of the research field by folding the bipartite graph of researchers and research interests.[8] In the resulting simple graph (shown in Figure 8.3) vertices represent concepts, while an edge is drawn between two concepts if there are at least a minimal number of researchers who are interested in that

---

[6] We have also experimented with normalization using the Jaccard-formula, but we found that it gives unsatisfactory results if there is a large discrepancy between the web-representation of two individuals. This is the case, for example, when testing the potential relationship between a Ph.D. student and a professor.

[7] Note that we do not factor in the number of pages related to the concept, since we are only interested in the expertise of the individual relative to himself. By normalizing with the page count of the interest the measure would assign a relatively high score —and an overly large number of interests— to individuals with many pages on the Web. We only have to be careful in that we cannot compare the association strength across interests. However, this is not necessary for our purposes.

[8] Bipartite graphs of people and concepts are known as affiliation networks (two-mode networks) in SNA practice. Two-mode networks can be used to generate two simple networks, showing associations between concepts and people [WFIG94].

particular combination of concepts. Note that this is different from the commonly used simple co-word analysis. By using a two-step process of associating researchers to concepts and then relating concepts through researchers we get a more accurate picture of the scientific community. Namely, the names of researchers disambiguate the meaning of words in case a word is understood differently by different authors.

Information from emails is processed in two steps. The first step requires that the emails are downloaded from a mail server and the relevant header information is extracted. In a second step, the individuals found in the collection are matched against the profiles of the members of the target list to filter out relevant profiles from the collection. (See Section 8.2.2.)

Although not used in the current experiment, FOAF profiles found on the Web can also be used as an information source. First, an RDF crawler (scutter) is started to collect profiles from the Web. A scutter works similar to an HTML crawler in that it traverses a distributed network by following the links from one document to the next. Our scutter is focused in that it only collects potentially relevant statements, i.e. those containing FOAF information. The scutter also has a mechanism to avoid large FOAF producers that are unlikely to provide relevant data, in particular blog sites[9]. Once FOAF files are collected, the second step again involves filtering out relevant profiles.

Lastly, bibliographic information is collected in a single step by querying Google Scholar with the names of individuals (plus the disambiguation term). From the results we learn the title and locations of publications as well as the year of publication and the number of citations where available.[10] An alternative source of bibliographic information (used in previous versions of the system) is the Bibster peer-to-peer network [HBE+04], which allows to export bibliographic information in an RDF-based format.

8.2.2 Representation, storage and reasoning

All information collected through the data acquisition layer is represented in RDF using the FOAF vocabulary (see Chapter 4).

In terms of data management for the social sciences, RDF is a key technology for aggregating information from heterogeneous information sources. The first step in this process is to express all information using a common representation, i.e. RDF. Personal information and social networks are described in FOAF, emails are expressed in a proprietary ontology, while publication metadata is expressed in terms of the SWRC ontology (see Section 6.2.2).

---

[9] The overwhelming presence of these large sites also make FOAF characterization difficult. See [PW04]. We ignore as we do not expect many Semantic Web researchers to maintain blogs and the amount of information would make it difficult to work with the data.

[10] Note that it is not possible to find co-authors using Google Scholar, since it suppresses the full list of authors in cases where the list would be too long. Fortunately, this is not necessary when the list of authors is known in advance.

After normalizing syntax, the next step is to bridge the semantic gap between the information sources. This consists of mapping the schema and instances of the ontologies used.

Schema matching is a straightforward task in our case. Since the ontologies are known, we can simply insert statements that link corresponding classes in related ontologies. For example, we can state that the Author class of the SWRC ontology is a subclass of the Person class of the FOAF ontology, reflecting the rather trivial knowledge that authors of publications are people.[11]

The matching of instances is a more difficult task and it would be close to impossible to automate without the use of advanced knowledge technology.[12] Identity reasoning is required to establish the identity of objects —in our case individuals— across multiple sources of information, based on the fragments of information available in the various sources. The technical details of this have been discussed in Chapter 5.

Semantic technology also enables us to reason with social relationships. For example, we have added a rule to our knowledge base which states that the co-authors of publications are persons who know each other. Similarly, the reasoning engine concludes that senders and receivers of emails know each other. In the future, the technology will also allow us to build more refined vocabularies of social relationships, for example to include negative relationships. (The current FOAF ontology only contains a single knows relationship).

8.2.3 Visualization and Analysis

The web interface of Flink allows visitors to browse and visualize the aggregated information about the social connectivity and professional interests of Semantic Web researchers. Researchers can also download their profiles in FOAF format. Although it is not possible to edit the information on site, researchers can take the FOAF files provided and store it at their own sites upon editing it. (The new information will be added at the next update of the website when it is found by the FOAF crawler.) The web interface is built using Java technology, in particular the Java Universal Network Graph (JUNG) API. We encourage the reader to visit the website at `http://flink.semanticweb.org`.

Besides visualization, the user interface also provides mechanisms for computing most of the statistics mentioned in this paper. It is also possible to download the network data and statistics for further analysis in the format used by the Pajek network analysis package [BM98]. Lastly, we provide marker files for XPlanet, an application that visualizes geographic locations and geodesics by mapping them onto surface images of the Earth (see Figure 1.4).

---

[11] That this may not be the case in the future has been demonstrated recently by a group of MIT students, who have created an application to automatically generate scientific papers. Interestingly enough, their works have been accepted at various conferences as legitimate publications.

[12] Manual solutions to the problem are completely excluded at the scale of our study.

8.3 Results

We have mapped the structure of the Semantic Web community by combining knowledge from three types of information sources as described in Section 8.2. The actual data set collected on March 17, 2005 contains ties based on 337000 Semantic Web-related web pages[13], a collection of 13323 messages from five mailing lists[14] and 4016 publications from Google Scholar.

The network extracted from e-mail is slightly more similar to publications than webpages (especially if we raise the threshold for emails), while webpages and publications are much more correlated. This confirms our intuition that webpages reflect publication activity more than the discussion networks of emails. (Table 8.1 shows the results of a QAP analysis performed with UCINET.)

Pearson	e-mail	pub	web
e-mail	1.000		
pub	0.072	1.000	
web	0.064	0.326	1.000

Table 8.1. Pearson correlations of the three networks extracted from e-mail lists, a publication database (Google Scholar) and web pages.

In the following, we take the aggregation of the networks as the object of our study, despite the high correlations between the networks. We do so because all networks contain a number of unique ties beyond the overlap. (For example, email lists reveal working group collaborations that may not be manifested in publications.) The aggregated network thus contains a tie between two persons if there is a tie in either the web, email or publication networks. We are not aggregating the weights from these underlying networks as these weights are measured in different units (association weight, number of emails, number of publications), which are difficult to compare.

8.3.1 Descriptive analysis

Out of the 607 actors, 497 belong to the main component of our network. This connected component itself shows a clear core-periphery structure, supporting our original choice for the boundary definition of the Semantic Web community. (This would not be the case if we would see, for example, two distinct cores emerging.) The single and continuous core/periphery analysis performed with UCINET suggest core

---

[13] This count does not take multiplicity into account, i.e. a web page may be tied to more than one name. At the time, there were altogether roughly five million pages on the Web where the term "Semantic Web" is mentioned. In general this shows that the community is highly visible on the Web: in comparison, there were about 13 million pages with the term "Artificial Intelligence" and about 1.2 million pages with the term "social networks".

[14] These are the rdf-interest, public-swbp-wg, www-webont-wg, public-webont-comments, semantic-web mailing lists, all maintained by the World Wide Web Consortium.

sizes of 66 and 114 respectively, where the membership of the larger core subsumes the smaller core with only three exceptions. (The concentration scores show a fairly even decline from their maxima, which suggests that the clusters outside the core are not significant in size and cohesiveness compared to the core.) The presence of a single, densely connected core also means that the measures of coreness, closeness and betweenness are highly correlated in our network.[15]

There is also compelling evidence that measures of the centrality of actors coincide with real-world status in the Semantic Web community. In Figure 8.1, we have listed the top ranking actors according to our centrality measures and labelled them with their positions held in the community. These positions include chairmanship of the ISWC conference series and editorial board membership at the Journal of Web Semantics[16], the IEEE Intelligent Systems journal[17], and the Applied Ontology journal[18], three main sources of Semantic Web-related publications. We also looked at the chairmanship of working groups of the World Wide Web Consortium (W3C), the most influential standards organization in the Semantic Web area.

Ian Horrocks, Dieter Fensel, Frank van Harmelen and Mark Musen have been the chairs of four international ISWC conferences held up to date (2002-2005). Stefan Decker and Deborah McGuinness were two of the four chairs of the Semantic Web Working Symposium (SWWS) held in 2001. Deborah McGuinness, Frank van Harmelen, Jim Hendler, Jeff Heflin, Ian Horrocks and Guus Schreiber have been co-chairs and/or authors of key documents produced by the Web Ontology (OWL) Working Group of the W3C. Guus Schreiber is also co-chair of Semantic Web Best Practices (SWBP) Working Group, a successor of the OWL group. Jim Hendler is also the current editor-in-chief of the IEEE Intelligent Systems journal. Carole Goble, Tim Finin, Rudi Studer and Stefan Decker have been joint editors-in-chief of the Journal of Web Semantics.

By looking at the table we can note that all of the common measures of centrality assign high scores to actors with real world status, and we can also ascertain that there are no key position holders of the community whose names would not appear among the first 20 ranks (first three columns). It is also clear that most of the influential members of the community are also successful in terms of the number of publications (fourth column). In terms of impact, i.e. the average number of citations per publication, however, there are members of the community who perform higher than the position holders (fifth column). The explanation is that some peripheral members of the community have highly successful publications in related areas

---

[15] In an ideal C/P structure, betweenness correlates highly with closeness, because actors in the core lie on a large portion of the geodesic path connecting peripheral actors. In other words, peripheral actors have to go through actors in the core to reach each other. Similarly, coreness and closeness correlate because actors in the core are close to each other as well as to actors on the periphery, while peripheral actors are only close to actors in the core, but not to each other.

[16] Elsevier, see http://www.websemanticsjournal.org/

[17] IEEE Computer Society, see http://www.computer.org/intelligent/

[18] IOS Press, see http://www.iospress.nl/loadtop/load.php?isbn=15705838

(e.g. agent systems or XML technology). These publications mention the Semantic Web, but are targeted at a different audience than the Semantic Web community.

Indegree		Closeness		Structural Holes		Publications		Impact	
Name	Value	Name	Value	Name	Value	Name	Value	Name	Value
Steffen Staab***	119	Ian Horrocks*	0.476	Ian Horrocks*	113	Steffen Staab***	81	Rakesh Agrawal	684
Dieter Fensel*	114	Steffen Staab***	0.469	Steffen Staab***	105	Dieter Fensel*	69	Daniela Florescu	191
Stefan Decker*	95	Dieter Fensel*	0.468	Dieter Fensel*	99	Mark Musen*, ***	65	David Kinny	180
Enrico Motta	61	Frank v. Harmelen*	0.467	Frank v. Harmelen*	91	Ian Horrocks*	57	Ora Lassila	166
Frank v. Harmelen*	59	Stefan Decker*	0.458	Stefan Decker*	80	Alexander Maedche	53	Honglei Zeng	153
Raphael Volz	59	Rudi Studer***	0.438	Rudi Studer***	63	Rudi Studer***	50	Stuart Nelson	117
Ian Horrocks*	55	Enrico Motta	0.434	Guus Schreiber*,**	48	Amit Sheth	47	Michael Wooldridge	91
Sean Bechhofer	48	Sean Bechhofer	0.427	Enrico Motta	44	Katia Sycara	46	Ramanathan Guha	85
Katia Sycara	48	Carole Goble***	0.425	Raphael Volz	43	Frank v. Harmelen*	42	Donald Kossmann	83
York Sure	47	Ying Ding	0.424	York Sure	43	Carole Goble***	42	Sofia Alexaki	61
Carole Goble***	46	Guus Schreiber*,**	0.421	Tim Finin***	43	Wolfgang Nejdl	42	Laks Lakshmanan	60
Guus Schreiber*,**	46	York Sure	0.408	Sean Bechhofer	42	Stefan Decker*	41	Paolo Atzeni	57
Rudi Studer***	46	Peter Crowther	0.407	Katia Sycara	41	Tim Finin***	41	Michael Uschold	56
Peter Crowther	40	Alain Leger	0.405	Carole Goble***	36	Chen Li	41	Richard Fikes	56
Deborah McGuinness*	37	Raphael Volz	0.405	Ora Lassila	27	Enrico Motta	40	Ray Fergerson	55
Ying Ding	35	Herman ter Horst	0.403	Chen Li	26	Nicola Guarino***	34	Boris Wolf	53
Jean F. Baget	34	Jim Hendler**,***	0.401	Richard Benjamins	25	John Domingue	33	Michael Lincoln	50
Jim Hendler**,***	33	David Trastour	0.401	Matthias Klusch	24	Gio Wiederhold	30	Fereidoon Sadri	46
Pat Hayes	32	Richard Benjamins	0.400	Michael Sintek	23	Anupam Joshi	30	Yannis Labrou	45

Figure 8.1. Network measures reflect real world status. We indicate the chairs of international Semantic Web events (*), the co-chairs of W3C working groups (**) and members of the editorial boards of Semantic Web related journals (***).

Despite the overwhelming presence of the core, we can still observe significant clusters outside the core and there is also some remaining clustering within the core. The analysis of overlapping cliques shows that the largest, most cohesive cluster outside the core is formed by researchers working on semantic-based descriptions of Web Services, in particular members of the DAML-S coalition. The recently popular topic of Semantic Web Services is rather an application of Semantic Web technology as opposed to the more foundational work on ontology languages (RDF, OWL), which are the main shared interest of those in the core. (The clustering could be partly also explained that many of the senior researchers have a background in agent-based systems and have worked together in the past in that area.) To show that this is clearly a topic-based cluster, we have mapped the association of researchers with the concept "DAML-S" against the social network. As Figure 8.2 clearly illustrates, most of these researchers belong to a relatively densely connected subgroup outside the core. (For more information on the method we use to associate researchers with research ideas, please refer to Section 8.2).

8.3.2 Structural and cognitive effects on scientific performance

The social network literature has debated the effect of structure on performance from the perspective of the effects of close interconnectedness versus a sparser network [Bur00]. The basic arguments for the positive effects of a dense interconnected network are that these ties foster trust, identification and these combined lead to an

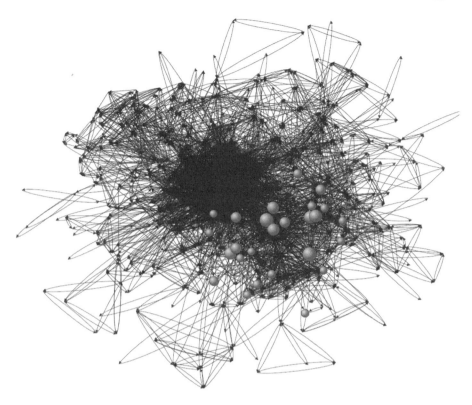

Figure 8.2. Researchers associated with the concept DAML-S form a cluster outside of the core.

easier exchange of information [Col88]. Opposite this argument stands the argument of diversity, by incorporating ties with diverse other groups through the occupation of a structural hole position more new ideas may be encountered and incorporated into one's work [Bur04].

In small scale situations it has been shown that communication ties that bridge a variety of different groups lead to higher performance as did network density [ZR01]. In a study of researchers working on the development of software, centrality measures have been shown to correlate with scientific productivity. An analysis of email messages in this group (about 50 members) showed that centrality correlated strongly with scientific performance [AGC03]. Centrality was found to be partly, but not completely, a consequence of functional characteristics of the researchers in the field. The reason centrality influences performance is suggested to be a consequence of the benefits a specific individual has from being receiver of a larger amount of (diverse) information.

In the following, we formulate our hypotheses concerning the effects of social networks on scientific performance. First, we test for the effect of ego-network structure, namely the size and density of ego networks. (As previously mentioned, the size

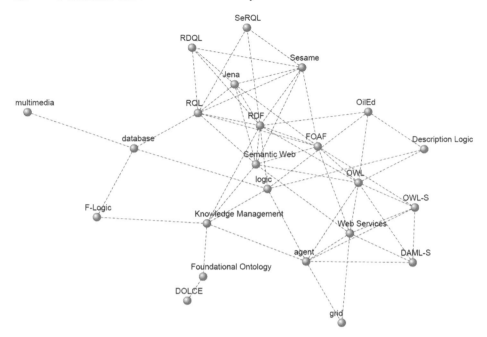

Figure 8.3. The cognitive structure (ontology) of research topics.

of the ego network is also highly correlated with the centrality of the individual.) Second, we look for the additional effects of cognitive diversity in the ego network.

Our primary measure of performance is the number of publications by a given researcher that has received at least a minimum number of citations (dependent variable TOPPUBLI). Based on the general distribution of the number of citations of all publications, we set this minimum at four, excluding 40% of all publications. (The exclusion of minimally cited publications is a commonly used method for filtering out publications that are unlikely to contain innovative results.) Our second, alternative independent variable is the average number of citations per publication (IMPACT). This is a different dimension than the number of publications, because the same impact can be achieved with less or more publications.

We chose the term performance instead of innovativeness when discussing our dependent variables, because publication-based measures offer a very limited way of measuring genuine innovativeness. For example, an article with innovative content may attract few citations if it is published in a journal with limited visibility. On the other hand a survey or review article with minimal innovativeness may attract a large number of citations due to its very nature, especially if published in a high-visibility journal. (These same arguments can also be raised against the usefulness of the impact factor for measuring journal performance.) Nevertheless, publication and citation numbers are still often used in real life to evaluate the performance of researchers.

In reporting our results, we control for experience as we are interested in the unique role of networks in explaining scientific performance. Experience is a personal factor (external to networks) that naturally correlates with both our network variables and our measures of performance.

We measure experience in years of research within the Semantic Web domain, based on the first publication in the area. Therefore, our measure of experience does not include (possibly extensive) research experience in other domains, before or in parallel to involvement in Semantic Web research. Further, we do not consider the case of researchers who give up Semantic Web research (or researcher altogether). However, we expect this to be quite rare at this point in time.

The effect of network structure on performance

A closer examination of Ronald Burt's measure of effective size reveals that a structural hole has two distinct components: the size and efficiency of the ego-network [Bor97]. In fact, in the simplest case of a network with undirected, unvalued ties, Burt's measure turns out to be equal to the number of direct ties of an actor (degree) minus the clustering coefficient scaled by a factor of $n - 1$, where n is the number of nodes.

In the following, we examine the separate contribution of these components.

Hypothesis 1a. The number of ties to alters is positively related to performance.

Experience	All	<= 5	<= 4	<= 3	<= 2
TOPPUBLI	0.665	0.494	0.350	0.299	0.376
sign.	0.000	0.000	0.000	0.000	0.000
df	496	318	248	172	92
IMPACT	0.009	0.286	0.195	0.254	0.269
sign.	0.848	0.000	0.002	0.001	0.009
df	496	318	248	172	92

Table 8.2. DEGREE controlled for NEWEXP

Figure 8.2 shows the partial correlation between the number of ties of an individual and our dependent variables, controlling for experience. The first column of the table shows the results for all cases, while the columns to the right show correlations for sections of the populations with less than five, four, three or two years of experience.[19]

---

[19] If we look at the separate effects of in- and out-degree instead of the full size of the ego network, we find that in-degree is more correlated with the number of publications, while out-degree is more correlated with impact. (Due to limitations of space, we omit the data.) Unreciprocated ties resulting from the analysis of web pages represent a relationship that is more important for the sending actor than the receiving actor.

In general, we can note that the number of ties explains a significant portion of the publication performance measured in the number of publications. A large social network is thus either the cause or the effect of publishing activity.

In the general population, however, degree is not significantly related to impact. In other words, high impact does not necessarily require a large social network and vice versa. However, it also seems that younger researchers are still able to turn the informational advantages of social access into a higher impact of their publications.

Hypothesis 1b. A dense network of ties among alters (closed network) is negatively related to performance.

As expected, clustering in the ego-network of the individual is negatively related to publication performance when measured in the number of publications. A dense network is thus an inefficient network as far as publishing is concerned.

The evidence for the negative effect of clustering on the impact of publications is much weaker. It seems that while clustering negatively impacts the number of publications, it has a much smaller effect on impact. We postulate that publications created in a dense network can still have a relatively high impact within a sub-community of researchers.

Experience	All	$<= 5$	$<= 4$	$<= 3$	$<= 2$
TOPPUBLI	-0.146	-0.129	-0.200	-0.179	-0.239
sign.	0.001	0.017	0.001	0.013	0.015
df	525	342	267	190	101
IMPACT	-0.066	-0.080	-0.072	-0.144	-0.205
sign.	0.128	0.140	0.236	0.047	0.037
df	525	342	267	190	101

Table 8.3. CLUSTER controlled for NEWEXP

The effect of cognitive network structure on performance

Burt's measure of structural holes ignores the actual content that moves through the connection provided. More precisely, Burt assumes that different, unconnected subgroups provide unique knowledge to the broker between them, leading to an advantageous position also in terms of access to knowledge. However, there are more direct ways to establish the link between accessing a diversity of knowledge sources and the performance of the individual.

In a number of previous studies the structural hole argument has been translated to the basic idea of a range of informational sources [RM03]. The manner in which this variety has been constructed differs in the studies that appeared until now. One example is a study in which organizational variety is taken as a proxy for diversity. Baum et al. considered companies, government agencies and firms with different industrial backgrounds as providing variety [BCS00]. In their study on knowledge transfer, Reagans and McEvily used a functional description of roles and variety of expertise [RM03].

In a relatively homogeneous research field, we expect that cognitive differences may drive the process of innovation. We expect that differences in the research profile of the ego and his alters may benefit the individual in addition to the already proven positive effect of a large and efficient social network.[20]

Hypothesis 2a. Access to cognitive diversity through networks is positively related to performance, especially for younger researchers.

In the following, we measure the cognitive diversity in the ego-network by looking at the difference between the research interests of the ego and his or her alters. We will say that a (structural) tie is a content tie, if there is at least one interest of the alter that is not a current research interest of the ego. We measure diversity by counting the number of content ties of an ego (content-degree). We stipulate positive effects on scientific performance in particular for younger researchers. We believe that senior researchers would be less susceptible to content effects as they can rely on junior researchers in their network (positional advantages) and their functional ties for greater publication performance.

Variable	Model 1	Model 2	Model 3	Model 4	Model 5	Model 6
(Constant)	0.736‡	0.883‡	-0.635†	2.452‡	2.946‡	1.106
	(0.000)	(0.000)	(0.041)	(0.000)	(0.000)	(0.265)
DEGREE	0.057‡	-0.036	-0.045	0.144‡	-0.239‡	-0.250‡
	(0.000)	(0.190)	(0.073)	(0.000)	(0.003)	(0.002)
CONTENTD		0.292‡	0.293‡		1.210‡	1.211‡
		(0.000)	(0.000)		(0.000)	(0.000)
NEWEXP			0.737‡			0.893†
			(0.000)			(0.027)
R^2	0.106	0.176	0.316	0.074	0.205	0.228

Figure 8.4. Results of linear regression with the number of publications (TOPPUBLI) as dependent variable (Model 1-3) and the average number of citations (IMPACT) as dependent variable (Model 4-6). N=172, $\dagger p < 0.05$, $\ddagger p < 0.01$

To show the unique contribution of cognitive diversity towards explaining scientific performance, we perform a linear regression with experience, degree and

---

[20] Note that while we take the cognitive structure as a given, related work by Mutschke and Quan Haase looks at social network-based explanations for the development of the cognitive structure of scientific communities [MH01]. The authors suggest that the most connected actors (actors with a higher degree centrality) are likely to work on the more central research themes. Renner hypothesizes that the opposite is also true, namely that new ideas are likely to originate from the most peripheral actors. However, such a hypothesis is difficult to prove or refute in practice: the boundary of a scientific network is always fuzzy and a peripheral actor may have many connections to actors outside of the community under investigation.

content-degree as predictors (independent variables) and the number of publications (TOPPUBLI) and average citation (IMPACT) as the outcome (dependent) variables. (We limit our investigations to scientists with at most four years of experience.) The results, shown in Figure 8.4, indicate that the unique contribution of content degree is significant in both cases. (In fact, in the final models the coefficient of degree is not significantly different from zero any more.) We also find evidence that access to cognitive diversity has a particularly large effect on the impact of the publications.

8.4 Conclusions and Future Work

With our interdisciplinary approach to the study of scientific communities, we are aiming to contribute to both the methods of network analysis and the social theory of research and innovation.

In our methodology, we build on the possibilities offered by Semantic Web technology in the aggregation of the data that we have collected from a number of freely accessible online information sources. The use of freely available electronic data (web pages, publications, mailing lists) not only lowers the cost of studying science communities, but also enables us to significantly increase the scale and longitude of our studies. Further, the reuse of multiple information sources allows us to gain a more complete picture of the community under investigation. Semantic technology is crucial for dealing with the arising heterogeneity.

With respect to our method, we note that it is applicable to a broader range of communities than the one featured in the current study. The few existing comparative studies in webometrics (web-based scientometrics) suggest that real-world networks of largely academic research communities are closely reflected on the Web [HHvdB03, KA04]. This suggest that our system could be used to generate networks of scientific communities in different areas, potentially on much larger scales. With different sources of data, the framework could also be used to visualize communities in areas other than science, e.g. communities of practice in a corporate setting. As our social lives will become even more accurately traceable through ubiquitous, mobile and wearable computers, the opportunities for social science based on electronic data will only become more prominent.

In the above, we have shown the immediate benefits of our methodology by applying it toward a network study of the Semantic Web community. Based on our data set, we have proved the positive effects of a large, efficient (sparse) network on the innovativeness of researchers, confirming the benefits attributed to Structural Holes [Bur04]. We have extended the well-known structural analysis of this scientific community with a novel analysis of the content of relationships. We have shown that diverse cognitive networks have a positive impact on performance beyond the structural effects. Our measure of content degree results to be a much better predictor than the conventional measure of degree for both the number of publications and the average number of citations.

We are planning to extend our work in this direction, e.g. by investigating whether cognitive diversity in the ego network could have a negative effect in cases where the distance between research areas is overly large. We are also developing measures to study the expected positive effect of achieving a diverse cognitive network with a minimal investment in social ties. Planned improvements to our information retrieval methods should also enable us in the future to determine more precisely the interests of individual researchers in the community. Lastly, we are tracking the development of the Semantic Web community over time using our electronic methods of data collection, providing a wealth of data for future work.

9

Ontologies are us: emergent semantics in folksonomy systems

According to the most cited definition of the Semantic Web literature, an ontology is an explicit specification of the conceptualization of a domain [Gru93]. Guarino clarifies Gruber's definition by adding that the AI usage of the term refers to "an engineering artifact, constituted by a specific vocabulary used to describe a certain reality, plus a set of explicit assumptions regarding the intended meaning of the vocabulary words" [Gua98]. An ontology is thus engineered by —but often for— members of a domain by explicating a reality as a set of agreed upon terms and logically-founded constraints on their use.

Conceiving ontologies as engineering artifacts allows us to objectify them, separate them from their original social context of creation and transfer them across the domain. Problems arise with this simplistic view, however, if we consider the temporal extent of knowledge. As the original community evolves through members leaving and entering or changing their commitments, a new consensus may shape up, invalidating the knowledge codified in the ontology.

To address the problem of ontology drift, several authors have suggested *emergent semantics* as a solution [ACMO+04]. The expectation is that the individual interactions of a large number of rational agents would lead to global effects that could be observed as semantics. Ontologies would thus become an emergent effect of the system as opposed to a fixed, limited contract of the majority. While the idea quickly caught on due to the promise of a more scalable and easily maintainable Semantic Web, the agreement so far only extends to the basic conditions under which emergence would take place. The vision is a community of self-organizing, autonomous, networked and localized agents co-operating in dynamic, open environments, each organizing knowledge (e.g. document instances) according to a self-established ontology, establishing connections and negotiating meaning only when it becomes necessary for co-operation. Beyond the reasonable belief that individual actions in such a social-semantic network would lead to ontology emergence, there is a lack of an abstract, empirically verifiable model of such a system that could also explain the process of emergence. Thus there appears to be a large conceptual gap in the literature between the vision and the details of implementations of various semantic architectures based on P2P, Grid, MAS and web technology.

In this Chapter, we take a step back and formulate a generic, abstract model of social-semantic networks (Section 9.1), which we will call the Actor-Concept-Instance model of ontologies. This model is built on an implicit (albeit crucial) realization of emergent semantics, namely that meaning is necessarily dependent on a community of agents. Inspired by social tagging mechanisms, we represent social-semantic networks in the form of a tripartite graph of person, concept and instance associations, extending the traditional concept of ontologies (concepts and instances) with the social dimension. We will show how lightweight ontologies of concepts and social networks of persons emerge from this model through simple graph transformations. In Section 9.2 we will demonstrate these effects based on two independent, large scale data sets. In Section 9.3, we evaluate one of our emergent ontologies (the result of a social-network based ontology extraction process) against the results of the traditional method of ontology extraction based on co-occurrence. Lastly, we conclude with a discussion of future work in Section 9.4.

9.1 A tripartite model of ontologies

While expert systems designed for centralized, controlled environments benefit greatly from the increasing expressivity of ontology languages such as OWL, especially in domains that lend themselves naturally to formalization such as engineering and medicine, lightweight ontologies expressed in RDF(S) have spread and caught on in the loosely controlled, distributed environment of the Web [MA04].

The tendency towards lightweight, easily accessible mechanisms for ontology and metadata creation is best evidenced by the recent appearance of folksonomies. Folksonomy (from folk and taxonomy) is a neologism for a practice of collaborative categorization using freely chosen keywords.[1] Folksonomies (also called social tagging mechanisms) have been implemented in a number of online knowledge sharing environments since the idea was first adopted by the social bookmarking site del.icio.us in 2004.

The idea of a folksonomy is to allow the users to describe a set of shared objects with a set of keywords of their own choice. What the objects are depends on the goal of the site: while bookmarks are the object of classification in del.icio.us, photos are shared in Flickr, scientific publications are tagged in CiteULike, while 43Things allows users to share their goals and plans (e.g. to travel or loose weight) by annotating their descriptions with keywords and connecting users with similar pursuits.[2]

It is important to note that in terms of knowledge representation, the set of these keywords cannot even be considered as vocabularies, the simplest possible form of an ontology on the continuous scale of Smith and Welty [SW01]. First, the set of

---

[1] "A portmanteau of the words folk (or folks) and taxonomy, the term folksonomy has been attributed to Thomas Vander Wal. Taxonomy is from 'taxis' and 'nomos' (from Greek). Taxis means classification. Nomos (or nomia) means management. Folk is people. So folksonomy means people's classification management." Source: Wikipedia.

[2] http://del.icio.us, http://www.flickr.com, http://www.citeulike.org, http://www.43things.com

words is not fixed. In fact, the users form no explicit agreement at all about the use of words, not even in the form of incremental, need-based, local and temporary agreements suggested by the research on emergent semantics [ACMO$^+$04]. Yet, the basic conditions of emergent semantics are given and as we will show there is semantics emerging at the scale of these systems. Second, although we use the term concept in the following, it is clear that there is no one-to-one correspondence between concepts and keywords. It is not always possible for the users to express a complex concept with a single keyword and thus they may use more than one tag to express the concept association that the item brings up in them. Lastly, the instances of folksonomies are instances only in the sense of classification.

In order to model networks of folksonomies at an abstract level, we will represent such a system as a tripartite graph with hyperedges. The set of vertices is partitioned into the three (possibly empty) disjoint sets $A = \{a_1, \ldots, a_k\}$, $C = \{c_1, \ldots, c_l\}$, $I = \{i_1, \ldots, i_m\}$ corresponding the set of actors (users), the set of concepts (tags, keywords) and the set of objects annotated (bookmarks, photos etc.) In effect, we extend the traditional bipartite model of ontologies (concepts and instances) by incorporating actors in the model.

In a social tagging system, users tag objects with concepts, creating ternary associations between the user, the concept and the object. Thus the folksonomy is defined by a set of annotations $T \subseteq A \times C \times I$. Such a network is most naturally represented as hypergraph with ternary edges, where each edge represents the fact that a given actor associates a certain instance with a certain concept. In particular, we define the representing hypergraph of a folksonomy T as a (simple) tripartite hypergraph $H(T) = \langle V, E \rangle$ where $V = A \cup C \cup I$, $E = \{\{a, c, i\} \mid (a, c, i) \in T\}$.

Tripartite graphs and hyperedges are rather cumbersome to work with. However, we can reduce such a hypergraph into three bipartite graphs (also called two-mode graphs) with regular edges. These three graphs model the associations between actors and concepts (graph AC), concepts and objects (graph CO) and actors and instances (graph AI). For example, the AC valued bipartite graph is defined as follows:

$AC = \langle A \times C, E_{ac} \rangle$, $E_{ac} = \{(a, c) \mid \exists i \in I : (a, c, i) \in E\}$, $w : E \rightarrow \mathbb{N}$, $\forall e = (a, c) \in E_{ac}$, $w(e) := |\{i : (a, c, i) \in E)\}|$

In words, the bipartite graph AC links the persons to the concepts that they have used for tagging at least one object. Each link is weighted by the number of times the person has used that concept as a tag. This kind of graph is known in the social network analysis literature as an affiliation network [WFIG94], linking people to affiliations with weights corresponding to the strength of the affiliation. An affiliation network can be used to generate two simple, weighted graphs (one-mode networks) showing the similarities between actors and events, respectively. (At this point it is recommended to dichotomize the graph by applying some threshold.)

The process of folding a bipartite graph (the extraction of a one-mode network) can be most easily understood by looking at the matrix form of the graph. Let's denote this matrix as $\mathbf{B} = \{b_{ij}\}$. As discussed before, $b_{ij} = 1$ if actor a_i is affiliated with concept c_j. We define a new matrix $\mathbf{S} = \{s_{ij}\}$, where $s_{ij} = \sum_{x=1}^{k} b_{ix} b_{xj}$. In matrix notation $\mathbf{S} = \mathbf{B}\mathbf{B}'$. This matrix, known as the co-affiliation matrix, defines a social network that connects people based on shared affiliations. In our case the links are between people who have used the same concepts with weights showing the number of concepts they have used in common. The dual matrix, $\mathbf{O} = \mathbf{B}'\mathbf{B}$ is a similar graph showing the association of concepts, weighted by the number of people who have used both concepts as tags. Note that in both graphs the diagonal of the corresponding matrices contains the counts of how many concepts or persons a given person or concept was affiliated with in the bipartite graph. We can use these values to normalize the association weights (e.g. by calculating the Jaccard-coefficient) and then filtering again based on the relative weights. In case of the $\mathbf{S}$ social network, for example, this means that we have taken into account the relative importance of the link between persons.

In summary, the AC graph, the affiliation network of people and concepts can be folded into two graphs: a social network of users based on overlapping sets of objects and a lightweight ontology of concepts based on overlapping sets of communities. Thus in this simple model, social networks and semantics are just flip-sides of the same coin: the original bipartite graph contains all the information to generate these networks, while it is not possible to re-generate the original graph from them.

The other two bipartite graphs that we derived from the original tripartite model can also be folded into one-mode networks in a similar fashion. In particular, the CI graph leads to another semantic network, where the links between terms are weighted by the number of instances that are tagged with both terms. This type of semantic network is of a much more familiar kind: it mimics the basic method applied in text mining, where terms are commonly associated by their co-occurrence in documents. The AI graph results in another social network of persons, where the weight of a pair is given by the number of items they have both tagged. We also get a network of instances, with associations showing the number of people who have tagged a given pair of instances.

In the following we focus our attention to the two lightweight ontologies based on overlapping communities (O_{ac}) and overlapping sets of instances (O_{ci}).[3] The analysis of the emergent social networks is outside the scope of the current Chapter.

9.1.1 Ontology enrichment

The community-based lightweight ontology O_{ac} that we extract from the affiliation network is rather peculiar from a knowledge representation perspective. Unlike the manually constructed thesauri known in the Semantic Web literature (such as Word-Net [Fel98]), it more closely resembles the association thesauri studied in linguistics. An example is the Edinburgh Associative Thesaurus (EAT)[4], which was collected in 1973 via an experiment using a group of university students as subjects [KAMP73]. The experiment consisted of handing a list of words to students who were instructed to write down against each stimulus word the first word it made them think of, working as quickly as possible. The obtained words were used in a next round of the

---

[3] Recall that $O_{ac} = \mathbf{B}'\mathbf{B}$, where $\mathbf{B} = \{b_{ij}\}$ with $b_{ij} = 1$ if actor a_i is affiliated with concept c_j; and $O_{ci} = \mathbf{D}'\mathbf{D}$, where $\mathbf{D} = \{d_{pq}\}$ with $d_{pq} = 1$ if concept c_p is used to tag the instance i_q.

[4] Consult the EAT online at http://www.eat.rl.ac.uk/

experiment. (The cycle was repeated three times, by then the number of different responses was so large that they could not all be re-used as stimuli.)

Our associative ontology is similar to the EAT in that the weights of the links between terms are expressed as the number of people who make that association. The difference is that in the EAT collection, people are prompted explicitly to create links between concepts, while we deduce such links by observing tagging behavior. More importantly, however, both methods have the crucial property that the result clearly depends on the community of people who take part in experiment. The method of ontology engineering is particularly revealing, because once the initial set of words is selected there is only one parameter to the process: the population chosen. (In particular, the knowledge engineer has no other role than handing out questionnaires and collecting the responses.) Some of the results are likely to hold for other communities (like the overwhelming reaction of saying *Noah* when hearing the word *ark*), but many of the aggregated associations are driven by the collective mind set of the subjects of the experiment. A collective mindset that is likely shaped by the well-known law of community formation: interaction creates similarity, while similarity creates interaction.

We can not only repeat the experiments with different communities, but given some information about the social structure of the community, we could also extract local ontologies by limiting our tripartite ontology to the associations of a certain sub-community of actors. Note that this is the principle of locality in action, one of the expected hallmarks of emergent semantics [ACMO+04]. We will demonstrate this effect in Section 6.2 where we extract an ontology of research topics in the Semantic Web domain.

In modern terms, the EAT is an emergent ontology based on empirical data. Unlike ontologies that are meant to codify fixed agreements, all graphs that we derive are also emergent in the sense of evolving dynamically with the Actor-Concept-Instance network. Changes in the original network can occur in a number of ways. Users may join or leave the community, changing the set of actors. The focus of the community may shift, affecting the set of items tagged and the concepts used. Last, the understanding and use of terms may change, reflecting in the set of associations between concepts and instances created by the users.

Although our association networks are very simple ontological structures, there are several opportunities of enriching them with additional semantics. We start by observing that a significant drawback of the EAT is the heterogeneity of terms. Our emergent ontologies are also likely to contain a diverse mixture of specific and generic terms, i.e. terms that we can unambiguously place in a clearly defined context (e.g. instances such as *Peter*) and terms that can occur in multiple contexts of use (e.g. *war*). From a network view, general words are therefore more likely to bridge different clusters of words, while specific terms are expected to exhibit a dense clustering in their neighborhood. This suggest an opportunity to distinguish between these two categories by computing the *clustering coefficient*, the *(local) betweenness centrality* or the *network constraint* on our terms (see Chapter 2). These well-known ego-network measures of Social Network Analysis are readily available in popular network analysis packages such as Pajek [BM98] and UCINET [BEF02]. Based on the same observation, we also expect that clustering algorithms can help us in finding synonym sets of the more specific terms. There is a wide range of clustering algorithms available in the above mentioned network analysis packages, based on different definitions of cohesiveness.

We may also extract broader/narrower term relations typical of thesauri using set theory. In an ideal situation, we would say that Concept A is a super-concept of Concept B if the set of entities (persons or items) classified under B is a subset of the entities under A ($B \subseteq A \leftrightharpoons A \cap B = B$). We might also add the criterion that the set of A should be significantly larger then the set of B, i.e. $|B|/|A| < k$ for some value of k. In principle, such an ordering allows us to define a Galois lattice using the subset relation. In practice, such a lattice would be very sparse (considering the number of entities and the number of possible subsets over them), so we will approximate this method by looking for near-perfect overlaps, i.e. $|A \cap B|/|B| < n$ for some value of n. Finding appropriate values for the k, n parameters of the model is the task of the researcher.

The reader should note that the meaning of these broader/narrower relations are very different, depending on whether we analyze the O_{ci} or the O_{ac} ontology. In the first case, the interpretation is that all (or most) of the items classified under the narrower term also appear under the broader term. In other words, what we extract is a classification hierarchy. In the second case, the meaning is that all the persons associated with the narrower term are also associated with the broader term. In other words, we extract a hierarchy based on sub-community relationships.

9.2 Case studies

In the following, we demonstrate the broad applicability of the Actor-Concept-Instance model of ontologies by looking at two different semantic social networks. Our first data set comes from an existing web-based social bookmarking tool called del.icio.us (Section 9.2.1), while the second case is built on synthetic data obtained by using web mining techniques (Section 9.2.2). We will show how the abstract model applies to the particular cases and demonstrate our method of ontology emergence based on the graph transformation described above.

9.2.1 Ontology emergence in del.icio.us

According to the definition of author Joshua Schachter, del.icio.us is a social bookmarking tool.[5] Much like the similar functions of browsers, del.icio.us allows users to manage a personal collection of links to web sites and describe those links with one or more keywords. Unlike stand-alone tools, del.icio.us is a web-based system that allows users to share bookmarks with each other. Bookmarks can be browsed by user, by keywords (tags) or by a combination of both criteria. Further, the user interface encourages exchange by showing how bookmarks are linked together via

---

[5] See http://del.icio.us

users and tags. In terms of the Actor-Concept-Instance model, registered users of del.icio.us are the actors who create or remove associations between terms and web-pages (instances) by adding or deleting bookmarks.

From the perspective of studying emergence, del.icio.us is remarkable for the dynamics of its user base. The young, technologically aware community gathering around the site closely follows the latest news and trends in web technology as well as the evolving vocabulary of the field. Beyond technology, del.icio.us users also post bookmarks related to current topics in politics, media, business and entertainment. The emphasis on timeliness is reinforced by listing bookmarks in a backward-chronological order as it is typical for blogs.

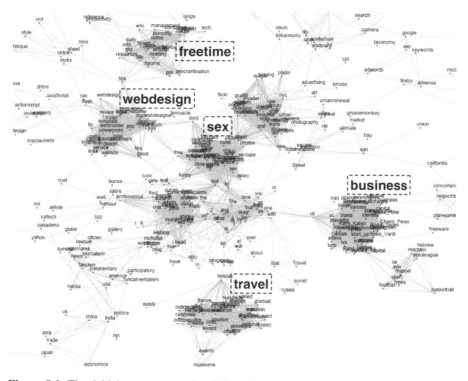

Figure 9.1. The del.icio.us tags associated through co-occurrence on items and the clusters emerging.

The process of annotation is made as easy as possible. A single textbox allows users to enter a set of words without any recommendations made by the system. On the downside, this means that synonyms are common in the folksonomy, e.g. "semanticweb", "semweb" are different keywords. Ambiguity is also present, since users often pick overly general terms to describe items (such as "web", "tool" and other popular terms). Further, users often make the mistake to enter key phrases instead of keywords (e.g. "Bill Clinton"), where the words are subsequently parsed

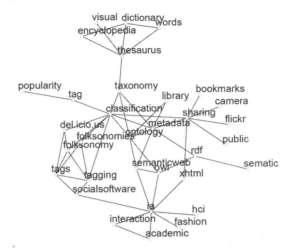

Figure 9.2. Detail view of the del.icio.us tags associated through users: a 3-neighborhood of the term ontology. Note that the term *sematic* is correctly associated, despite the obvious typo.

as separate tags ("Bill" and "Clinton"); or they escape the one-word-only limitation by concatenating words. Case sensitivity and the use of punctuation marks further pollute the del.icio.us namespace. However, at the scale of system (over 30 thousand registered users in December, 2004) the imperfections of tagging are reduced to an acceptable level. On the plus side, users benefit from instant gratification in the form of linkage to other relevant, timely, socially-ranked posts.

del.icio.us exposes tagging data in the form of RSS feeds, which we have collected using a focused RDF crawler. The crawler was initialized with the single most popular tag ("web") and have traversed the RSS network in a breadth-first-search manner, following links to tags mentioned in the descriptions of items. The sample data that we collected —over a million triples of RDF— was stored using the Sesame storage and query facility [BKvH02]. The sample represents 51852 unique annotations of 30790 URLs, by 10198 persons using 29476 unique tags.[6]

Next, we have generated both the Actor-Concept and Concept-Instance graphs. In order to scale down the data set (without loosing much information) and to avoid strong associations with a low support we have filtered out those entities that had only a minimal number of connections, i.e. those tags that had less than ten items classified under them and those persons who have used less than five concepts.

Subsequently, we have extracted the above mentioned two kinds of ontologies by folding these graphs using the network analysis package Pajek. As a reminder, the first ontology (O_{ac}) is based on actors sharing concepts as interests, i.e. the associations reflect overlapping communities of interests, while the second network (O_{ci}) reflects the co-occurrence of tags on items. We have filtered the networks based on

---

[6] This is a sample of the complete data set because the RSS feeds expose only the latest thirty items for each tag. Further, we stopped crawling after reaching this size. To our knowledge this is still the largest ontology annotation data set ever studied.

the absolute strength of associations. Next, we applied geometric normalization to the resulting graphs and filtered edges again based on the relative strength of the associations. We have chosen the thresholds in such a way that we obtain networks of equal size (438 concepts). Figure 9.1 shows a high level view of the O_{ci} graph, Figure 9.2 shows a detailed view of the O_{ac} graph.

The results show clear evidence of emerging semantics in both cases, but the networks we obtain still show very different pictures. With an equal number of vertices, the densities of the two networks are quite different (0.01 for the O_{ci} network, 0.006 for the O_{ac} network), and so is the amount of clustering present (the average clustering coefficients are 0.2 and 0.03, respectively).

The selection of concepts in the two networks is also very different: only 64 concepts are present in both networks of the total of 438 nodes in each graph. (A sample is included in Table 9.1.) A closer look reveals that the concepts within the clusters of the first network are often very specialized terms, while those in between the clusters are overly general terms. A look at the terms with the lowest clustering and highest betweenness centrality confirms this hypothesis. The top five terms with highest betweenness are *up, cool, hot, in, to*. Noticeable also is that the terms with the highest clustering and lowest network constraint are those related to sex. As mentioned before, the second network shows much less clustering: overly general and overly specific terms are both missing.

O_{ci}	*/GoogleHacks, _0, 04, 1, 2, 2005, 3g, a, A, a9, Aaron_Mankovski, actona, actors, adult, aduva, advice, ajax, all, Allegrini, america, an, and, angeles, apparel, Apple, as, assembly, attempt, attention, attention.xml, aviv, axml, azur
O_{ac}	.net, 3d, 43folders, academic, accessibility, acronym, actionscript, activism, ad, ads, adsense, advertising, advice, advisories, adwords, agile, ajax, amazon, america, analysis, and, Apache, apache, api, app, apple, application, architecture, archive, Art, art, articles, asia, astronomy, atlas, Audio

Table 9.1. Terms starting with "A" or "a" in the two lightweight ontologies generated from the del.icio.us network.

The clue to the different qualities of these networks lies in the difference in the way associations are created between the concepts. In the first case, there exists a strong association between concepts if they share a large percentage of items, *independent of the number of users interested in them and regardless whether these associations were added by the same users or not*. The resulting distribution of association weights shows a very slow decline, the average weight is fairly high. In the second case, there is a strong association in the network if two concepts share a large fraction of the users among them, *independent of the number of instances associated with them and regardless whether these terms were added to the same instances or not*. The resulting weight distribution shows a very steep decline, the average weight is fairly low.

This suggests that the first network (O_{ci}) is more appropriate for concept mining. In fact, a λ-set analysis performed with UCINET on a slightly larger network of

travel	cote, provence, villa, azur, mas, holiday, vacation, tourism, france, heritage
business	venture_capital, enterprise, up, start, venture, newspaper, capital, Segev, pitango, vc
free time	procrastination, info, advice, gtd, life, notes, planning, daily, reading, forums
sex	hot, to, street, pictures, on, photos, free, celeb, adult, lesbian
web design	design, designer, webdesign, premium, logo, logos, dreamweaver, templates, best, good

Table 9.2. The five main clusters of interest based on the Concept-Object network.

Broader	Narrower
rss	atom
cmyk	rgb
cell	umts, wcdma, ev-do
phone	cell
ajax	json
xml	xslt
rdf	owl
flickr	gmail, picasa
ruby	rails
mac	iphoto
java	j2ee
google	gds
search	a9, engine
linux	ubuntu, gnome
flash	actionscript
flickr	lickr, photoset
javascript	xmlhttprequest, dom, sarissa

Table 9.3. Broader/narrower term relations in the technology domain, based on sub-communities in del.icio.us.

751 concepts resulted in meaningful clusters of specific terms, representing various domains of interest in the del.icio.us community. At a level of $\lambda = 20$, we found 5 cohesive groups of concepts that we identified as interests related to travel, business, free time, sex and web design (see Figure 9.2 and Table 9.2).

However, the O_{ci} semantic network ignores the relevance of the individual concepts from the user perspective and as such it gives an inaccurate picture of the community. Concepts related to sex, for example, get a misleadingly high centrality in the network due to the specificity and extent of the vocabulary used to describe sex-related sites. On the other hand, the more evenly distributed community-based network (O_{ac}) contains concepts that are actually important to del.icio.us users. These concepts almost all come from the computer domain, the apparent core interest of users. The strength of links between the concepts are also a more accurate representation of reality as they are not biased by the actual number of items that have been tagged with them.

The ignorance of the item-based extraction method towards the number of users also makes it problematic to extract taxonomic relations. Namely, many of the relations we extracted are based on the word usage of a small number of users, and in the worst case a single user. The Concept-Actor ontology yields much more easily interpretable results, shown in Figure 9.3. As discussed before, these are sub-community relations: the community associated with a narrower term is a sub-community of the community associated with the broader term. Nevertheless, even here we find an association created by a single story marked by a large number of users. This suggests an improvement to our original method, namely filtering out concepts that have only a limited number of items or persons associated to them. We take this into account as we move on to generalize our method to community-based ontology extraction from Web pages.

We conclude by noting the potential application of the results to improving del.icio.us itself, e.g. by offering search and navigation based on broader/narrower terms. Considering the dynamics of the community and the extent of neologism, the ontologies emerging from folksonomies such as del.icio.us also have a large potential for enriching established, but slowly evolving linguistic ontologies such as WordNet [Fel98].

9.2.2 Community-based ontology extraction from Web pages

Folksonomies such as del.icio.us are effective, because they attract sizeable sub-communities of users pursuing similar interests. Nevertheless, the community of del.icio.us is still a niche compared to the general web population, just as the number of web sites tagged is only a fraction of the number of pages on the Web.

We would like to show in the following that even without explicitly assigned tags, it is possible to extend the idea of community-based ontology extraction to the Web. Let's suppose that we have a selected a community, whose members will play the role of Actors in our model, and we have prepared a list of terms whose associations we are interested in. The instances of our model are the pages of the Web. Further, we assume that a web page is tagged by a concept if the concept occurs on the page.

Based on these assumptions, the Concept-Instance ontology is straightforward to create: we can use a search engine to obtain page counts for all pairs of concepts and then normalize by their separate page counts. This is the basic co-occurrence analysis method of text mining.

Generating the Actor-Concept ontology requires another broad assumption. We will say that there is an association between a concept, a person and a web page if the name of the person and the label of the concept co-occur on the page. This association represents a weaker commitment than in the case of folksonomies, because it is not guaranteed that the association is made *by* the person. Nonetheless, we can now generate the bipartite graph of persons and concepts by measuring the association using page counts from the search engine.

First, we measure the association between a person (e.g. *"Peter Mika"*) and a concept (e.g. *"Semantic Web"*) by submitting a boolean query combining the two terms (e.g. *"Peter Mika" AND "Semantic Web"*). We normalize the result with the number of pages where the concept occurs. We then repeat this with the same concept and the names of all other members of the target community. We calculate the mean strength of association with the concept of *"Semantic Web"*. Lastly, we associate those members of the community with this concept whose association strength is at least one standard deviation higher than the mean. (Note that this is a slightly more sophisticated method of filtering than a general threshold.) We can now fold the bipartite graph of actors and concepts to obtain the O_{ac} ontology.

Our method of community-based ontology extraction have been implemented as part of the Flink system (see Section 6.2). The system is a web-based presentation of the social networks and research interests of Semantic Web researchers. The community of researchers represented in Flink includes all authors, program committee members and organizers of all past international Semantic Web events from 2001, altogether 607 persons. The system extracts the social network of researchers as described in [Mik04] and associates them with research topics using the search engine Google. [7]

Flink can also be used to perform co-occurrence analysis and generate the O_{ci} ontology. We improve the basic method by adding the disambiguation term *"Semantic Web" OR ontology* to the queries sent to the search engine, limiting the items returned to those relating to the Semantic Web.

The resulting ontological structures are not included here due to limitations of space, but we strongly encourage the reader to consult them online[8]. To make the networks comparable, we have included only the 100 strongest associations in each network. Again, we see a significant difference in the set of concepts remaining in the networks. Namely, from the original 60 terms (selected manually from the proceedings of the ISWC events), the method of text mining found the strongest associations between more general terms. Specific concepts related to the Semantic Web seem to float to the periphery and are misplaced in general. For example, the term *FOAF* is related to *XML* and *OWL-S*, technologies not directly related to FOAF. *Annotation* is related to *alignment* and *databases*. The term *ontology* is associated, among others, with *HTML*, *XML* and *databases*, concepts not directly related to the understanding of ontologies in the Semantic Web community.

The O_{ac} association network represents a clear improvement in these respects. The method found correct associations between domain specific concepts. For example, the term *FOAF* is linked here to *Redland* and *Sesame*, the triple stores pre-

---

[7] Note that the page counts returned by Google violate some of the assumptions of our set theoretic interpretation of boolean logic. For example, OR queries in Google typically return less items than the terms separately, i.e it is possible that $|"A" \wedge "B"| < |"A"|$. Further, the boolean operators are not symmetric: $|"A" \wedge "B"| \neq |"B" \wedge "A"|$.

[8] http://www.cs.vu.nl/~pmika/research/iswc2005/

ferred by FOAF developers for their scalability. Terms related to ontology languages (*OWL*, *RDF*, *OIL*, *DAML+OIL*, *ontology languages* etc.) are correctly clustered together, just as the technologies related to ontology storage (query languages, triple stores), with terms related to ontology development (*OilEd*, *OntoEdit*, *ontology development*) connecting the two clusters. More general technologies are also placed correctly in context, i.e. corresponding to the way they are used in the Semantic Web. For example, *NLP* is tied to the notions of *annotation* and *ontology learning*.

The difference in the node sets can be explained in a similar way as in the case of del.icio.us: the O_{ci} network ignores the overall relevance of these concepts to the Semantic Web community. Considering the associations, we believe that there is another effect in play. By querying the associations of persons first and then linking concepts through overlapping communities, we simulate the effect of first asking the members of the community to associate themselves with certain research interests and then relating these interests through overlapping communities. Overlapping communities turn out to be a stronger link than overlapping sets of web pages. A possible explanation is that even after including the disambiguating term in the query, the search engine still suffers from *knowing too much*, blurring away community-specific interpretations.

9.3 Evaluation

In absence of a golden standard, evaluating the results of ontology learning or ontology mapping is a difficult task: inevitably, it requires consulting the community or communities whose conceptualizations are being learned or mapped. In order to evaluate our results, we have thus approached in email 61 researchers active in the Semantic Web domain, most of whom are members of the ISWC community and many of them are in the graph-theoretical core of the community[9]. The single question we asked was *In terms of the associations between the concepts, which ontology of Semantic Web related concepts do you consider more accurate?* Lacking a yardstick, there is no principled correct answer to this question that we expected to receive. Instead, we were interested to find out if there is a majority opinion emerging as an answer and if yes, which of the two ontologies (produced by the two different methods) would that majority accept as more accurate.

Many respondents expressed difficulty in answering the question due to the (intentional) lack of further explanations or instructions, e.g. what the associations mean, but also due to the very different node sets of the two semantic networks. Nonetheless, out of the 33 respondents only three persons were not willing to express any preference (even if a slight one) for one network or the other. 23 respondents were members of the ISWC community and 15 of them belong to the core of the community.

---

[9] We performed a categorical core/periphery analysis with correlation optimization using UCINET 6 based on the connected part of the Flink social network data (N=528), available at `http://prauw.cs.vu.nl:8080/flink/graph`. The results show a clear C/P structure with 63 persons in the core and 465 persons on the periphery.

	N	O_{ac}	O_{ci}	Ratio	Sign.
All	30	22	8	73.3%	0.0055
ISWC	23	18	5	78.3%	0.0040
ISWC-core	15	13	2	86.7%	0.0032

Table 9.4. Results for the comparison of the community-based (O_{ac}) and item-based (O_{ci}) ontology extraction methods.

The distribution of the answers for the various subgroups are summarized in Table 9.4. First, taking all responses into account, we can conclude that the participants consider the O_{ac} network as a more accurate representation of associations between the concepts than the O_{ci} network (the result is significant at a level of $p = 0.01$). The majority vote becomes even stronger if we consider only the members of the ISWC community, i.e. the persons whose name has been used to extract the semantic network. Thus as a second finding we can also conclude that the O_{ac} network is considered more accurate particularly by those whose names were used in the extraction process. The results become even more conclusive if we only consider the votes from the core members of the community. Based on this finding and assuming a continuum, we can state that the O_{ac} network better reflects the conceptualizations of those closer to the core of the community. Combined together, our findings confirm that the O_{ac} network better reflects the conceptualizations of those involved in Semantic Web research, and this holds especially for those most actively involved in Semantic Web research.

9.4 Conclusions and Future Work

The Semantic Web is a web for machines, but the process of creating and maintaining it is a social one. Although machines are helpful in manipulating symbols according to pre-defined rules, only the users of the Semantic Web have the necessary interpretive and associative capability for creating and maintaining ontologies. Ontology creation necessitates a social presence as it requires an actor to reliably predict how other members of the community would interpret the symbols of an ontology based on their limited description. With incorporating the notion of semantics into the web architecture, we have thus made the users of the system a critical part of the design.

We have argued elsewhere for a three layered view of the Semantic Web, namely the layer of communities and their relations, the layer of semantics (ontologies and their relations) and the layer of content items and their relations (the hypertext Web) [Mik05b]. In this Chapter, we have formalized this view as a tripartite model of ontologies with three different classes of nodes (actors, concepts, and instances) and hyperedges representing the commitment of a user in terms of classifying an instance as belonging to a certain concept. We have shown the usefulness of this model by generating two kinds of association networks: the well-known co-occurrence network of ontology learning and a novel semantic network based on community relationships.

Among the future work is the study of the two emerging social networks, based on object and concept overlaps.

The general advantage of the incorporation of the social context into the representation of ontologies is the possibility of studying emergence from user actions. Emergent semantics is likely to best complement well-established, but slowly evolving ontologies such as WordNet [Fel98], which lack the associative component.[10] We have also compared the two networks based on object and person overlap and noted the advantage of the second network: the possibility to extract semantics pertinent to a sub-community of the user network. In a sense, this is the opposite of mining general knowledge from search engines as in the work of Cimiano et al. or Etzioni et al. [CHS04, ECD+04]. In comparison to these systems, our community-based ontology extraction has a great potential in extracting ontologies that more closely match the conceptualization of a particular community. For example, when trying to find associations between concepts used by the Web Services community, it is natural to consider only the associations created (explicitly or implicitly) by those involved in developing Web Services. As we have shown, by using this method the resulting ontology is more likely to be accepted as accurate by the community itself.

It seems that ontologies are us: inseparable from the context of the community in which they are created and used. A greater acknowledgement of this state —by incorporating the link between actors and concepts into the model of ontologies— have only benefits to bring in terms of more meaningful and easily maintainable conceptual structures. While we are only at the beginning of realizing these benefits, there is a clear magic as we see semantics emerge from the individual actions of a community at work.

---

[10] For example, according to WordNet the distance of the terms *Noah* and *ark* is quite large: their closest common ancestor in the hypernym tree is *object, physical object*. Yet, the Edinburgh master's students overwhelmingly associate the term *Noah* with *ark* and vice versa. The association is so strong in fact (78 and 79 percent of all terms mentioned in response, respectively) that it is safe to say that in the mind of the students these terms are solely defined by each other, in the context of the biblical story of Noah's ark.

Part IV

Conclusions

The perfect storm

Hurricane Katrina formed as Tropical Depression Twelve over the southeastern Bahamas on August 23, 2005 as the result of an interaction of a tropical wave and the remains of Tropical Depression Ten. The system was upgraded to tropical storm status on the morning of August 24 and at this point, the storm was given the name Katrina. The tropical storm continued to move towards Florida, and became a hurricane only two hours before it made landfall between Hallandale Beach and Aventura, Florida on the morning of August 25. The storm weakened over land, but it regained hurricane status about one hour after entering the Gulf of Mexico. The storm rapidly intensified after entering the Gulf, partly because of the storm's movement over the warm waters of the Loop Current. On August 27, the storm reached Category 3 intensity on the Saffir-Simpson Hurricane Scale, becoming the third major hurricane of the season (see Figure 10.1). An eyeball replacement cycle disrupted the intensification, but caused the storm to nearly double in size. Katrina again rapidly intensified, attaining Category 5 status on the morning of August 28 and reached its peak strength at 1:00 p.m. CDT that day, with maximum sustained winds of 175 mph (280 km/h) and a minimum central pressure of 902 mbar. The pressure measurement made Katrina the fourth most intense Atlantic hurricane on record at the time, only to be surpassed by Hurricanes Rita and Wilma later in the season; it was also the strongest hurricane ever recorded in the Gulf of Mexico at the time as well (a record also later broken by Rita).

By August 26, the possibility of unprecedented cataclysm was already being considered. Many of the computer models had shifted the potential path of Katrina 150 miles westward from the Florida Panhandle, putting the city of New Orleans right in the center of their track probabilities; the chances of a direct hit were forecast at 17%, with strike probability rising to 29% by August 28. This scenario was considered a potential catastrophe because 80% of the city of New Orleans and 20% of the New Orleans metropolitan area is below sea level along Lake Pontchartrain.

Figure 10.1. Satellite image of Hurricane Katrina on August 27, 2005. This image also depicts a 3-day average of actual sea surface temperatures for the Caribbean Sea and the Atlantic Ocean, from August 25-27, 2005. Courtesy of NASA.

At a news conference at 10:00 a.m. on August 28, shortly after Katrina was upgraded to a Category 5 storm, New Orleans mayor Ray Nagin ordered the first ever mandatory evacuation of the city, calling Katrina "a storm that most of us have long feared". The city government also established several "refuges of last resort" for citizens who could not leave the city, including the massive Louisiana Superdome, which sheltered approximately 26,000 people and provided them with food and water for several days as the storm came ashore.
Source: Wikipedia, the online encyclopedia.[1]

10.1 Looking back: the story of Katrina PeopleFinder

Hurricane Katrina was the deadliest US hurricane since 1928 and the costliest of all times. However, Hurricane Katrina was not only the perfect storm in a meteorological sense but in the way it exposed the failings of our infrastructure in times of emergencies. While the weaknesses of the physical infrastructure and the failings of the organizational structures of the emergency management are well documented, much less has been told about the story of the inadequacy of the current Web in dealing with emergency.

---

[1] http://en.wikipedia.org/w/index.php?title=Hurricane_Katrina&oldid=78783928

We are all familiar with the way levees and floodwalls designed to protect New Orleans have been breached, leaving 80% of New Orleans under water. Just as well known are the failures of the rescue operations which have left people stranded on roofs for days. Those who reached the packed Superdome waited in almost complete darkness and without access to food, water, sanitation or fresh air. Those who survived described the Superdome as a concentration camp where rape, riots, armed violence and suicide were the order of the day.

Over time, however, the evacuees of the SuperDome joined the ranks of a total of 1.1 million who were displaced by Hurricane Katrina and moved to other shelters in the region. Shelters that varied in size from large to small, from the Houston Astrodome —where some 125 000 found temporary refuge— to housings set up in schools, churches and private homes.

However, it was unavoidable in the chaos of rescue and evacuation that families and friends were torn apart. As all of us would do the first thing the victims of Hurricane Katrina have done after finding shelter is to seek out their missing loved ones. As central coordination was lacking on the ground and communication options were limited, they invariably turned to the Internet for doing so.

Inevitably, evacuees have logged on to a number of different web sites for posting their notifications of missing persons and looking for survivors. The Mississippi coast area newspaper, the Gulf Coast News, for example started a Katrina survivor database as it was the natural source of news for the region.[2] Katrina survivor notices have also started to appear *en masse* on national bulletin boards such as Craigslist[3]. CNN started to collect submissions of notices from its viewers.[4] New discussion lists and forums for Katrina survivors have popped up by the minute (see Figure 10.2).

The problem with the resulting situation was blatantly apparent: how would family members, friend and co-workers find each other if they are all looking for information at different sites? The situation threatened to complement the physical suffering of the survivors with the emotional toll of being separated from their loved ones. Traditional search engines offered little help as they typically index information on a monthly basis, much too infrequent for websites that are updated by the minute. A central website put up by the authorities on time could have funnelled much of the information pouring in to a single database. But it could not have fully prevented the scenario that emerged. In fact, the diversity of sources is the result of those features of the Web that we cherish the most: a scalable, distributed design without a single point of failure that is open end-to-end and not controlled by any single authority.

In the absence of government action and just a few days after the disaster it was a volunteer effort that made the crucial steps toward a solution. A core group of bloggers and activists (most of whom have known each other from the Web and their

---

[2] This database is still online at the time of writing and contains 77,000 records, see `http://www.gulfcoastnews.net/katrina/status.aspx`.

[3] `http://neworleans.craigslist.org/laf/`

[4] At one time, CNN's Katrina Safe List contained over a thousand pages of messages of safe and missing, although it has been taken off-line since then. See `http://www.cnn.com/SPECIALS/2005/hurricanes/list/`

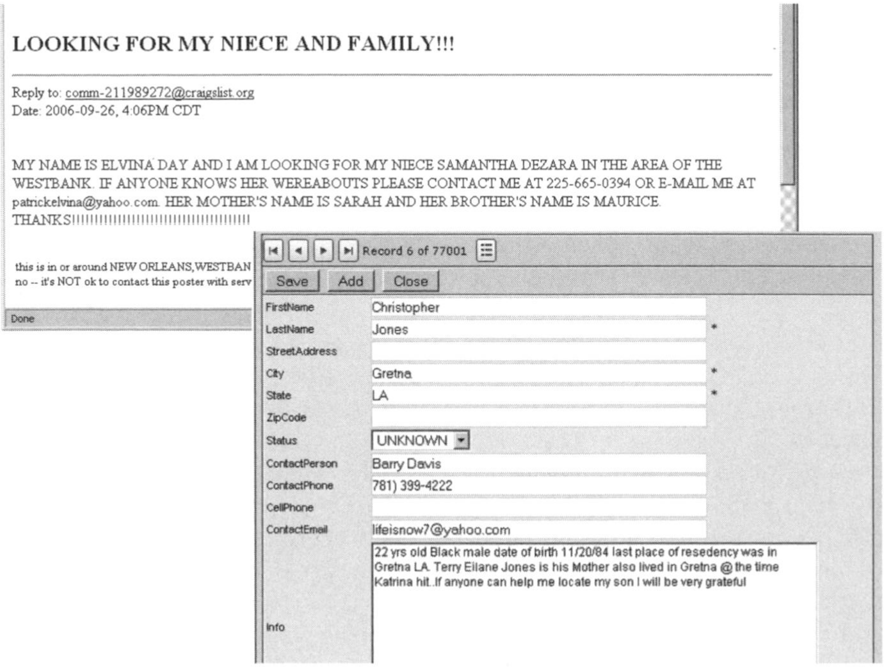

LOOKING FOR MY NIECE AND FAMILY!!!

Reply to: comm-211989272@craigslist.org
Date: 2006-09-26, 4:06PM CDT

MY NAME IS ELVINA DAY AND I AM LOOKING FOR MY NIECE SAMANTHA DEZARA IN THE AREA OF THE
WESTBANK. IF ANYONE KNOWS HER WEREABOUTS PLEASE CONTACT ME AT 225-665-0394 OR E-MAIL ME AT
patrickelvina@yahoo.com. HER MOTHER'S NAME IS SARAH AND HER BROTHER'S NAME IS MAURICE.
THANKS!!

this is in or around NEW ORLEANS,WESTBAN

no -- it's NOT ok to contact this poster with serv

Done

				Record 6 of 77001

Save   Add   Close

FirstName	Christopher
LastName	Jones
StreetAddress	
City	Gretna
State	LA
ZipCode	
Status	UNKNOWN
ContactPerson	Barry Davis
ContactPhone	781) 399-4222
CellPhone	
ContactEmail	lifeisnow7@yahoo.com
Info	22 yrs old Black male date of birth 11/20/84 last place of resedency was in Gretna LA. Terry Eliane Jones is his Mother also lived in Gretna @ the time Katrina hit..If anyone can help me locate my son I will be very grateful

Figure 10.2. Survivor posting at Craigslist and the Gulf Coast News website.

volunteering in many previous efforts) started to band together using their blogs and
IRC as a communication means.

On Friday, September 2 they came up with the key part of the technological
solution: an XML format (called the PeopleFinder Information Format or PFIF) for
records that describe missing or located individuals. The PFIF specification (written
in less than 24 hours!) also defined the embedding of PFIF records in RSS feeds. The
Salesforce.com Foundation committed to providing the back end database and search
engine. The group also immediately begin to organize the social part of solution: they
sent out urgent calls on volunteer mailing lists for people who would be willing to
help in entering data manually into the database through a web form. They were also
looking for people who would help to write scrapers to automatically extract content
from other sites or to help other website owners write code to export data in PFIF
format. They set up a Wiki[5] and mailing lists[6] to coordinate the work of data entry
and technical development.

By Saturday, the first volunteers started entering data primarily from Craigslist.
(Sites to be visited were collaborative tagged using the social bookmarking site
del.icio.us.) As news of the project spread in the blogosphere it almost became a

---

[5] The project Wiki is available at http://katrinahelp.info/wiki/index.php/
Katrina_PeopleFinder_Project

[6] Archives of the Katrina developer mailing list are available at http://orwant.com/
katrina/by_date.html

victim of its own success: the Wiki slows to a crawl as several hundred people are trying to edit the same page at times, the database needs to be taken down for update and the data collection efforts bring other sites to a halt. There are also unexpected technical challenges along the way: for example, *chunking*[7] is problematic in cases like Craigslist where the content of the pages changes continuously and the posts are not numbered sequentially.

Nevertheless, problems are fixed immediately as volunteers work around the clock, even if the solutions are often practical hacks. The effort also learned to scale up organizationally and everyone in the community found a specific role, e.g. assisting newbies with questions, developing training material, gardening, maintaining the Wiki, chunking, promoting the project etc. There are 7,000 records by Sunday morning, and over 50,000 by the end of Monday. In time, over 4000 volunteers contributed and over 640,000 records are collected manually or automatically. A number of libraries and tools have been written in a variety of programming languages for dealing with PFIF data.

The Katrina PeopleFinder project has also spawned a sister project, the ShelterFinder. The ShelterFinder addresses the problem of collecting up-to-date information about shelters (their location, capacity, status etc.) Similar to personal status, this information is also scattered around the Web in case of emergencies or passed along between agencies in various formats such as Excel sheets. ShelterFinder brings this data into a central search facility and also integrates geographic visualization (GoogleMaps) to make it easier to find shelters by location.

While ShelterFinder still exists, the Katrina PeopleFinder project came to an end before the end of the month just as quickly as it started. The data that has been collected has been merged into even larger databases set up by Google and a co-operation between the American Red Cross and Microsoft and eventually almost all victims were reconnected.[8] Much of survivor data on the Web have been also removed[9] due to privacy concerns once the emergency was gone. The project itself was mired in a legal debate already after two weeks of existence. One of the sources scraped, the Gulf Coast News (GCN) has sent a cease and desist letter to the project citing copyright violation. Katrina turned out to be also a business opportunity for many who have seen the traffic of their websites (and their advertising revenue) increase in the wake of the disaster.

The emergency wasn't gone, however. Hurricane Rita, the fourth most intense Atlantic hurricane ever recorded hit Florida less than a month after Hurricane Katrina. Hurricane Wilma, the most intense Atlantic hurricane ever recorded followed Rita on October 18, 2005. With Hurricanes Wilma, Emily, Katrina, and Rita, 2005

---

[7] The technical term invented by the community for the breaking up of large sites into portions manageable by a single volunteer.

[8] None of these databases are available any more, although by far not all have returned to New Orleans and certainly not all have found each other: even after a year there are still friends and former co-workers looking for each other on Craigslist and other remaining sites.

[9] Removed from its original location that is...

became the first year on record in which four Category 5 hurricanes developed in the Atlantic basin.

10.1.1 The Semantic Web

The Katrina PeopleFinder is a remarkable project because it has shown a glimpse of the power in combining novel web-based technologies and civil activism.[10] Some call this idea *Recovery 2.0* (a combination of Web 2.0 and recovery efforts), others term it *social source*, the mix of social support and open source. (As one of the founding project members have phrased it: "Sometimes code is the solution. Sometimes 2,000 loosely organized people are the solution."[11]) As a result of the efforts of those involved an immeasurable number of people were saved from the emotional toll of being separated from their loved ones.

Yet those involved on the technology side of the project are the first to admit that they tackled an important problem with inadequate tools. However, an emergency is not the time to innovate or educate: as one of member phrased it "the technology has to be pre-positioned, accessible, and you can't need to 'ask permission' or even involve the folks that 'own'/maintain the technology to use it for your purposes." Needless to say, most of the developers involved in the project were only marginally aware of semantic technologies if at all, which has yet to find its way to mainstream web developers.

The reader who has read this book, however, knows the difference that semantic technologies could have made. In the following we highlight two key issues where the technologies discussed in this book might have made a significant impact on the capabilities of the system.

Reducing interdependence on the schema level

The choice for XML in the project was a conscious technical decision due to the wide availability of XML tools, e.g. XML Schema validators that could be used to validate data against the XML Schema contained in the PFIF specification. XML as an interchange language was ideal in connecting disparate systems on a syntactic level.

The reliance of XML schema languages, however, introduced a significant dependency in the design. In particular, after the initial release of PFIF standard project members have quickly found out that their XML schema is far from perfect: some sites collect much more detailed information than the simple contact fields of the PFIF schema. But there was no way to change the schema any more: by that time a

---

[10] Unfortunately, the story and the lessons from the Katrina PeopleFinder project have not been widely publicized. The best records are the blog entries from some of the core members, including Ethan Zuckerman `http://www.ethanzuckerman.com/blog/?p=170` and David Geilhufe `http://socialsource.blogspot.com/2005/10/personal-history-of-katrina.html`

[11] `http://www.ethanzuckerman.com/blog/?p=170`

number of other sites and a host of tools were supporting it. The dependency of these tools on a particular version of the PFIF format created a dependency that had to be continuously reckoned with from then on.

And in an emergency all dependencies are costly: ideally actions need to be parallelized as much as possible. Dependencies between developments introduce delays through the necessary communication involved. In the case of PFIF, this would have essentially entailed notifying all developers and synchronizing the switch to the new schema. The costs in terms of time loss would have been so high that introducing a second version of the schema was never even considered. Instead additional information was shoe-horned into plain text fields where their semantics was completely lost. In essence, this information could not be searched other than by keywords.

We know that RDF and OWL would have offered a way to remove much of this interdependency through greater flexibility in modelling. RDF offers all the advantages of XML in terms of shared syntax and tool support is improving rapidly. More importantly, web-based knowledge representation languages are prepared for exactly the kind of scenario that is present on the Web, in particular supporting the independent, parallel evolution of schemas (ontologies). For example, adding a new field such as birthdate to the definition of the concept *foaf:Person* can be done independently of the maintainers of FOAF schema. Further, it is possible to describe this new notion in such a way that other parties will have at least a partial understanding of it. For example, we could state that the value of the birthdate property is a point in time (a date). Other agents would then at least know that a birthdate can be visualized along a timeline, it can be compared with other kinds of dates etc.

Other implementors may take over our use of the term birthdate, but they may also come up with their own separate property for exporting birthdates. In particular in cases where an existing database is converted to PFIF or some other interchange format, it saves time and effort to export the database using the original database schema.[12] If that happens, two properties with the same semantics can still be mapped to each other either manually or automatically (*ontology mapping*), allowing processing agents to understand that two or more properties have the same intended meaning and treat them uniformly.

An ontology-based approach would have also made it easier to combine the collected data with available sources of background knowledge and web services. For example, in order to visualize shelters on a map in ShelterFinder there was a need to locate the geographic coordinates of the shelters. Such a task could have been done by combining shelter data with the freely available database that contains the mappings from US zip codes to geo-coordinates. Standards such as the SPARQL protocol and query language allow to query such data sources remotely, without the need of adding them to the local knowledge base. For more precise location, the system could also have been more easily connected to external geo-locator services that return geographic coordinates based on place names or complete addresses.

---

[12] In fact, tools such as PHPMySQLAdmin allow the export of a database directly to XML. With similar tools for RDF, there would be no coding effort involved in making data available in RDF.

The kind of bottom-up, emerging ontologies (*folksonomies*) that we have seen in Chapter 9 could have also played a key role in breaking down the complexity of the emergency management task. Folksonomies represent a different trade-off in formality versus control than manually engineered ontologies. Tagging is a simple activity that even those unaware of ontologies can easily do as shown by the success of many folksonomy systems in Web 2.0 applications. Tagging systems can thus be built in the user interface of web applications without adding much complexity.

Tagging also offers much more flexibility than traditional ontologies at the cost of loosing explicit semantics. In the PeopleFinder project, for example, as the project went along the need came up to mark records that need correction or due for removal. As this need was not anticipated there wasn't an appropriate field in the schema of the project. Using tagging, however, such records could be easily tagged with some specific keyword using the interface, without even the need to adjust the underlying ontology. Once the action has been completed, the tag could have been removed just as easily. In this case, the semantics of the tag only needed to be understood by the project members and only by those concerned with gardening and thus the loss of explicit semantics would have been an acceptable price to pay for increased flexibility and user convenience.

In summary, emergencies have the inherent property that they can cannot be completely planned for. In such cases technologies that offer the greatest flexibility will allow to adapt to changing conditions with the least delay. The RDF and OWL languages introduced in this book have been specifically designed for knowledge representation in web-based settings, which could have been exploited in the Katrina PeopleFinder to reduce the interdependency between data and services maintained by project members or third parties.

Aggregation of social individuals

PeopleFinder served as a search interface to a collection of data gathered from the Web. The system was designed in a way that users (evacuees themselves) would be expected to come to the site searching for their loved ones among the announcements of missing and safe persons.

However, the system was not able to aggregate information or automatically match descriptions of missing persons against descriptions of safe persons. Using the technologies we have described in this book it would have been very well possible to automate the tasks of merging identical records and matching descriptions of persons. Ultimately, the system could have brought families and friends directly in contact after matching their records instead of waiting for them to search for each other.

We have seen in this thesis what is needed for that in terms of technology. RDF as a knowledge representation language offers a good starting point as it provides a globally unique mechanism to identify resources. We have shown how to use OWL and rules to describe in a specific domain what it means for two things to be equal and how reasoners can be applied to the task of instance unification or *smushing* (see Chapter 5). We have implemented the general framework for this method in the

Elmo API and used it to disambiguate person references in the Flink system which provided the data for our research on the Semantic Web community (see Chapter 6).

When I joined the ShelterFinder project I quickly realized that it was not the time to educate the volunteer community about the Semantic Web. However, the costs of not using any automated technology for removing duplicate records was also painfully clear. In this project, duplicate records of shelters were either found by searching the database (and noticing the duplicates) or by sorting Excel sheets on certain columns. It was clear that while the first method relies on chance and human effort, the second is hardly fool-proof as it only works if prefixes of strings overlap. This was a clear case where a little semantics went a long way. I have donated a converter from CSV format (supported by Excel) to RDF and wrote a simple smusher that matched the names of shelters based on string similarity. While hardly rocket science in terms of research, it could be used by the project in filtering out already known shelters from incoming Excel sheets.

The reader may note that before semantic technologies could have been brought to bear in matching descriptions of missing persons with reports of safe persons, the PeopleFinder project would have also needed to enrich their schema with personal characteristics that could have been used for matching. (As discussed in the previous section the PFIF was rather limited and could not be extended due to necessary freezing of the schema.) An additional problem the project would have needed to deal with is that many of the records imported from other sites contained person descriptions in natural language (see for example the postings in Figure 10.2). To some extent automatic information extraction techniques could have been applied to extract some of this metadata. As such techniques are hardly fool-proof, it is likely that human effort would have been necessary to check and eventually re-enter some of the metadata. However, what the project has also shown is that such help is nearby when it's needed the most.

10.1.2 Social Networks

Much of the help the PeopleFinder project received came through the online social networks of activists. Thanks to internet-based communication technologies such networks were promptly activated as the situation escalated and served as a critical factor in mobilizing resources for the project. Evacuees themselves also tried to re-connect their personal networks. In fact, the records of PeopleFinder are not only descriptions of individuals but rather descriptions of two persons —the one creating the note and the one addressed— and their relationship.

Conceptualizing the system as a social network application would have allowed to make connections between people who could not be directly connected to each other, but could be reached through a third person. Studying the data using the methods of Social Network Analysis would have made it possible to gain important insights into how precisely networks are used in times of emergencies, allowing us to build even better applications for crisis management.

Although not a discussion that have entered in detail, we would also note the urgent need to clarify the legal and ethical boundaries of carrying out social science research on the Web. The story of the Katrina PeopleFinder serves as a reminder of the possible collision between the public interest on side and the law and the markets as regulators on the other side.

When aggregating data from multiple electronic sources one is particularly liable to accusations that sensitive personal data has been used in ways that were not intended (and could not have been foreseen) when making some information available on the Web. Collecting information from the Web is also likely to cross the boundaries of national legislations and ethical guidelines. With respect to our web mining method we can also state that asking permission for the reuse of every individual piece of information on the Web would not have been a real possibility either. Such possibilities have not even been foreseen in existing ethical codes for Social Science research that involves the handling of personal data.

Networks in science

Our research has focused on networks that form under less strenuous circumstances: we have studied the networks of researchers working on realizing the Semantic Web. Our inspirations, however, have been similar: understanding the role of networks in science is an important first step toward organizing the scientific process in more efficient ways.

The scientific domain offers an ideal terrain to demonstrate our methodology for social network analysis based on electronic sources. Not only researchers are present on the Web and carry out discussions on electronic forums of all kinds but the very objects produced by science itself are undergoing a thorough digitalization. This means that more and more of science is visible through the Web and can be manipulated by computers.

The move towards *e-science* is clearly visible, for example, in the changing role of libraries and publishers, the traditional facilitators of the scientific process. The library system is rapidly turning into networks of repositories of digital objects instead of books and periodicals, while publishers more and more require scientists to publish their data in electronic formats alongside with the text of their articles. Ultimately, the scientific article itself will be decomposed into its two main constituents (data and argumentation) so that we can analyze the data separately and apply various argumentations to it just as we can apply different stylesheets to webpages today.

That social networks matter in science is also an important lesson that everyone who has done a PhD would learn. In the case of PhD students, collaborating with more senior researchers is the primary way a PhD student would acquire the necessary skills to write successful articles. And because reputation is an important organizing factor in communities with no formal rules, it is an advantage to co-author with more senior researchers. It is equally important to build (preferably) direct relationships with those key members of the research community who have roles in managing journals and conferences, the outlets of scientific production. (This has informational advantages but may also result in some minor favors such as the softening of a deadline.) Lastly, for more senior researchers social networks are also intensively activated when acquiring research funding: some funding agencies such as the EU allow only multinational research teams to apply and both the assignment of total funding to certain research areas and the individual grant decisions are determined by experts who are necessarily members of the community.

In our case we have been interested in the impact of social networks on scientific outcomes as measured by publication performance. In particular, we would test the common intuition that the most successful works come about by combining one's own ideas with that of researchers at different research groups, possibly in different specialties. We have proved that indeed a cognitive diversity in the personal networks of researchers has benefits beyond the well-known structural advantages of large and sparsely connected networks (see Chapter 8). While this has been a traditional study in terms of analysis, we introduced a set of novel methods in the representation and management of social network data. In particular, our semantic-based representation of network data made it possible to automatically aggregate a number of electronic sources that contained information about the relationships in our target community, the community of researchers working on the Semantic Web. Among others, we have exploited the content of Web pages for social network mining, which provided us with plentiful data for analysis. Our automated methods allowed us to scale up our effort significantly when having to deal with multiple data sources containing information about the same set of social individuals and their relationships. Further, the possibility to use multiple data sources allows to design studies that are more robust and allow multiple viewpoints on the social structures within a community.

Beyond our own study, semantic technologies offer advantages to the whole of *e-social science*. Shared ontologies for representing data in a scientific domain allow researchers to exchange and reuse data more effectively. Just as it is already common in some of the natural sciences, there are also attempts in the social sciences to set up repositories of research data instead of repositories of publications. Such repositories will need representations that are formal (machine processable), commonly agreed upon yet flexible enough to serve a variety of viewpoints on what is the specific object of a study and how it is to be performed.

As a benefit on the side, the necessary formalization of social science concepts will no doubt lead to important discussions. Although Social Network Analysis is one of the most formalized field of Social Science, there are still significant differences in the definition of some of the very basic concepts of the field as we have seen from the many ways to capture the idea of tie strength. Formalization can lead to a clarification of the existence of these different viewpoints, what measures they induce and how these measures ultimately relate to each other.[13]

10.2 Looking ahead: a Second Life

There is only one area that captures most succinctly the mesmerizing opportunities and the mind-boggling challenges ahead of Social Networks and the Semantic Web. This is the area of artificial worlds.

---

[13] For a broader view on the mutual influence of Computer Science and Social Science methodologies see also [AG06a, AG06b].

Systems such as Second Life present alternate realities buzzing with life.[14] Second Life is a simulated environment populated by human controlled avatars; three-dimensional characters in a three-dimensional environment. The virtual reality of Second Life is inhabited by over 800,000 avatars (the size of Amsterdam) at the time of writing[15], who live their lives in an environment where flying is normal and nobody dies. Second Life caters to a primitive desire we most likely carry since we gained consciousness: what if we could step out of our self and redefine who we are?

Second Life allows just that by allowing to customize our self and in fact, allowing us to have as many personae (represented by different avatars) as we like. Yet Second Life is *realistic* in many respects and certainly more serious than to be described as a game. For example, Second Life has a striving economy based on the Linden Dollar, which is freely convertible to US dollars. Just in the last 24 hours 350,000 US dollars have been spent in Second Life. In fact, many residents of Second Life have already given up their real world jobs to make a living in the alternate reality by selling, for example, virtual clothing, teaching classes, by acting in movies shot in the virtual reality or by performing music in bars. (Needless to say, one has to be really good to get into the hottest venues.) The company that runs Second Life earns money by selling real estate in the virtual world; but they are not the only one: BusinessWeek devoted a recent cover story to Anshe Chung, who earns hundreds of thousands of (actual) dollars as the most prominent real-estate mogul in Second Life [Hof06].

Most of all, however, Second Life residents socialize, build relationships and yes, have sexual affairs in specifically marked Adult areas. (Although Second Life policy prohibits giving out real identities, there have been real world marriages that started with a relationship in SL.) Not only can they talk to each other, but also use gestures and body languages (see Figure 10.3). And in this new level of interaction lies a grand new Challenge for AI: how to introduce machine intelligence into the world of Second Life?

Surely, a machine that would pass the Turing test would not be considered realistic enough for a Second Lifer: a computer standing behind a curtain would be promptly exposed as a cheat no matter how wittily it answers our questions. In order for our computer driven avatar to be accepted it would certainly need to have a social life.

Social Network Analysis, the study of the structure, formation and impact of social networks could come to the rescue. But Second Life could teach just as much to Social Network Analysis. Doing social science research through a researcher-avatar in the virtual reality of Second Life would be certainly low cost (no need to leave the room) and fast (hey, you can fly from subject to subject!). Such research could no doubt also rely on electronic data (e.g. collected by intelligent objects placed in the environment) and would need to be liable to the same questions as Social Science research on the Web, i.e. how much of what we learn in the VR world holds for the real world. If that is what we are trying to understand... it is also very well possible

---

[14] http://secondlife.com, http://lindenlab.com
[15] October 1, 2006

Figure 10.3. Who said they can't dance? While some sit around the bar, some Second Lifers take on the dance floor at a party thrown by the Second Life Herald, SL's in-game newspaper covering the politics, society and events that occur inside Second Life.

that SNA would find applications inside Second Life, e.g. for predicting the effects of word of mouth marketing campaigns under way by some major corporations (real and un-real).

Systems like Second Life may also mark the future of the Web as they can be easily integrated with Web content. Many applications may directly benefit from being conceptualized in the virtual space. Not only real world retailers such as Amazon would be interested to show their merchandize, but also projects like the Katrina PeopleFinder could be built in a special part of Second Life. In this space Katrina evacuees would get together and meet rescue workers, explore shelters laid out on a simulated terrain of the real disaster area etc. Creating the application in a 3D reality would play to our inherent strength of processing information faster when presented in a familiar context of space, using human interactions instead of written text.

There are also ample opportunities for improving our understanding of semantics. Part of the difficulty in developing technologies for the Semantic Web is that ultimately the truth of statements (and thus the correctness of inferences) is determined against an external reality: *the truth is out there*. As a consequence, for example, evaluating ontology construction or ontology mapping methods is a human-complex problem. We as humans can determine (or agree upon after some discussion) on some golden standard based on what we believe is true about the segment of the world to be modelled. We can then evaluate our algorithms against this understanding and design new ones that match our intuitions better.

The interesting aspect of Second Life is that *the truth is inside the system* at least to some extent. The statement "people can't fly" is true in our reality but easily falsified in Second Life *even by a machine*. (If only we equate avatars with people and apply our usual definition of what flying is.) Machines in Second Life has a much greater access to the grounding of statements, which in theory enables them to be much more intelligent in their own reality. Second Life will probably also vividly demonstrate our statements about the socially constructed nature of ontologies. Second Life residents will no doubt create many abstract, socially-constructed concepts expressed in words whose meaning is relative to some or all Second Life residents.

In fact, that "people can fly" is not in conflict with our own mental model as we know that such semantics is relative to the context of Second Life. There is some danger that we loose this grip if we immerse too much in the virtual reality: cognitive science tells us that when faced with an observation that contradicts our own beliefs we have two basic choices: reject the observations on some grounds or adapt our mental model. The theory of cognitive dissonance dictates that we will choose the option that can most easily reduce the tension [Fes57]. If the virtual reality is compelling enough (or we spend long enough time there) would there be a danger that we adopt our mental models and believe that people can fly?

That is a scary thought. But here is happy one: I turned 19 yesterday. That is: one of my avatars has turned 19. It was a hell of a party... with lots of friends and *all of me*.

References

[AA05a]   Lada Adamic and Eytan Adar. How to search a social network. *Social Networks*, 27(3):"187–203", 2005.

[AA05b]   Eytan Adar and Lada A. Adamic. Tracking Information Epidemics in Blogspace. In *Web Intelligence*, Compiegne, France, 2005.

[AB06]   Ben Adida and Mark Birbeck. RDFa Primer 1.0, May 2006.

[AC99]   Manju K. Ahuja and Kathleen M. Carley. Network Structure in Virtual Organizations. *Organization Science*, 10(6):741–757, 1999.

[ACMO⁺04] Karl Aberer, Philippe Cudré-Mauroux, Aris M. Ouksel, Tiziana Catarci, Mohand-Said Hacid, Arantza Illarramendi, Vipul Kashyap, Massimo Mecella, Eduardo Mena, Erich J. Neuhold, Olga De Troyer, Thomas Risse, Monica Scannapieco, Fèlix Saltor, Luca de Santis, Stefano Spaccapietra, Steffen Staab, and Rudi Studer. Emergent Semantics Principles and Issues. In *Database Systems for Advanced Applications 9th International Conference, DASFAA 2004*, volume 2973 of *LNCS*, pages 25–38, 2004.

[ADR06]   Sören Auer, Sebastian Dietzold, and Thomas Riechert. OntoWiki A Tool for Social, Semantic Collaboration. In *Proceedings of the Fifth International Semantic Web Conference (ISWC 2006)*, number 4373 in Lecture Notes in Computer Science (LNCS), pages 736–749. Springer-Verlag, 2006.

[AE06]   Anjo Anjewierden and Lilia Efimova. Understanding weblog communities through digital traces: a framework, a tool and an example. In *International Workshop on Community Informatics (COMINF 2006)*, Montpellier, France, 2006.

[AG05]   Lada A. Adamic and Natalie Glance. The Political Blogosphere and the 2004 U.S. Election: Divided They Blog. In *Workshop on Link Discovery: Issues, Approaches and Applications (LinkKDD-2005)*, 2005.

[AG06a]   Hans Akkermans and Jaap Gordijn. Ontology Engineering, Scientific Method, and the Research Agenda. In *Proceedings of the 15th International Conference on Knowledge Engineering and Knowledge Management (EKAW06)*, 2006.

[AG06b]   Hans Akkermans and Jaap Gordijn. What is This Science Called Requirements Engineering? In *14th IEEE International Requirements Engineering Conference (RE'06)*, pages 266–271, Los Alamitos, CA, USA, 2006. IEEE Computer Society.

[AGC03]　Manju K. Ahuja, Dennis F. Galletta, and Kathleen M. Carley. Individual Centrality and Performance in Virtual R&D Groups: An Empirical Study. *Management
Science*, 49(1):21–38, 2003.

[App05]　Daniel Appelquist. Enabling the mobile web through semantically-driven user
experiences. In *Third Workshop on Emerging Applications for Wireless and
Mobile Access (MobEA III)*, 2005.

[AR99]　Albert-László Barabási and Réka Albert. Emergence of scaling in random networks. *Science*, 286:509–512, 1999.

[AvH04]　Grigoris Antoniou and Frank van Harmelen. *A Semantic Web Primer*. MIT
Press, 2004.

[BAT97]　W.N. Borst, J.M. Akkermans, and J.L. Top. Engineering ontologies. *International Journal of Human-Computer Studies*, 46:365–406, 1997.

[BBJ97]　Baldwin, Timothy T., Bedell, Michael D., and Johnson, Jonathan L. The social
fabric of a team-based m.b.a. program: Network effects on student satisfaction
and performance. *The Academy of Management Journal*, 40(6):1369–1397, dec
1997.

[BCS00]　Joel A. C. Baum, Tony Calabrese, and Brian S. Silverman. Don't go it alone:
alliance network composition and startups' performance in Canadian biotech-
nology. *Strategic Management Journal*, 21:267–294, 2000.

[BEF02]　Stephen P. Borgatti, Martin G. Everett, and Linton C. Freeman. UCINET for
Windows: Software for Social Network Analysis. Technical report, Analytic
Technologies, 2002.

[BEH⁺01]　U. Brandes, M. Eiglsperger, I. Herman, M. Himsolt, and M.S. Marshall.
Graphml progress report: Structural layer proposal. In *Proceedings of the 9th
International Symposium on Graph Drawing (GD '01)*, volume 2265 of *LNCS*,
pages 501–512. Springer, 2001.

[BEL04]　Ulrik Brandes, Markus Eiglsperger, and Jürgen Lerner. GraphML Primer, June
2004.

[BHKL06]　Lars Backstrom, Dan Huttenlocher, Jon Kleinberg, and Xiangyang Lan. Group
Formation in Large Social Networks: Membership, Growth, and Evolution. In
Proc. 12th ACM SIGKDD Intl. Conf. on Knowledge Discovery and Data Mining,
2006.

[BHWR06]　Jeffrey Boase, John B. Horrigan, Barry Wellman, and Lee Rainie. The Strength
of Internet Ties. Technical report, Pew Internet & American Life Project, January 2006.

[BJN⁺02]　A.L. Barabási, H. Jeong, Z. Néda, E. Ravasz, A. Schubert, and T. Vicsek. Evolution of the social network of scientific collaborations. *Physica A*, 311(3-4):
590–614, 2002.

[BKvH02]　Jeen Broekstra, Arjohn Kampman, and Frank van Harmelen. Sesame: An Architecture for Storing and Querying RDF and RDF Schema. In *Proceedings of
the First International Semantic Web Conference (ISWC 2002)*, number 2342
in Lecture Notes in Computer Science (LNCS), pages 54–68. Springer-Verlag,
2002.

[BLFD99]　Tim Berners-Lee, Mark Fischetti, and Michael L. Dertouzos. *Weaving the Web :
The Original Design and Ultimate Destiny of the World Wide Web by its Inventor*.
Harper San Francisco, 1999.

[BLFM98]　Tim Berners-Lee, Roy Fielding, and Larry Masinter. Uniform Resource Identifiers (URI): Generic Syntax, August 1998.

[BLHL01]　Tim Berners-Lee, James Hendler, and Ora Lassila. The Semantic Web. *Scientific
American*, May 2001.

[BM98]   Vladimir Batagelj and Andrej Mrvar. Pajek - Program for Large Network Analysis. *Connections*, 21(2):47–57, 1998.

[BM05]   Ron Bekkerman and Andrew McCallum. Disambiguating Web Appearances of People in a Social NetworkE. In *Proceedings of the 14th International World Wide Web Conference (WWW2005)*, pages 463–470. ACM Press, 2005.

[BMI06]   Danushka Bollegala, Yutaka Matsuo, and Mitsuru Ishizuka. Disambiguating Personal Names on the Web using Automatically Extracted Key Phrases. In *Proceedings of the 17th European Conference on Artificial Intelligence*, 2006.

[Bor97]   Stephen P. Borgatti. Structural Holes: Unpacking Burt's Redundancy Measures. *Connections*, 20(1):35–38, 1997.

[Bur95]   Ronald S. Burt. *Structural Holes: The Social Structure of Competition*. Harvard University Press, 1995.

[Bur00]   Ronald S. Burt. The network structure of social capital. *Research in Organizational Behaviour*, 22:345–423, 2000.

[Bur04]   Ronald S. Burt. Structural Holes and Good Ideas (in press). *American Journal of Sociology*, 110(2), 2004.

[Che76]   Peter P. Chen. The entity-relationship model - toward a unified view of data. *ACM Trans. Database Syst.*, 1(1):9–36, 1976.

[CHS04]   Philipp Cimiano, Siegfried Handschuh, and Steffen Staab. Towards the Self-Annotating Web. In *Proceedings of the 13th International World Wide Web Conference*, pages 462–471, New York, USA, 2004.

[Cic73]   Aaron V. Cicourel. *Cognitive Sociology*. Penguin Books, Harmondsworth, England, 1973.

[Cla06]   Kendall Grant Clark. Sparql protocol for rdf, April 2006.

[Col88]   James Coleman. Social capital in the creation of human capital. *American Journal of Sociology*, 94:95–120, 1988.

[Cra71]   Diana Crane. Transnational networks in basic science. *International Organization*, 25:585–601, 1971.

[DFJ+04]   Li Ding, Tim Finin, Anupam Joshi, Rong Pan, R. Scott Cost, Yun Peng, Pavan Reddivari, Vishal C Doshi, and Joel Sachs. Swoogle: A Search and Metadata Engine for the Semantic Web. In *Proceedings of the 13th ACM conference on information and knowledge management*. ACM Press, November 2004.

[DFvH03]   John Davies, Dieter Fensel, and Frank van Harmelen, editors. *Towards the Semantic Web: Ontology-Driven Knowledge Management*. John Wiley & Sons, 2003.

[dP65]   Derek J. deSolla Price. Networks of scientific papers: The pattern of bibliographic references indicates the nature of the scientific research front. *Science*, 149(3683):510–515, 1965.

[dSHNW06]   H. Van de Sompel, T. Hammond, E. Neylon, and S. Weibel. The 'info' URI Scheme for Information Assets with Identifiers in Public Namespaces, April 2006.

[DZFJ05]   Li Ding, Lina Zhou, Tim Finin, and Anupam Joshi. How the Semantic Web is Being Used: An Analysis of FOAF Documents. In *Proceedings of the 38th International Conference on System Sciences*, January 2005.

[ECD+04]   Oren Etzioni, Michael Cafarella, Doug Downey, Stanley Kok, Ana-Maria Popescu, Tal Shaked, Stephen Soderland, Daniel S. Weld, and Alexander Yates. Web Scale Information Extraction in KnowItAll (Preliminary Results). In *Proceedings of the 13th International World Wide Web Conference*, pages 100–111, New York, USA, 2004.

[Fel98]   Christiane Fellbaum. *WordNet: An Electronic Lexical Database*. MIT Press, 1998.

[Fes57]   Leon Festinger. *A theory of cognitive dissonance*. Stanford University Press, Stanford, CA, 1957.

[FHH04]   Richard Fikes, Patrick Hayes, and Ian Horrocks. OWL-QL—a language for deductive query answering on the Semantic Web. *Journal of Web Semantics*, 2(1):19–29, 2004.

[Fow03]   Martin Fowler. *UML Distilled: A Brief Guide to the Standard Object Modeling Language*. Addison-Wesley, Third Edition edition, 2003.

[GB00]   Martin Gargiulo and Mario Benassi. Trapped in Your Own Net? Network Cohesion, Structural Holes, and the Adaptation of Social Capital. *Organization Science*, 11(2):183–196, 2000.

[GGLNT04]   Daniel Gruhl, Ramanathan V. Guha, David Liben-Nowell, and Andrew Tomkins. Information diffusion through blogspace. In *Proceedings of the 13th International World Wide Web Conference*, pages 491–501, New York, USA, 2004.

[GH06]   Jennifer Golbeck and James Hendler. FilmTrust: Movie recommendations using trust in web-based social networks. In *Proceedings of the IEEE Consumer Communications and Networking Conference*, 2006.

[Gil93]   Richard Gillespie. *Manufacturing Knowledge: A History of the Hawthorne Experiments*. Studies in Economic History and Policy: USA in the Twentieth Century. Cambridge University Press, 1993.

[GLDZ03]   Peter A. Gloor, Rob Laubacher, Scott B. C. Dynes, and Yan Zhao. Visualization of Communication Patterns in Collaborative Innovation Networks - Analysis of Some W3C Working Groups. In *CIKM '03: Proceedings of the Twelfth International Conference on Information and Knowledge Management*, pages 56–60. ACM Press, 2003.

[GM02]   Marko Grobelnik and Dunja Mladenic. Approaching Analysis of EU IST Projects Database. In *Proceedings of the International Conference on Information and Intelligent Systems (IIS-2002)*, 2002.

[GM03]   Aldo Gangemi and Peter Mika. Understanding the Semantic Web through Descriptions and Situations. In Robert Meersman, Zahir Tari, and Douglas Schmidt et al., editors, *On The Move 2003 Conferences (OTM2003)*. Springer Verlag, 2003.

[GN02]   Michelle Girvan and Mark E. J. Newman. Community structure in social and biological networks. *Proc. Natl. Acad. Sci. USA*, 99(12):7821–7826, 2002.

[Gra73]   Mark Granovetter. The strength of weak ties. *American Journal of Sociology*, 78(6):1360–1380, 1973.

[Gra92]   Mark S. Granovetter. Problems of explanation in economic sociology. In N. Nohria and R. Eccles, editors, *Networks and Organizations: Structure, Form, and Action*, pages 25–56. Harvard University School Press, 1992.

[Gru93]   Tom R. Gruber. Towards Principles for the Design of Ontologies Used for Knowledge Sharing. In N. Guarino and R. Poli, editors, *Formal Ontology in Conceptual Analysis and Knowledge Representation*, Deventer, The Netherlands, 1993. Kluwer Academic Publishers.

[Gua98]   Nicola Guarino. *Formal Ontology in Information Systems*. IOS Press, 1998.

[Hay04]   Patrick Hayes. Rdf semantics, February 2004.

[HBE$^+$04] Peter Haase, Jeen Broekstra, Marc Ehrig, Maarten Menken, Peter Mika, Michal Plechawski, Pawel Pyszlak, Björn Schnizler, Ronny Siebes, Steffen Staab, and

Christoph Tempich. Bibster — a semantics-based bibliographic peer-to-peer system. In Sheila A. McIlraith, Dimitris Plexousakis, and Frank van Harmelen, editors, *Proceedings of the Third International Semantic Web Conference (ISWC 2004)*, pages 122–136, Hiroshima, Japan, November 2004. Springer-Verlag.

[HEC⁺04]   Lewis Hart, Patrick Emery, Bob Colomb, Kerry Raymond, Sarah Taraporewalla, Dan Chang, Yiming Ye, Elisa Kendall, and Mark Dutra. Owl full and uml 2.0 compared, 2004.

[HH01a]   Jeff Heflin and James Hendler. A Portrait of the Semantic Web in Action. *IEEE Intelligent Systems*, 16(2):54–59, 2001.

[HH01b]   Julie M. Hite and William S. Hesterly. The evolution of firm networks. *Strategic Management Journal*, 22(3):275–286, 2001.

[HHvdB03]   Gaston Heimeriks, Marianne Hoerlesberger, and Peter van den Besselaar. Mapping communication and collaboration in heterogeneous research networks. *Scientometrics*, 58(2):391–413, 2003.

[Hit03]   Julie M. Hite. Patterns of multidimensionality in embedded network ties: A typology of relational embeddedness in emerging entrepreneurial firms. *Strategic Organization!*, 1:11–52, 2003.

[HL73]   P. W. Holland and S. Leinhardt. The Structural Implications of Measurement Error in Sociometry. *Journal of Mathematical Sociology*, 3:85–111, 1973.

[Hof06]   Robert D. Hof. My Virtual Life. *BusinessWeek*, May 2006.

[HPSB⁺04]   Ian Horrocks, Peter F. Patel-Schneider, Harold Boley, Said Tabet, Benjamin Grosof, and Mike Dean. Swrl: A semantic web rule language combining owl and ruleml, May 2004.

[HSB⁺05]   Peter Haase, Björn Schnizler, Jeen Broekstra, Marc Ehrig, Frank van Harmelen, Maarten Menken, Peter Mika, Michal Plechawski, Pawel Pyszlak, Ronny Siebes, Steffen Staab, and Christoph Tempich. Bibster — a semantics-based bibliographic peer-to-peer system. *Journal of Web Semantics*, 2(1), 2005.

[IA93]   H. Ibarra and S. B. Andrews. Power, social influence and sense-making: Effects of network centrality and proximity on employee perceptions. *Administrative Science Quarterly*, 38:277–303, 1993.

[KA04]   Hildrun Kretschmer and Isidro Aguillo. Visibility of collaboration on the Web. *Scientometrics*, 61(3):405–426, 2004.

[Kah03]   Leander Kahney. Making Friendsters in High Places. *Wired*, July 2003.

[KAMP73]   G.R. Kiss, C. Armstrong, R. Milroy, and J. Piper. An associative thesaurus of English and its computer analysis. Edinburgh University Press, 1973.

[Kle04]   Michel Klein. *Change Management for Distributed Ontologies*. PhD thesis, Vrije Universiteit Amsterdam, August 2004.

[KNRT03]   Ravi Kumar, Jasmine Novak, Prabhakar Raghavan, and Andrew Tomkins. On the Bursty Evolution of Blogspace. In *Proceedings of the 12th International World Wide Web Conference*, 2003.

[Kra90]   David Krackhardt. Assessing the Political Landscape: Structure, Cognition, and Power in Organizations. *Administrative Science Quarterly*, 35:342–369, 1990.

[Kre02]   Valdis Krebs. Uncloaking terrorist networks. *First Monday*, 7(4), April 2002.

[KSS97]   Henry Kautz, Bart Selman, and Mehul Shah. The Hidden Web. *AI Magazine*, 18(2):27–36, 1997.

[KT06]   Maksym Korotkiy and Jan L. Top. MoRe Semantic Web Applications. In *Proceedings of the End-User Aspects of the Semantic Web Workshop (UserSWeb)*, 2006.

[Lem03]   Charmianne Lemmens. *Network Dynamics and Innovation*. PhD thesis, Technical University of Eindhoven (TUE), 2003.

[MA04]   Peter Mika and Hans Akkermans. Towards a New Synthesis of Ontology Technology and Knowledge Management. *Knowledge Engineering Review*, 19(4):317–345, 2004.

[May33]   Elton Mayo. *The Human Problems of an Industrial Civilization*. Macmillan, Cambridge, MA, USA, 1933.

[MC84]   Peter V. Marsden and Karen E. Campbell. Measuring tie strength. *Social Forces*, 63(2):482–501, 1984.

[MH01]   Peter Mutschke and Anabel Quan Haase. Collaboration and cognitive structures in social science research fields. *Scientometrics*, 52(3), 2001.

[MHT$^+$06] Yutaka Matsuo, Masahiro Hamasaki, Hideaki Takeda, Junichiro Mori, Danushka Bollegara, Yoshiyuki Nakamura, Takuichi Nishimura, Koiti Hasida, and Mitsuru Ishizuka. Spinning Multiple Social Networks for Semantic Web. In *Proceedings of the Twenty-First National Conference on Artificial Intelligence (AAAI2006)*, 2006.

[Mik02]   Peter Mika. Integrating Ontology Storage and Ontology-based Applications Through Client-side Query and Transformations. In *Proceedings of Evaluation of Ontology-based Tools (EON2002) workshop at EKAW2002, Siguenza, Spain*, 2002.

[Mik04]   Peter Mika. Social Networks and the Semantic Web: An Experiment in Online Social Network Analysis. In *Proceedings of the IEEE/WIC/ACM International Conference on Web Intelligence*, Beijing, China, September 2004.

[Mik05a]   Peter Mika. Flink: Semantic Web Technology for the Extraction and Analysis of Social Networks. *Journal of Web Semantics*, 3(2), 2005.

[Mik05b]   Peter Mika. Social Networks and the Semantic Web: The Next Challenge. *IEEE Intelligent Systems*, 20(1), January/February 2005.

[Mil67]   Stanley Milgram. The Small World Problem. *Psychology Today*, 1(1):61–67, 1967.

[MKB98]   A. Mehra, M. Kilduff, and D. J. Brass. At the margins: A distinctiveness approach to the social identity and social networks of underrepresented groups. *Academy of Management Journal*, 41(4):441–452, 1998.

[MKB01]   Ajay Mehra, Martin Kilduff, and Daniel J. Brass. The Social Networks of High and Low Self-monitors: Implications for Workplace Performance. *Administrative Science Quarterly*, 46(2), 2001.

[MM04]   Frank Manola and Eric Miller. Rdf primer, February 2004.

[MMIF04]   Junichiro Mori, Yutaka Matsuo, Mitsuru Ishizuka, and Boi Faltings. Keyword Extraction from the Web for FOAF Metadata. In *Proceedings of the 1st Workshop on Friend of a Friend, Social Networking and the (Semantic) Web*, 2004.

[MOGS04]   Peter Mika, Daniel Oberle, Aldo Gangemi, and Marta Sabou. Foundations for Service Ontologies: Aligning OWL-S to DOLCE. In *Proceedings of the 13th International World Wide Web Conference (WWW2004)*. ACM Press, 2004.

[MSLB06]   Miller McPherson, Lynn Smith-Lovin, and Matthew E. Brashears. Social isolation in america: Changes in core discussion networks over two decades. *American Sociological Review*, 71:353–375, June 2006.

[MVB$^+$04] Claudio Masolo, Laure Vieu, Emanuele Bottazzi, Carola Catenacci, Roberta Ferrario, Aldo Gangemi, and Nicola Guarino. Social roles and their descriptions. In *Proceedings of the Ninth International Conference on the Principles of Knowledge Representation and Reasoning*. AAAI Press, 2004.

[MvH04]   Deborah L. McGuinness and Frank van Harmelen. OWL Web Ontology Language Overview. Technical report, World Wide Web Consortium (W3C), February 2004.

[New01]   Mark Newman. Who is the best connected scientist? a study of scientific coauthorship networks. *Physics Review*, Nov 2001.

[NG98]   Janine Nahapiet and Sumantra Ghoshal. Social Capital, Intellectual Capital, and the Organizational Advantage. *The Academy of Management Review*, 23(2):242–266, April 1998.

[OR02]   Evelien Otte and Ronald Rousseau. Social network analysis: a powerful strategy, also for the information science. *Journal of Information Science*, 28(6):441–453, 2002.

[PK99]   R. Petke and I. King. Registration Procedures for URL Scheme Names, November 1999.

[PMW05]   John C. Paolillo, Sarah Mercure, and Elijah Wright. The Social Semantics of LiveJournal FOAF: Structure and Change from 2004 to 2005. In *Workshop on Semantic Network Analysis (SNA'05)*, 2005.

[Pow03]   Shelley Powers. *Practical RDF*. O'Reilly Media, July 2003.

[PP06]   Katie Portwin and Priya Parvatikar. Building and managing a massive triple store: An experience report. In *Proceedings of XTech 2006*, Amsterdam, The Netherlands, may 2006.

[PS06]   Eric Prud'hommeaux and Andy Seaborne. SPARQL Query Language for RDF, April 2006.

[Put93]   Robert D. Putnam. The Prosperous Community: Social Capital and Public Life. *The American Prospect*, 4(13):35–42, 1993.

[PW04]   John C. Paolillo and Elijah Wright. The Challenges of FOAF Characterization. In *Proceedings of the 1st Workshop on Friend of a Friend, Social Networking and the (Semantic) Web*, 2004.

[QK04]   Dennis Quan and David R. Karger. How to Make a Semantic Web Browser. In *Proceedings of the 13th International World Wide Web Conference*, pages 255–265, New York, USA, 2004.

[RDH$^+$04]   Alan Rector, Nick Drummond, Matthew Horridge, Jeremy Rogers, Holger Knublauch, Robert Stevens, Hai Wang, and Chris Wroe. Owl pizzas: Practical experience of teaching owl-dl: Common errors and common patterns. In *14th International Conference on Knowledge Engineering and Knowledge Management (EKAW 2004)*, 2004.

[RM03]   Ray Reagans and Bill McEvily. Network Structure and Knowledge Transfer: The Effects of Cohesion and Range. *Administrative Science Quarterly*, 48(2):240–267, 2003.

[Rob02]   Colin Robson. *Real World Research: A Resource for Social Scientists and Practitioner-Researchers*. Blackwell Publishing, second edition edition, 2002.

[Rua98]   Danching Ruan. The content of the General Social Survey discussion networks: an exploration of General Social Survey discussion name generatornext term in a previous termChinese context. *Social Networks*, 20(3):247–264, 1998.

[SAA$^+$99]   A. Th. Schreiber, J. M. Akkermans, A. A. Anjewierden, R. de Hoog, N. R. Shadbolt, W. van de Velde, and B. J. Wielinga. *Knowledge Engineering and Management. The CommonKADS Methodology [version 1.1]*. MIT Press, November 1999.

[Sal89]   Gerard Salton. *Automatic text processing*. Addison-Wesley, Reading, MA, 1989.

[Sco00]   John P. Scott. *Social Network Analysis: A Handbook*. Sage Publications, 2nd edition, 2000.

[Smi99]   Marc A. Smith. Invisible Crowds in Cyberspace: Measuring and Mapping the Social Structure of USENET. In Marc Smith and Peter Kollock, editors, *Communities in Cyberspace*. Routledge Press, London, 1999.

[Ste95]   Mark Stefik. *Introduction to knowledge systems*. Morgan Kaufmann Publishers Inc., San Francisco, CA, USA, 1995.

[SW01]   Barry Smith and Chris Welty. Ontology: Towards a new synthesis. In *Formal Ontology in Information Systems*, pages iii–x, Ongunquit, Maine, 2001. ACM Press.

[SWM04]   Michael K. Smith, Chris Welty, and Deborah L. McGuinness. OWL Web Ontology Language Guide. Technical report, World Wide Web Consortium (W3C), February 2004.

[tH05]   Herman ter Horst. Combining rdf and part of owl with rules: Semantics, decidability, complexity. In Yolanda Gil, Enrico Motta, V. Richard Benjamins, and Mark A. Musen, editors, *Proceedings of the Fourth International Semantic Web Conference (ISWC 2005)*, volume 3729 of *LNCS*, pages 668–684, Galway, Ireland, November 2005. Springer-Verlag.

[TWH03]   Joshua R. Tyler, Dennis M. Wilkinson, and Bernardo A. Huberman. Email as spectroscopy: automated discovery of community structure within organizations. In *International Conference on Communities and Technologies*, pages 81–96, Deventer, The Netherlands, 2003. Kluwer, B.V.

[vAKOS06]   Wouter van Atteveldt, Jan Kleinnijenhuis, Dirk Oegema, and Stefan Schlobach. Knowledge Representation of Social and Cognitive Networks. In *Procedings of the Social Networks Analysis workshop of the 3rd European Semantic Web Conference (ESWC06)*, 2006.

[vdB99]   Gerhard van de Bunt. *Friends by Choice; An Actor-Oriented Statistical Network Model for Friendship Networks through Time*. PhD thesis, Rijksuniversiteit Groningen, 1999.

[VKV+06]   Max Völkel, Markus Krötzsch, Denny Vrandecic, Heiko Haller, and Rudi Studer. Semantic Wikipedia. In *Proceedings of the 15th International World Wide Web Conference*, pages 585–594, Edinburgh, United Kingdom, 2006.

[VOSS03]   Raphael Volz, Daniel Oberle, Steffen Staab, and Rudi Studer. Ontolift prototype. WonderWeb Deliverable 11, January 2003.

[vR79]   C.J. van Rijsbergen. *Information Retrieval*. Butterworth-Heinemann, London, 2nd edition edition, 1979.

[Wat99]   Duncan J. Watts. Networks, dynamics and the small-world phenomenon. *American Journal of Sociology*, 105(2):493–527, 1999.

[WFIG94]   Stanley Wasserman, Katherine Faust, Dawn Iacobucci, and Mark Granovetter. *Social Network Analysis: Methods and Applications*. Cambridge University Press, 1994.

[WHAT04]   Fang Wu, Bernardo A. Huberman, Lada A. Adamic, and Joshua R. Tyler. Information flow in social groups. *Physica A*, 337:327–335, 2004.

[WL41]   Willam Lloyd Warner and P.S. Lunt. *The Social Life of a Modern Community*. Yale University Press, New Haven, CT, USA, 1941.

[WS98]   Duncan J. Watts and Steven Strogatz. Collective dynamics of 'small-world' networks. *Nature*, 393:440–442, 1998.

[WSD+96]   Barry Wellman, Janet Salaff, Dimitrina Dimitrova, Laura Garton, Milena Gulia, and Caroline Haythornthwaite. Computer Networks as Social Networks: Collaborative Work, Telework, and Virtual Community. *Annual Review of Sociology*, 22:213–238, 1996.

[ZR01]   Ezra W. Zuckerman and Ray E. Reagans. Networks, Diversity, and Performance: The Social Capital of Corporate R&D Teams. *Organization Science*, 12(4):502–517, 2001.

Index

CREATIVE

MACHINE

DESIGN

Creative
Machine
Design

DESIGN INNOVATION

AND THE RIGHT SOLUTIONS

by Ben-Zion Sandler, Ph.D.
BEN-GURION UNIVERSITY OF THE NEGEV, BEER SHEEVA, ISRAEL

A Solomon Press Book

PARAGON HOUSE PUBLISHERS

The Solomon Press
Publishers Creative Services Inc.
89-31 161 Street; Suite 611
Jamaica, New York 11432
United States of America

The author and publisher wish to thank the copyright owners
who have given their permission to use copyrighted material.
Any ommissions or errors in giving proper credit are unin-
tentional and will be corrected at the first opportunity after
the error or omission has been brought to the attention of the
author or publisher.

Creative Machine Design is a joint publication of Paragon
House Publishers and The Solomon Press (a division of Pub-
lishers Creative Services Inc.) It is distributed by Paragon
House Publishers, 866 Second Ave., New York, NY 10017.

Library of Congress Cataloging in Publication Data

Sandler, B.Z., 1932-
Creative machine design.

Bibliography: p.
Includes index.
1. Machinery—Design. I. Title.
TJ233.S25   1985   621.8'15   85-11964

ISBN: 0-913729-28-0

Manufactured in the United States of America.

TABLE OF CONTENTS

LIST OF TABLES

LIST OF
FIGURES

ACKNOWLEDGMENTS

I express my deep gratitude and appreciation to my colleagues at the Mechanical Engineering Department of the Ben-Gurion University of the Negev for their spiritual support and cooperation in accumulating the material for this book and assistance in writing it.

I am especially grateful to those who transformed my poor Russian English into something readable, particularly Inez Muerinik. I wish to thank Evelyn Tucker of The Solomon Press for her excellent copyediting, as well as the many who contributed to the editing, who typed, and to those who offered their advice in developing the manuscript. I thank Dr. Vladimir Maxson who made many valuable suggestions. My appreciation to Morion Milner for her valuable assistance. And, of course, many, many thanks to my wonderful family and my wife whose warmth and humor help me in all aspects of my life.

PREFACE

In my work as a professional engineer, designer and teacher, I have had many inquiries about specific machine design problems and general inquiries about the creative process as it applies to this area of engineering. These questions have come from fellow engineers, faculty colleagues and from students.

This book was conceived as a result of my own frustration at not being able to refer people to a book that would have an answer to these vital questions. In developing the content of the present work I have highlighted the creative-imaginative aspects and related this to the creative-practical side of engineering design. I have tried to keep in the forefront the end-result of the design process, namely the creation of a new, useful and saleable product.

Part I deals with the methodology for seeking technical solutions to design problems, the development of ideas and concepts, and the organization and execution of creative thinking. Problems are described as assignable to two planes: "what" to design and "how" to design it. The former are of interest to salespeople, marketing executives, and the like, and the latter to engineers and designers. It encompasses Chapters 1–4.

In Part II the reader is led directly into the stages of design after the "what" problem has been solved. Here the pathway from engineering principles to design is charted. This section consists of Chapters 5–9.

5. The design of the processing layout of the machine or device, in which the principles of action and the operation sequences are defined.

6. The design of the kinematic layout of the machine or device, which defines the way by which the elements are caused to move in the desired order.

7. A list of rules, conventions, and methods relating to the design of machine parts. A wide range of situations is illustrated for which the designer must know how to provide satisfactory reliability of the machine part. No classic design course treats these aspects of design. Nevertheless knowledge of the rules is very important in the machine design process, and this information can be useful not only to a beginner in the field, but also to the experienced engineer.

8. The use of computers in technical creativity; a discussion of the nature of creativity and how it can be computerized—if at all.

9. Some marketing problems.

Academic reasoning, which can cause difficulties for inexperienced readers, is kept to a minimum. Highly detailed classification is more suitable for the specialist than for the beginner, and thus example is preferred to discussion. The examples are simple enough to illustrate clearly the development of the engineering thought process. They do not require long explanations, in contrast to those presented in some books in the field, which suffer from the drawback of being too specific and professional. The cases described here should be familiar to most students.

The text includes a number of exercises and questions on different types of creative thinking, most of which have been tried out in class, in various projects, or in the laboratory.

We believe that in this book we have achieved an important objective—to introduce the beginner in engineering to the main approaches to the different stages of design. We have tried to accomplish this by classifying the methods involved in the creative search for technical solutions.

CREATIVE

MACHINE

DESIGN

Part I

INTRODUCTION

The past 150–200 years have been years of incredible progress in technology. And the main criterion on which such an evaluation is based is one that is easily measurable—it is productivity or efficiency in industry and manufacturing, or more simply, the number of units produced per unit of time. Thousands of examples can be cited to illustrate this tremendous progress. Here are just a few.

Today metal is cut at a velocity of 15 kg of chips per minute at a relative speed between the cutter's edge and the blank of 500 meters per minute. In 1825 the same parameters were about 0.15 kg of chips per minute at a speed of 5 meters per minute. Writing is another example. A modern typewriter can reach a speed of about 300 typed symbols per minute, and produce some ten copies simultaneously. In addition, with modern copying equipment an original can be reproduced many times per minute, exactly and ready for use. Compare this achievement with the production of books and manuscripts by hand 500 years ago. The classical example of progress, however, is weaving. The output of a modern loom is about 300–500 woofs per minute versus the 10–20 woofs per minute produced a hundrd years ago.

The most impressive technological achievements of the past two centuries have been in the realm of transportation—on the surface of the earth, on the sea, in the air, and, of course, in space. Before the advent of the steam engine, practically the only means of maintaining communication between geographical points on land was by horse. A team of horses can attain a speed of almost

30 kilometers per hour in a relatively short time, with the average velocity 10–15 kilometers per hour. A journey by sailing ship from Europe to America took six to ten weeks and was completely dependent on the weather and the winds, but ships were the only means of transportation available to those early travelers across the ocean. The same limits existed for communications: cablegrams, telegrams, air mail, and radio are all "youngsters" in terms of history. During the past 200 years, the speed of delivering information has increased by at least 50–100 million times. Compare the time required for a telephone call from the United States to Europe with that to deliver a letter via a sailing vessel, or even a steamship.

We could continue giving examples indefinitely, but even the few described here should lead to the conclusion that while technology has leapt forward, the productivity of thinking, especially creative thinking, has barely increased. The brain of a modern man or woman does not evaluate situations much faster than did the human brain 100, 200, or even 1000 years ago. It is true that people today know much more and are equipped with many kinds of technical devices, but the situations with which people now have to deal are much more complicated and cumbersome than those of the past. As a result, we often make decisions that are ridiculous. To quote only one example: To modify an item such as a modern machine tool to suit the production of a new product may take the production staff of a factory six months, and to design a new machine may take a year or two. This time is somewhat longer than the ever-changing market for tool machines will allow. In those two years, new concepts can appear and the new machine may be hopelessly obsolete at the very moment of its birth. Consequently it may be better not to initiate the process of implementing the new product in the factory. The design time is critical here. One may offer the objection that today we have sophisticated computing equipment that enables us to obtain information about hundreds of variations within a few hours, including all the auxiliary time-intensive operations connected with the system. Gear-speed reducers, for instance, can be completely calculated in minutes, including the time required for walking to the computer terminal room, punching the cards, and returning with the sheets bearing the calculation results. The process can be further speeded up with the help of a auxiliary devices, such as aids for pencil sharpening, erasing incorrect lines on drawings, and copying. Modern desks equipped with rulers that are firm, straight, and perpendicular are available, and these considerably ease the work of the drafter. We also have computer-operated design systems in which the computer actually prints out the drawing of the object being designed. These systems have the ability to present tens, or even hundreds, of visual variations of the design pattern in several spatial positions in a few moments. This is of great importance for automobile and aircraft design and for other fields involving machine design and building.

However, all these "miraculous" mechanisms can be utilized only after a certain stage of design or thinking. Before these heavy weapons can be brought out, it is necessary to know what is going to be designed and what principles will be used for this purpose. We do not, as yet, have any automatic system that can invent a device, create a new product, or propose a new principle. Even today this part of the creative process must be performed by human beings. What can help us at this stage is possibly an effective "thinking organization" and the knowledge of the basic "laws" that control this process.

Although many mechanisms, devices, and methods look familiar, are well known, and have been used for a long time, someone may suddenly propose an original and unexpected solution to a particular problem. Ask how this splendid way of solving the problem was arrived at and very seldom will its inventor have a definite answer. Mostly the answer will take the form: "I thought, it took a long time, and *suddenly*!" What is this "suddenly"? It is the problem with which the first part of this work will deal.

It appears that the process of developing a new product occurs on two planes. The better known plane is related to typical engineering calculations, and its basics are taught at educational institutions. As a result of scientific research, this plane develops rapidly. Each year reports and scientific conferences add new information to this computative domain. However, the other plane of engineering activity—the process of creative seeking of new ideas, solutions, and approaches—must precede the calculations. Before one can begin to calculate, one must be able to create a model or to have a picture of the object under design. This latter domain will constitute the subject of this work. The engineer or inventor has to overcome a number of obstacles during the design process—"what" to develop and "how" to go about it.

The solution to the problem may be found with the help of Figure I-1. Here we see a ream of sheets. Each sheet represents a coordinate plane in which we call one axis "what" and the other "how." Each sheet represents a separate design stage. Let us illustrate the use of this figure with an example—the creation of an electromobile (an automobile driven by electric power).

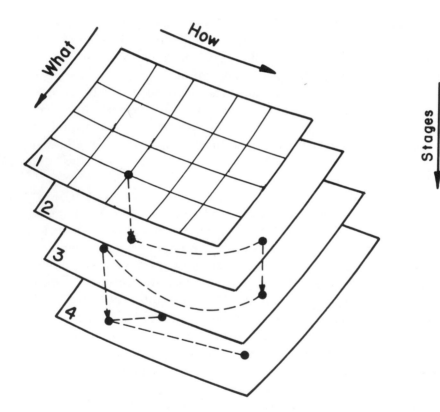

Figure I-1 The "what" and "how" model of technical creativity. Each sheet represents a coordinate plane in which one axis is denoted "what" and the other "how." Each sheet also represents a specific design stage. The dotted line is the trajectory of the design process.

For the first stage or sheet, one has to define *what* is to be designed and *how* to operate it:

What—a self-driven vehicle.
How—driven by a horse, a steam engine, an internal-combustion engine, an electromotor, and so on.

Once the choice to use an electromotor has been made, one passes on to the second sheet. Here:

What—an electromobile.
How—source of electricity can be chemical batteries, accumulators, solar cells, an autonomous generator, ultrahigh-frequency supply, and so on.

Once the decision to use an accumulator has been made, one passes on to the third sheet:

What—an electromobile with an accumulator-type energy source.
How—accumulator can be alkaline, acidic, or something unknown, charged from a stationary energy source located at home, from distribution points cited on the streets, or from charging stations.

After that choice has been made, one proceeds to the fourth sheet:

What—an electromobile with an alkaline accumulator that may be charged at home.
How—for the building of the car, how to design the driving mechanisms and the energy sources, and how to ensure the necessary parameters such as load, speed, and distance.

As one passes on to the following sheets, the solutions and details of the design become more specific and detailed. Each step is realized as a result of long and deep thinking.
The creativity factor appears in both the "what" and "how" coordinates on each sheet. Each sheet places an enormous stress

on the intellectual power of the designer, who attempts to make the best decisions at each stage, and it may take months, or even years, to go through the ream. This process has not significantly changed during the past 50, 100, or 200 years. It is no small wonder that attention is being paid to ways of speeding up the process of creative thinking.

The "what" problem encompasses a wide spectrum of questions, including the marketing, economic, and manufacturing possibilities at our disposal.

What should we develop?
What should we produce?
What will be in demand?
What will bring the best profit?
What will attract the customers' interest?

The most unpredictable solutions are possible here, but the problem of how to stumble on them remains. This is the problem of generating new ideas; it is the problem of speeding up the generating.

To solve the "how" problem, a wide range of knowledge in physics, chemistry, and technology is required. Much scientific erudition is the result of the striving to find an optimal solution to a previously formulated task. Here lies the source of the engineering calculations that are not the current object of our interest. We shall consider only the first, creative part of the "how" problem, although there is obviously always an interaction between "what" and "how" and the chain develops from "what" through "how" to calculation.

1

PRINCIPLES OF CREATIVITY IN ENGINEERING

The examination of a familiar example should help to understand the role of creative thinking in the principles of design. The process of weapons' development is such an example. Unfortunately weaponry is a subject of common knowledge: each of us is familiar with its main concepts from childhood. It is, therefore, not difficult to define the requirements a weapon must fulfill:

1. To hit the target from as far away as possible.
2. To hit the target as strongly as possible.
3. To hit the target as accurately as possible.
4. To hit as many targets as possible at one time.
5. To conform to any economic restraints that may be placed on the weapon's production.

Having neither patent offices nor educational establishments at their disposal, primitive people used stones, pieces of wood, or sticks to throw at enemies or at animals they wanted to kill for food.

THE PRINCIPLES OF CREATIVE DESIGN

The First Principle

We should now be ready to formulate the first principle of creative thinking in design.

The designer copies or duplicates the events, phenomena, or processes taking place in nature, in neighboring fields of human activity, or even in far-removed fields of activity. Let us look first at the "copying" nature of machines. Here it would certainly be wrong to assume that borrowing from nature was typical only of ancient times. For example, the design of one of the most modern navigation devices is based on a navigation principle used in nature by the beetle. This insect finds its way by means of a "tuning fork," which excites the ganglion responsible for the direction of flight when the plane of the "tuning fork's" oscillations changes. The steam engine is another example of this principle: Many inventors tried to design their engines in a horse-like form. The mere fact that the engine was created to pull a load instead of to push it confirms this idea. The way in which the steam engine mimics nature was beautifully described by H.G. Wells (1866–1946), who said that the shadow of a horse runs in front of every steam engine.

If we think about "borrowing" from adjacent fields of human activity, we see that many modern machines and tools have hand-operated predecessors. The inventors of these machines tried to duplicate the manual process, for example, in the sewing machine and the loom. Although the needle and thread were tools, the sewing process was manual. Similarly, for thousands of years weaving was a completely manual process.

Over the years hunters learned to shape their stones to get sharp edges or to sharpen their stick to inflict greater damage on their enemies or prey. When metals were "discovered," these hunting tools were transformed into knives and spears. The steps described conform to the second requirement—to increase the effectiveness of the thrust. As the skill and experience of the ancient hunters and warriors grew, they came to understand that a straight stick hits more precisely and flies further and that a sharpened stone cuts better. They also found that by shaping a stick in a specific way, it could be made to return to the hunter's feet if it missed the prey—an important property, since it saves energy and decreases the danger to the owner of the weapon. We are still familiar with this kind of hunting tool in the boomerang.

Today we often apply the expertise gained in one field to the development of a device in another. For example, the idea of using a reversed wing in the design of sports cars was "borrowed" from aviation. (Figure 1-1). This modification provides the car with an

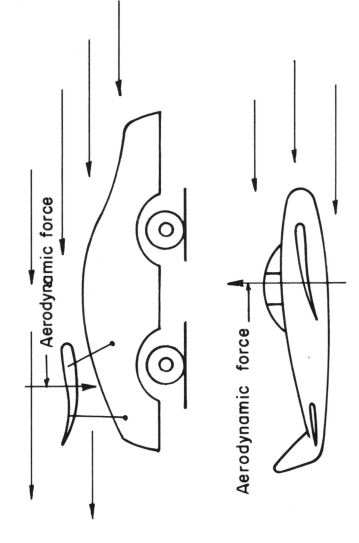

Figure 1-1 The reversed wing "borrowed" from aircraft design provides an automobile with an additional force that presses the wheels onto the road at high speeds.

additional force that presses the wheels onto the road at high speeds. The aerodynamics of the wing creates a force which, in this case, is equal to the carrying capacity of the wing and is directed toward the ground.

The Second Principle

The second principle of creativity can also be derived from the examples given, and can be stated as follows:

II. *The existing features of a tool, device, or product are improved by streamlining and emphasizing the most important features.* Sharp edges, better materials, and smoother surfaces of the stone, stick, and knife made them more effective and more dangerous tools. The better the streamlining of the throwing tool, the deeper it penetrates in spite of the fact that the initial value of mV (m mass, V velocity) does not change. In addition, the better the material, the longer the tool will last. As the use of new materials becomes widespread, new shapes sometimes become available, and the dimensions of many devices also change as technology becomes more sophisticated. An increase in the capacity of tools, weapons, or devices is often achieved by increasing their dimensions. For example, people began to build bigger bows and to use stronger materials, including steel, which led to the production of arbalests and ballistas. Similarly, after the introduction of gunpowder into military technology, there was a tendency to increase the dimensions of guns. Toward the end of World War I, for example, the Germans built their "Big Bertha" to shell Paris. (The results were disappointing from a military point of view.) Conversely, as technology develops, dimensions sometimes tend to decrease. The history of timepieces is an excellent illustration of this process, ranging from traditional large, tower clocks to today's tiny wristwatches.

The application of the second principle thus leads to the development of new products and the creation of new tools. It also involves the possibility of combining different tools to produce new ones. For instance, the spear was created from a stone or a metal tag fastened to the edge of a stick, and the ax by a differently shaped stone or metal body fastened to a thicker stick.

A classic example of new devices created by combining two existing technologies is the family of "geared linkages." These devices consist of a combination of a linkage mechanism, for instance, a four-bar mechanism, and a gear transmission. These new mechanisms have very interesting and important kinematic properties, as shown in Figure 1-2. In this figure the wheel 1 is the driving link. It rotates around its center 0_1. As a result of the action of links 3–4 and of a block of geared wheels 5, the wheel 2 is driven around its center 0_2. The ratio of this mechanism and the angle ϕ_2 as a function of the angle ϕ_1 are shown in the accompanying graph. We can see that there is an interval $\Delta\phi$ during every revolution of wheel 1 when wheel 2 is practically motionless. This property is very useful in some cases.

The Third Principle

We can now formulate the third principle of creativity as follows:

III. New tools and products can be created as the result of a combination of known elements. We are perhaps now approaching the most important point. The excellently shaped ancient tools were the outcome of the skill and experience of generations of craftsmen, their successes and failures. But no matter what they did, a sword remained a sword and a spear was still a spear. A new concept was necessary to push the development of the weapon further, and this modification was achieved by separating the weapon from the hands of the hunter or the warrior. The bow and arrow and the sling are the most important examples of this family of weapons (Figure 1-3).

The Fourth Principle

Let us now formulate the fourth principle.

IV. At a certain stage in the development of a new approach to the solution of a problem, it becomes necessary to introduce further advances in the product under consideration. What is the big difference between the bow and its predecessors? A hunter

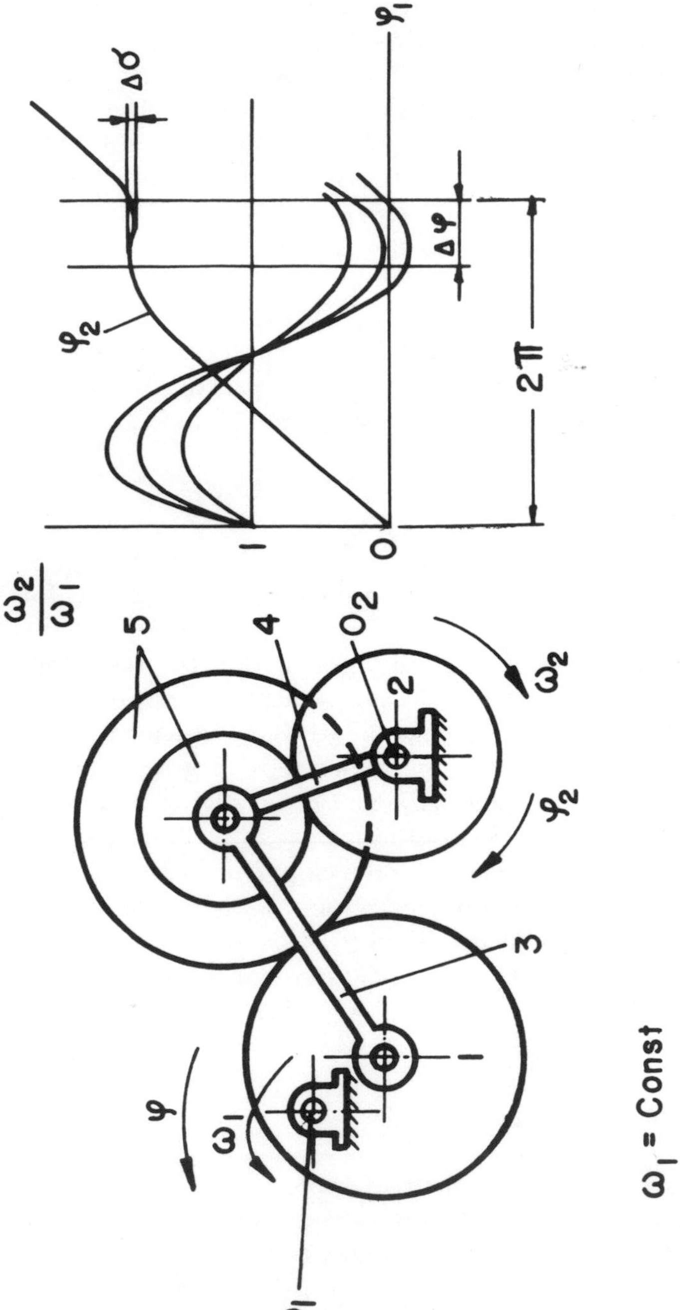

Figure 1-2 A four-bar linkage and a gear train illustrate a combination of two existing technologies—as the result of which a new kinematic property is derived. As is clear from the graph, the speed of the wheel 2 is close to zero during the interval of the rotation of wheel 1.

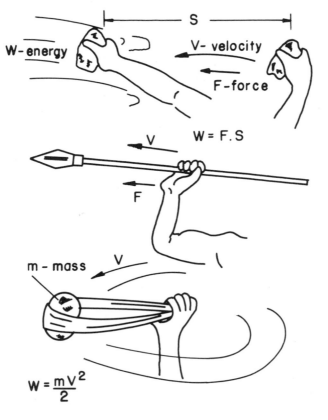

$$W = F \cdot S$$

$$W = \frac{mV^2}{2}$$

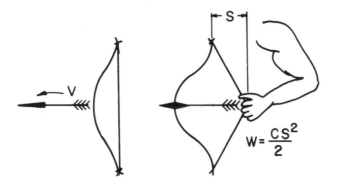

$$W = \frac{CS^2}{2}$$

C - stiffness of the bow

Figure 1-3 What is the difference between using a bow or sling and throwing a stone or a spear? The warrior accumulates the energy necessary for "throwing" the arrow by stretching the bow string (or rotating the sling). A new concept is thus achieved by separating the weapon from the hands of the warrior.

accumulates the energy necessary for "throwing" the arrow by stretching the bowstring and bending the bow. This is the first stage of the action. The second stage begins after the hunter has aimed: the hunter frees the bowstring and thus shoots the arrow. The same separation of actions can be seen in the use of the sling. The first energy-accumulating stage involves the rotating of the sling, and the second stage comprises freeing the sling and allowing a stone to fly in the desired direction. The first stage is manual, but the second is automated. The duration of the first stage depends on the capacity P, of the user, who has to attain a certain amount of potential energy W. Thus the time T is

$$T = \frac{W}{P}$$

The capacity of the device does not depend on the user, but the user's power can be used to actuate the device or tool. The efficiency of solutions of this type depends largely on the skill and personal attributes of their operators. The accumulated energy W is transformed into kinetic energy during a definite interval T_o, which depends on the bow's capacity P_o. Thus $T_o = W/P_o$. The value P_o is usually bigger than P, and therefore $T_o < T$.

Anybody who knows how to aim, has good eyes, and is trained to use a weapon can propel that weapon over a longer distance than would be possible in a completely manual case. The efficiency of the weapon thus is no longer a function of the hunter's physical properties as it was before the bow was invented. As a further illustration of the fourth principle, we can compare advances in technology with those achieved in sport. Today each centimeter, each fraction of a second, in sport requires great effort, sophisticated training, and a high level of scientific investigation. As in the technical field, after the main aims have been achieved, each additional improvement in an existing concept requires both a tremendous amount of research and large investments. We can depict this process in technology as well as in sport in a graphical manner. In the diagram shown in Figure 1-4, at points A_I and A_{II} it is no longer worth expending more effort on improvements; a new concept must be found because the "ceiling" of the concept has been reached.

To deepen our understanding of the fourth principle, let us look at another example—the history of the development of the bearing (Figure 1-5). The ancient bearing consisted of a wooden or stone shaft enveloped in a simple wooden or stone sleeve. Difficulties in the treatment of these materials resulted in low accuracy of the joint elements. With the use of metals, the quality of the bearing improved, especially after the invention of turning. A large contribution to and a new concept in the further development of the bearing was the use of lubricants, and by the choice of the right combination of materials, the limits of improvement were reached (Figure 1-5I).

The next step was therefore a new concept—the use of rolling elements in the bearing (i.e., the transition from sliding friction to rolling). With this improvement the losses in the bearing were decreased by ten or more times (Figure 1-5II). The first roller bearings were invented in 1862 for use in bicycles. The mass

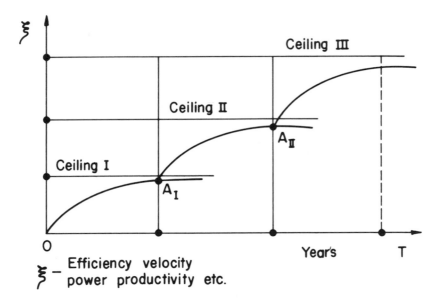

Figure 1-4 The interrupted nature of the development of technical concepts. At points A_I, A_{II}, . . . it is no longer worth expending effort on additional improvement of an existing concept. A new concept must be found where the "ceiling" of the concept has been reached.

Lubricant

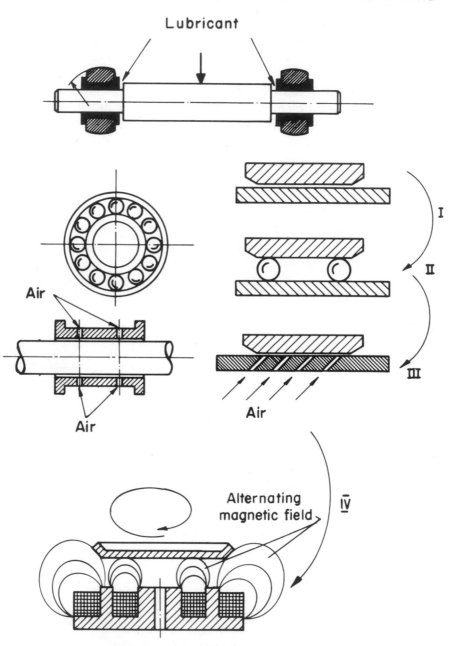

Air

Air

Air

Alternating
magnetic field

Figure 1-5 The concept described in Figure 1-4 is
illustrated by the history of bearing
development—from simple, lubricated friction I, to
rolling friction II, to the air cushion III, and finally to
electromagnetic suspension IV.

production of roller bearings and their applications in general machine manufacture began in 1898, and since then many kinds of roller bearings have been created. But for some technical requirements, these bearings are not smooth enough; that is, the resistance caused by friction due to the rolling movement is sometimes very large in comparison with the needs of a mechanism such as the gyroscope. To reduce this negative effect, a special "driven bearing" was proposed. The main concept behind this solution is illustrated in Figure 1-6. The external ring of the bearing is allowed to rotate, and the relative motion between the rings and rolling elements is thus decreased, as are the losses due to friction. We can see that this solution is very complicated. Moreover, although this solution improves one feature of the device, it introduces other troubles, such as vibration, noise, and loss of accuracy.

The next new idea was the use of pneumatic and hydraulic bearings (Figure 1-5III). In this type of bearing, the shaft "floats" in the sleeve on a thin layer of compressed air or liquid, and there is no direct contact between rigid surfaces. Friction is very much reduced, especially when compressed air is used. The rotation speed can be considerably increased without increasing the resistance, which is of great importance for gyroscopes and other

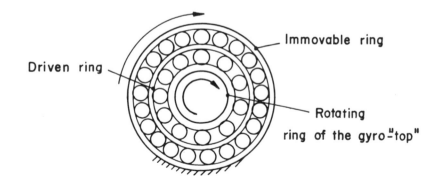

Driven ring

Immovable ring

Rotating
ring of the gyro-"top"

Figure 1-6 A double bearing for diminishing friction losses. The external ring of the bearing rotates so as to decrease the relative motion between the rings, thus reducing the losses due to friction.

devices that rotate at very fast speeds. It should be pointed out that the hydraulic bearing is similar to the lubricated slide bearing. The only difference lies in the fact that for the hydraulic bearing modern technology allows the elements to be fitted together with such a high degree of precision and such lubricant feeding systems to be produced that a thin liquid layer becomes realistic.

The next, and perhaps most revolutionary, idea was the suspension of the rotating body in a vacuum by means of a magnetic field. (Figure 1-5IV). In this case the speed of rotation reaches millions of revolutions per minute. This value is greater than the speed that most materials are able to resist because of the forces of inertia caused by the rotation.

Here we should remember that when one problem results in the appearance of a number of inventions, it is obvious that the most effective solution has still not been found, and we remain on the plateau of the exponent. A "revolutionary" solution is still required.

The Fifth Principle

At this point we can formulate the fifth principle of creativity.

V. A new solution can be found in the past history of the subject under consideration. The development of many products follows a spiral-like path. The same solutions return, but in significantly improved forms that impart to the product new qualities and properties.

The history of aviation is an outstanding example of this statement (Figure 1-7). In 1783 the Montgolfier brothers built the first fire-powered balloon and embarked on the first real flight known to mankind. This balloon was, in fact, the first flying aircraft. The concept underlying the use of this "lighter-than-air" device was borrowed from Archimedes' principle (in an application of Principle I). Difficulties in navigating this type of airborne craft resulted in the creation of a new device—the airship (dirigible)—which was a combination of a balloon and propelling equipment (Principle III). The first airship took off in 1852 after the "parent" balloon-type craft had been improved in many ways. New materials, such as aluminum were used for constructing the body, and

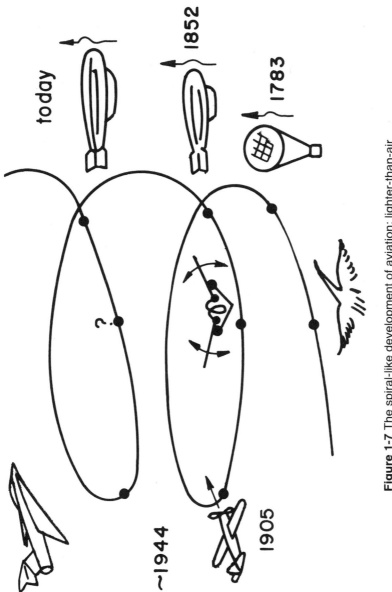

Figure 1-7 The spiral-like development of aviation: lighter-than-air devices, heavier-than-air devices, and waving-wing devices. Each turn of the spiral brings the old concept to a new technological level.

hydrogen replaced warm air (which had to be heated by a bonfire) as the "lighter-than-air" gas. The zeppelin disaster of 1937 put an end to this kind of flying for about 30 years. At present we are, however, witnessing the restoration of this concept, but with helium replacing the dangerous hydrogen gas. Thus the spiral that began in 1783 completed its first turn at the junction of the nineteenth and twentieth centuries with the creation of the airship and will make its second turn during our lifetimes.

A second line of development appeared on the spiral with the invention of the "heavier-than-air" aircraft by the Wright brothers. Orville and Wilbur Wright built their first airplane in 1903, and made their first practical flight in 1903.

There is a third line of development of flying devices (Figure 1-7) that should not be forgotten. It appears that a flying apparatus with moving wings (like those of a bird) is much more efficient than conventional aircraft, that is, the amount of the useful flying weight per unit of fuel weight or per unit of spent power is larger. Modern technology has enabled the construction of such a waving-wings model. This type of craft may well be the airplane of the future, or at least the small airplane of the future—it is difficult to imagine a jumbo jet waving its wings. Thus the third line on the spiral winds from the bird through Icarus, the son of Daedalus, to the experimental flying ornithopter.

Another excellent example of the spiral development of technical ideas is provided by a commonplace instrument—the razor. We suppose that in ancient times it was a variation of knife, but it is unlikely that a stone-made knife could afford much pleasure to the user. In more modern times, with the improvement of the properties of steel and the invention of stainless steel (and the development of shaving foams), the straight razor came into use. These instruments are still used by barbers today. Gillette then invented a practical, cheap, and convenient blade for the safety razor, which precluded the need to sharpen the blade. The manufacturers of razors subsequently produced various kinds of blades, razor handles, and auxiliary accessories for shaving.

In the middle of the twentieth century, the industry was struck by the invention and swift introduction to the market of electric and mechanical razors. A large number of patents were granted, differing in the mode of mechanical or electric drive, as well as in the cutting method. It then took some 15 to 20 years for blade manufacturers to recover and to revive the concept of the blade. The new manual razors appearing on the market incorporated achievements in steel technology and the latest developments in plastic materials. The high quality of beard cutting combined with extremely high safety and "productivity" have rendered the "old fashioned" razor highly competitive with electric and mechanical models.

The turns of the spiral depend on the state of technology at the time in question. Thus it is obviously important to study the history of technical solutions and to check whether now is perhaps the time to apply some long forgotten ideas.

The Sixth Principle

Let us proceed to the next principle.

VI. *This is the principle of inversion, that is, the exchange of positions, functions, or movements of the elements or links of the system under development.* This principle may be applied at any level of consideration or on any "what" or "how" sheet. The following examples illustrate this principle. It has been known since the beginning of the nineteenth century that when an electric current flows through a conductor, a magnetic field is set up. In 1831 Faraday demonstrated the inverted idea that when a conductor moves through a magnetic field in a certain manner, an electric current will appear in the conductor. This idea is known as the law of electromagnetic induction.

An outstanding example of inversion is the IBM Selectric typewriter. The classic typewriter, which has been in existence for about 120 years, consists of a linkage mechanism system to drive each type bar regardless of the kind of machine (electric or manual), a paper roller mounted on a carriage, and a housing. The paper roller and the carriage constitute a relatively massive body, which has to accomplish rapid, accurate periodic movements during typing. Obviously the larger the paper sheets and the more copies required, the higher are the accelerations and declarations of the carriage and the stronger and more harmful are the impacts of the moving parts of the mechanism; the typing rate thus may be restricted. Even electrically powered machines of classical design suffer from the same inherent problems as the strictly manual machines. Typewriter design thus reached the "top" of the exponential curve, and a revolutionary idea had to be found. The design of the IBM Selectric typewriter is an illustration of the inversion principle. In this machine the massive carriage is fixed and a light globe-shaped printing element is allowed to move along the paper. Thus the dimensions of the paper and the number of copies required do not influence the dynamics of the mechanism. A single typing head with a small mass can be moved faster and more accurately than the massive carriage. It should be noted that this concept became realistic only because of the development of electronics. It is difficult to imagine that such a solution could have been found 50 years ago.

The development of the gas turbine was also based on an inversion approach. The Laval steam turbine, invented in 1889, had an inherent balancing problem as a result of the high speed of rotation (about 30,000–42,000 r/m). Attempts to increase the accuracy and the strength of the shaft did not provide a solution to the problem. The answer lay in an inversion of these attempts: A flexible, thin shaft was introduced and its self-balancing property solved the problem. This improvement opened the way for the introduction of high-speed steam turbines, and later gas turbines, into industry.

And last, is not a rocket or jet-propelled missile an inverted gun? The recoil of a gun is utilized to propel a rocket, and the body of the rocket can be considered a moving gun tube. Later we consider a number of examples of inversion at different levels of complexity.

The principle of inversion does not always involve a change in a directly opposite manner, such as up–down, move–stop, or rigid–flexible. Let us look, for example, at the arc lamp. The original arc lamp consisted of two carbon electrodes between which an electric arc was maintained. Since it is difficult to provide a constant gap between the edges of the electrodes, special regulating devices had to be used to control this gap as well as the brightness of the light. To overcome this problem, Yablochkov, in 1876, changed the relative positioning of the electrodes: He placed them one next to each other with a layer of special insulation, comprised of nonconducting clay, between them. In this setup the gap between the burning electrodes remains constant, the electrodes burn uniformly, and they shorten at the same rate. This invention made the arc lamp cheap enough to be used for many public needs, for instance, the illumination of Opera Square in Paris and many other streets.

The Seventh Principle

The inversion principle is a very effective tool in the creation of new concepts and the improvement of existing ones. But the efficiency of the drilling process, for instance, can be increased by multiplying the number of drill heads in a drilling instrument instead of seeking a new concept, such as punching or burning out the required holes. This example brings us to the next principle.

VII. The joining together of identical elements can result in a new effect—the principle of multiplication. One of the oldest examples of the application of this principle is Archimedes' tackle, which was an assemblage of pulleys. Another example may be found in the fifteenth century, in Leonardo da Vinci's weapon consisting of 33 gun tubes—three rows of tubes, each containing 11 tubes, arranged one above the other in such a way that the shooting and charging of each row was accomplished separately in a certain sequence. (Bear this in mind when considering Principle VIII.)

In 1884 an English engineer, Charles Algernon Parson, applied the principle of multiplication to the development of the steam engine by creating a multistage turbine. With this device the utilization of steam energy was improved. A more modern example is the type of drilling machine used in mass production. These tools are equipped with a number of drills located in positions corresponding to those of the holes required in the part being processed.

A note of caution must be introduced here. Care must be taken in applying this principle (as with Principle II): the number of components cannot be increased infinitely. It is ridiculous to put together, say, 100 gun tubes or 1000 drill heads. However, when used properly, the multiplicative principle improves productivity. For instance, six gun tubes assembled on a revolving drum create the possibility of increasing the shooting efficiency six times. At any moment each of the six gun tubes is undergoing a different action—charging, closing, shooting, and so on. For each gun tube, the shooting pace is the same as that of a single-barrel gun, but as a result of the combined action, the system shoots six times faster.

The Eighth Principle

The eighth principle is a logical extension of the foregoing principle.

VIII. Simultaneous execution of a number of actions of a device can enhance its productivity and result in the achievement of new effects. The general case for this principle can be represented by the diagram shown in Figure 1-8. A number of actions, say three, are carried out simultaneously, and despite the relative slowness of the process, the final output rate is three times faster. If we suppose that mechanism B carries out the final operation of some process that takes time T and consists of three actions A, B, and C, then a combination of three machines I, II, and III will manufacture the final product, within a time interval t, where $T = 3t$. When the number of separate actions exceeds three, the advantage of simultaneous execution is even more important. For example, a combination of this principle and that previously described is used in the design of $4-$, $6-$, $8-$, and $12-$ cylinder (and more) internal combustion engines. The pace of the working strokes depends on the number of cylinders. As the number of cylinders is increased, the power increases, and the rotation becomes smoother.

It is obvious that the use of this eighth principle is based on the use of semi- or completely automatic solutions. For example, the crossbow machine gun unit designed by Leonardo da Vinci in about 1500 illustrates the fact that this principle cannot be applied to nonautomatic systems: An archer was suspended independently and aimed and fired bows charged by 20 big men on the outside of a wheel, which was responsible for activating the system. The bow charging force was estimated at 120,000 pounds.

The Ninth Principle

Automatic machine tools are often based on principles of multiplication as well as on the ninth principle.

IX. *Automation (electronics, pneumatics, hydraulics, mechanics) produces new effects and improves the product, device, or tool.* The effects of automation are a result of its "tirelessness," its smaller "response time," its independent manner of action, and its ability to carry out a task under conditions in which a human being cannot function.

What are the reasons for the difficulties in product improvement as the advancement approaches the top of the curve? What are the restrictions that make each subsequent step in the devel-

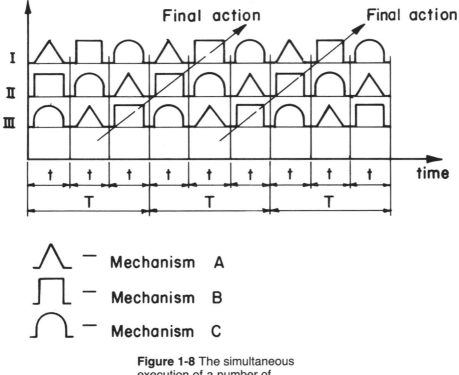

Figure 1-8 The simultaneous execution of a number of actions by a single device can enhance its productivity and result in the achievement of new effects.

opment of any technical concept less effective? The answers to these questions are not simple, but they may be said to revolve about three basic ideas:

1. The dynamics of mechanical, electrical, thermal, and chemical processes.
2. The properties of materials and substances.
3. The level of technology at our disposal.

For example, the IBM Selectric typewriter provided a revolutionary solution to the dynamically overloaded conventional typewriter. Similarly, the Otto internal-combustion engine was "replaced" by the diesel engine when the thermodynamics of the Otto engine had become "exhausted." The maximal efficiency of the Otto engine is about 35 percent while that of the diesel engine is 42–45 percent. An excellent example of the role played by technology may be found in the lagging behind of the Soviet Union in the "moon race" of the 1960s and 1970s. The low thermal resistance of the metals used for constructing rocket jets forced the designers of one Russian spaceship to propel the craft with 20 "low-temperature" engines (multiplication principle), whereas the Americans were able to drive their Saturn rocket with as few as four engines. The Soviet program was thus hampered by larger fuel requirements and heavier missiles. In addition, the lag in electronics technology reduced both the maneuverability of the Russian spaceship and its ability to join up with other craft in space.

What are the difficulties facing an engineer, a designer, or an investigator seeking a new solution or an effective concept? What are the main factors restricting such thinking? We consider them to be:

1. The absence of information in particular fields of knowledge.
2. The level of technology at the time under consideration.
3. "Psychological inertia."

The first two points do not require an explanation, but let us dwell briefly on the third point. The phrase "psychological inertia" is used to describe a common phenomenon from which all of us suffer, whether or not we are creators, investigators, developers, or designers. The phenomenon may also be termed "conservative thinking." Let us take an example from ancient Rome. The Romans built hundreds of miles of aqueducts from force of habit because they knew that water can flow from a high point to a lower one. They could, however, have transported water in any direction by means of pipelines, since they knew how to manufacture pipes and they could easily have discovered the principle of syphoning.

This inertia thus may be described as the ever-constant striving to transfer the shape, concept, or structure of an old solution to a new one. The principle of copying solutions is generally useful, but in the particular case of transferring elements from an old concept to a new one, this principle becomes useless, and may even be harmful. We should be very careful to avoid this conservative thinking, this psychological inertia.

Three additional simple examples are appropriate here. The first steamships were propelled by paddle wheels partly because force of habit dictated that moving objects should have wheels. The first self-driven automobiles were carriage shaped (someone even fixed a sculpture of a horse to the front of these cars). One of the first electric motors was built like a steam engine: Two coils (like cylinders) pulled the armature, and a crank mechanism transformed the linear motion of the armature into rotation of the flywheel; a special switch mechanism (like a steam valve) controlled the coils.

Let us review the principles of creativity once more, this time as applied to the history of the development of gear transmission. We thus start with a brief study of the evolution of the art of gearing, which began about 5000 years ago. Unfortunately we do not know when the ancient "inventors" first proposed the idea of the wheel in general, but the inventors of the first geared wheels obviously borrowed the shape of the rotating wheel to utilize the remarkable properties of equidistant points rotating about a constant pin (Principle I). The principle of the engagement of two or more bodies for purposes of movement was also borrowed by these inventors of gears, who were familiar with this principle from their daily activities and skills. The teeth of the gears of that time had the shape the manufacturer was able to produce; that is, the level of technology dictated the structure of gearing. However, even in those centuries parallel, perpendicular, and crossing shafts could be driven by means of gears. At this stage we approach the top of the first exponential* curve (see Figure 1-4, point A_1).

In the fifteenth century, the German scholar and mathematician Nicholas of Cusa (1451) began to study the application of cycloidal teeth to gearing, and in 1525 Albrecht Durer (of Germany) discovered epicyclic transmissions. These advances were followed by the development of involute gearing in 1694 by Philip de la Hire (France) and in 1754 by Leonard Euler (Russia) (Principle IV). At this time many mechanical clocks and watches were being built, and gear wheels of all dimensions were used for clocks from the size of Big Ben to tiny wrist, necklace, and pocket watches (Principle II). The demand for these types of mechanisms stimulated the art of gearing and the development of the gear industry. For example, the involved mechanisms needed for driving "puppet shows" led to the development of gear chains and complicated interlacings of shafts, wheels, and spindles (Principle V). The calculated cycloidal or involute teeth profile brought new qualities to gearing, that is, the motion became uniform, higher speeds became possible, and the ratio became constant. In 1852 Edward Sang (Scotland) wrote his general theory of gearing and teeth generating, and the top of the second exponential curve was thus reached. Setting aside many minor although important details, we notice that during that period the main struggle was directed toward increasing the durability of the teeth. In general their ability to withstand bending was much greater than their contact strength, since two convex profiles cannot provide good contact conditions. There is only one case in which involute teeth do allow good contact, that of inner engagement. Because of their structural disadvantages, these kinds of gears are used relatively infrequently. Increased dimensions, better materials, thermal treatment, and spiral and "herring-bone" (Principle VII—two helical gears together) teeth have all contributed to narrowing the gap between the bending and contact capacity of gears (Figure 1-4. point A_{II}). Although these factors improved gearing, they did not close the gap completely (Principle II).

The next exponential section was born with the introduction, by Wildhaber (of the United States) in 1921 and Novikov (of the U.S.S.R.) in 1955, of a fundamental change in the implementation of the basic gearing rules—that during wheel rotation, the pressure

---

* The curve may be described as being exponential because its shape may be approximated by an expression such as $A(I - e^{-at})$.

line must pass through the instantaneous center of the mechanism, and that the profile contact point that lies on the pressure line must slide along this line (as in involute engagement) or along some other curve (as in cycloidal engagement). In both cases the pressure line and the trajectories of the contact points are situated in planes perpendicular to the rotation axes. The innovation of Wildhaber and Novikov lies in the fact that the basic rule can be implemented in other planes, for instance, in a plane tangential to the pitch cylinders. The contact point slides along the teeth (which have to be spiral). In applications of this innovation, the profiles of the pinion teeth are usually convex while those of the wheel teeth are concave, both being helicoidal. Wildhaber and Novikov thus overcame the psychological inertia of traditional thinking and obtained a new effect (Principle IV). The contact capability of this arc-shaped convex–concave profile is about twice as high as that of the involute wheels. At this stage bending begins to become the major limitation. The matching of the concave and convex profiles of circular arc gearing is shown in Figure 1-9a and 1-9b.

PROFILES

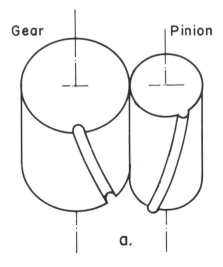

Gear   Pinion

a.

b.

Figure 1-9 The gear-and-pinion circular-arc wheels shown (a) are provided with concave and convex teeth, respectively (b). This gearing concept is novel in that the line of action lies in the plane perpendicular to the plane of rotation of the wheels.

There is still room for improvement of these circular arc gears, particularly by finding solutions to problems of grinding, measuring, and other manufacturing difficulties. We are now at the beginning of the third exponential; point A_{II} (Figure 1-4) is behind us.

Chapter *2*

COMPLEXITY OF PROBLEMS

The technical problems we have to solve today are varied in their subject matter and differ in their levels of complexity. Each level of complexity requires its own tools and means for problem solving, and, obviously, the intellectual power required for each level also differs.

ALTSHULLER'S METHOD

Altshuller[1] has proposed a method of classifying problems according to their complexity, which is based on the following criteria:

1. The way in which the problem is chosen.
2. The way in which the concept of the solution is chosen.
3. The way in which the necessary information is gathered.
4. The way in which the principle of the solution is chosen.
5. The way in which the design is carried out.

Table 2-1 shows how the criteria change in accordance with the level of complexity. The level of complexity of a problem may be said to be the one corresponding to highest level into which any of the criteria fit. There are, of course, no "rigid" borders between the levels. But in typical cases there is no doubt as to

31

Table 2-1
Level of Complexity According to the Criteria of Altshuller

Level of Complexity	Method of Choice of Problem	Method of Choice of Concept	Means of Gathering Information	Method of Choice of Solution	Method of Design (Creative Stage)
I	Trivial problem	Use of existing concept	Common knowledge	Trivial solution	Trivial design
II	A problem selected from several problems	A concept selected from several possibilities	Information gathered from several sources	A solution picked from several possibilities	The design selected from several choices
III	The initial problem is changed	The concept is changed in accordance with the problem	The information is treated according to the changed problem	The solution is changed	The initial design is changed
IV	A new problem is found	A new concept is found	New data relating to the problem are obtained	A new solution is found	A new design is used
V	A new domain of problems is discovered	A new method is discovered	New data relating to the new method and the problems are obtained	A new principle is discovered	New design principles are created

which level the problem under consideration belongs. We shall illustrate the concept of complexity levels by a number of examples.

THE LEVELS OF COMPLEXITY

The first complexity level includes, for instance, problems that can be formulated as follows:

Making something lighter.
Making something stronger.
Making something more accurate.
Emphasizing particular properties, such as heat transfer or heat insulation.
Combining certain simple functions.
The concepts employed to solve these problems are trivial and may include the use of alternative materials, such as plastics or special alloys for reinforcement; the use of special shapes or structures, such thicker parts, crossbars, ribs, openings, or special cross sections; or changes in the methods of manufacturing, such as precise casting and grinding.

The information used to solve these problems can be found in engineering textbooks, handbooks, and catalogs. This information often belongs in the "common knowledge" category, and no printed matter is needed to find the solution. Thus the solution and design do not require special creativity and are based on the utilization of information.
Let us look at three examples:

1. The problem is to prevent a door from knocking against a wall when the door is being opened. This problem is trivial enough to be included in the first level of complexity. An existing concept may be applied for its solution, that is, a mechanical support can be used to limit the movement of the door. No special information is needed to solve the problem. Thus the solution is also trivial, as is the design. The door had to be stopped and a support was used for this purpose.

2. The problem is to prevent the overheating of a transistor under an electric load. This problem is also trivial. The concept underlying the solution is the provision of good heat transfer from the transistor to the air. The necessary information can be found in any electronics handbook. The solution lies in the use of a heat radiator. The design is trivial: an aluminum body provided by ribs to increase the air contact area.

3. The problem is to provide a high degree of stiffness to a long shaft in a case in which no additional support or weight increase is permitted. The concept is mechanical. Any textbook dealing with the strength of materials will give the solution. The design involves the use of a hollow shaft constructed in such a way as to maximize the resistance moment of its cross-section and in this way to decrease the possible deflections under load.

The second complexity level can be illustrated by the following examples.

1. The problem is to produce a door that closes automatically after a person has passed through it. Here one first must formulate the conditions of closing. What will the speed be? Must it be uniform during the closing or is deceleration needed near the closing point (to avoid a strong stroke and noise)? What should the value of the closing force be? Must it change when a disturbance (entrance by a child or elderly person) occurs inside the doorway? How must the closing device behave during door opening? At this level obviously, one first must select the particular problem. Then one has to decide whether a mechanical, pneumatic, hydraulic, or electrical concept will be chosen for its solution. The sources of information will then correspond to the type of problem and the concept to be applied in its solution. Likewise, the solution itself and the design must correspond to the concept.

2. The problem is to create an automatic tablet dispenser that would ensure proper distribution of medicine for a sick person who has an active timetable during the day. When a person who leads an active life has to take three or more kinds of medicine in strict succession, at different times of the day, adherence to the medicine-taking schedule can become a serious problem.

Figure 2-1 shows the development of the design used to solve the second problem. The initial device had the form of a round box provided with a time scale and 24 sockets, 12 on each face (analogous to a watch). In the morning the patient would insert the pills into the relevant sockets, and during the day he would take them according to the sequence shown on the device. Experience showed that in practice 12 sockets were sufficient, since most patients do not take medicine at night. The second picture shows the addition of an electronic timer to the 12-socket device. This timer beeps at predetermined times to remind the patient to take the medicine. The number of sockets can thus be further reduced; the dosage time is monitored by an electronic device, rather than indicated by the location of the sockets. As shown in the third picture, a further reduction of size could be accomplished by separating the electronic timer from the tablet dispenser. At this stage "psychological inertia" had to be overcome before the round shape of the socket box could be changed. In the last picture, we see that the shape of the box is now right-angled, the number of sockets is reduced to six, and the volume of the box is efficiently utilized. Such a medicine dispenser can be conveniently kept in a pocket and will remind the patient to take the necessary medicine in the right sequence with no major interference with a busy day. Further improvements are, of course, possible.

We can see that, at least at the design stage, the designer has to choose the best of several designs. This case thus fits into the second complexity level.

Let us now look at two examples illustrating the third complexity level.

1. The problem is to find a way to fasten the parts to be ground to the table of a grinding machine where the parts are composed of non-magnetic materials. The widely used "electromagnetic table" is suitable only for steel and other iron alloys. What can be done when nonmagnetic material has to be treated? We must change the fastening concept. Obviously the trivial case in which the parts are provided by special claws that can be fastened by mechanical means is not universal enough. Here we see that the initial concept has been changed. For the purpose of finding a

1. The initial design is of a round box provided with 24 (or 12) sockets, analogous to a watch.

3. The size of the dispenser is reduced by separating the dispenser from the timer.

Figure 2-1 Four stages in the design of a tablet dispenser.

2. An electronic timer is inserted into the 12-socket box.

4. The size and shape of the device are changed so as fully to utilize the dispenser.

universal solution, a cooling device is mounted on the moving table of the grinding machine, and the part or blank is fastened to the table by allowing a liquid to freeze in such a way that it holds the part to the table.

2. The problem is to produce an electric starter for a high-powered three-phase asynchronous motor. For this type of motor, at the instant at which the rotor is stationary, the current is approximately twice as high as that under nominal rotation conditions. The conventional starter consists of a number of contactors (about four) actuated by special means that switch out the active resistances in the rotor circuit to limit the current (Figure 2-2). A new electric starter, which differs from the conventional starter, has been designed for this type of motor (Figure 2-3). The following section from the manufacturer's prospectus for the new starter explains its principles of action.

An inductive winding, connected in series with the rotor circuit of a slip-ring motor, is wound on an iron tube which

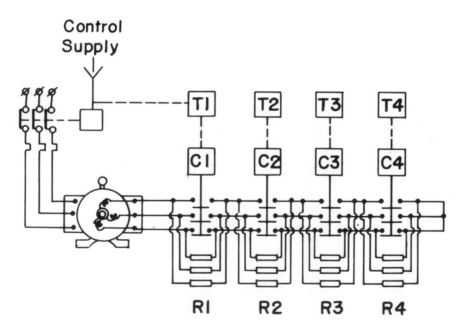

Figure 2-2 Principal layout of the electric circuit for conventional starting of a three-phase electric motor.

acts as a short-circuited secondary of one turn. The iron losses caused by the eddy currents in the core result in an impedance in the rotor circuit which has a high resistive component.... This impedance is at its maximum at the instant that the mains voltage is applied and while the rotor is still stationary. The increase in the rotor speed during start-up decreases the iron losses which are a function of the rotor current frequency. This, in turn, results in a smooth, stepless reduction in the starter impedance as the rotor gains speed. In this manner, the rotor speed reaches approximately 92% of its synchronous speed, and at this point the rotor impedance is shorted out automatically. This operation is normally carried out at a predetermined number of seconds after the motor start button is pressed, but for special applications the shorting-out of the starter may be determined by the rotor current amplitude, speed or torque.

In comparing Figures 2-2 and 2-3, we can see that the new solution has considerably simplified the electric layout. This solution has

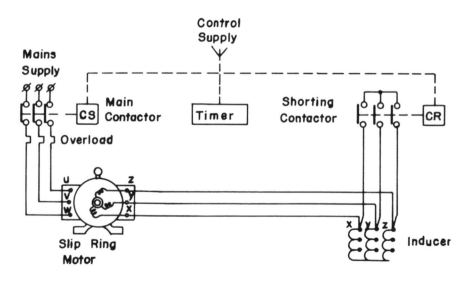

Figure 2-3 Principal layout of the electric circuit for starting a three-phase electric motor, where the starter is based on eddy-current effects.

the added advantages that it obviates stepped current increases (as takes place with resistor switching) and that it provides continuous, stepless acceleration.

Thus in the second problem the initial concept has been changed (a new approach is used, Principle IV), and the design has changed accordingly. Obviously we have a third-level technical solution. Note that we have not changed the main basic idea, that is, the dissipation of energy from the rotor in the form of heat in the starter. What is changed is the means by which the electricity is transformed into heat.

Let us now consider a problem illustrating the fourth complexity level.

The problem is to provide a plant with an optimal amount of irrigation water.

In solving this problem we note that there are many types of sprinklers that result in the soil being saturated with water. These irrigation methods entail a serious waste of water (evaporation from the air during sprinkling, evaporation from the open soil areas, etc.). A drip irrigation device was invented as an alternative solution. With this device water is supplied only to the roots of the plant via a pipe, that is, the water reaches its target in the shortest way with minimal losses. Thus a new problem was found (to irrigate the roots, not the soil);

a new concept was found (to create a dripping device);

a new solution and a new design were accomplished (a dripping system was created); and a method for calculating its parameters was developed.

As an example of the fifth complexity level, let us briefly consider holography. This technique is based on new electronic-optics methods whose introduction opened up a completely new domain of problems and applications. New data were gathered (and this gathering continues today) and a new principle for creating three-dimensional images, or holograms, was discovered. Special devices for producing the images, which can be viewed from different angles, were designed and constructed and are still being further developed.

3

GENERATING SOLUTIONS

We have become familiar with some of the general principles we can use, consciously or unconsciously, in the development of new products. Let us put ourselves in the position of an inventor or developer and try to find what we can do to make the process of generating new ideas and new solutions more effective. It is easy to discuss the utilization of these principles and to illustrate them with examples, but it is much more complicated to solve a new problem when we do not know exactly at which "point" on the exponential we happen to be or whether a new solution can be found only by a leap in the technology. In other words, the process of seeking new solutions and generating new ideas is a system of overcoming contradictions. The point of the process is to find out what the contradictions are and to be clever enough to know how to resolve them. For instance, the contradiction that the Montgolfier brothers had to overcome was the fact that a human being is heavy and does not have the tools to fly. They followed (as was discussed earlier) the path proposed by Archimedes and built a device that had an average density less than that of air. The Wright brothers, on the other hand, chose an aerodynamic solution to overcome the same contradiction.

At this stage it would be useful to study some methods for the seeking of new ideas. Because thinking itself is under consideration, the methods must be psychological. It is useful to represent the solution-search process in a graphical manner. In Figure 3-1 we see the solutions plane. Each mark on this plane represents a

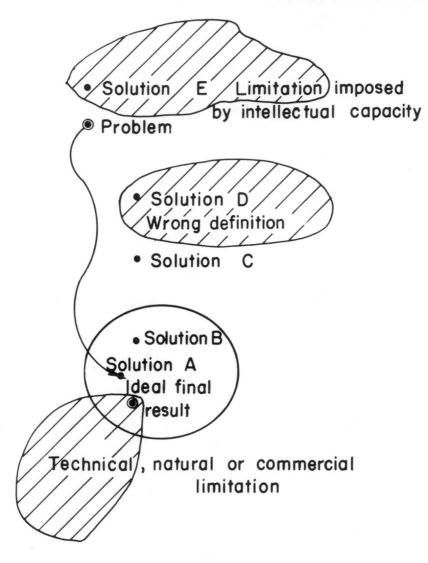

Figure 3-1 Graphic representation of the solution-search process. The shorter the trajectory of the search, the closer is the solution to the ideal and the higher is the efficiency of the design.

possible solution. The closer the marks, the closer are the solutions. The optimal case would be that in which an engineer travels from point to point—that is, from one solution to a better one—until the best solution is found or the time limit for the search is reached. But the restricted knowledge and mind of the designer will not permit following this optimal course, and an accidental solution is often chosen. In addition there are some restricted areas in the solutions plane. In Figure 3-1 we can see that there are three types of restricted areas:

1. Technical, natural, or commercial limitations. The example of the Soviet space program discussed earlier is an illustration of technical limitations.

2. Limitations imposed by false restrictions defined by the designer, by wrong formulations, by imprecise initial information, or by "psychological inertia." For example, it was thought that smooth cast-iron wheels rolling on rails would not be able to develop the friction essential to driving a train. The first steam engines, therefore, were equipped with teeth on the wheels (and rails) or "legs" to push them forward.

3. Limitations imposed by the intellectual capacity of the designer. For instance, a weak knowledge of electronics will lead a mechanical engineer to apply purely mechanical concepts to the solution of a problem, and some outstanding possibilities based on the use of electronics thus can be overlooked.

The following are methods used in the search for solutions.

1. Trial and error.
2. Brainstorming.
3. Analogy.
4. Empathy.
5. Inversion.
6. The morphological approach.
7. The systematic approach.

TRIAL AND ERROR

The most popular method used in the search for solutions is based on the knowledge and skill acquired by means of trial and error. The designer asks: "What will happen if I do this?" This is the simplest, and least effective, way of thinking. It was, however, the thinking and working style of Thomas Edison (1847–1931), who was the author of some 1200 patents in many different fields. His co-worker Nikola Tesla (1856–1948), the inventor of the three-phase synchronous electromotor, once said that if Edison had to find a needle in a haystack, he would be ready to disassemble the stack straw by straw. This was the way he found the "lighting material" for his electric bulb. The effectiveness of the method when employed by Edison can be explained in two ways: in terms of the staff that worked with him, and in terms of his own genius. We are, however, discussing methods for ordinary people. In Figure 3-2 we can see the leaps of a designer's thoughts, the "idle strokes" of the thinking process, until the solution dawns, as if by chance. This was the method used by the alchemists. Although they did a lot of work in vain, they managed to gather the large body of information that gave birth to modern chemistry. Many substances were discovered as "by-products." In 1674, for example, the alchemist Brand, in trying to recover from human hair a liquid for the transformation of silver into gold, discovered phosphorus. This trial-and-error method also resulted in the discovery of some important metal alloys. An outstanding example is dur-aluminum, a strong, hard, lightweight alloy widely used in aircraft construction, which was patented in 1910 in Germany by Alfred Wilm. He carried out about 10,000 different trials before he obtained an alloy with the properties he required. Of course, Wilm knew what he was seeking—which is an essential difference between this example and the previous one.

This manner of thinking is very widespread. All of us—children at play, dedicated technicians, lazy pupils, and even physicians—at one time or another espouse the slogan: **"Let us try it this way! Let us see what the response will be!"** Sometimes this is the only way to succeed. Relatively often, some very curious and amazing "by-products" are obtained. For example, a compass needle accidentally left near a wire carrying an electric current

led to the discovery of electromagnetism and the formulation of the laws of induction; a silver spoon forgotten on a metal plate stimulated the invention of the photograph; and a phosphorescent screen left near an active cathode tube gave birth to X-rays.

Trial and error is the natural response of human beings (and not only human beings) to difficult intellectual situations. It is the simplest way to gather skill and experience. The disadvantage of the "what if I do this" method is that the process of finding a solution to a problem involves moving from the beginning to the result, while the thought pattern moves in the direction of the vector of psychological inertia of the individual. Later we show that in many cases much more effective solutions exist in moving

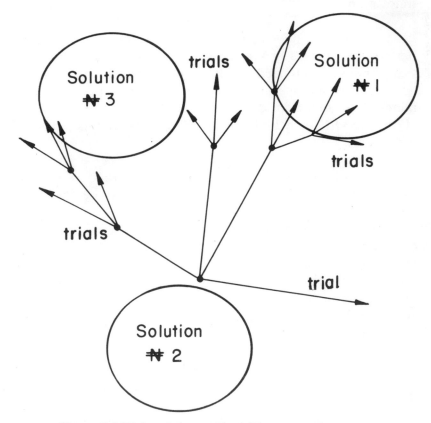

Figure 3-2 Trial-and-error method. We can see the leaps in the designer's thoughts—the "idle strokes"—until the solution dawns, as if by chance.

from the result to the beginning. All too often we are caught in the trap of straight thinking in which logic governs the mind, whereas creative, roundabout thinking requires logic to serve the mind.

BRAINSTORMING

The brainstorming method, which was proposed in 1953 by a U.S. psychologist, A.F. Osborn, is an improvement over the trial-and-error method. The novelty of this proposal lies in two main innovations:

1. A group of people, as opposed to a single individual, take part in the process of seeking a solution to a problem; that is, many brains are activated simultaneously (Principle VII).
2. The people who generate the ideas or solutions are completely separated from those who analyze the gathered solutions (Principle VIII, many brains are working both simultaneously and in parallel).

Note: Since this proposal of Osborn is a method of improving the solution-making process, we feel that it may be classified in terms of Principles (VII and VIII).

With the brainstorming technique (Figure 3-3), the chances of covering the solutions plane uniformly are increased, since the vectors of psychological inertia of the participants are randomly directed. The time required for generating new ideas is shorter because the technique involves a number of brains working separately and almost independently. The main conditions and requirements for a brainstorming session are:

1. The brainstorming group should include about ten persons.
2. These people can (or sometimes must) be specialists in several fields.
3. Each participant can express any ideas briefly, no matter how ridiculous they may sound.
4. The time limit for each pronouncement is about 1 minute.

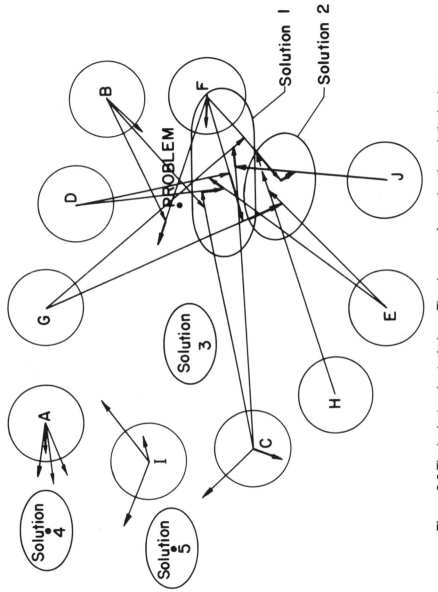

Figure 3-3 The brainstorming technique. The chances of covering the solution's plane uniformly are increased, since the vectors of the psychological inertia of the participants are randomly directed.

5. No criticisms or other remarks relating to the pronouncements are allowed.

6. The relationships among the participants must be free and friendly.

7. The session is to last about 40 minutes.

8. A group of analysts should record all statements and then rethink them carefully.

The main disadvantage of this method is that there is no control over the thinking process and a fruitful line of thought can be cut off by a participant's sudden suggestion.

Sometimes a lone creator can organize a brainstorming suggestion by speaking, for instance, into a tape recorder. In such a session, no doubts should be expressed, but only ideas without any restrictions, and with any amount of "ridiculousness."

An example of brainstorming session held by a group of about 15 students is presented here. The problem for which solutions were sought was how to steady a bicycle when its speed is low or even zero, as happens when it approaches traffic lights or is caught in a traffic jam.

Brainstorming Session

An idea for the design of a "steady-when-stationary" bicycle is required.

A: A collapsible support is needed.

B: A gyroscope would provide the required steadiness.

A: A collapsible wheel.

C: The gyroscope can be constructed in two planes—horizontal and vertical.

D: A gyroscope driven by a chain and treadle.

E: In this case the gyroscope can be placed inside the wheel—the rear wheel, for instance. No additional chain is needed.

C: Then a special coupling will be required.

F: It is possible to locate the gyroscope in a parallel plane, next to the wheel.

G: The gyroscope can be driven by an air turbine. An air compressor will be driven by the cyclist's feet.

E: A small roller can drive the gyroscope by friction from the wheel.

H: Then the system has to be arranged so that before braking the roller is pressed against the wheel, and when the riding speed decreases, it is freed.

B: Such a gyroscope can return its kinetic energy to the bicycle.

F: Such a gyroscope will, in general, smooth the running of the cycle.

H: It will promote steadiness during low-speed riding in traffic jams.

I: Two automatically controlled jets may keep the bicycle steady.

A: Instead of collapsible supports or auxiliary wheels, the whole frame can be lowered to the road.

F: An automatic device can press the roller to the wheel during acceleration and release it during deceleration.

C: I propose an air balloon to suspend the bicycle during its stops.

I: Or a propeller, like a helicopter, for balancing.

G: A horizontal gyroscope seems to be better; it will resist the bicycle turns to a lesser degree.

J: One merely needs a handle to switch the drive from the wheel to the gyro. Turning the pedals on the spot on will keep the balance.

C. A vertical gyroscope will not disturb the rider essentially, just as the wheels do not. It will help to incline the machine.

G: An electrically driven gyroscope. A bicycle provided by accumulators.

It was decided to use a gyroscope for the bicycle problem.

ANALOGY

Thinking in terms of analogies is a further development of Principle I. We can say that the copying of nature, of previously created devices, or of manual processes relates to "analogy thinking" just as arithmetic relates to algebra. (Note that to clarify the point, we had to use an analogy.) This method of thinking is very

useful in the conceptual stage of creating. When Rutherford pro-
pounded his concept of atomic structure, he described the atom
as being like the solar system, although he knew that such a model
could not exist. (Ten years later Niels Bohr improved this model
by introducing some revolutionary explanations.) For decades this
planetary analogy of atomic structure has been quoted in textbooks to help students understand the basic nature of the atom.

Let us consider some other well-known examples. There is an
analogy between some electric and hydraulic phenomena; that is,
some properties of direct electric current and the current of a
liquid may be described analogously, such as potential difference
and the resistance of wires and pipes. Another example is that of
parametric vibrations in mechanical and electric circuits. Similarly,
there is a direct analogy between the phenomenon of resonance
in electric circuits and the vibrating of mechanical systems, and
thus the mathematics used to describe the behavior of electric
and mechanical oscillators is identical. This fact led to the development of analog computation. A wide range of electronic analog
computers has been developed for many mechanical, hydraulic,
and other investigations. In analog computations electric resistance plays the role of mechanical damping, inductance the role
of inertial mass, and electric capacitance the role of stiffness. By
knowing some special rules, one can translate mechanical values
into electrical language, go through the computation, and then
retranslate the results into terms of mechanics.

Another example of the application of analogies may be seen
in the use of fluidics—the technology of employing the flow characteristics of a liquid or a gas to operate a control system. (The
term fluidics is a combination of two words, fluid and logic.) This
technique, which became commercially viable in the 1960s, is
analogous to the electric relay control technique. The properties
of fluidics render the technique unsuitable for some operations,
and in such cases mechanical or electrical approaches have to be
used.

All of these examples are examples of direct analogy, which
is illustrated schematically in Figure 3-4. Here the domains of two
phenomena are considered. We state that an analogy exists if there
are parallel transformations from situation A_I to B_I and from A_{II} to
B_{II}. Let us take domain I to be electricity and domain II to be

magnetism. The changes of electric current A_I to B_I and magnetic flow A_{II} to B_{II} can be described by identical analytic expressions. Thus an analogy exists. Analogy may now be used as a tool for discovering new facts. Let us consider an event in domain I—for instance, semiconductivity C_I to D_I—and ask ourselves whether an analogous situation, semiconductivity of the magnetic flow C_{II} to D_{II}, exists in domain II. Try to propose a layout that would conduct a magnetic field of only one polarity. In contrast to direct analogy, inverse analogy can be used; that is, if within a domain certain conditions A_I lead to a situation B_I, then by forcing the situation B_{II} in another domain, conditions A_{II} are obtained (see Fig. 3-5). For instance, when the junctions in a loop of dissimilar conductors are kept at different temperatures (A_I), an electromotive force (B_I) appears—the Seebeck effect. Inversely, when an electric current is maintained in a loop of dissimilar conductors (B_{II}), one junction of the conductors becomes cooler and the other one warmer (A_{II})—the Peltier effect.

A number of other examples may be quoted. Oersted discovered the connection between electric current and the behavior of the compass needle in 1826. Inverse analogy led Faraday to

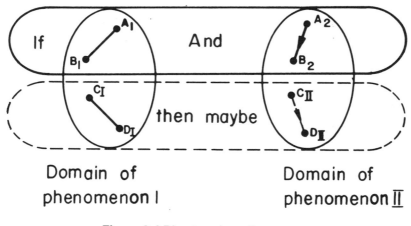

Domain of
phenomenon I

Domain of
phenomenon II

Figure 3-4 Direct analogy diagram. If two transformations A_I to B_I and A_2 to B_2 are alike in the domains of two different phenomena, then there is the possibility of finding a transformation C_{II} to D_{II} if C_I to D_I is known.

predict, and later to show (in 1831), the phenomenon of electromagnetic induction. The diffraction theory of a coherent light beam enabled the physicist Dennis Gabor to "invent" holography, which is an inverse phenomenon, in 1948. With the advent of lasers in the 1960s, a source of coherent light beams became a reality, and Dennis Gabor received the Nobel prize for physics in 1971.

As a practical example of the analogical approach, let us consider the creation of a remote-control irrigation system.

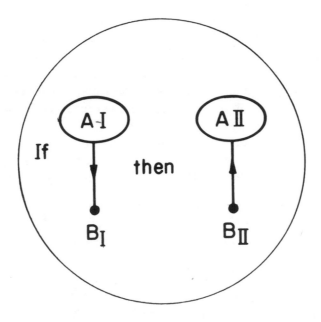

Figure 3-5 Inverse analogy diagram. If certain conditions A_I within a domain lead to a situation B_I, then by forcing the situation B_{II}, we can expect the appearance of conditions A_{II} in another domain.

Remote-Control Hydraulic System

Here we describe the analogous application of the electric frequency technique used in communications to a remote-control approach to the design of specific hydraulic systems. In some hydraulic systems, it is necessary that the opening and closing of valves or taps be carried out by remote control, such as in the case in which the response time of the hydraulic servo devices must not be small and the distances between the control and serve units are significant. An automatic irrigation system is a good example of this type of remote-control hydraulic device. Our discussion will relate to this kind of system, regardless of whether or not the proposed approach can be used for other applications.

The overall layout of the type of system under consideration is given in Figure 3-6. A pipeline 1 connects the water (or other liquid) supply station 2 to the irrigation sprinklers S1–S6. The pipe has a number of branches, each of which is provided with a valve (or tap) V1–V6. These valves are controlled by control units C1–C6, which receive commands from the central command unit CO. A communication channel 3 connects the central command unit CO to the control units C1–C6. Energy sources E1–E6 are used for amplifying the commands arriving at units C1–C6. The power for actuating the valves is obtained from the water pressure by means of connections P1–P6. The communication channel 3 may be hydraulically, pneumatically, electrically, or radio controlled. Whichever means of control is used, an additional channel has to be constructed parallel to channel 3 to facilitate the remote control, and additional energy sources have to be installed. For instance, if radio control is chosen, the receivers have to be supplied with electricity from batteries or from an autonomous electric power generator (which may, for example, be wind driven). If a hydraulic system is chosen, a parallel pipe for transmitting control commands has to be installed. If an electrically operated variant is used, then at least one cable has to be laid along the system. The necessity for an additional control channel in pipes or wires makes the system cumbersome and expensive.

Let us now ask ourselves whether it is possible to design a simplified system without an additional control channel. Such a system is shown in Figure 3-7. In this new layout, there are two new elements (shown on the right-hand side) in addition to the elements shown in Figure 3-6 (on the left-hand side). These new elements are a frequency generator FG and a transmitter TR. When a command has to be sent to one of the valves or taps, the frequency generator produces pulses of a particular frequency that corresponds to the chosen valve and the required action (opening

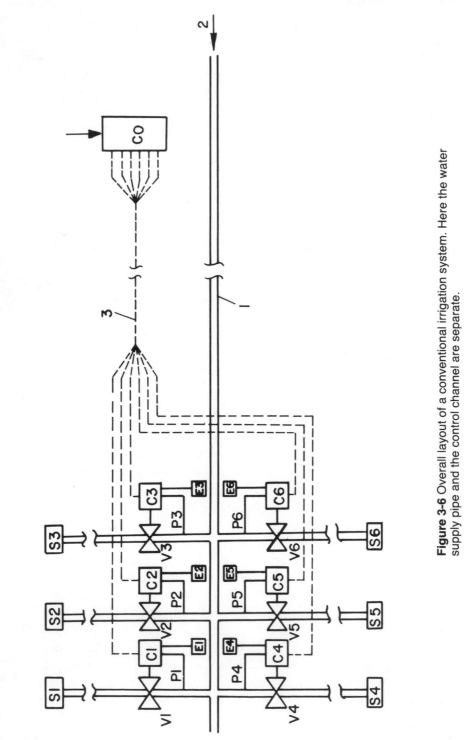

Figure 3-6 Overall layout of a conventional irrigation system. Here the water supply pipe and the control channel are separate.

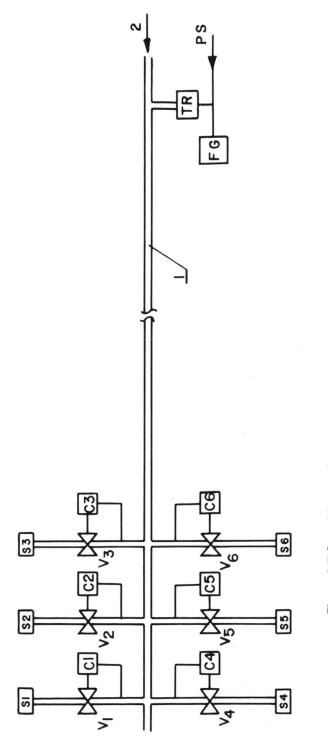

Figure 3-7 Overall layout of proposed irrigation system, in which the water-supply pipe also serves as the control channel.

or closing). The transmitter then transforms these pulses into pressure oscillations, which are set up in the pipe, so that the command is transmitted by pressure waves running along the pipe. The shape of the pressure waves is shown in Figure 3-8. The pressure *P* is the average pressure of the water supply. P_i describes the amplitudes of the alternating pressure. Each command requires a "package" of waves in a time interval if $\tau_1, \tau_2 \ldots \tau_i$ and a frequency ω_i given by

$$\omega_i \ \frac{2\pi}{\tau_i}$$

Thus the instantaneous pressure *p* can be expressed as follows:

$$p = \bar{p} + p_i \sin \omega_i t$$

where *t* is the running time.

To examine this principle, we built an experimental device that would enable us to investigate the following points:

1. The influence of the length and shape of the pipe on the pressure-extinguishing process along the pipe.
2. The maximum possible number of different controllable elements that could be included in the system.
3. The nature and range of the disturbing events in this remote-control system.

To make it easier to understand our experimental device, let us look at Figure 3-9. Here one can see a transmitter consisting of a membrane 1, which is in contact with the liquid in the main pipe 2. The frequency generator FG actuates, for example, an electromagnetic valve EV, which connects (or disconnects) the membrane with the pressure source PS (in our case, we used compressed air). In this manner the pressure "package" can be added to the static pressure in pipe 2. The receiver consists of two membranes 3, which are connected by a rigid body 4. A bypass 5 is used to balance the static pressure in the system and to relieve the static pressure on the membranes. An orifice 6 is used to restrict the transfer of rapid pressure changes below the

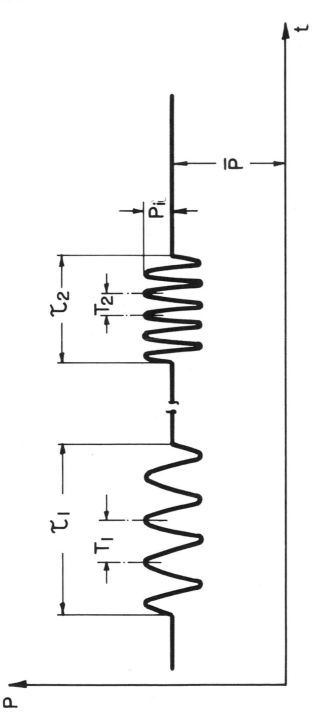

Figure 3-8 Shape of the pressure waves in the water pipe. The pressure comprises a constant pressure $\bar{P}$ (the water supply) and a variable pressure P_i (the control signal).

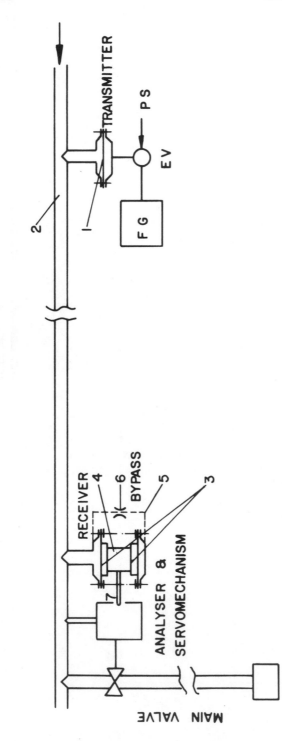

Figure 3-9 Layout of an experimental device consisting of a transmitter for generating P_1, a receiver for receiving the variable pressure P_1, an analyzer for separating frequencies of the pressure P_1, and a servomechanism for actuating the faucet.

lower membrane. As a result the body 4 oscillates with a frequency corresponding to the pressure changes in the pipe, and thus actuates the frequency analyzer (by means of a pin).

The mechanical design of the frequency analyzer is illustrated in Figure 3-10. From the figure we can see that the frequency analyzer consists of a shaft 1 driven by a pin 2. The pin receives oscillations from the oscillating body 4 shown in Figure 3-9. The free-mounted pendulums 3 are connected to the shaft by springs 4. The moment of inertia of the pendulums and the stiffness of the springs determine the natural frequencies of the receiver. When conditions at which resonance occurs are approached, one of the pendulums will begin to oscillate with increasing amplitude.

In our system each pendulum controls a single action; that is, the opening or closing of one tap. Each tap or valve is provided

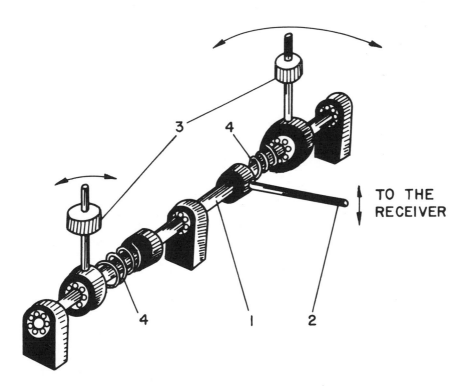

Figure 3-10 Mechanical design of an experimental water-pressure frequency analyzer.

with an identical device tuned to a different frequency. The oscillations are transformed into action of a tap or a valve by means of a hydraulic amplifier, which is shown in Figure 3-11. It consists of a housing 1 into which a piston 2, two plugs 3, and a system of channels are inserted. When the water pressure is transmitted to channels A, the piston 2 is balanced. If, while oscillating, a pendulum hits one of the levers 4, and in this way opens one of channels B, the balance of the piston becomes disturbed and it begins to move in the direction of the lower pressure. This forms a connection between channel C and either channel D or E; this last action transmits water pressure to the hydraulically actuated valves, causing them to open or close. Springs 5 press on levers

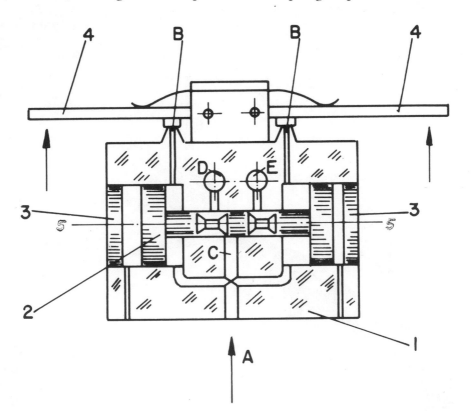

Figure 3-11 Pressure amplifier. The analyzer actuates the levers 4, thus changing the balance of the pressure in the chambers. The plunger 3 moves, and in keeping with its movement, channels D, E, C, and A are connected.

that close the openings B to the channels when there is no signal from the amplifiers.

One of the experimental devices, consisting of a receiver, analyzer, and amplifier, is shown in Figure 3-12.

In practice, for a 100-meter-long pipe, we did not observe any loss of pressure. The receivers we used are able to distinguish about 0.3 Hz. This means that in the range of 0.5 to 4 Hz, about 14 different signals can be transmitted and acted upon.

We found that there are two main obstacles that still must be overcome:

1. The system is sensitive to gas pressure in the pipes, and so some means of removing gas bubbles from the system must be incorporated.

2. A feedback device must be included to indicate the state of the valves or taps.

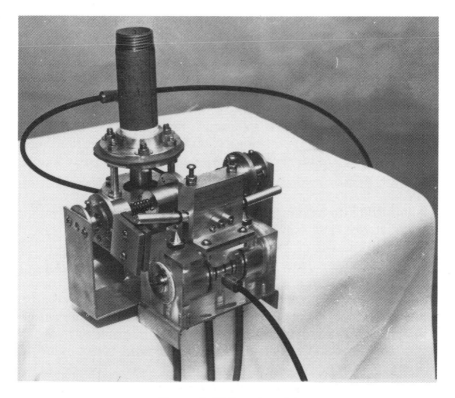

Figure 3-12 Experimental device described in Figures 3-7, 3-9, 3-10, and 3-11.

EMPATHY

This method can be considered as a particular case of the analogy method; it is an individual analogy. When employing empathy, we have to put ourselves into the situation with which we have to deal. We then have to act as though we are inside the problem and seek analogous paths of action for its solution. We can, for example, imagine that we can change our position, our size, or our proportions. Let us imagine that a colleague, John, has to solve such a simple problem as extracting a cork from a wine bottle. Put him inside the bottle, and let him take the place of the wine that "wants to get out of the bottle." After a number of manipulations, he can position himself along the length of the bottle, resting his legs against the bottom and his hands against the cork. Then by exerting himself to the limit, he can release the cork. We can thus draw the conclusion that a force from inside the bottle is able to open the bottle. What can the nature of this force be in reality? The solution is simple. It is pressure. Create pressure inside the bottle and the cork will pop out. This pressure can be generated by inserting a hollow needle through the cork and introducing air into the bottle by means of a syringe.

Empathy is a very specific method that is useful only in a limited number of cases. It is most often applied as an auxiliary method. Let us, nevertheless, look at one more example. The problem is to pass information from a rotating body to a resting one, without the use of sliding contacts. An empathy session may sound as follows:

> I am sitting on a wheel; all is going around and there is no point at rest. The only more or less stationary place is the center of the wheel. I have an insuperable desire to grip it. I could keep my hands on the shaft, but they slip around it. Perhaps I could pull a wire through a hollow shaft. But the wire will twist. This solution works only with a limited number of revolutions of the wheel, but in our case the wheel makes an indefinite number of revolutions per unit of time. It would be good to have a thin, liquidlike wire. What about a cup of mercury or some other molten metal? This could be a solution—no slipping, no friction. But there are two

limitations: the plane of rotation has to be horizontal, and mercury is harmful to human beings. Something else? I can scream from the wheel and I can hear someone else screaming. I can blink with a flashlight or a lamp, but how can I stop the rotation of the beam? How about a mirror? I will put a mirror above the center of the rotating wheel and direct the beam along the hollow shaft. The beam does not twist, since it is a light beam. Light is an electromagnetic phenomenon as radio is. Stop! Radio—this opens the possibility of transmitting information from the rotating body and back; moreover it opens the possibility of supplying energy to equipment located on the wheel.

The answers to a lot of questions are not yet clear, but the principle on which the solution is based has been established. It is possible that this concept will be too expensive or too cumbersome, or that too much effort will have to be invested to make the concept applicable, but at least the possibility of a specific kind of solution has been discovered and analyzed.

INVERSION

Inversion is a very powerful tool in the creating of new ideas. We have already discussed it in our description of the principles used for developing new solutions. We also encountered it as a tool in the use of analogies. At this stage we will confine ourselves to a brief consideration of inversion at different levels. Here we must keep in mind the fact that this method is an effective means for the seeking of new concepts in engineering.

An example of inversion was the discovery in 1880 by Pierre and Jacques Curie of piezoelectricity—the generation of electric charges in a nonconducting crystal subjected to pressure and, conversely, the change in volume of certain crystals subjected to an electric field. One can see that it is worth keeping any thought "under suspicion" for the potential possibility of inverting it and thus obtaining a new effect, product, or solution. In the Curie case, the gap between the direct and inverse phenomenon was covered simultaneously. In the case of Oersted and Faraday, it took about ten years for the inverse effect to be discovered.

We should not think that this creative tool is applicable only to physical laws. It also can be applied to more abstract problems, as the following example illustrates. How can the windows of a workshop be cleaned properly so as to provide proper illumination? It is apparent that the main problem is that of illumination. It is therefore worthwhile to invert the approach. Rather than spending money and effort on a complicated mechanical solution (window cleaning), it might be better to provide optimal electric lighting in the workshop. At least the pros and cons of the two approaches should be weighed.

Another example: How can a spiral electric resistance be produced? This resistance may be obtained directly by winding a wire on an insulator (see Figure 3-13a), or the inverse solution may be found by taking an insulator covered with conducting material and cutting out a spiral groove (see Figure 3-13). The inverse approach allows us to deal with very thin layers of conducting materials, and by changing the cutting pitch, high values of the resistance can be obtained. The latter process appear to be cheaper and more effective than the former one.

Further examples of inversion will be brought up during subsequent discussions.

MORPHOLOGICAL APPROACH

The morphological approach is based on the simultaneous consideration of as many situations as possible. By application of this method, the designer tries not to miss any opportunity in the "field of solutions." The morphological approach fits both the "what" and "how" problems. Let us consider an example of its application to the "what" problem, in this case, one concerning the domain of car users. The simplest case can be illustrated with the help of Table 3-1.

Some factors relevant to car users appear in the left-hand column and again at the top of the table. We now have a two-dimensional domain of possibilities. (*Note:* The domain is symmetric relative to its diagonal.) In analyzing combinations of the factors, we may obtain, for instance, the following:

1. Fuel-consumption meter (dashboard + fuel consumption).

2. Tire-pressure meter (dashboard + tire pressure).

3. Exhaust-gas-composition meter (dashboard + exhaust gases).

4. Device for inflating tires with exhaust gases (exhaust gases + tire pressure).

5. Device for cleaning by the use of exhaust gases (exhaust gases + cleaning).

6. Inflatable covering blown up by the exhaust gases (exhaust gases + covering).

7. Indicator of the state of the ignition system (dashboard + ignition).

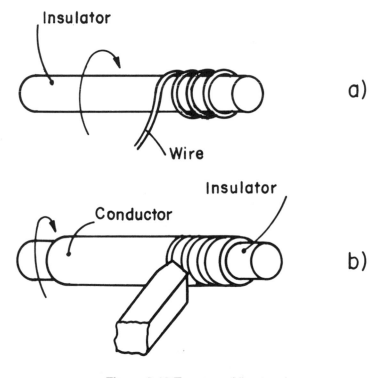

Figure 3-13 Two ways (direct and inverse) of producing electrical resistance. In (a) a wire is wound on an insulator and in (b) a spiral groove is cut into a conducting material (say carbon), which has been laid over an insulator.

Table 3-1
Morphological Approach

8

1. Speed	2. Distance	3. Fuel consumption	4. Tire pressure	5. Exhaust gases	6. Cleaning	7. Cooling	8. Dashboard	9. Ignition	10. Covering

1. Speed

2. Distance

3. Fuel consumption

4. Tire pressure

5. Exhaust gases

6. Cleaning

7. Cooling

8. Dashboard

9. Ignition

10. Covering

At this stage we do not need to decide how to realize these proposals, but rather whether there will be any demand for them and thus whether it is worthwhile to develop them. Some of the potential products are discussed later.

Let us now pass on to the "how" stage. For this purpose the designer must first ennumerate all the possible directions available, and then must consider all the steps in each direction and all the elements of each step. The combinations of elements then must be analyzed. It is easier to understand the application of the morphological approach to the "how" problem in terms of an example. For this purpose we will consider a fuel-consumption meter. The function of this device is, by definition, the continuous supplying of data to the driver about the fuel consumption of the car per unit of distance—liters per kilometer or gallons per mile. Of course, the inverse values—kilometers per liter or miles per gallon—are also acceptable. It is clear from the definition of the device that its design must include an aspect that treats information about the amount of fuel burned and an aspect that deals with the distance traveled by the car. In this case we met with difficulties in solving the first aspect, which is why we are using it in our discussion.

In our example the directions for solution seeking are as follows:

1. The structure of the flowmeter.
2. The way in which the measured results are to be indicated.
3. The means of computation.

To simplify the consideration, we stopped at three variables, that is, at the three-dimensional representation. With regard to the structure of the flowmeter, we can imagine a purely mechanical approach, an electric one, a hydraulic one, and so on (Figure 3-14). The kind of display can be chosen in accordance with Figure 3-14—digital, analog, acoustic, or colorific. For the computation method, continuous, interrupted, and analog approaches can be considered. The three-dimensional volume of the solution space is covered by 54 (in this case) possible combinations, from which, after thorough analysis, the most promising one can be chosen.

The solution space shown in Figure 3-14 can be represented in a different manner, as shown in Table 3-2. Here the multidimensional "spaces" can be better and more simply portrayed.

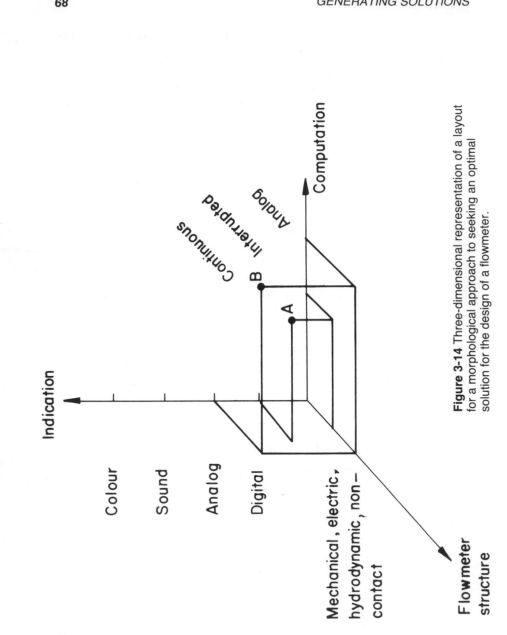

Figure 3-14 Three-dimensional representation of a layout for a morphological approach to seeking an optimal solution for the design of a flowmeter.

Table 3-2
Example of "Solution Space"

Direction	Step I	Step II	Step III	Step IV
		IV		
1. Flowmeter structure	Mechanical	Electric	Hydrodynamic	Noncontact
2. Means of indication	Digital	Analog	Acoustic	Calorific, etc.
3. Computation	Continuous	Interrupted	Analog	

Note the following points:

1. The morphological method does not add information to the problem, but it puts the considerations in better order.

2. If $1, \ldots, i, \ldots, k$ is the number of consideration directions, and A_i is the number of steps on the *i direction, then the number of possible combinations will reach*

$$N = \prod_{i=1}^{k} A_i$$

3. If N is large, the method ceases to work.

SYSTEMATIC APPROACH

The systematic approach is based on a previously mentioned idea that it is better and more effective to solve a problem by moving from the end to the beginning than vice versa.

If the final result is properly formulated, then the problem can be solved in the best possible way. Serious consideration, therefore, must be devoted to this first and very important stage of problem solving. An extremely simplified idealized form of the final aim has to be formulated and imagined. This step is not as easy as it seems, some psychological obstacles first must be overcome.

Rules for Formulating the Problem

1. The first rule we have to remember is that the formulated problem must not sound like

To change A and B for achieving C and D

or like

To change A and B

but rather like

To achieve C and D

Let us consider the following example. The higher the speed of a car, the smaller will be the traction between the wheels and the road, which is an undesirable factor. In the context of the example, let us compare the following formulations of the task.

a. To increase the weight of the car to increase the traction of the wheels.

b. To increase the weight of the car.

c. To increase the traction.

The first two statements are wrong because they automatically exclude, for example, the aerodynamic possibility (Figure 1-1). These two statements would be better phrased as:

a. To increase the pressure of the wheels on the road to increase the traction.

b. To increase the pressure of the wheels on the road.

But the best formulation remains the third (i.e., the most general) statement. This formulation does not exclude the possibility of putting chains on the tires, of using sand, of designing special-purpose tires, of adding wheels, and so on.

2. The second rule may be briefly stated as: When formulating the aim *do not* think how or by what means you will reach it.

3. The third rule may also be briefly presented: Do not *guess* whether or not it is possible to solve the problem and thus attain the aim.

4. The fourth rule requires a short explanation: Do *not* be afraid of solving "old" or "perpetual" problems. Often the older the problem, the easier it is to solve. The explanation for this is simple: The complexity of the problem does not change but the means for solving it (knowledge, technology, tools, etc.) *do* develop. This rule perhaps can be best expressed in the words of Jules Verne (1828—1905), who wrote that all that one human being can imagine, others will succeed in carrying out in reality. We should remember that many of Jules Verne's fantastic predictions have been realized, or even surpassed.

Definition of the Approach

The systematic approach offers a certain system for the seeking of solutions or a definite sequence that should be followed for overcoming contradictions. In simplified form the process may be described as follows:

1. Define the ideal final aim or result. What do you want to obtain in the optimal case?

2. Define the factors that may complicate the achieving of the ideal result. What is (are) the obstacle(s) on the way to success?

3. Define why the obstacles present a problem. What is the direct cause of the stumbling block(s)?

4. Define the conditions under which nothing will prevent the achievement of the desired result. What conditions will cause the obstacles to disappear?

Do not think that by following this sequence you will automatically succeed. Obviously reality is more complicated. For instance, the first step in this list requires a certain thinking procedure, which itself consists of some auxiliary steps.

Auxiliary Questions in Problem Formulation

1. What is the final aim of the sought solution?

2. Is it possible to reach the aim in a roundabout manner?

3. Which way appears more promising—the direct or the roundabout?

4. What are the major and minor requirements that the solution must provide?

The implications inherent in these questions can be understood in light of a detailed example: The problem we will consider is how to indicate to a driver whether or not the pressure in the tires of the car is correct. This would facilitate the prevention of the danger caused by a sudden flat tire. Let us follow the foregoing sequence.

1. Final aims:
a. To indicate the state of the tires, that is, to indicate the value of the pressure in them.
   b. To indicate whether the pressure is less than a certain allowed value.
2. Definition of the roundabout solution:
a. To indicate the distance between the drum of the wheel

and the surface of the road, which is obviously correlated with the pressure.

b. To indicate the deformation of the tire.

3. Direct or roundabout way: At this stage the roundabout way does not appear attractive—potential roundabout solutions do not seem better than a direct solution.

4. Requirements:

a. The price of the device built in accordance with the solution must be reasonable.

b. The device must be applicable to existing cars.

c. The indicator showing which tire is bad must be both acoustic and visual.

d. A minor requirement: An accoustic indication of a bad tire is sufficient; the driver is responsible for defining which is bad by climbing out of the car and seeing which tire is flat.

Now we can pass on to the solution-seeking procedure—steps 1 through 4. This procedure may be repeated several times, each time narrowing the domain of the search. Thus the "first round" will take the following form.

1. The ideal final result: An accoustic and visual indicator of "dangerous pressure in the tires" would be installed on the dashboard.

2. Complicating factors: A mechanical solution with the installation of a complicated piping system connected to the tires by means of rotating sealed couplings on the wheels is not acceptable because this solution requires that the wheels have a special design.

3. Cause of the obstacles: The mechanical solution is too expensive and is not applicable to existing cars because of the need to interfere with the mechanical structure of the wheels.

4. Solution to the obstacles: The mechanical concept must be changed for, say, an electrical one.

The "second round" will narrow the problem as follows:

1. The ideal final result: An electronic "dangerous-pressure-in-the-tires" indicator would be installed on the dashboard.

2. Complicating factors: An electric pressure transducer in each tire creates an electric signal that has to be transferred to the dashboard. The difficulties are the powering of the electronic circuit on the wheel and the receiving of the information from the wheel.

3. Cause of the obstacles: The difficulties arise from the rotation of the wheel. To overcome this obstacle, we need to find a non-contact and nonwired electric connection. (See the example under "Empathy.")

4. Solution to the obstacle: A radio-wave connection can be used for both energy feeding and information receiving purposes.

The proposed solution is shown schematically in Figure 3-15. A pressure relay PR is installed in the valve of the tire. When the

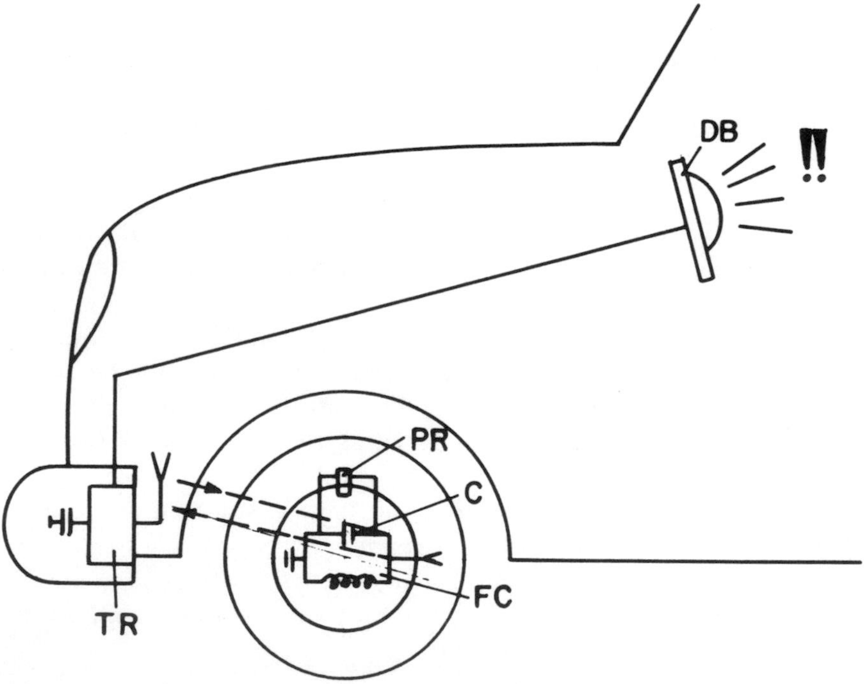

Figure 3-15 Radio-wave connection system for a "dangerous-pressure-in-the-tires" indicator located between the wheel and the dashboard.

pressure in the tire is correct, the contacts in PR are closed and thus short-circuit the capacitance C. When the pressure decreases and reaches dangerous values, the contacts of the PR open and the circuit of the wheel becomes a frequency loop with natural frequency ω. A transmitter TR fastened to the bumper continously transmits radio waves of frequency ω to the frequency loop FC. Thus when the pressure drops, the power used by the transmitter changes as a result of resonance, and this event appears on the dashboard DB in the form of sound signals and (if desired) as a visual indication of which tire is flat.

Chapter 4

AFTER THE
SOLUTION IS
FOUND

Almost all methods of generating solutions are suitable for solving both the "what" and the "how" problem. This is illustrated in Table 4-1.

These methods are suitable for the initial stages of creation, but there is another side to the question. This aspect, which we call synthesis, becomes apparent only after a solution has been found, or even after a device has been built. Synthesis is made up of three components—the "expansion" principle, the "complementary" principle, and the "excess" principle.

Table 4-1
Comparison of Solution Methods

Method	What	How
Trial and error	+	+
Brainstorming	+	+
Analogy	+	+
Empathy	−	+
Inversion	+	+
Morphological approach	+	+
Systematic approach	−	+

THE EXPANSION PRINCIPLE

To clarify the expansion principle, let us reconsider the example of a fuel-consumption meter for cars. The device (which measures two values in a digital manner and then divides one value by the other) comprises a flowmeter for relatively low flow rates (0.15–0.25 cm³/sec) and a distance meter. Let us suppose that we own such a device and ask ourselves what new ideas we can extract from it and how we can propagate the ideas and solutions peculiar to it to other technical fields. We call this approach the *expansion principle*.

Such a flowmeter, which is relatively cheap and sensitive, can be used in any situation in which digital information about low flow rates of any liquid is required. Gas flows can also be measured. In our case the same device, with minor modifications, can measure air consumption at rates around 2.5 cm³/sec. Thus what we have really invented is a universal flowmeter, and our next step should be a comparison with existing equipment of this type and examination of the demand and marketing conditions for these devices.

We also have designed an instrument in which the distance covered is divided by the fuel consumption, or vice versa. Why not seek other applications in which the consumption of a fluid has to be divided by any other physical value—time, speed, or even the consumption of some other substance?

Let us take another example, the tire pressure indicator. That solution was based on the "separation" of the rotating part of the car from the source of energy supply and information gathering. Where else could this type of radio solution be useful? The answer, of course, is for any other rotating object. Besides this particular case, it could also be applied to any process taking place in a closed space in which there are limitations on direct means of communication, for instance, in the burglar alarm system for automobiles presented in Figure 4-1. When someone tries to break into the car, the mechanical oscillations cause the alarm relay AR to short-circuit the LC circuit, and this action changes the energy balance of the transmitter. The latter component then actuates an alarm device located, for instance, in the car owner's home.

As another illustration we can consider the expansion of "Ru-

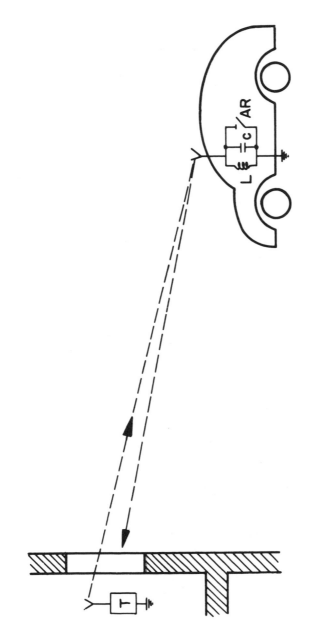

Figure 4-1 Burglar alarm system for automobiles. The alarm device in the car owner's home is connected by radio to a transmitter in the car.

bik's cube." One direction of expansion may be to change the number of constituent small cubes (which we call cubicles). Another direction may be to alter the shape. Why only a cube? What about a pyramid or a sphere? (Psychological inertia). For instance, if we take a 4 × 4 cube and round its apexes, we produce a sphere. This operation gives the game new properties. Let us print a map of the earth on this sphere. By changing the relative positions of the eighths, we obtain a perfect illustration of our topsy-turvy world and its political ambitions (Figure 4-2). Furthermore, we can print any portrait on the surface of the sphere, thus transforming the dry mathematical exercise of the initial cube into an amusing game that can fascinate many different types of people.

We can expand the concept even further by asking: Why not use a definite form? Figure 4-3 shows some of our fantasies as to how to execute this idea. Imagine that the small attractive elephant or pig in the picture could each appear in approximately $2.6.10^8$ combinations. Is this not fascinating? Try to move the parts and then put them back in order!

Figure 4-2 A topsy-turvy world built on the surface of Rubik's cube. A 4 × 4 cube with round apexes forms the basis for this puzzle.

Another possibility of applying the expansion principle is to combine (Principle III) the "cube" with another game, for instance, "15" (the Samuel Lewis game). Let us propose a cube with 2×2 cubicles on each facet, that is, eight cubicles altogether, which creates $8! \times 3^8 = 2.6453 \times 10^8$ combinations. The six visible facets of the cubicles consist of $6 \times 4 = 24$ squares on which we place, by special constructive means, 23 movable numbered squares. By moving the numbered squares through the empty square and turning the cubicles, we create a new entertainment by bringing the numbers into the desired order. This yields another $23! = 2.6.10^{22}$ combinations.

THE COMPLEMENTARY PRINCIPLE

The analysis of a new product often leads to the revealing of some previously unknown properties of the product. One must think these new facts over and then decide whether they can be useful. When the characteristics of the flowmeter described earlier were reexamined, it became evident that there was a definite relationship between the viscosity of the liquid flowing through the device and the slope of the line in a rotation versus flow-rate plot. The thought occurred to us the device could be used as a viscometer. Thus we can see that the utilization of the newly discovered properties of a device forms the basis of the comple-

Figure 4-3 Why should Rubik's cube have a cubic shape? These figures could each appear in approximately $2.6 \cdot 10^8$ combinations.

mentary principle; that is, some complementary properties of a solution are applied to solving another problem. For instance, the same fuel-consumption meter can also be used to remind the driver that the time has come to change the lubricating oil. The information on the distance traveled is, in any case, stored in the memory of the device, so there is no difficulty in arranging for a visual signal to appear on the dashboard every 3000 km (or any other distance)—"change the lubricant!" This is a complementary aspect of the solution to the main problem.

Let us look at another example of the complementary principle, this time the design of an accelerometer. When engaged in an experiment with reproducing analog images by means of carbon paper, the author noticed that the contact pressure influenced the results. This property (which is easily explainable) led to the creation of an inexpensive accelerometer (U.S. Patent no. 4114453).

The structure of this accelerometer is shown in Figure 4-4A. It consists of a housing 1 in which an inertial mass 2 is placed, variable resistances 3, a casing 4, and electric wires 5. In this example a simple bridge layout is used for the measurement of the acceleration (or force). The electric voltage corresponds to the acceleration components A along the coordinate axis X. A battery B provides the voltage for the bridge. Changes in the voltage of the battery will influence the measuring scale and the sensitivity of the device. A possible solution for the construction of the variable resistances is shown in Figure 4-4b. It can be seen that basically the variable resistance consists of a thin insulator film 7 (for example, paper) covered with a conductive or semi-conductive layer 8 (for example, carbon). In this case the film is criped so that one end of layer 8 comes into contact with the inertial mass 2 and the other with the cover 4.

THE EXCESS PRINCIPLE

To help us understand this principle, let us look at Figure 4-5, which shows schematically the structure of an air compressor that is actuated by the exhaust gases of a car (see Problems 4 and 5 in the discussion of the morphological approach). This compressor

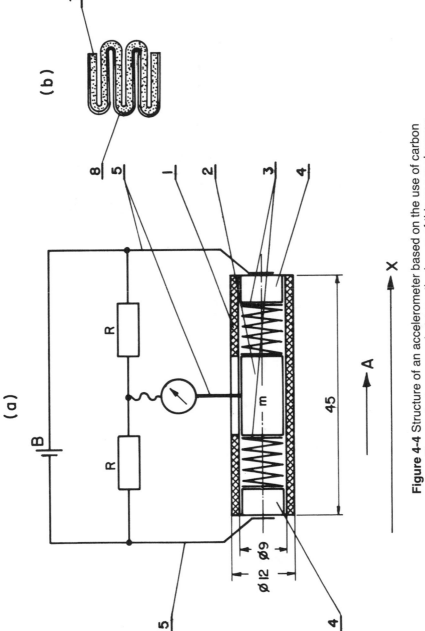

Figure 4-4 Structure of an accelerometer based on the use of carbon paper. The contact pressure between the layers of this paper changes the electric resistance of the device.

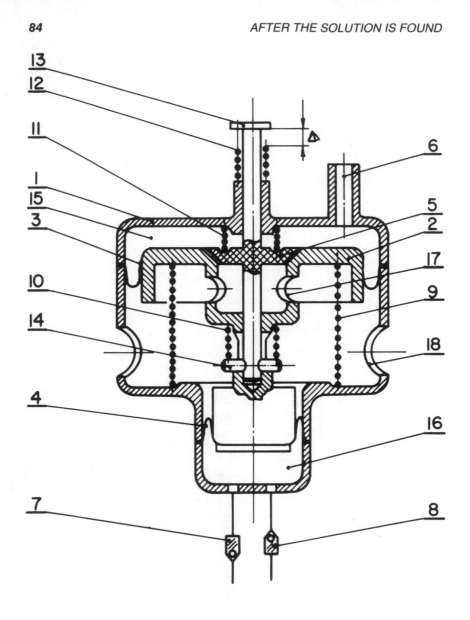

Figure 4-5 Structure of an air compressor actuated by the exhaust of a car. This device can be used for inflating tires as well as for actuating other pneumatic equipment.

utilizes car exhaust gases for the production of compressed air. The figure shows that the compressor consists of the following components: 1—housing; 2—plunger; 3—"large" diaphragm; 4—"small" diaphragm; 5—valve; 6—low-pressure inlet; 7—atmospheric air inlet valve; 8—high-pressure outlet valve; 9, 10, 11, and 12—springs; 13 and 14—supports; 15—low-pressure chamber; 16—high-pressure chamber; 17 and 18—openings.

When the low pressure is connected to the inlet 6 and chamber 15, the plunger 2 begins moving downward as a result of the pressure of diaphragm 3 on the spring 9. At this time the valve 5 is closed because of the pressure in the chamber 15, the action of spring 10 on support 14, and, at the very beginning of this stroke, the action of spring 11. During the downward stroke, the small diaphragm 4 compresses the air in the chamber 16 and forces it through the outlet valve 8. When the plunger 2 has moved a certain distance, the support 13 reaches the spring 12. When its deformation becomes considerable, the spring 12 opens the valve 5. At this moment the low pressure rapidly disappears because of the low aerodynamic resistance of the openings 17 and 18. This results in the lifting of the plunger 2 due to the action of spring 9. The small diaphragm 4 sucks fresh air into the chamber 16 through the inlet valve 7. The correct choice of the mass of the plunger 2, the stiffness of the spring 9, and the geometry of the openings will facilitate a close-to-resonance working regime of the device. The outlet pressure and the productivity of the device will depend on the ratio of the areaas of the diaphragms, on the input pressure, on the consumption of the exhaust gases, on the volumes of chambers 15 and 16, and on the dynamic properties of the moving system. In our case the input pressure is about 0.4–0.6 psi and the output pressure is about 28–32 psi, the productivity being about 3.5 liters per minute. By changing the parameters of the device, a different set of figures can be obtained.

At this stage a word of warning is in order. When a new idea appears, do not become too optimistic; first check whether the same new effect cannot be achieved in a simpler way. It is, however, a general rule to examine whether a new solution may contain more possibilities than are required. For example, when we apply the expansion principle to the air compressor, we must conclude that we also have a vacuum source (via the air inlet valve). The next step naturally would be the creation of a vacuum cleaner actuated by the exhaust gases of a car. Here we must be careful! We must examine other possibilities, and perhaps we will find something cheaper and easier to produce. The type of "danger" inherent in the application of the excess principle has its roots in psychological inertia. Figure 4-6 shows a simpler solution based on the ejector principle. In this design there are neither moving parts nor superfluous properties.

To deepen our understanding of the excess principle, let us look at another example—a "swimming" device. There are many different kinds of swimming devices driven by human power, most of which are propelled by paddle wheels. This means that a person must drive a mechanical transmission cumbersome enough to maintain the rotation of the paddle wheels, the latter driving the water backward while the craft travels forward.

Why do we need an intermediate agent—the transmission? All we need to provide is a stream of water, or a water jet, in the backward direction. Thus the idea of a swimming craft propelled by a human-driven water jet was born. Calculations show that the speed of such craft is about 1–1.5 m/sec, taking into account the fact that the capacity of an average person is about 0.2 hp (or even 0.4 hp for less than 2 minutes of action). Figure 4-7 shows a possible design for such a swimming device, which consists of a plastic or rubber float 1 and a propulsion unit 2. Figure 4-8 shows the structure of the propulsion unit comprising two bellows

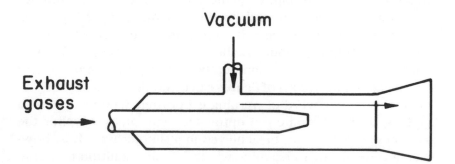

Figure 4-6 Vacuum generator actuated by the exhaust of a car is based on the ejector principle.

1, which can be activated independently or together. In both cases valves 2 and 3 ensure that the propelling water flow is directed rearward.

The traveling speed can be increased by enlarging the driving power. In accordance with Principle VII of creativity, let us put a number of people on the float, thus increasing the power. Note that if the cross section of the flat does not change (as is the case when the people sit one behind the other), the speed will be approximately proportional to $\sqrt{n}$, where n is the number of people. There is, however, the possibility of increasing the speed in another way, by copying the idea of the bow and arrow (Principle I), by accumulating the energy. The layout of such an energy-accumulating propelling device is shown in Figure 4-9. The bellows 1 pumps the water via valves 2 and 3 into an elastic bag, thus compressing the air in a solid vessel 5. Then, at a given moment, the driver frees the water via valve 6 and it flows through the nozzle 7.

Further increases in speed demand other energy sources, and this is where the excess principle can be applied. Vessels propelled by water jets currently are built according to the layout shown in Figure 4-10. The water is sucked in through inlet 1 by means of a compressor or pump 2 and is ejected from the chamber 3 through the outlet 4. The pump is driven by an engine 5 (for example, an internal-combustion engine). By applying the excess principle to this design, we obtain a solution based on the shortening of the process from the combustion of the fuel to the expulsion of the water from the jet. In this solution we are aiming

Figure 4-7 Manually actuated swimming device propelled by water jets.

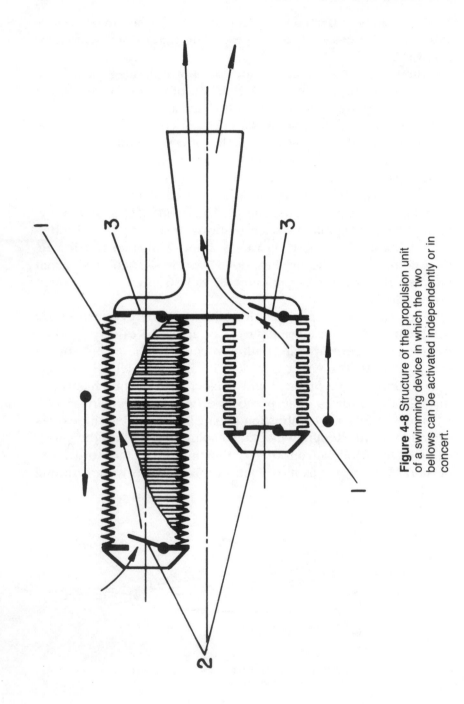

Figure 4-8 Structure of the propulsion unit of a swimming device in which the two bellows can be activated independently or in concert.

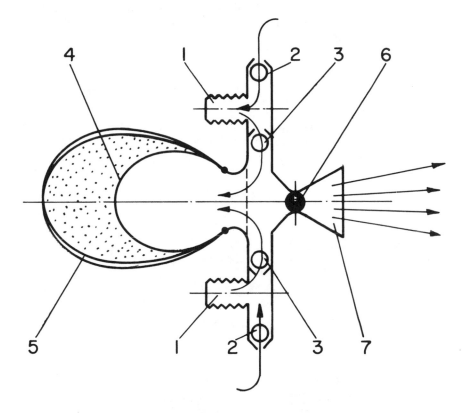

Figure 4-9 A propelling water jet
provided with a pneumatic energy
accumulator. At a given moment,
the driver frees the water via valve
6, increasing the traction of the
swimming device.

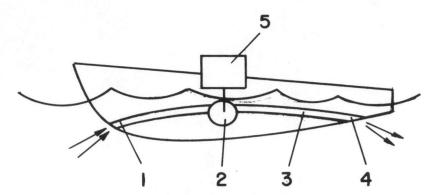

Figure 4-10 Layout of vessel
propelled by water jets.

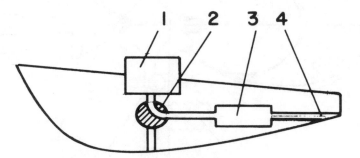

a)   b)

Figure 4-11 Layout of a vessel
driven by a water jet where the
propulsion is obtained by the direct
action of the expanding gas
(generated by burning fuel) on the
water.

a. The valve in the propulsion
position.
b. The valve in the gas-
generating position.

at finding a means of expelling a particular volume of water per unit of time. To this end we propose to burn a fuel to produce a gas that will, in a direct manner, push the water out of the jet chamber 4. This concept is presented schematically in Figure 4-11a. Gas source 1 is connected to the jet 4 via a valve 2 (which has two positions, *a* and *b*). The chamber 3 is filled with water through valve 2 in position *b*, and when the pressure reaches a certain value in the gas source 1, the valve 2 will move to position *a*, and the water will be pushed out, causing traction. When the chamber 3 becomes empty, the valve 2 moves into the *b* position, providing the time for the chamber to fill with water and for another batch of gas to be produced from the burning fuel in the gas source 1.

CONCLUSIONS

We have considered some topics relating to the processes of generating new technical (and, nontechnical) ideas and of seeking new technical solutions. We have tried to show the development of technical thinking and ways of overcoming pitfalls. Let us make it clear, however, that a knowledge of such techniques does not automatically convert the reader into a technical genius. But this way of thinking does open up certain possibilities:

1. It allows us to analyze existing technical solutions, their history, and the solutions of our colleagues and co-workers, and in this way to accumulate skills in effective thinking.

2. It allows us to organize our approach to overcoming technical problems and, at certain stages, to perfect our craft and to improve our techniques (just as a chess player improves by practicing).

3. It allows us to accumulate a number of example solutions, which (when a considerable number have been stored in our memories) will serve us in our professional lives, either directly as ready solutions or as analogies and stimulants for finding new solutions.

We recommend that you start a notebook and keep it with you at all times so that you can make brief notes of your thoughts (even seemingly stupid ideas); that you read; that you listen; and that you use sketches and layouts. Do not be embarrassed if your solution to a problem seems trivial—nobody reads your notes. When the number of notes you have made reaches 300, you will find that you are much more able to reach technical solutions. When the number approaches 500 to 600, you will be a person of technical erudition.

Although our discussion has not touched on engineering calculations, we must remember that after the solution has been conceived, we must check whether it is practical, whether it can be realized, whether it contradicts the laws of nature, and what dimensions and expenses are involved. Sometimes the concept of a technical solution occurs as a result of an analytic investigation; that is, the engineering calculations precede the creative process. For example, a two-mass system may be described by the following system of differential equations.

$$m_1\ddot{x}_1 + b(\dot{x}_1 - \dot{x}_2) + c(x_1 - x_2) + c_0x_1 = c_0X$$
$$m_2\ddot{x}_2 - b(\dot{x}_1 - \dot{x}_2) - c(x_1 - x_2) = 0 \tag{1}$$

The symbols are in accordance with the schematic model given in Figure 4-12a and their physical meanings are as follows:

m_1, m_2 oscillating masses
c, c_0 stiffnesses of springs
b damping coefficient, or a coefficient that describes the rate of energy dissipation in the system
X the excitement, which is some external movement
x_1, x_2 displacements at the masses m_1 and m_2 respectively

Let us substitute $x = x_1 - x_2$ into equation (1). Then
$$m_1\ddot{x} + b\dot{x} + cx + c_0x_2 + m_1\ddot{x}_2 = c_0x$$
$$m_2\ddot{x}_2 - b\dot{x} - cs = 0 \tag{2}$$

Now the dissipated energy E can be found by using the expression

$$E = b\int_0^t \dot{x}^2 dt \tag{3}$$

It is easy to imagine, as an application of such a mathematical model, a body m_1 floating on the open seas, on which another mass m_2 is suspended by means of a springlike device that has a stiffness c (Figure 4-12b). The energy is dissipated via a system that transforms the relative moment $x = x_1 - x_2$ of the masses into some kind of energy (compressed air, water, or electricity). Here the excitation X is performed by the sea waves, and the water plays the role of the second spring characterized by stiffness c_0 (in the mathematical model). Thus at least the concept of a utilizer of the energy generated by sea waves has been created. In this case the "mathematics" is the forerunner of the creation.

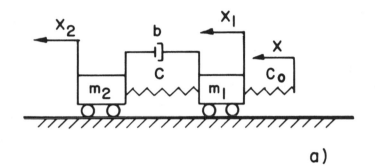

a)

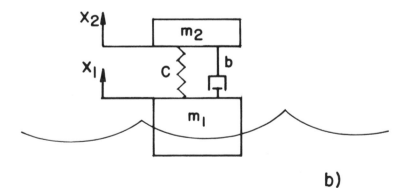

b)

Figure 4-12
    a. Model of a two-mass oscillator.
    b. Application of the model to the idea of a sea-wave-energy utilizer. The relative motion of the bodies $X_1 - X_2$ can be transformed into energy.

The invention of radio communication is another example of mathematics giving rise to creativity. The theoretical existence of electromagnetic waves—later known as radio waves—was first proposed by Maxwell in 1873. His computations, in turn, led to the experimental discovery of radio waves by Hertz in 1885, and to the first practical application of radio communication by Marconi in 1897. Similarly the diesel internal-combustion engine was invented analytically through theoretical calculations of the thermodynamic cycle.

EXERCISES

The following exercises may serve as the first steps on the road to technical creativity. Good luck!

I. Study the history of the development of creativity. Indicate which principles of creativity are applied to the following subjects.

1. Cars.
2. Propellants for traveling on land.
3. Propellants for traveling on water.
4. Bicycles.
5. Cooking.
6. Home heating.
7. Faucets.
8. Furniture.
9. Door locks.
10. Sewing machines.
11. Washing machines.
12. Vacuum cleaners.
13. Heat engines.
14. Refrigerators.
15. Radio and TV receivers and transmitters.

II. Propose and create technical solutions for following problems (after finding the solutions, define the complexity level of the problem).

1. Design a device for cleaning the air of tobacco smoke; it may be something that switches on automatically when

the concentration of the smoke reaches a certain level. It should be suitable for offices, trains, and so on.

2. Design a shower actuated automatically when a person walks under the shower head; electrical devices are not allowed because of the danger inherent in a combination of electricity and dampness. The device could be suitable, for example, for public showers at the beach.

3. Propose a design for a hydraulic-pressure amplifier that is fed (for instance) by a water pressure of $P_1 \approx 10$ atm without the use of any other energy source. Such a device might be useful for irrigation.

4. Existing water-pressure regulators include an elastic element whose deformation dictates the control policy. Create a water-pressure regulator that is free of the influence of nonstable elastic elements (its properties change with time).

5. Create an inflatable umbrella. It should have a minimum of rigid mechanical parts, and should not interfere with its carrier's entrance into a car, a bus, or a shop, or with passersby.

6. Existing DC electric motors are provided with a commutator or collector that has sliding contacts. This results in losses in torque, and small motors, in particular, suffer from this problem. Find a solution that avoids the torque losses due to mechanical friction of the contacts.

7. Propose a device able to move on walls or, generally speaking, on vertical surfaces.

8. Figure 4E-1 shows a common assembly. The body 1 has to be fixed on the support 2 while rollers 3 must separate the two bodies. The problem is that this procedure has to be accomplished by one worker, who has difficulty in controlling both the body and the rollers. Propose a solution that simplifies this activity.

9. Roller bearings consist of two rings and a special body that separates the rolling elements. Although the separator is not loaded, it causes friction. Propose, for example, a roller bearing that does not have these inherent losses.

10. Night driving involves the driver having to switch the bright lights of the car on and off. It causes inconvenience to all drivers on the road. Propose a way to decrease, or completely avoid, this inconvenience.

11. You have a hungry baby who does not care about your problems and cries at night, disturbing your rest. Find a harmless solution that will, at leaast partially, allow you to get a night's rest.

12. Propose a "telltale" device to be installed in a car that will show a traffic inspector that the speed limit has been exceeded. The design of the device must take into account that honesty is not an inherent property of human beings.

13. Design a device that will inform the handlers of a parcel or package that it is suffering undesirable shocks or positioning during its transportation (for instance, a parcel labeled "fragile").

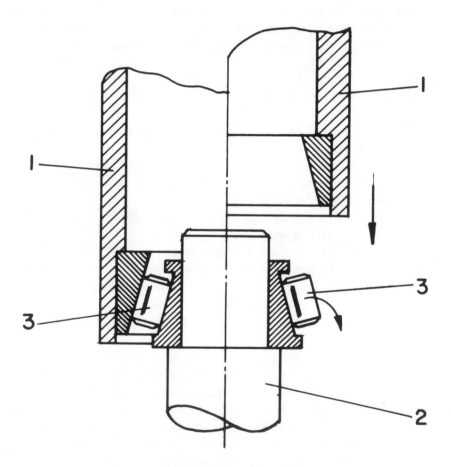

Figure 4E-1 Exercise II-8.

14. Design an automatic bathroom lock. When one enters the bathroom, the door is automatically locked and can be opened only from inside. After one leaves the bathroom, the door is not locked.

15. Propose a way of utilizing the wave energy of an open body of water to charge accumulators for illumination of a buoy or for its radio transmitter.

16. Propose a solution to the problem of measuring small speed oscillations in a rapidly rotating shaft.

17. When approaching the resonance speed a rapidly rotating shaft begins to vibrate. Try to find a solution that provides "smooth" working conditions regardless of the rotating speed.

18. In many places the shore is soiled by crude oil spills. Can you propose a device or method for cleaning the sand?

19. Create an accurate automatic mixer for two or more gas components.

20. Working the soil on slopes of hills for agricultural purposes is difficult, especially since the usual type of tractor can overturn on such a slope. What is your proposal?

III. What are the inverse solutions to the following system?

1. The peristaltic pump shown in Figure 4E-2 consists of a housing 1, a rotor 2 provided with two rollers 3, and an elastic pipe 4. When the rotor 2 rotates, the rollers 3 are pressed on the pipe 4 and push out the portion of the liquid enclosed between points A and B (it is possible to use more than two rollers). In this manner a continuous flow of the liquid through the pipe is produced.

2. The magnetohydrodynamic device shown in Figure 4E-3 consists of a trough containing seawater 1 connected to a pair of electrodes 2. A magnetic field is produced by means of magnets 3. The interaction of two fields causes the flow of water.

IV. Propose technical solutions by combining the following elements (Principle III).

1. Pneumatics with hydraulics.
2. Cam mechanism with gearing.
3. Cam mechanism with a linkage.

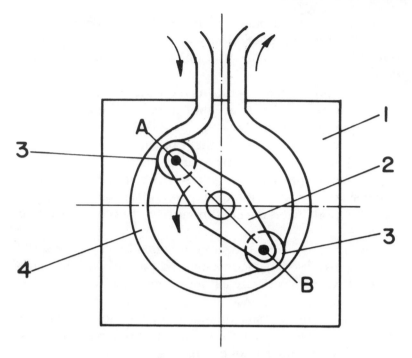

Figure 4E-2 Exercise III-1.

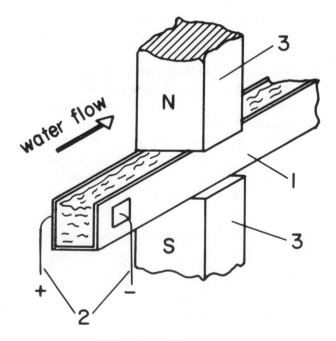

Figure 4E-3 Exercise III-2.

PART II

INTRODUCTION

The engineering design process must begin with a clear definition of the action the object to be designed has to perform. An excellent description of this aim is given in Edward V. Krick's book *An Introduction to Engineering and Engineering Design:* "Each problem can be formulated as a change of the state *A* into a state *B*." Each problem takes the form of a "black box" in which state *A* exists at the input and state *B* at the output. A number of examples illustrating this statement are given in Figure II-1. The "what" problem is solved by defining the nature of the states *A* and *B*, and the "how" problem is embodied in the black box.

For example, the 300- to 400-year-old desire to transmute fuel into mechanical torque culminated in the creation of the engine, with the type of engine depending on the kind of fuel and the thermodynamic cycle. Similarly, the path from flour, water, and eggs to bread might be described as an ancient manual process or as a modern mass-production technique (the product of the latter perhaps being less tasty). The path itself depends on which "how" is embodied in the black box.

Thus, in brief, after *A* and *B* have been defined, the designer has to "unravel" the contents of the black box. We consider the black box to contain, in general, three stages of design:

1. The design of the "processing" layout.
2. The design of the "kinematic" layout.
3. The design of the structure.

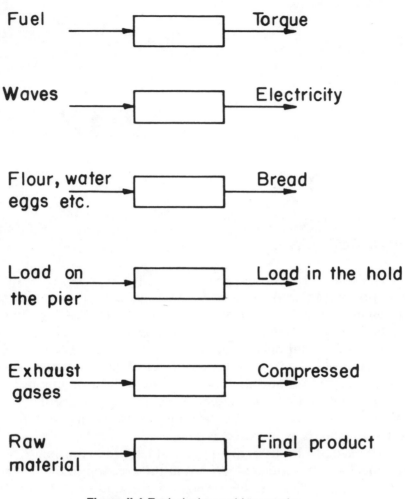

Figure II-1 Each design problem can be formulated as a change of the state *A* into a state *B*.

5

DESIGN OF THE PROCESSING LAYOUT

During this stage the designer has to put on paper in a schematic way the sequence of processes the black box must carry out, the means or tools involved in these processes, and the main movements that the tools produce. At this stage kinematic (i.e., the transmission of movement) considerations are not invoked. Similarly, the designer does not consider how to obtain the sequence and type of displacements of tools and other elements in the proposed processing layout. The following examples will serve to clarify the foregoing statement.

EXAMPLE 1—A CRANE

Stage A: The load is on the pier.
Stage B: The load is in the hold of a ship.
The processing layout is shown in Figure 5-1. The tool in this case is a hook (for a fork-lift truck, the tool would be a fork). The arrows show the chosen trajectory of the load and the idle stroke when the hook returns to the pier to pick up the next load.

Later we investigate how such a motion can be obtained, but at this stage all we need to know are the dimensions or ranges of the hook displacement in all directions, the allowed and desired lifting and horizontal speeds of the traveling load, and the parameters of the load to be moved by means of the crane.

EXAMPLE 2—AN INTERNAL-COMBUSTION ENGINE

State A: A certain fuel.

State B: A particular torque and speed on a rotating shaft.

From Figure 5-2 we can see that the fuel is placed in a special tank 1 from where it is pumped by means of a fuel pump 2 into a mixing system in which the combustion mixture is prepared. A carburetor serves as the mixing system and consists of a fuel-splashing device and an air channel. The air is cleaned by passing it through a filter. To create the air flow, a piston moves down inside a cylinder. As soon as the combustion mixture has been

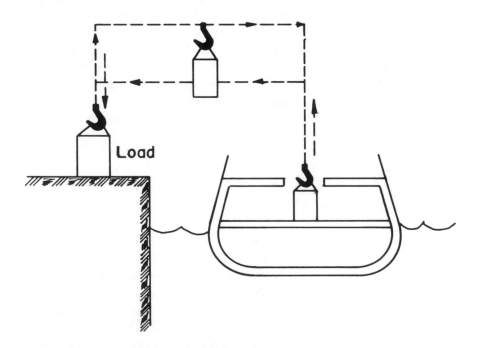

Figure 5-1 Processing layout for a case in which: state *A*—the load is on the pier; state *B*—the load is in the hold of a ship

103

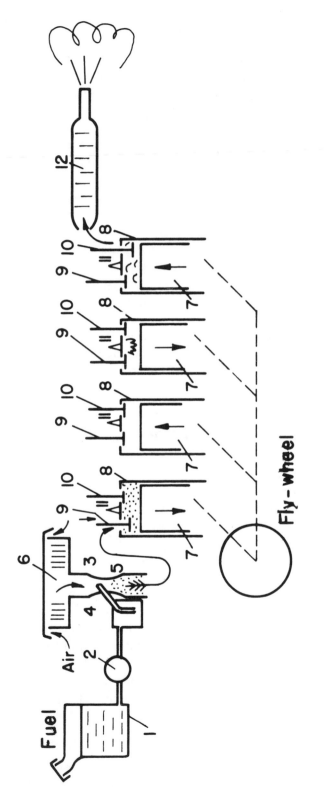

Figure 5-2 Processing layout for a case in which: state *A*—a certain fuel is supplied; stage *B*—a particular speed and torque are obtained on a rotating shaft.

prepared, the inlet valve is opened and the mixture is sucked into the combustion chamber. The space created between the cylinder walls and the top of the piston, which will serve as the place where the mixture is burned, we call the combustion chamber.

In accordance with the desired thermodynamic cycle, the next stroke of the piston must compress the mixture in the combustion chamber. Thus the piston moves upward and the valves are closed. When the pressure in the chamber reaches about 10 atm, the critical point of combustion has been reached, and an electric spark from the plug ignites the mixture. The working stroke thus begins, and it pushes the piston downward. A fourth stroke is used to empty the combustion chamber. During this stroke the piston moves upward and pushes the exhaust gases via the open outlet valve into the noise extinguisher and from there out to pollute the air. To guarantee continuous movement of the piston during the four strokes, the use of a flywheel has been proposed. This device is somehow driven (at this stage we do not think about how) by a mechanism converting the reciprocating displacement of the piston into the rotation of the flywheel.

EXAMPLE 3—THE WEAVING PROCESS

Stage A: Yarn.
Stage B: A fabric.

This process is almost as old as the history of humankind. The layout shown in Figure 5-3 has not changed over the centuries—from Penelope to modern times. The warp (the lengthwise threads) is divided into two (not necessarily equal) sets of threads, A and B, in such a way as to generate a clearance gap. A special body called a shuttle, which is provided with yarn from a coil, is moved through the gaps from A to B to A, and so on, thus generating the weft. A comblike reed pushes the weft forward, thus thickening the fabric. Thereafter sets A and B change places, and the process is repeated. The fabric formed is wound onto a coil.

Let us consider ways of moving the shuttle. It can be moved manually, as was done by Penelope, or mechanically, as shown in

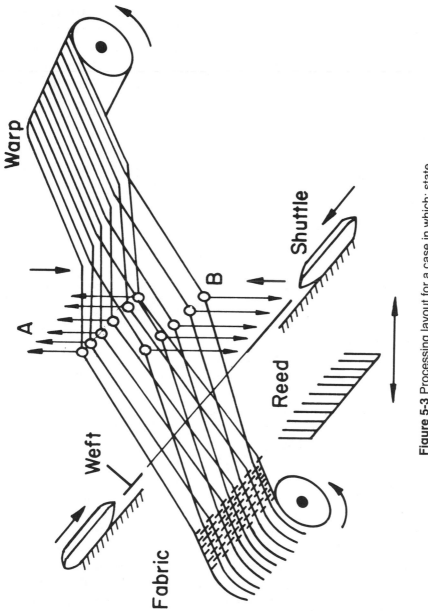

Figure 5-3 Processing layout for a case in which: state A—the yarn; stage B—the fabric.

Figure 5-4. In case I, the most common case, a mechanical "arm" hurls the shuttle through the gap between the two sets of threads constituting the warp (sometimes over a distance of 7–10 meters). In Case II a "pneumatic gun" shoots the shuttle, and in case III an "electromagnetic gun" serves the same purpose. A different mechanical solution is given in case IV—two permanently rotating rollers "clasp" the shuttle, and generate the initial speed required to throw it.

An excellent example of Principle IV is shown in Figure 5-4V. Instead of a "pneumatic gun" to shoot the shuttle, a "gun" to shoot the yarn was created, and looms that do not use shuttles were thus built. The advantage of this solution lies in the considerable reduction of the mass with which the mechanism must deal.

EXAMPLE 4—THE WIRE-DRAWING PROCESS

This example is illustrated in Figure 5-5. The wire is pulled, by means of rollers, through a series of drawplates, and in this way its diameter is reduced. Of course, as the rotation speed of the roller increases, the diameter of the wire is decreased. The essential difference between this and the three previous examples is that wiredrawing is a continuous nonperiodic operation whereas the other processes are periodic.

It is important to note that the same "processing" concept may be realized in a number of different ways. For example, Figure 5-6 illustrates a metal-cutting process carried out in five different ways, depending on the tools employed and their movements.

A continuous nonperiodic process is preferable to a periodic operation, since there is no waste of time in a continuous process; each working moment is exploited. During the wire-drawing process, for example, wire is produced continuously, whereas during weaving fabric is produced step by step. Here each operation is followed by the next, and only at the end of a certain period can another piece of fabric be considered ready. The periodicity of the weaving process is the result of the actual sequence of operations: the weft has a limited length, the sets of yarn in the warp have to move to two defined, final positions, and the reed can act

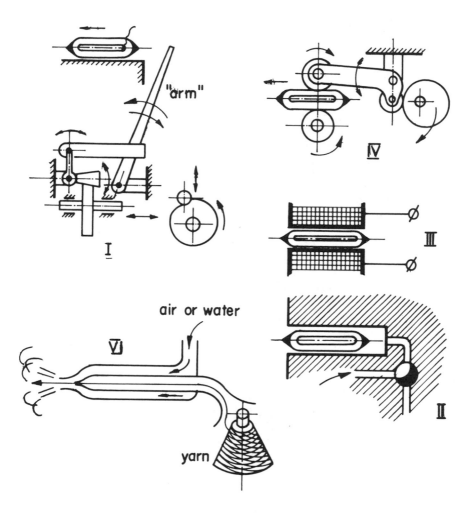

Figure 5-4 Different ways of moving the shuttle of a loom:
    I—Conventional mechanical drive.
    II—Pneumatic "gun" to shoot the shuttle.
    III—Electromagnetic "gun" to shoot the shuttle.
    IV—Frictional drive of the shuttle.
    V—Ejection of the weft without any shuttle.

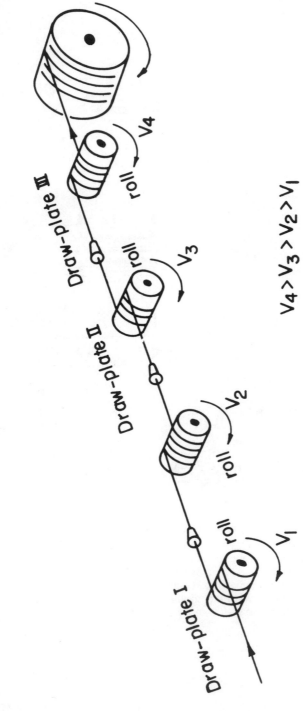

Figure 5-5 Processing layout of a wire-drawing machine. This is an example of a continuous process whereas the other processes presented are periodic.

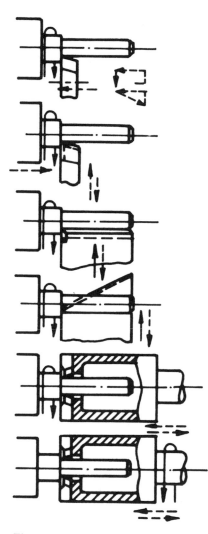

Figure 5-6 The same "processing" concept (in this case metal cutting) may be realized in a number of different ways, as shown (from top to bottom):

(1) The part rotates, and the cutter executes a two-dimensional movement.

(2) The part rotates and moves in an axial direction and the cutter moves only transversally.

(3) The part rotates, and a wide cutter moves only transversally.

(4) The part rotates, and a specially shaped cutter moves only transversally.

(5) The part rotates, and a tool-head moves axially.

(6) The part is immovable and a tool head carries out the required movements.

only after the waft has been woven. The weaving process can be transformed into a nonperiodic operation only if these limitations are overcome. An idea for such a process is shown in Figure 5-7. In this design the warp forms a cylinder, as does the finished fabric. A cross section of the warp yarns is shown in the figure, from which it can be seen that the two sets of threads form two over-lapping circles. The crossing points *A* and *B* rotate continuously at equal speeds, thus forming gaps in which the continuously moving shuttles are placed, leaving behind them two wefts. In this type of loom, all the operations proceed simultaneously. These looms are used for the production of rough-weave fabrics, such as burlap bags. The limitations on their wider application lie in their kinematics, for example, the difficulty of moving the "sur-rounded-by-yarn" shuttles.

Return for a moment to Example 2, the internal-combustion engine, and remember that it too has a nonperiodic successor—the

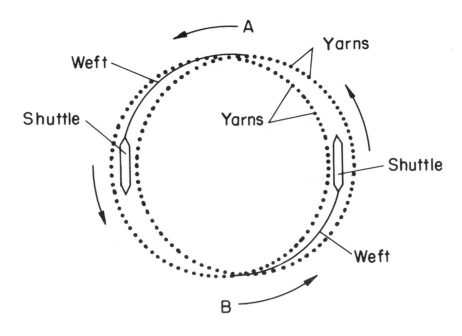

Figure 5-7 An idea for a continuous weaving process. The shuttles move around pulling the weft and the yarns "open" the way for the shuttles.

gas turbine. Thus we see that the chief characteristic of a periodic producing process is a particular sequence of actions for each tool or element. To clarify this sequence, and to make it easy to estimate the time required for each operation, we must design a sequence "program," which we call a "cyclogram."

There are two ways to express a cyclogram on paper: (1) in a cycle form; and (2) in a linear form. The cycle form is convenient because it represents the process and its component parts in direct relation to a rotating body, which we call the "main shaft." In general, most machines do actually contain a main shaft, and the time it takes to complete one or more revolutions defines the period of the process. Figure 5-8 presents a cyclogram of an internal-combustion engine (Otto cycle) according to the layout in Figure 5-2. In this case the main shaft is the crankshaft of the engine, and one period requires two revolutions of the shaft. The rest is clear from the Figure. The angles α_1, α_2, α_3, α_4, and α_5 define,

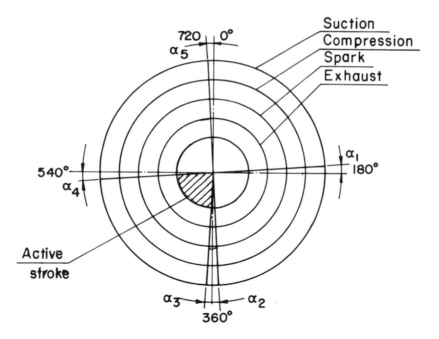

Figure 5-8 Cyclogram of an internal-combustion engine (Otto cycle).

with a high degree of accuracy, the opening and closing moments of the valves and the time at which the mixture burns. The angles of rotation of the main shaft can easily be translated into time units by knowing the value of the rotating speed (and assuming it to be uniform). Two inherent disadvantages of this cyclic cyclogram are:

1. Although the relative values of the angles are represented in a most obvious manner, the absolute lengths of the arcs that represent these angles depend on the radius of the corresponding circle. This fact sometimes has a psychological influence on the "reader" of the cyclogram.

2. The course of the motion or action of each tool or element cannot be fully described; only the times at the beginning and end of the action can be pinpointed. In the case of the internal-combustion engine, for example, the displacements of the valves as functions of time cannot be seen.

These disadvantages can be avoided by the use of a linear cyclogram. In Figure 5-9 a cyclogram of the same engine is presented, but this time in linear form. Note the graphical interpretation of the valve motion. Here it is possible to show the maximum displacement of any valve by using the vertical coordinate and a defined scale. (If required, the forms of the acceleration and deceleration can also be shown.) Obviously the spark action does not require the use of this coordinate.

The vertical coordinate can also be related to other physical values, such as pressure, temperature, and voltage, if the action being considered requires it, and the form of the changes in these physical values can appear on the linear cyclogram. These cyclograms show:

1. The sequence of action.

2. The relationships between the time intervals required for each action.

3. The time reserves that may help to decrease that period.

4. The "shapes" of the movements or other changes in various parameters as functions of time.

5. The initial information needed for the design of the kinematic layout.

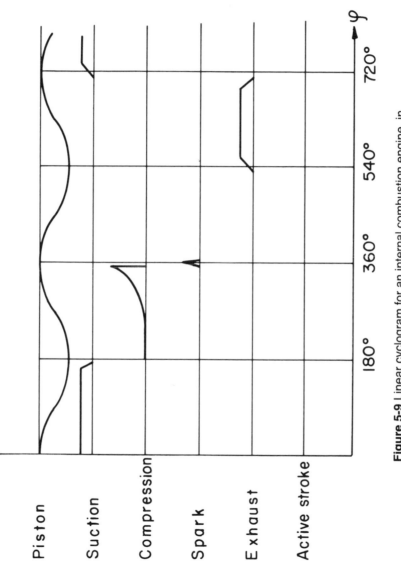

Figure 5-9 Linear cyclogram for an internal combustion engine, in accordance with Figures 5-2 and 5-8.

At this stage the conceptual design once again comes into contact with engineering calculations. The designer has to estimate the operation times of each of the elements regardless of the nature of the process under consideration. Both the designer's knowledge of mathematics, physics, mechanics, hydraulics, and so on, and the designer's skill determine the quality of the design. This is the point at which the limitations described when design principles were discussed will become evident.

Let us now try to design a processing layout—for example, a process for the automatic manufacture of an aluminum antenna, as in Figure 5-10. Since about half a million antennas are manufactured each year, it is natural that the raw material should be in the form of a coil of aluminum wire.

The coil of wire 1 is placed on a freely rotating turret 2 and is unwound by a pulling force, as shown in Figure 5-11 (position *a*). The unwound wire, which is now bent into a spiral form, must be straightened out before anything can be made from it, and for this purpose a classic "straightening" tool is used, as follows: The wire is passed through a rapidly rotating bushing 4 fitted with five pins 3 (as shown in Figure 5-11, position *b*), in which it undergoes plastic deformation. The straightened wire is pulled out of the bushing by two rotating rolls, which create the required pulling force by means of friction (Figure 5-11, position *c*). The next step is the measuring off of the length of wire needed to produce a single antenna, about 1186 ± 5 mm. A high degree of accuracy is not required, and a simple electric contact 6 placed in the path of the running wire (Figure 5-11, position *d*) can be used. This contact has a dual purpose: it stops the pulling and straightening devices and activates the cutting and bending tools. The measured section of the wire is then cut off (Figure 5-11, position *e*) by means of a cutter moving upward. The piece of wire is fixed in a horizontal position by some means (see horizontal view) and the bending operations can begin. Since the antenna is symmetric, the bending operations on each side of it can be carried out simultaneously, thus saving time.

The first operation is the bending of the two ends to form two vertical 40 ± 5-mm sections. This is achieved by moving the tools 8 upward and bending the wire around two fixed pins 9 (Figure 5-11, position *f*).

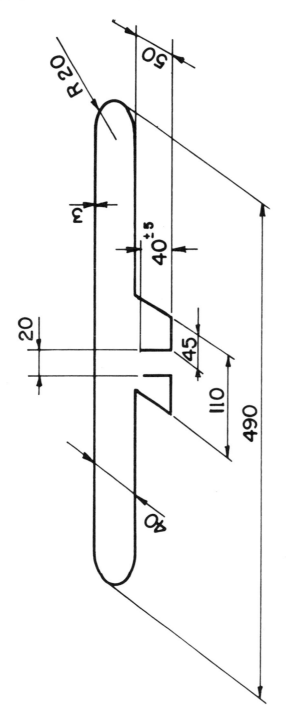

Figure 5-10 An aluminum antenna. The design process of an automatic machine for manufacturing this type of antenna is shown in Figures 5-11 and 5-12.

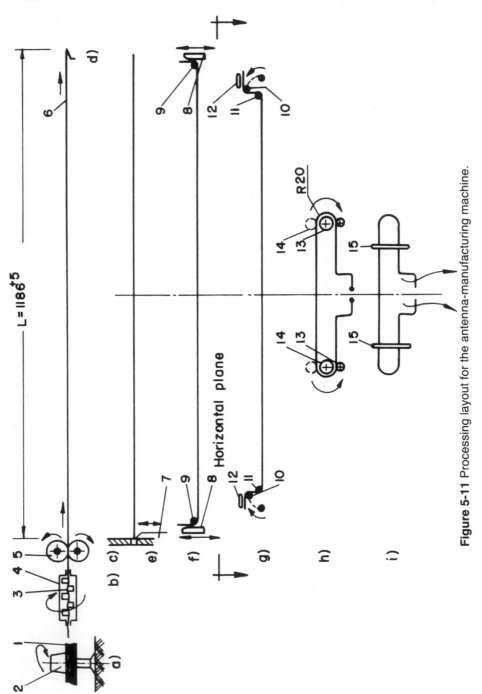

Figure 5-11 Processing layout for the antenna-manufacturing machine.

The subsequent bending operations are carried out in the horizontal plane and thus all the diagrams are drawn in that plane. The bending of the 45-mm and 50-mm sections into a steplike configuration at each end of the wire can be achieved in a single operation, as follows (Figure 5-11, position *g*): On each side a rotating pin 10 bends the wire around a fixed pin 11 to meet a fixed support 12, and in this way the steplike section is completed. The last bending operation, the formation of the curved sections with radius R20, is achieved by bending the wire around two fixed cylinders 14 by means of rollers 13 (Figure 5-11, position *h*).

The final operation (which we call extraction) is the removal of the completed article from the machine. In the layout this step is illustrated in the vertical plane. A lifting body 15 raises the new antenna and it slides into a packing case (Figure 5-11, position *i*).

Figure 5-12 shows a linear cyclogram for this process. Each line corresponds to one of the operations described. In general each action of any tool has three phases: an increase in movement, a uniform phase, and a slowing down. For instance, under the influence of the pulling mechanism (whatever it may be), the motion of the wire first increases (θ_1), then there is an interval of uniform pulling (θ_2), and finally, after the wire has been measured, the mechanism slows down (θ_3). However, sometimes the action of a tool consists of only two phases: increase in movement and slowing down. In our case, for instance, the bending operations do not involve a uniform-motion phase, and a rest period is often needed between the forward and backward strokes.

The process has to be designed in such a way that predetermined time intervals between operations will avoid interference by the different phases with one another.

The dashed lines in Figure 5-12 show a more efficient use of the same process. The period is shortened by eliminating the time intervals wherever consecutive operations, or parts of them, can be carried out simultaneously. For instance, the first bending operation can begin before the cutter has completely returned to its initial position. Similarly, the wire-pulling and -measuring process can begin before the "extraction" tool returns to its initial position. Once again, to know how much time can be saved, we have to move from a conceptual approach to an engineering and computational one. In our case the initial value of the period *T* equals:

$$T = t_i + t_2 + t_3 + t_4 + t_5 + t_6 + 5\delta \quad 7 \text{ seconds}$$

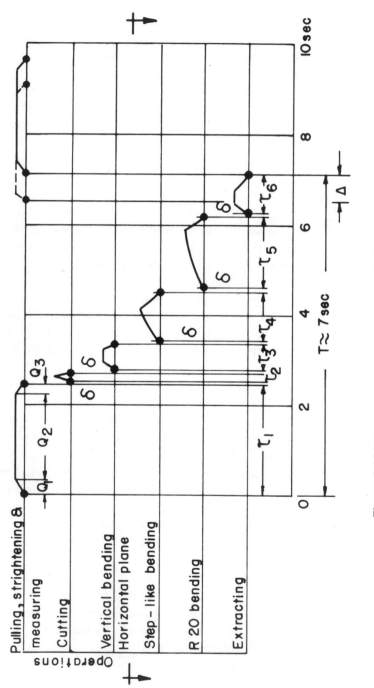

Figure 5-12 Linear cyclogram for processing of the antenna in accordance with Figure 5-11.

The improved value of $T' = T - \Delta = 6.5$ seconds.

While working as a design engineer, this writer was requested to design an automatic, highly productive, machine for manufacturing silver contact needles (Figure 5-13). To understand better the difficulties facing the design team, we have to keep in mind that silver is a very soft material. Thus grinding, for instance, is not a suitable treatment because the silver clings to the grinding stone and blocks its pores. The same problem occurred with the file, the tool used in the manual production of the needle. Consequently our first idea—to borrow from the manual process—failed. It is difficult to imagine how any machine, after the production of each batch of 30 pieces, could clean the file with a metal brush, as did the worker who produced the silver contacts manually. An attempt to treat the contact by cutting—a manufacturing principle borrowed from the metal-turning process—also failed, because of the small dimensions of the part and its inherent softness, which led to bending of the silver wire. We then set about designing a process using the "systematic approach."

• What is the aim?
To produce a part from a particular material in accordance with the given specifications.

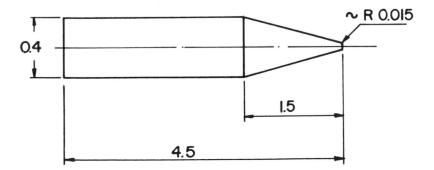

Figure 5-13 Diagram of a silver contact needle. A processing layout and a tool for sharpening the needle are required. (The other operations, such as measuring and cutting, are trivial.)

• What are the obstacles?

The properties of the material and the small dimensions of the part.

• How are the obstacles manifested in the processing?

Grinding and filing are not acceptable because of sticking, and cutting is not possible because of the bending of the wire and the small dimensions of the part.

• What is the way out of the situation?

Perhaps to create a grinding tool with very small pores so that the silver will not clog them.

This last thought led to the creation of the tool shown in Figure 5-14. It consists of two disklike bodies assembled, as is shown in the figure, in such a way that the triangular slot so formed shapes the tip of the needle. To avoid bending the wire, we decided that it should be rotated so as not "to allow time" for curving. A machine rotates the wire at about 600 r/min and pushes it into the slot of the disks, which, in turn, rotate at about 1500 r/min. This method proved very successful. The other operations (feeding and cutting) are trivial.

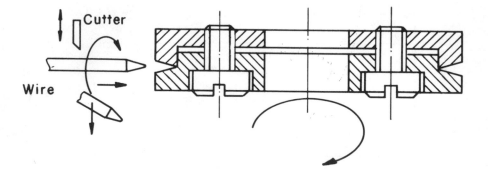

Figure 5-14 The silver needle in Figure 5-13 was sharpened by a rapidly rotating hardened steel tool of the shape shown here.

EXERCISES

What would be your proposed processing layout for each of the following?

1. Automatic or semiautomatic manufacturing of a chain corresponding to Figure 5E-1.
2. Automatic manufacturing of a spiral spring in accordance with

    a. Figure 5E-2a.
    b. Figure 5E-2b.
    c. Figure 5E-2c.

3. Automatic wrapping of bars of soap.
4. Automatic gluing of labels on cans or bottles.
5. Automatic packaging of eggs in boxes.
6. Automatic or semiautomatic conductor winding on a ferrit ring for:

    a. A large number of turns.
    b. A small number of turns.

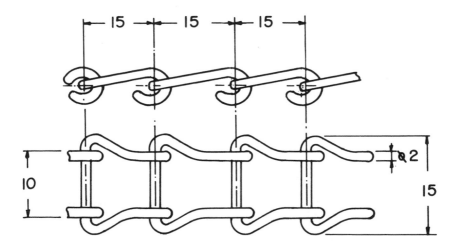

Figure 5E-1 Exercise 1. How would you design a processing layout for automatic or semiautomatic manufacturing of the chain shown?

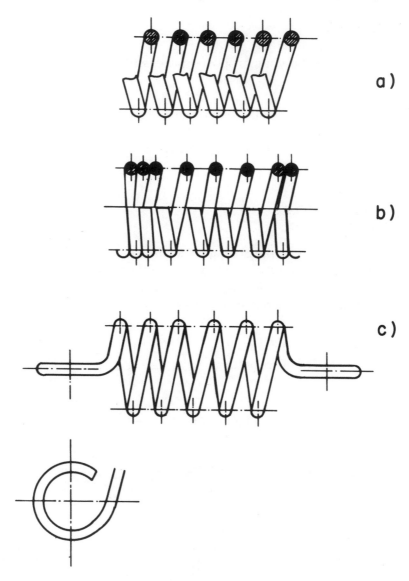

a)

b)

c)

Figure 5E-2 Exercise 2. How would you design a processing layout for automatically manufacturing the spiral springs shown in a), b), and c)?

6

KINEMATICS

At this stage of the design, the designer has to find ways to produce the desired movements of the tools, or other working parts, and determining their significance according to the "processing" layout. At the designer's disposal are mechanical, pneumatic, hydraulic, and electrical methods. To make the right choice, one must know the main characteristics of these techniques, and their comparative advantages and disadvantages. A combination of two or more of the four methods may provide a suitable solution, but this must be justified by sound reasoning. Too many communication lines and auxiliary accessories will be required by a "mixed" solution and the expense must be balanced by a definite benefit.

This stage of the kinematic design can be considered to be complete when a layout of the kinematic solution is ready. Of course, a large number of calculations (ratios, and numbers of teeth, belt drive wheels, cylinders, etc.) will be involved in the work, but we do not consider these here. Our discussion is limited to concepts and methods of invoking them.

The layout must include all the necessary elements—wheels, shafts, bearings, supports, cylinders, valves, switches, and so forth. The single aim at this stage is the clarification of the kinematic solution. The designer does not have to bother with scales, locations, or proportions.

THE VARIOUS SYSTEMS

The advantages and disadvantages of the various systems are given in the following.

Mechanical Systems

Advantages

1. The relative obviousness of mechanical layouts (in comparison with an electronic circuit, for instance).

2. The absence of the need for a specific power supply.

3. The possibility of implementing different kinds of movements or different displacement laws.

4. The relative ease of achieving accurate displacement.

6. The rigidity of mechanical links.

7. The high accuracy of ratios in movement transmission.

Disadvantages

1. For spatially extended constructions, the cumbersomeness of the mechanical kinematic solution.

2. Difficulties in creating relatively rapid movements.

3. Difficulties in creating very large forces.

4. The necessity for special protecting devices to avoid breakage of expensive links.

Hydraulic Systems

Advantages

1. The possibility of achieving very large forces.

2. The possibility of carrying out slow and smooth movements.

3. The relative simplicity of carrying out spatial location of moving elements.

4. The possibility of changing velocities of displacements in a smooth manner.

5. The fact that it is not explosive (pressure sharply drops when the liquid leaks).

Disadvantages

1. The difficulties resulting from the use of high pressures.

2. Mechanical supports or complicated control layout required for accurate displacements.

4. Leakage influence on the pressure inside the system.

5. Variation of the viscosity influenced by temperature changes.

Pneumatic Systems

Advantages	Disadvantages
1. The relative ease of providing complicated spatial locations of moving elements (e.g., pipes can be bent into any shape).	1. The difficulties in creating special displacement laws.
	2. The need for mechanical supports for obtaining accurate displacement.
2. The relative ease of carrying out rapid movements (dependent on the thermodynamics of gases).	3. The dependence of the action on the pressure in the piping.
3. The relative ease of creating large forces (which are the product of the pressure and the area of the piston or diaphragm).	4. The need for special auxiliary equipment.
	5. The need for means to avoid leakage.
	6. The danger of explosion.

Electrical Systems

Advantages	Disadvantages
1. Spatial locations of working elements easily achieved.	1. Problems of reliability.
2. High rate of automation easily obtained.	2. The need for relatively well-educated maintenance personnel.

We shall illustrate the design of a kinematic layout using the automatic machine for manufacturing an antenna (Figure 5-10) as our example. As with the processing layout, the first stage of the kinematic layout must provide for the straightening of the wire and its simultaneous feeding into a bending position. These two simultaneous processes must be stopped when the wire has reached the required length (about 1186 mm), and remain motionless during the bending process. For this purpose a mechanical approach is the means of choice, the driving being carried out by an electromotor with a rotation speed of about 1500 r/min.

Figure 6-1 shows this part of the kinematic layout. The motor

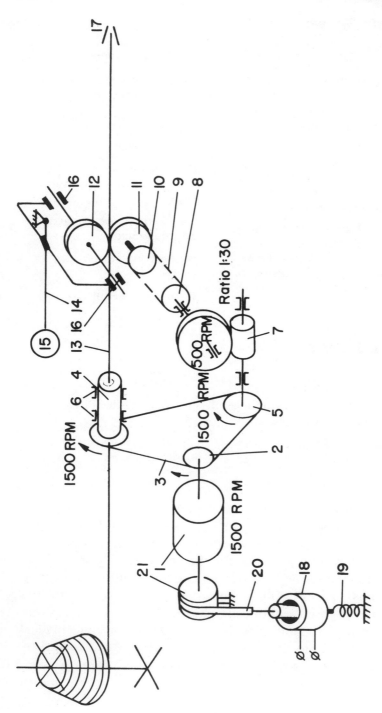

Figure 6-1 Kinematic layout of the antenna-processing machine, showing the mechanical portion.

1, via pulley 2 and trapezoidal belt 3, drives pulleys 4 and 5, pulley 4 being fixed to the straightening device placed on bearings 6. The ratio between the motor and this device is about 1:1. The pulley 5 drives the worm speed reducer 7, which has a chain wheel 8 on its outlet shaft. The chain 9 connects wheel 8 to the other chain wheel 10. The rotation speed of this wheel is about 30 r/min as a result of the action of reducer 7. The wheel 10 drives the lower feeding roller 11. Friction forces between roller 11, the upper roller 12, and the wire 13 have to be sufficiently large to pull the wire. The value of these forces is controlled by the lever 14 and the load 15. The weight of this load is increased by the lever 14, which, via the bearings 16, presses the shaft of the upper roller 12 onto the wire. When the wire 13 reaches the contact 17, it actuates the electrical layout, which disconnects the motor 1 and the coil 18 of the electromagnetic brake from the electric supply, thus stopping the feeding of the wire. The brake is closed by the spring 19, which pulls the belt 20 around the drum 21. The particulars of the electrical layout are given later.

Knowing the rotation speed of the motor and the desired velocities of the rotation of the straightening device and the pulling rollers (to provide the required feeding speed), we can define the necessary ratio values; that is, the diameters of the belt pulleys, the number of teeth, and so forth.

When the feeding of the wire has been accomplished, the required length of wire is available, and this must be cut so that the bending processes can begin. Because of the considerable distances between the bending positions, we decided to use a pneumatic solution for this purpose (Figure 6-2).

A sequence of pneumocylinders acting in concert with the processing layout is provided by a rotating pneumatic valve 22 driven by a motor 23 and a speed reducer consisting of a worm 24 and a wheel 25. The first action to be carried out is the cutting of the wire. For this purpose a piston 26 placed in a cylinder 21 (position *A*) is actuated by air pressure for the working stroke and by a spring 28 for the idle stroke. The piston rod is connected by a link 29 to a lever 30, onto which a cutter 31 is fastened.

Two identical cylinders (position *B*) are used to provide the first bending operation. A punch 32 is fastened to the end of the piston rod, and the wire is bent around a pin 33.

128 KINEMATICS

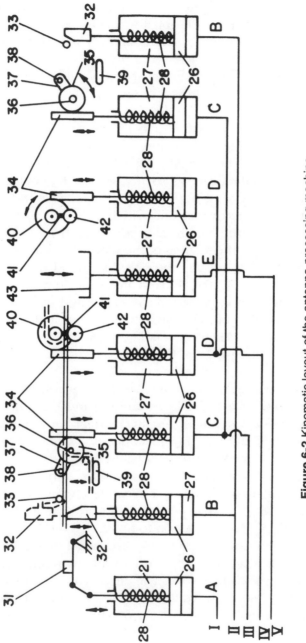

Figure 6-2 Kinematic layout of the antenna-processing machine, showing the pneumatically driven elements.

Another two identical cylinders (position C) perform the second cranklike bending process. A toothed rack 34 constitutes the piston rod, which is geared to a toothed wheel 35 in such a way that the reciprocative motion of the piston 26 is transformed into rotation of a shaft 36. The bending tool 37 is fastened to the end of the shaft and is supplied by two pins 38 and 39. The bending is performed as a result of the rotation of this tool through 90 degrees.

The final bending operation—the formation of a curved section with a radius of 20 mm—is carried out by a third pair of cylinders (position D). Here the piston rod 34 also consists of a toothed rack that transforms the movement of the pistons into the rotation of the wheels 40. The wheels drive a shaft, to the ends of which are fastened another bending tool 41 provided with a roller 42.

The final cylinder (postion E) is used to take the finished product out of the machine. For this purpose a fork 43 is fastened to the end of the piston rod. During the working stroke, the fork raises the antenna and it slides out into a special box, or some other suitable container.

As shown in Figure 6-3, each cylinder is connected by a corresponding pipe I, II, III, IV, or V, to the rotating valve 22 (Figure 6-3). This valve consists of a housing 44 provided with five slots 45, each connected to a corresponding pipe, and a rotating plate

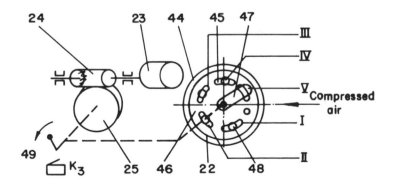

Figure 6-3 Kinematic layout of the pneumatic controller (valve) drive that provides the normal sequence of action of the cylinders (see Figure 6-2).

46 provided with one long slot 47 and five openings 48. The plate 46 is driven by the motor 23. During the rotation the plate 46 connects, by means of the slot 47, the compressed-air source with the corresponding cylinder groups. At that time the other cylinder groups are open, via the openings 48, to the atmosphere, thus allowing the springs 28 to carry out the idle strokes. It is clear that the plate 46 and the housing 44 are well sealed. During the feeding process, the drive of the valve 22 is stopped in such a position that the slot 47 is located in an intermediate sector (i.e., between slots 45) and the cylinders are connected to the atmosphere via openings 48.

The motors are controlled by the electric circuit shown in Figure 6-4. The motors 1 and 23 are three-phase asynchronous machines controlled by contactors K_1 and K_2 respectively. (The contacts of these contactors are denoted by the same letters.)

In the very beginning, at the beginning of the wire-feeding process, the normally closed contacts K_1 in the circuit of motor 1 facilitate the rotation of the motor and actuate the brake's coil 18. This action frees the brake (the electromagnet works against

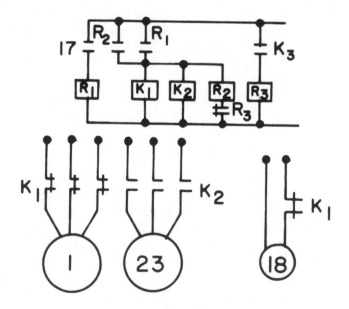

Figure 6-4 Electrical layout of the two motors used to drive the kinematics of the antenna-manufacturing machine.

the spring 19 and prevents friction between the belt 20 and the drum 21). At this time the normally open contacts K_2 are open because both contactors K_1 and K_2 are off. When the desired length of the wire has been obtained and the end of the wire has closed the contact 17, the coil of the relay R_1 is actuated, and its contact R_1 closes the loop and actuates the coils of the contactors K_1 and K_2. As a result the normally closed contacts K_1 must open and the motor 1, together with the coil of the brake 18, is disconnected. The motor 1 stops almost immediately (due to the action of the brake) and the motor 23 begins to rotate, driving the valve 22 and beginning the process of producing an antenna.

Note that after the first bending (cylinders in position B) has been carried out, the contact 17 is off, and to prevent the influence of this fact on the action of the circuit, a block relay R_2 is used. Its coil is actuated at the very moment the contact R_1 is closed and the relay R_2 of the parallel contact R_2, which provides the normal continuation of the circuit's work whether the contact R_1 is on or off. When the valve 22 has completed the circle (all operations are fulfilled), a special lever 49 (see Figure 7-3) acti- vates the position switch K_3; this action closes the circuit of the coil of the relay R_3. Its normally closed contact R_3 opens, discon- necting the coil from the relay R_2, which opens the contact R_2 and brings the circuit to the starting position.

The example discussed seems to contradict the statement made earlier that, whenever possible, different, energy sources should not be mixed in one machine. We will now justify our decision. The first part of the kinematic layout is purely mechan- ical. One can find similar designs in other industrial applications. The second part of the layout is based on the use of pneumatics. The reasons for this choice are:

1. A mechanical solution would be too cumbersome because of the dimensions of the antenna.

2. A mechanical solution is not as flexible as a pneumatic one. If, for instance, one of the dimensions of the antenna has to be changed, the pneumatic solution facilitates such an alteration with only minimal changes in the system; for example, cylinders can be moved if necessary or changes can be made in the diameter of pins with relative ease. Similarly, if we want to produce a part other than an antenna from the same wire on the same machine,

the changes needed will be less for a pneumatic solution than for a mechanical one.

The choice of an electrical layout for synchronizing the work of the motors and brake is obvious.

The design of a kinematic layout often represents a creative process. Sometimes the conventional solution does not fit, and a special solution must be sought. There are also cases where a solution cannot be found in the available printed matter.

The following exercises will help the reader to sharpen his or her skills in this field.

EXERCISES

1. Propose a system that will rotate the lights of a car by an angle ψ, corresponding to the rotation of the steering wheel, through an angle ϕ. *Note:* Small rotations of the steering wheel must not affect the lights (Figure 6E-1).

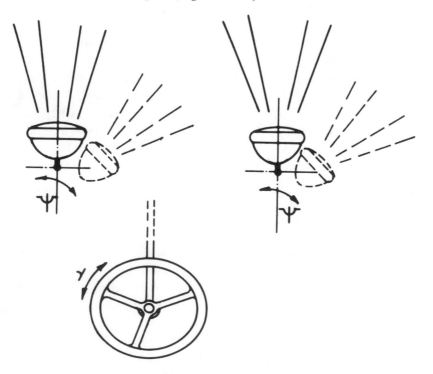

Figure 6E-1 Exercise 1.

2. The diagram shows two handles located as illustrated. Design a device that will permit the movement of only one of the handles when the other one is fixed in the "O" position (Figure 6E-2).

3. The same as Exercise 2 (Figure 6E-3).

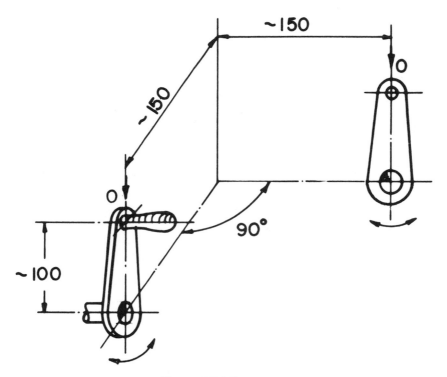

Figure 6E-2 Exercise 2.

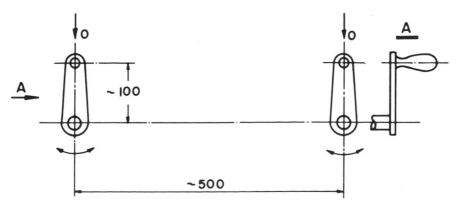

Figure 6E-3 Exercise 3.

4. A number of pushbuttons are given. Find a solution that prevents two or more of the buttons from being pressed simulaneously. Consider the following options:

a. By pressing any button, the previously pressed one is released.

b. A depressed button must be released before another one can be pressed (Figure 6E-4).

5. The layout shows a shaft I rotating at a uniform speed of about 120 r/min and a body II in a plane parallel to the shaft I. Propose a mechanical solution that will enable the movement of the body II (driven by shaft I as shown in Figure 6E-5).

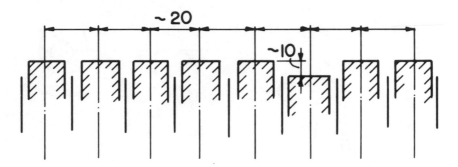

Figure 6E-4 Exercise 4.

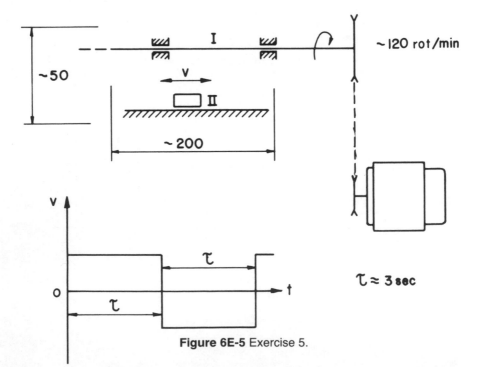

Figure 6E-5 Exercise 5.

6. The diagram shows glass bottles packed in a case. Propose a system for the automated removal of the bottles from the packing case for purposes of cleaning (Figure 6E-6).

7. The diagram shows two pistons I and II housed in a cylinder. Find a solution that will cause piston I to move when $P = P_1$ and piston II to move when $P = P_2$, where $P_2 > P_1$ (Figure 6E-7).

8. The rotating cutter shown in the diagram cuts wire into 20-mm pieces. Propose a solution for feeding the wire and stopping its movement during the cutting process (Figure 6E-8).

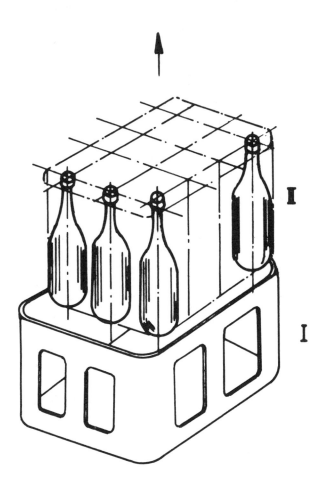

Figure 6E-6 Exercise 6.

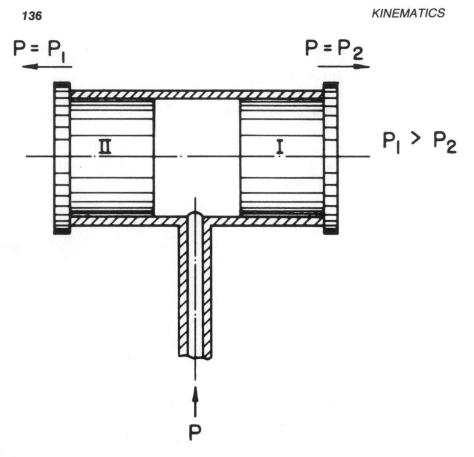

Figure 6E-7 Exercise 7.

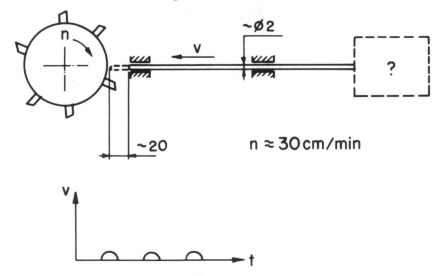

Figure 6E-8 Exercise 8.

9. A coil of wire is given (the diameter of the coil changes as the wire is used up). Propose a system for providing a constant pulling stress F (Figure 6E-9).

10. The layout shows a constantly rotating electric motor and a shaft provided with a tap (for forming an internal screw thread) on its end. Propose a system for facilitating rotation of the shaft with speed n_1 for producing the thread and with speed n_2 for extracting the tap from the threaded part. The axial movement of the shaft is caused by a variable force P (Figure 6E-10).

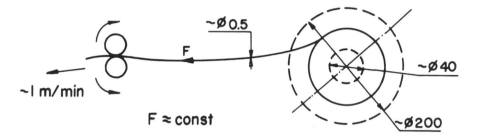

Figure 6E-9 Exercise 9.

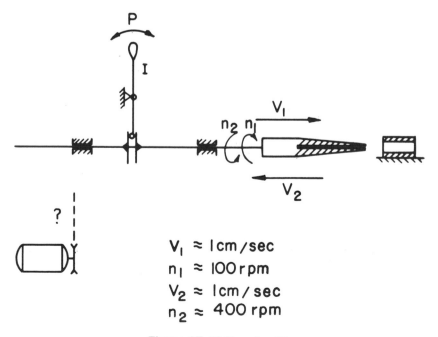

$V_1 \approx 1\,cm/sec$

$n_1 \approx 100\,rpm$

$V_2 \approx 1\,cm/sec$

$n_2 \approx 400\,rpm$

Figure 6E-10 Exercise 10.

11. The diagram shows a punch for cutting certain items out of a moving metal tape. Propose a device for facilitating the movement of the tape in accordance with Figure 6E-11.

12. A set of helicopter blades is shown in the layout. How is it possible that during horizontal flight each blade has an inclination of α_1, α_2, α_3, and α_4 while passing through positions I, II, III, and IV respectively? Take into account that the pilot can change the absolute and relative values of the angles (Figure 6E-12).

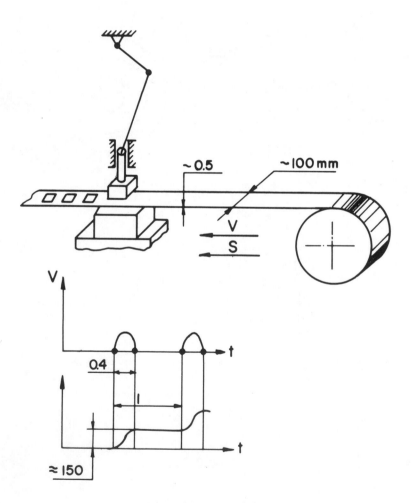

Figure 6E-11 Exercise 11.

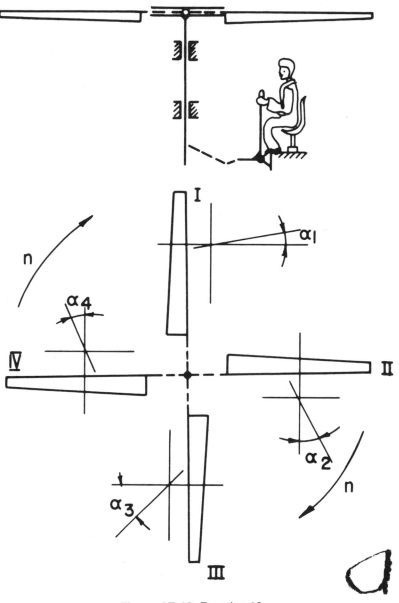

Figure 6E-12. Exercise 12.

13. Two shafts rotating with speeds ω_1 and ω_2 are shown in the figure. How can you arrange for the third shaft to rotate with speed ω_3 in accordance with the given expression (Figure 6E-13)?

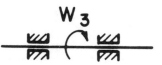

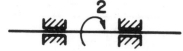

$$W_3 = K (W_1 + W_2)$$

$$K = const$$

Figure 6E-13 Exercise 13.

14. Body I travels as is shown in the diagram with an amplitude of about 150 mm. How can the body II be forced to move in accordance with Figure 6E-14?

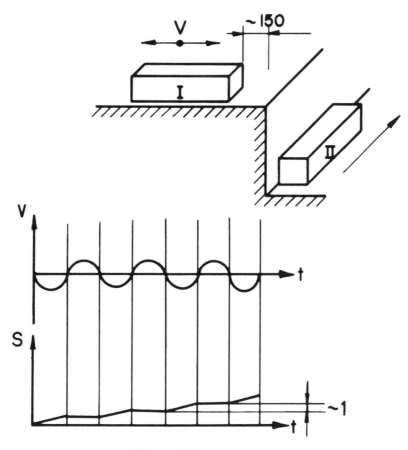

Figure 6E-14 Exercise 14.

15. The diagram shows a drilling device in which a motor constantly drives the drill. Design a system that restricts the torque M (if M reaches M, the drill will have to be disconnected from the drive). (See Figure 6E-15.)

16. Two shafts I and II are shown in the layout. Shaft I has a variable speed ω_1 that vacillates continuously between o and ω_{max}. Design a coupling that connects the shafts when $\omega \geqslant \omega_1^*$ (not before) is reached. In accordance with the diagram when $\omega_1 \geqslant \omega_1^*$, then $\omega_2 = \omega_1$ (Figure 6E-16).

17. Two parallel shafts I and II are given in the diagram. The speed of shaft I is uniform and is equal to ω_1. Design a system that enables shaft II to rotate at speed ω_2 in accordance with the graph (Figure 6E-17).

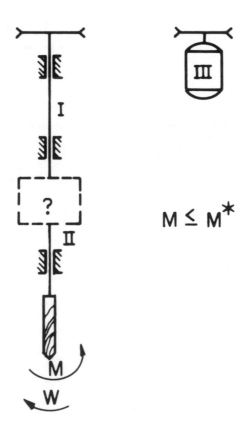

Figure 6E-15 Exercise 15.

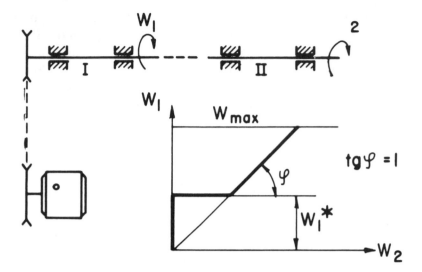

$$M \approx 0.1 \, KG \, sm$$

Figure 6E-16 Exercise 16.

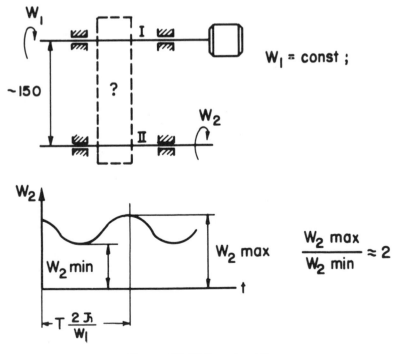

Figure 6E-17 Exercise 17.

18. A pair of railroad car wheels VII and their axes are shown in the diagram. The braking system is actuated by a pneumocylinder VI. Design the transmission from the lever V to the rods I, II, III, and IV, which will force the brakeshoes to be pressed against the wheels during the deceleration process. The transmission must provide a uniform pressing force that is independent of the wear on the shoes (Figure 6E-18).

19. An elevator car is presented in the diagram. Propose a solution for stopping the car immediately if the cable should tear (Figure 6E-19).

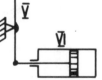

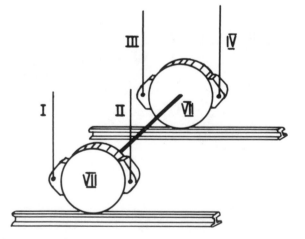

Figure 6E-18 Exercise 18

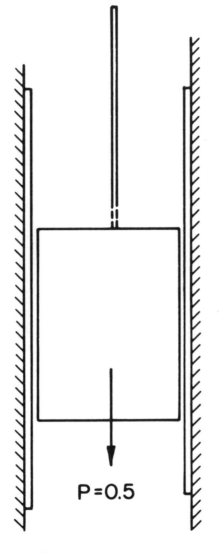

$P = 0.5$

Figure 6E-19 Exercise 19.

20. Two shafts rotating at the same speed $\omega_1 = \omega_2$ are given in the diagram. Design a coupling that allows the shaft free motion around point "o" in the plane of the paper during its rotation (Figure 6E-20).

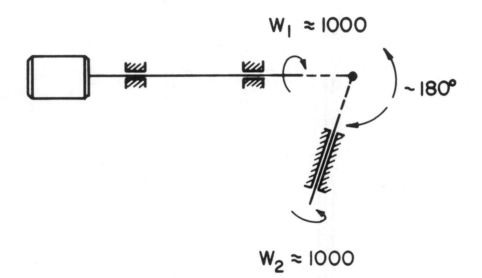

Figure 6E-20 Exercise 20.

21. The diagram shows a propelling device of a boat. An improvement that permits a change in the inclination of the blades during the rotation of the shaft (for reversing or speed changes) is required (Figure 6E-21).

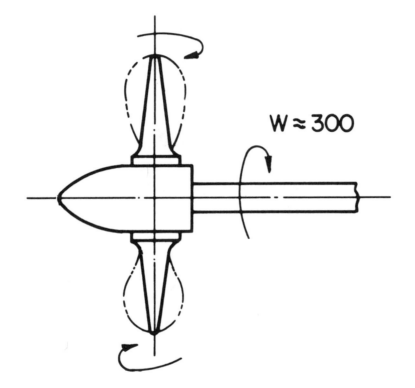

$W \approx 300$

Figure 6E-21 Exercise 21.

22. The layout shows a shaft I rotating at a uniform speed of about 100 r/min and a body II in a plane perpendicular to the shaft I. Propose a mechanical solution that will enable the movement of the body II (driven by shaft I) as shown in Figure 6E-22.

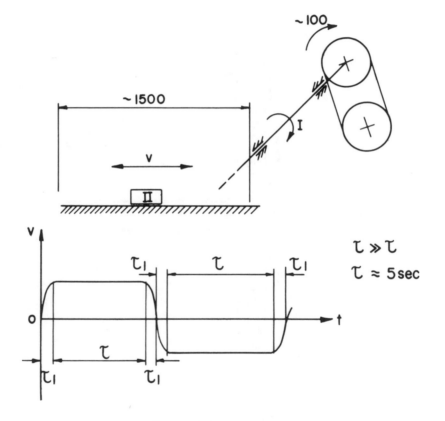

Figure 6E-22 Exercise 22.

Chapter 7

SOME RULES OF DESIGN

When the concepts have been clearly defined and the layouts are ready, the real design begins. The following are some rules the designer must follow in order to create a reliable device. This collection of rules constitutes the "grammar" of design. Most of them do not involve calculations, and so classical engineering books do not deal with them. However, they are based on the experience of generations of engineers, and should be valuable to new engineers to enable them to avoid some of the pitfalls they will encounter in the course of practicing their profession. Here, of course, we can present only a small part of this grammar. The examples are taken from an excellent book written by the Russian engineer Orlov.[6]

The first example illustrates that what sometimes appears to be a negligible element in a particular design may turn out to be of great importance.

Problem: A conical plug located in a housing must provide sealing between the conical surfaces. Which of the four designs shown in Figure 7-1 is the correct one? As we can see, the only differences between the layouts are the relative dimensions of the plugs and the housings. In case 1, after the grinding-in process, the upper diameter *m* of the plug becomes larger than the housing hole (regadless of whether or not the plug material is softer than that of the housing). This fact prevents the plug from moving closer to the housing surface, and, as a result, sealing will not be satisfactory. In cases 2 and 3, after grinding, the lower diameter

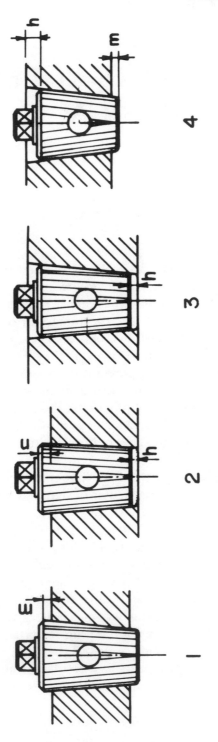

Figure 7-1 Try to decide which of these four designs is the correct one.

h of the housing will prevent the plug from moving deeper, and thus will cause the same problem as in the previous case. The best solution is that shown in case 4: the grinding-in process does not affect the sealing and is independent of the hardnesses of the plug and housing materials—the plug "finds" the best position to close the gap between the conical surfaces.

In light of this example, we can outline one of the most general design rules as follows: *Two adjoining parts should make contact only via one surface each.* Figure 7-2 illustrates this rule. Case 1 is completely incorrect. Case 2, in which backlashes *h* prevent unnecessary contacts, and case 3 offer the correct solutions. Another example of the application of this rule is shown in Figure 7-3. Case 1 is completely wrong, but cases 2 and 3 are satisfactory.

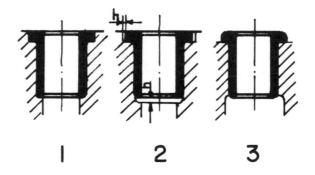

Figure 7-2 Bushing design.

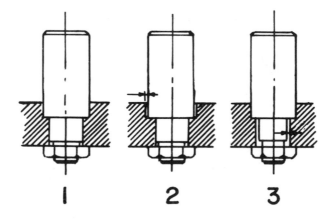

Figure 7-3 Fastening of a pin.

In the coupling shown in Figure 7-4, the connection between the two parts is provided by teeth. Case 1 not only is wrong, but it is harmful because the centering by the cylindrical part of the coupling prevents complete contact between the teeth. On the other hand, in case 2 a backlash S facilitates better contact between the teeth and hence improves transmission of the load.

Another rule states that *a precise movable joint or mechanism has to be released from external forces that can cause intensive wear and disturb normal action of the part*—that is, working surfaces must be protected from the influence of superfluous forces. This rule is illustrated in Figure 7-5 with the example of a conical

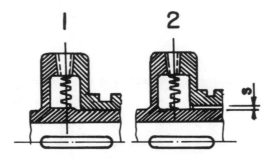

Figure 7-4 Coupling.

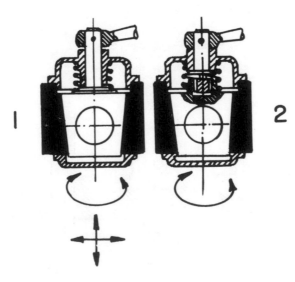

Figure 7-5 A conical faucet with a handle.

plug tap with a handle. In case 1 the turning is precipitated by the conical surfaces. Axial forces applied to the plug by the operator impair the normal action of the tap by causing disturbances in the sealing. The self-centering of the plug is hampered by the drive shaft, which, in turn, is centered by the cover. Consequently the manufacturing process becomes very expensive, since the production and maintenance of the two guiding surfaces require a high degree of accuracy. In the design shown in case 2, the handle and drive shaft are separate from the plug, thus releasing the plug from all forces other than the torque when the handle is rotated.

As another example consider the drive of a valve of an internal combustion engine (Figure 7-6). In the first illustration, the cam pushes the rod of the valve directly. The cam creates a tangential friction force when pushing the valve open. This force causes warping of the valve within the limits of the backlashes. As a result the disk of the valve cannot close the opening promptly, and the exhaust gases flowing through the chink intensify the nonuniform errosion of the valve. In the second case, the valve is designed in such a way that the influence of tangential friction forces on the valve is prevented: only axial, centrally attached forces act on it. This improvement is achieved by the introduction of an intermittent plunger 2. However, this solution entails an increase in the mass of the moving parts. This disadvantage is obviated in the mechanism shown in the third case. Here a lever 3 prevents the influence of tangential friction on the valve.

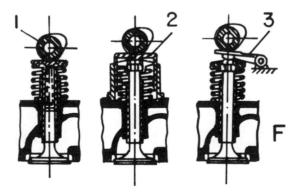

Figure 7-6 Drive of a valve of an internal combustion engine.

A third example is the clamping device shown in Figure 7-7. In case 1, the fixing force acts only at one point on the surface of the object being clamped. In addition the thread of the bolt undergoes bending. The design of case 2 is free of this disadvantage. The ridged surface of the clamping arm finds its position independently of the size of the object. The same applies to the bolt. Also, the clamping process in this case is faster.

The main rule *applicable to the thread is that it must be free of bending and shear stresses.* Let us consider the example presented in Figure 7-8 and compare the six technical solutions. Case 1 is completely unsatisfactory. The maximum bending torque and shear stress caused by the force *P* are located on the threaded

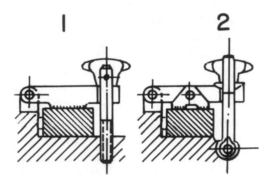

Figure 7-7 Clamping device.

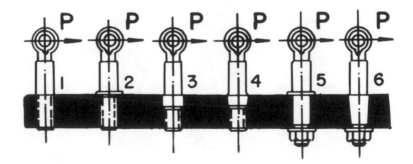

Figure 7-8 Design of a thread.

section of the part. The addition of a collar (case 2) scarcely helps, since the bending deformations are decreased only by the additional friction forces between the collar and the surface of the base. Solutions 3 and 4 are much better. The smooth surface takes the load, thus freeing the threaded section of the part from the bending and shear stresses. The only disadvantage of such a solution is the necessity to provide concentricity of the smooth and threaded sections. Therefore, the thread has to be made with a backlash. The best solutions are offered by cases 5 and 6. Here the thread is loaded only by tension stresses. Bending and shear stresses are taken by the smooth part, which may be conical or cylindrical in shape.

The bending of bolts is often a result of incorrect positioning. The five examples of fixing a support shown in Figure 7-9 will be used to explain this statement. There are two errors in the design of case 1: the lack of an element capable of resisting shear, and the eccentricity of the load due to the force *P* on the bolts, which in turn causes them to bend. In case 2 the base of the support is turned through 90 degrees. Here one bolt is almost not loaded and the other is loaded by the same force that acts centrally. Solutions 3 and 4 are similar, but case 4 obviously is preferable: In case 4 the triangle-like base facilitates the division of the load

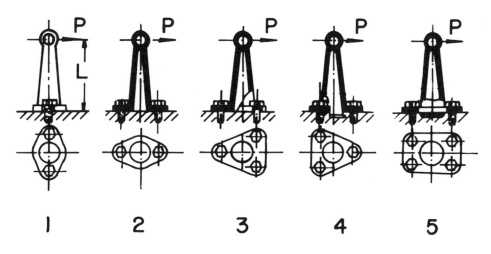

Figure 7-9 Location of bolts.

between two bolts (the disadvantages of case 3 are the same as those for case 2). In addition, in case 4 on the bottom of the support is a lug located in a socket on the base. Case 5 offers the best solution. Here the rectangular base of the support facilitates an increase in the contact area and in the size of the lugs, thus decreasing the load on the bolts and the shear stress.

The designer must avoid, if possible, processes that involve the bending of elements of machine parts, utilizing instead tension, pressing, or shear. For example, it is worth substituting for the lever shown in case 1 of Figure 7-10 the design shown in case 2; the extra rib prevents bending.

Another example is given in Figure 7-11, which illustrates an improvement of a support roller. The best solution is case 3; the worst is case 1.

In the cam follower shown in Figure 7-12, case 2 offers a better solution than case 1. In the latter case, the rod of the follower undergoes considerable bending, which worsens the action conditions of the mechanism. The follower can be jammed in its guide rails.

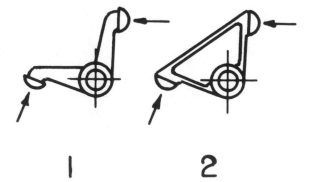

Figure 7-10 Design of a lever.

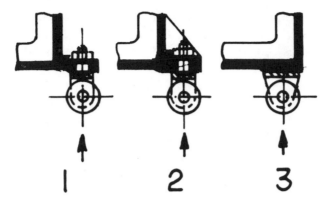

Figure 7-11 Design of a support.

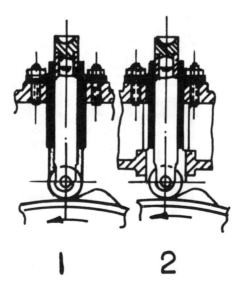

Figure 7-12 Design of a cam follower.

The fast rotating wheel shown in Figure 7-13 must be designed in accordance with diagram 3. In cases 1 and 2, the centrifugal tension forces due to rotation will cause spatial bending of the disk.

The designer must avoid axial fixation of any part at two points along its length, especially if the points are far apart. Such a situation is typical for bearing assemblies. Figure 7-14 shows a comparison of the correct (*2*) and incorrect (*1*) designs. The former allows the left bearing to find its place in accordance with the thermal expansion of the housing and the shaft. In addition, errors that may occur during the manufacturing process will not influence the normal action of this assembly.

A part should be centered on a base by a surface with the smallest possible diameter to increase the accuracy of centering and decrease the influence of the temperature changes. Figures

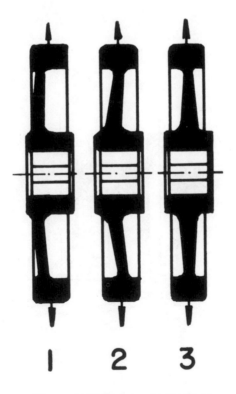

Figure 7-13 Design of a flywheel.

7-15 and 7-16 illustrate this statement. In both cases design 3 is better than 2, with the latter preferable to design 1. For instance, if the support presented in Figure 7-16 is centered on its larger diameter, say about 200 mm, the backlash should be about 0.12 mm: in the optimal case, the backlash can be made three times less, and for the same fit it will be about 0.037 mm. This example should serve to clarify the nature of the rule under consideration.

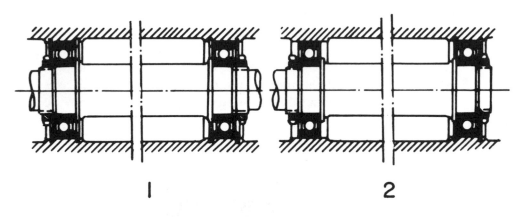

Figure 7-14 Design of a bearing assembly.

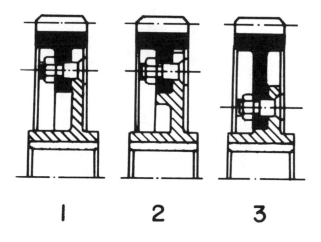

Figure 7-15 Gear-wheel design.

When designing an assembly on the principle of shrink, the designer must remember that the assembly will be under load, even before the working load is attached. It is unacceptable to fit a part on two cylindrical surfaces of equal diameter, as shown in Figure 7-17, case 1. The sizes of the surfaces must be different, as in case 2. In addition, the axial dimensions of the part should be chosen in such a way that the narrower end is fitted into its hole before the wider end enters its hole, as shown in case 3.

Similarly, it is incorrect to design an assembly corresponding to Figure 7-18, case 1. To save the cost of precision processing, the designer has divided the contact surface between two cylinders. The error lies in the fact that the diameters of these cylinders are equal. When the lower cylinder passes through the hole, it will be damaged and will not be able to function properly. Cases 2 and 3 not only offer a better solution, but they also provide higher accuracy.

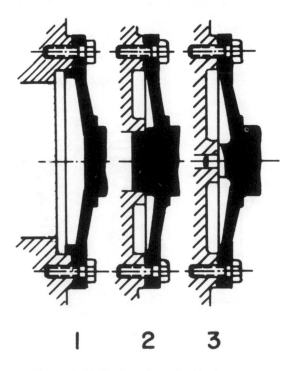

1   2   3

Figure 7-16 Design of a cylindrical support.

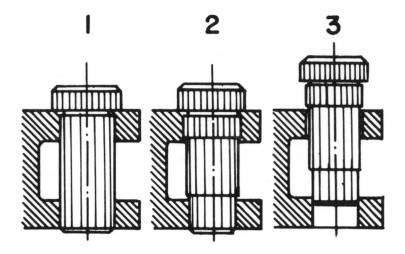

Figure 7-17 Assembly of a pin.

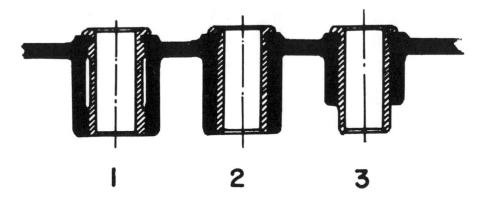

Figure 7-18 Assembly of a sleeve.

Thermal stresses cause serious problems in the construction of machines, especially parts that are subjected to changes in temperature. The following example will help us to understand this point. Figure 7-19 shows the cooling jacket of the cylinder of an engine. The temperature differences between the internal and external surfaces, and hence differences in thermal expansion, give rise to stress. A possible solution lies in the use of a material with a very small expansion coefficient, but in most cases this solution is not acceptable because of other restrictions. The solution offered by case 1 is incorrect because of the straight shape of the walls. Here the stresses reach high values. The shape of the external wall in case 2 facilitates an increase in the elasticity of the jacket and a consequent decrease of the stress.

Some "grammar" *rules relating to cantilever shafts can be explained with the help of* Figure 7-20. It is easy to see that in case 1 the reaction forces in the bearings are significantly different, which results in the bearings having different lifetimes. (The use of different bearings complicates the device.) Solution 2 improves the relationship between the forces. In principle they can be made

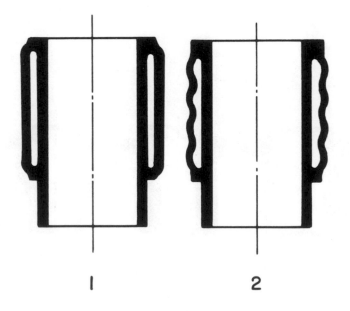

1   2

Figure 7-19 Cooling jacket.

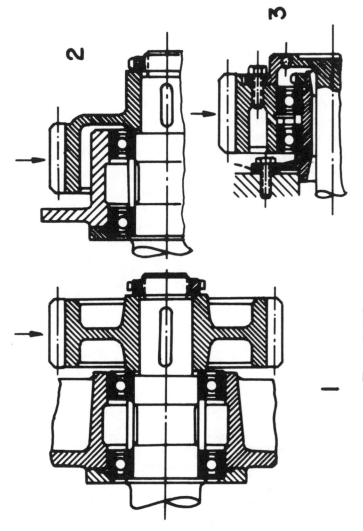

Figure 7-20 Design of a cantilever shaft.

completely equal. The third case eliminates the cantilever. The loads on the bearings are identical and the bending stresses in the shaft are eliminated. The shaft is loaded only by torque. The disadvantage of this solution is the shorter life of the bearings as a result of the rotation of the external rings. (Try to answer the question: Why is this kind of rotation worse?)

The inversion method is a very useful tool in design, and a "grammar" rule based on it may be formulated as follows: *To improve the design, try to invert the chosen solution.* Sometimes this rule permits the designer to achieve the required effect in a less expensive way. The pros and cons of each possibility should be weighed before making a final decision.

This rule is illustrated in Figure 7-21. In case 1 the rod is driven by a forklike lever that pushes or pulls the pin fastened to the rod. The inverse design 2 differs in the location of the pin. Here the pin is fastened to the lever and the fork to the rod. Design 2 is better from the point of view of the distribution of the forces. On the other hand, the advantage of the first design is that it has smaller dimensions.

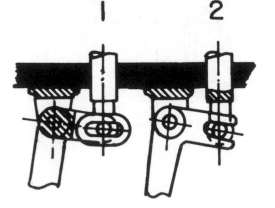

Figure 7-21 Design of a forklike lever.

In Figure 7-22 cases 1 and 2 show two variations of a pipe joint. In the first design, there is an external screwnut, and in the second design, an internal one. The first design has larger diametric dimensions but smaller axial ones. The second mode is smaller in diameter but greater in length.

Figure 7-23 shows two possibilities for fastening a turbine blade. The first provides better conditions for manufacturing the wheel and the second for production of the blade roots.

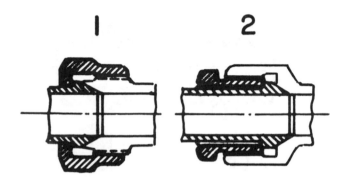

Figure 7-22 Design of pipe joints.

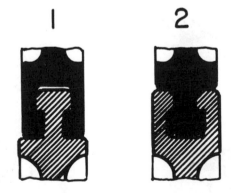

Figure 7-23 Fastening of a turbine blade.

Figure 7-24 illustrates two solutions for connecting a rod to a forkpiece. In the first solution, the connecting rod has one bearing; in the forkpiece, the pin is fixed. The dimensions can be made smaller but lubrication then becomes a problem. In the second case, the rod is fixed on the pin and the bearings are placed in the fork piece. The dimensions are increased, and in general lubrication is facilitated.

The hydraulic cylinders presented in Figure 7-25 differ in that

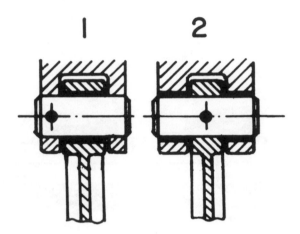

Figure 7-24 Means of connecting a rod to a forkpiece.

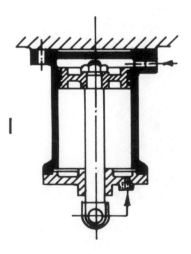
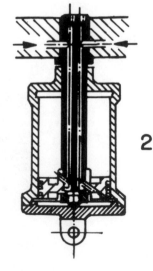

Figure 7-25 "Direct" and "inverse" hydraulic cylinder.

in case 2 when pressure is applied, the cylinder moves while the piston rod is stationary. In the first, more usual, case, the principle is the inverse: when pressure is applied, the piston and the piston rod move, while the cylinder is fixed. Under certain conditions this inversion is very useful.

EXERCISES

Which of the following proposed designs is the best? Try to explain your decision.

1. A bolt joint (Figure 7E-1).
2. A cylindrical support (Figure 73-2).
3. Securing of a housing (Figure 7E-3).

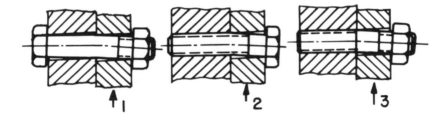

Figure 7E-1 Execise 1.

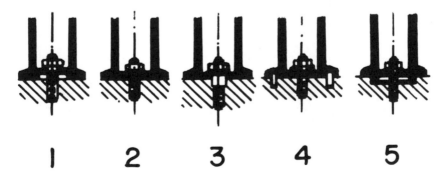

Figure 7E-2 Exercise 2.

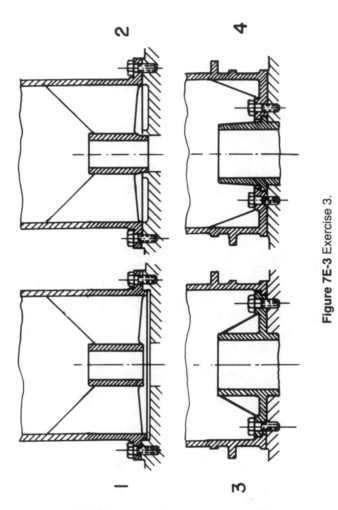

Figure 7E-3 Exercise 3.

4. A housing subjected to different temperature conditions (Figure 7E-4).

5. A welded lug (Figure 7E-5).

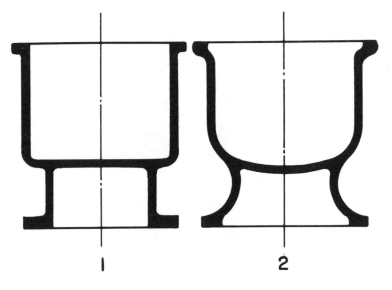

Figure 7E-4 Exercise 4.

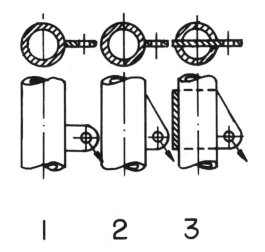

Figure 7E-5 Exercise 5.

6. A joint element (Figure 7E-6).

7. A two-step plunger of a compressor (Figure 7E-7).

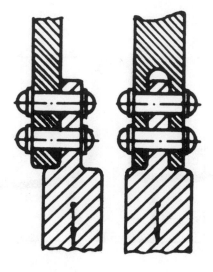

Figure 7E-6 Exercise 6.

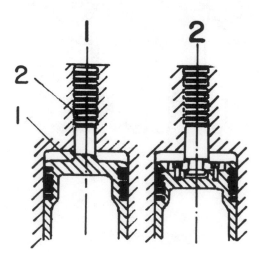

Figure 7E-7 Exercise 7.

8. A cover closing either of two pipes (Figure 7E-8).
9. The roller assembly of a cam follower (Figure 7E-9).

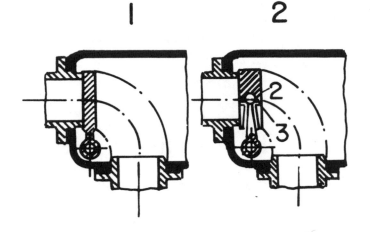

Figure 7E-8 Exercise 8.

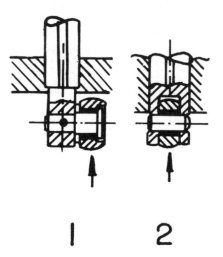

Figure 7E-9 Exercise 9.

10. A thrust-bearing support (Figure 7E-10).
11. A conveyer link joint (Figure 7E-11).

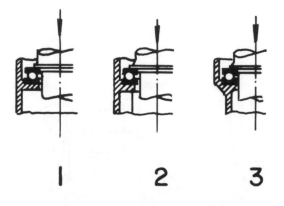

Figure 7E-10 Exercise 10.

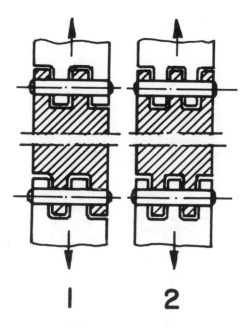

Figure 7E-11 Exercise 11.

8

COMPUTERS IN TECHNICAL CREATIVITY

No discussion of any technical process is complete these days without considering the possible role of the computer, that ubiquitous superservant that promises to take all the drudgery out of life—from planning our meals, and cooking them, to managing our finances. Thus our question here is: How can the creative process be computerized, if at all? The key word, of course, is "creative." It seems we know more about why it is not feasible to computerize creativity than about how computers can be applied in creative design.

The natural conclusion to this book is a consideration of the role of computers in creative design. This chapter thus is devoted to some ideas about the nature of creativity in general, and of technical creativity in particular, and about how creativity can be computerized—if at all.

Creativity produces information and knowledge, and whoever controls information and know-how will inherit the productive world. Computerization of this process of knowledge production could contribute much to science and technology. The process of creating a new product, machine, or technical solution can be described as a "game" with nature, a game in which nature is essentially an indifferent partner. Thus we confront the unknown without a definite apponent. Richard Bellman[1] has expressed this idea differently: "The assumption that the universe is completely hostile is not a feasible one, since it is too expensive."

After beginning our in-depth discussion of the subject with a brief description of the state of the art of computer-aided activities in engineering, we compare the known applications of computerization with the less-well-investigated field of the role of computers in technical creativity.

CAD, CAG, AND CAM—STATE OF THE ART

In modern engineering we are familiar with a number of computer-aided processes:

computer-aided design (CAD);
computer-aided graphics (CAG); and
computer-aided manufacturing (CAM).

CAD can be applied in industry and technology for the design of machines, apparatus, circuits (pneumatic, hydraulic, mechanical, electronic, etc.), tools, structures, and systems. It is particularly useful in the design of gear transmissions and cam mechanisms, turbines and missiles, engines, and manufacturing processes and plants. In machine design the following specific domains of computerization are worthy of mention.

1. CAD can be applied to the investigation of the kinematics of mechanisms and machines, which includes the study of the motion of the links of the mechanism. For example, it is often very important to define the displacement of some specific point or element as a function of time (or of some other displacement), the trajectory of a specific point, the velocities of certain links, or, of course, the accelerations of links, which are the sources of dynamic loads, vibrations, and noises.

2. The forces acting between and within links constitute another important factor that must, and can, be elaborated by means of a computer. The importance of this application of CAD cannot be sufficiently emphasized.

3. Computerization can also be used in the design of machine parts, including the determination of their main dimensions, the choice of materials (as well as special treatments), and, often, the mode of manufacture.

To help us understand this brief (and incomplete) list of CAD domains, let us consider the example given in Figure 8-1. Here we have a four-link, two-slider mechanism. By defining the motion of the slider *A* in the form

$$x = Vt \qquad V = \text{const} \tag{1}$$

where

$$V = \text{the speed of motion}$$
$$t = \text{time}$$

we can calculate the motion of the slider *B*. Obviously, corresponding to Figure 8-1 we have

$$y(x) = \sqrt{l^2 - x^2} \tag{2}$$

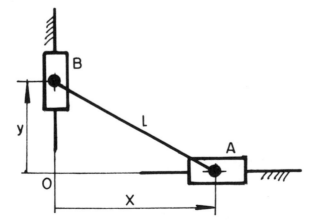

Figure 8-1. Four-link two-slider mechanism.

Expressing *y* in terms of time, we obtain from equations (1) and
(2):

$$y(t) = \sqrt{l^2 - V^2 t^2} \tag{3}$$

If this formula and the values of *l* and *V* are entered into the
computer memory, the computer will be able to process the value
of *y* for any time *t*. Of course, the speed and acceleration of the
slider *B* can be obtained immediately by differentiating equation
(3) once and twice respectively. It is important to note that this
is not the only computation algorithm for this mechanism. For
example, we can use the following expression for the definition
of *y*:

$$\bar{y}(x) = \bar{x} \tan \varphi \tag{4}$$

where

$$\varphi = \text{arc cos } Vt/l \tag{5}$$

Thus

$$\bar{y}(t) = Vt \tan [\text{arc cos } Vt/l] \tag{6}$$

The programmer must decide which of the two algorithms is more
convenient for the computer in question, will enable faster processing of the data and the like.

When the acceleration A_B of the slider *B* has been obtained,
the force of inertia $F = A_B m_B$ can be found, and thus the load on
the rod *l* can be determined. The rod's cross section can be calculated after computation of the stresses that the force *F* develops
in the rod. We can choose to take into account only compressing
stresses, or we can investigate, in addition, the ability of the rod
to withstand buckling. For this purpose, another set of formulas,
dependences, and constants must be introduced into the computer's memory.

An additional example of this type is the case described in
Chapter 4 by the set of equations describing the model shown in
Figure 4-12. A computerized analysis of this system would be of
use in studying the behavior of the float on the waves and the

influence of the "springs" on the effectiveness of utilization of the wave energy. Computer-aided solutions are especially useful for nonlinear equations. In the case under consideration, for instance, when the shape of the "float" is conical (and not cylindrical), the force of buoyancy is essentially not proportional to the float's diving depth and thus equation (1), which describes its motion, becomes nonlinear.

Another kind of CAD problem is that of optimization. To illustrate this point, let us seek the minimal weight of a beam that can withstand a certain load (Figure 8-2). The weight can be minimized by changing the shape of the beam's cross section, within certain restrictions of the cross section's dimensions, and by changing the construction material. It is clear that here the moment of inertia I and the areas of the cross section are under discussion. The restrictions may be formulated as follows:

—The thickness of any element of the cross section cannot be less than δ.

—The height of the cross section cannot be more than H.

—The width of the cross section must be less than B.

By dividing the cross section into a number of elements, we can express its area of the following.

$$S = \sum_{i=1}^{k} s_i \tag{7}$$

where $\quad s_i$ = the area of the ith element
$\qquad k$ = the number of elements

and the moment of inertia as

$$I = \sum_{i=1}^{k} I_i + \sum_{i=1}^{k} s_i D_i \tag{8}$$

where $\quad I_i$ = the moment of inertia of the ith element
$\qquad D_i$ = the distance of the ith element's mass center from the symmetry axis of the cross section

The computer can be programmed to check different combinations of shapes and materials (the latter give us different values of allowed bending stresses and density of the material). The computer searches until it obtains the minimal values of beam weight that provide the required strength.

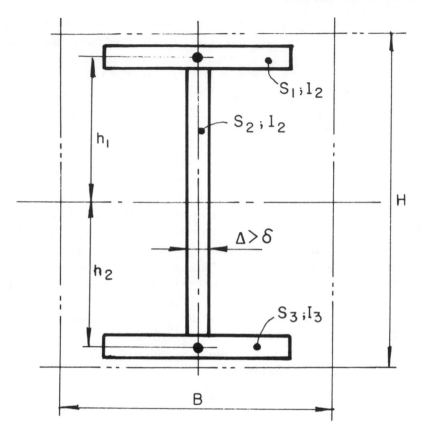

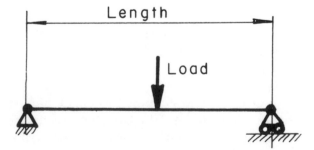

Figure 8-2. Example of a cross section of a beam.

If we introduce, in addition, a cost criterion (for the cheapest beam), the optimization will be more complicated. Figure 8-3 shows this phenomenon graphically. Here we see the "material" versus "cross section's shape" plane and above it the "cost" surface. The cost *C* is a function of the material and the cost of processing.

$$C = c(\text{material, processing}) \qquad (9)$$

Thus the computer manipulates the numbers introduced into the memory in accordance with equations (7), (8), and (9). To accomplish such a design manually would require a tremendous

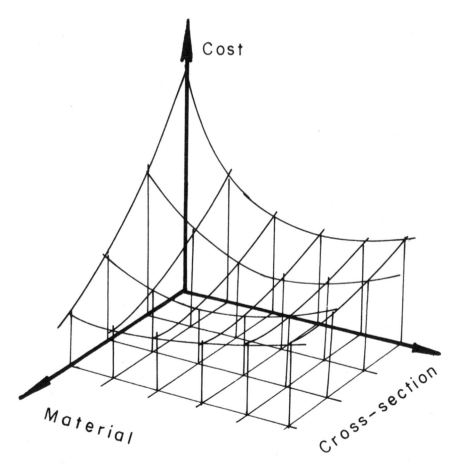

Figure 8-3. Graphic representation of a minimization surface.

amount of trial and error. The use of a computer facilitates the trial-and-error approach to produce the desired results incomparably faster.

By analogy, any other mechanical part—such as a shaft, gear wheel, key, or screw—can be designed in terms of known formulas developed analytically or experimentally. The speed of the computer facilitates the introduction of some very effective calculation methods, for instance, the finite elements method, which is based on relatively simple principles but requires a large number of repetitive computations. Only computerization of such methods can provide accurate and reliable results.

After the dimensions of the part or machine have been determined, the graphic stage begins. The computer parameters must be documented on paper for the manufacturer. The application of CAG at this design stage can be illustrated by the example of a gear wheel. The main diameters, the width, and the teeth modulus are determined by calculations and by the restraints imposed by the structure into which the wheel must fit, as shown in Figure 8-4. However, other dimensions can be chosen almost arbitrarily, such as those dictated by the manufacturing requirements and method or those that depend on the properties of the material of the part (in this example). The dimensions of the part may also be determined by the shapes and dimensions of auxiliary details, such as bearings or sealings. The convenience of CAG lies in the fact that the operator can manipulate proportions and dimensions on the screen until the optimal solution is found, and only then commit it to paper. Moreover, this graphic image and its program can be stored in memory and the design of other analogous wheels accomplished simply by pushing the relevant buttons.

Another application of CAG is in the graphic animation of images. The simplest way to illustrate this is again to use an example—the mechanism shown in Figure 8-1 modified to the view in Figure 8-5. (Point C traces an arc of a circle with a radius of one-half while point D traces a straight line dividing the coordinate angle.) If we want to know the trajectory of motion of some point belonging to a specific link, the animation technique is very useful. It is based on the analytic description of the coordinates of the chosen point. In other words, by substituting current values of time $t_1, t_2 \ldots, t_n$ in a suitable expression, we obtain, on the screen, the trace of the chosen point. By changing the values of sections

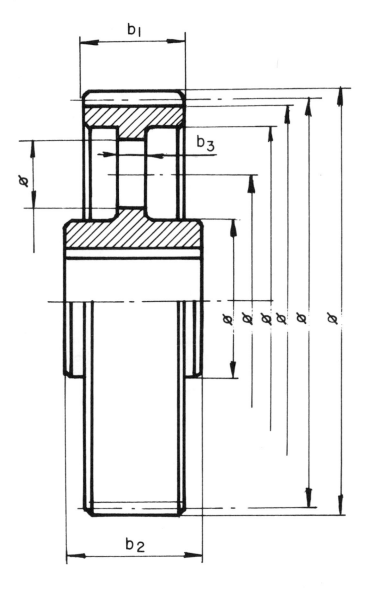

Figure 8-4. Gear wheel.

a and *b*, the operator can seek the proportions that provide the chosen trajectory.

Still another important application of CAG lies in the computer's ability to provide a spatial image of a particular structure by, as it were, rotating the structure in "space," thus allowing the operator to observe the design from different sides and different points of view. The time that can be saved by the use of CAG for this purpose in comparison with manual drafting simply cannot be estimated. Thus complex structures or structural elements with complicated shapes can be treated by CAG, and the influence of changes in the structure or elements can be studied with ease. An excellent example of the utilization of this CAG property is in the design of turbine or propeller blades, or of the bodies of cars or naval vessels. Obviously images are built on the screen by fast coordinate computing based on numbers and formulas or equations stored in the computer's memory.

CAM is the final stage in this chain of computerized activities. During this stage, a blank is transformed into a ready-for-assembly or ready-for-action detail. Only a limited number of manufacturing processes currently can be computerized, and there are some that are not suitable for computerization at all. To the former group belong material cutting and some assembly procedures. The latter group includes molding, stamping, and other kinds of processing based on plastic material deformation.

The principles constituting the basis of computerized manufacturing relate to the calculation of tool coordinates in accord-

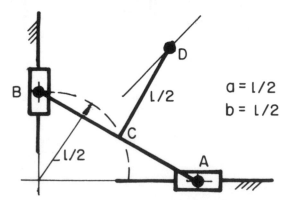

Figure 8-5. Trajectories of two specific points belonging to the connecting rod of a four-link two-slider mechanism.

ance with programs that the machine follows. In considering a computerized numerically controlled (CNC) milling machine, we can describe the motion of the cutter by some analytic expression or by a set or matrix of coordinates defining its location. The dimensions of the cutter can also be taken into account with ease. For example, to cut the profile given in Figure 8-6, the coordinates of the arc centers O_1, O_2, and O_3 must be defined, as must the radii R_1, R_2, and R_3 of the arcs. Then the current coordinates of the cutter's center O_4 are calculated while the coordinates x and y must satisfy the obvious expression:

$$(x - x_1)^2 + (y - y_1)^2 = (R_3 - r)^2$$
$$(x - x_1)^2 + (y - y_1)^2 = (R_2 + r)^2 \tag{10}$$
$$(x - x_2)^2 + (y - y_2)^2 = (R_1 + r)^2$$
$$(x - x_3)^2 + (y - y_3)^2 = (R_3 - r)^2$$

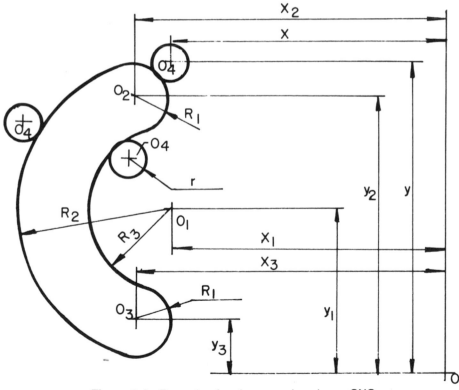

Figure 8-6. Example of a shape produced on a CNC milling machine.

In addition, such a CNC machine can change tools in accordance with previously defined requirements and cutting regimes to provide optimal surface quality in minimal time and with minimal tool wear.

An electronic circuit assembly machine can be analogously programmed. The components (capacitors, resistors, transistors, etc.) that must be positioned are described by codes, and the plate on which the assembly is carried out is positioned in accordance with a coordinate matrix loaded into computer memory. The system can be improved by programming the computer to calculate the shortest trajectories and minimal times of the positioning mechanism. Such improvements obviously increase the efficiency of the process.

Thus we see again that despite the fact that the task that CAM must achieve is physically different from the aims of CAD and CAG, the underlying principles are similar.

The main conclusion that we can derive so far is that any computer-aided activity must be based on:

1. Known mathematical models (formulas, equations, and inequalities) for CAD, CAG, and CAM.
2. Known sets of constants and parameters (coefficients of friction, stiffness coefficients, specific weight, safety factors, allowed stresses, etc.) for engineering purposes.

CAN THE COMPUTER BE CREATIVE?

"The human is smart, creative, and slow. The computer is stupid, noncreative, and fast."[12] In other words, the computer does not possess such human attributes as curiosity, imagination, intuition, and the ability to take the initiative; it does not know how to formulate questions. For this reason the child who is asking, "How much is 3 plus 2?" is much more creative than the computer, despite the fact that the computer "knows" how to solve differential equations. The behavior of a computer is instinctive rather than creative: it follows blindly the program introduced into its memory. From this point of view, its thought pattern is similar to that of an insect or a bird. For millions of years, the seasonal migration of birds has been controlled by an unknown navigation technique. A variety of explanations have been offered for this phenomenon. Some experts feel that visual markers such as seashores are the guides that direct the flight path; others believe the sun or the magnetic field of the earth serves this purpose. The point we wish to make here is that birds are able to find their way without an understanding or a knowledge of astronomy and geography, and without the ability to compute a course. (The sad truth is that those who lose their way die.) When, however, faced with a nonstandard situation, birds and insects become completely "illiterate." Modern science explains such phenomena in terms of innate instincts, genetic codes, or inherent abilities.

The rigid behavior of a migrating bird is reminiscent of that of a computer. For example, a conventional CNC milling machine will continue its cutting process (as shown in Figure 8-6) blindly even if it encounters a hard grain (say, in the cast iron) accidentally present in the material, with the outcome being dictated solely by good or bad luck. Either nothing detrimental will happen (if the grain is small and weak), or the result may be a broken tooth on the cutter, a spoiled part, a slip in one of step motors, or the loss of control. Or let us take the example of a programming error. If in the calculation of the moment of inertia of the beam (Figure 8-2) the expression had accidentally been written incorrectly (say, instead of $I = bh^2/12$, the wrong $I = bh^3/12$), the computer would have continued processing the data without hesitation. How would a creative creature respond in such situations? We can suppose that upon feeling a growing resistance to the cutter's blades, such a creature would stop cutting and start analyzing the source of the resistance, and then derive conclusions and act accordingly—perhaps by decreasing the cutter's speed or changing the blank. In the second example, the error would be revealed practically immediately after the first few results had been obtained, since an experienced engineer would intuitively feel that the values obtained were greatly disparate from the anticipated results. Of course, a torque meter or sensor could be installed in the milling machine and some computerized checking routine used to stop the machine's activity, but such measures are effective only when possible problems can be predicted. The computer is not able to deal with failures that have not been predicted by the programmer.

In contrast to an insect, or a computer, human beings have inherited the ability to handle *nonprogrammed, nonstandard situations*, as well as to create ideas, tools, and concepts. Take the case of the famous actor who had forgotten to darken his arm when appearing in the role of Othello. The astonished audience reacted with whispers, smiles, and laughter as the actor continued his performance. During his next appearance, the audience was even more surprised when, at one point, the actor pulled off a white glove and exposed a dark-colored arm. Only the human brain is capable of this type of creative behavior.

Let us try to understand what makes a certain action creative, whereas another, though much more complicated, is not creative at all. Why should a child at play putting one block on top of another be creative, but a computerized manipulator, a so-called robot, assembling a complicated electronic circuit be considered noninnovative? We do not purport to analyze the nature of creativity or how it can be related to artificial intelligence, but we do intend to examine computer-aided technical creativity. We thus must define where the boundaries of creativity lie.

To return to the playing child, we can ask: "What makes the child creative or innovative?" It is the ability to see in the pile of blocks a tower or a building and to associate it with other things and events. In other words, the capacity for imagination and for formulating and asking questions—the child's curiosity—are the main features determining creativity.

When James Watt encountered a fuel-consumption problem with the steam engine, he responded by questioning what could be done to rectify the waste of fuel. He answered this question by improving piston sealing, applying steam from both sides of the piston, and exploiting the advantages of compound engines. He also created a rotating output and a centrifugal speed governor. Finally, he invented a device that graphically indicated the pressure inside the engine cylinder and then used the device to monitor the performance of the engine and to adjust it to facilitate maximum efficiency.

Some people seem to be born with the ability to play chess well, to "feel" a good move. The chess-playing computer must overcome by blind exhaustive search what the human brain is able to "jump over" by intuition, by inspiration, or by using rules of thumb. Concepts such as esthetics or a sense of elegance are foreign not only to a computerized chess player, but also to a computer-aided creator in any field.

Let us return to the delineation of creativity. We can say that creativity begins when a system (electronic or live) is able to initiate a question or recognize a problem and then devote itself to seeking an answer. The pessimistic view of computerized creativity is that the computer can never be anything other than a high-speed "number cruncher" (it knows how to handle zeros and ones, and it can carry out simple operations such as addition and subtraction millions of times per second). In addition, the computer does not have the ability to make chance discoveries. For example, the computer could not have discovered radioactivity, as did Henry Becquerel when he observed in 1896 that certain salts of uranium were particularly active in spoiling photographic film. The computer also could not have been capable of discovering Newton's law of gravity. Richard Bellman[11] has said: "At present, and most probably forever, we cannot use a computer to recognize structure. However, there is no proof of this conjecture and it may well be possible that tomorrow someone will find a way to use a computer for this purpose."

If computers have such limited capabilities, one might ask, then why continue the search for applications? Computers do have positive features, and a look at these will indicate what awaits us in the field of computer-aided creativity—at least how the computer can be applied in the preparatory stages of design, the preliminary draft work.

The speed at which the computer works is but one of its advantages. The human brain often relies on feelings, while the computer, in a blind, stubborn, but very fast way, may attain the same result. In some instances a "good human brain" may shorten a search by intuitively rejecting deadlocks, but often will wander aimlessly among blind alleys and take many years to find the way out of scientific or technical impasses. This psychological inertia is one of the most serious obstacles to human creativity, especially in applied domains and technical fields. Perhaps computer-aided creative activity will suffer less from psychological inertia (or stereotyping as it is also known). For good or for bad, the computer is not influenced by tradition, and so will not be "embarrassed" to find and to offer an unusual or unfashionable solution. A computer-aided creativity (CAC) system would not have been surprised or felt unsure when offering a front-wheel-drive concept for a car, despite the fact that rear-wheel drive was the convention, or when proposing a circular-arc tooth profile instead of the usual involute or cycloidal profile. A computer could have proposed micromini bathing suits years ago because they would have appeared functional, convenient, and healthful and the computer would not have taken into account norms or prejudices.

Another advantage of CAC systems over human thinking results from the fact that the computer "deals" with collective knowledge. Here we come to the requirement for limiting the volume of the computer's memory. In principle there are no limits to the size of the memory and the amount of information that can be stored. The bigger the volume of stored knowledge, the closer it approaches the so-called ideal. (Ideal knowledge is based on the supposition of an infinitely large memory.)

To be creative a system must possess some knowledge or information. There are two ways of storing information. The first, the direct, way consists of tables or matrixes of numbers. For instance, specific weights of different materials can be simply introduced in the form of a two-dimensional table of friction coefficients, shown in Table 8-1.

The other way to store information is based on the generation of information, that is, the memory is loaded only with the analytic expressions that are used to compute a required number in accordance with required conditions. For instance, the cross-sectional areas, static moments, and moments of inertia or round rods produced by a particular company can be calculated at any time, in accordance with stored formulas, by feeding the computer only the diameters of the rods.

Another advantage of the computer is that it does not become tired (even without coffee breaks). It is able to continue searching where the human brain would be saturated and require rest. In addition, the computer's memory does not forget the input data or, more important, the results obtained.

Thus there is a spark of hope that the advantages of the computer can be applied to creativity, and efforts to attempt to get computers to simulate intellectual activities may be worthwhile. This explains the appearance of the relatively new concepts of artificial intelligence, computerized heuristics. In the field of medicine, for example, computer-aided solution search has already been successfully applied. The question is: How can computers be utilized best in the domain of engineering and technical creativity?

COMPUTER-AIDED CONCEPTUAL DESIGN

We already have discussed some aspects of computer-aided creativity and have seen that this is a very complex problem. Nevertheless, in spite of the limitations imposed by machine-design conceptual constraints, we hope to find some justification for

Table 8-1.
Example of Organization of Information

	Material 1	2	...	i	...	n
Material 1	f_{11}	f_{21}	$\cdots$	f_{i1}	$\cdots$	f_{n1}
———— 2	f_{12}	f_{22}	$\cdots$	f_{i2}	$\cdots$	f_{n2}
· · · · · ·	· ·					
———— i	f_{1i}	f_{2i}	$\cdots$	f_{ii}	$\cdots$	f_{ni}
· · · · · ·	· ·					
———— n	f_{1n}	f_{2n}	$\cdots$	f_{in}	$\cdots$	f_{nn}

Note: f_{in} is the friction coefficient for the pair of materials number i and number n.

the development of algorithms useful in creative machine design. The main problem in introducing the computer into the design stage is the lack of mathematical models describing the solutions. Previously, we saw that any computer-aided activity in engineering is based on the existence of a more or less accurate mathematical description of the phenomenon under investigation. Galileo once said that "mathematics is the language of science"; this is also true for computerization. We must find some way to formalize the processes used in conceptual thinking. But because we do not know what human thinking really is, we cannot try to copy this process. (And, as we showed, earlier, directly copying nature is not always the best way to proceed.)

In this section we show that some computer-aided means of releasing human energies for more interesting and difficult activities are indeed available (although we doubt that there is anything more fascinating than finding new solutions). Algorithms are not necessarily intended for finding high-level solutions; some algorithms can provide computation results that enable the user to make the final decision. Thus the system under consideration really illustrates the interaction of the person with the machine.

The computer deals with binary numbers, with zeros and ones, and so can be used effectively for handling logical operations. As an example, let us formulate two attributes of some set of technical entities:

$$T_1 = \text{high flying speed}$$
$$T_2 = \text{high take-off speed}$$

The 0 denotes the absence of a property, and the 1 the existence of that property. Thus we have Table 8-2.

Table 8-2 automatically gives us a list of all the technical possibilities that relate to the chosen attributes:

0. Slow take-off and slow flight.
1. Fast take-off and slow flight.
2. Slow take-off and fast flight.
3. Fast take-off and fast flight.

Analysis of this list brings us to the idea (case 2) of creating an aircraft (an answer to the "what" problem, but not "how" to achieve it) that does not require long and expensive runways but still achieves high cruising speed. Thus if we load the computer with k attributes, it offers us 2^k combinations. We then provide the computer with information for which combinations already exist, and perhaps also with information as to which combinations do not interest us, and we obtain a list of the remaining possibilities. In our example, case 0 (a helicopter) and case 3 (a conventional airplane) are known, and case 1 seems ridiculous. Therefore, case 2—a brilliant solution of a plane with rotatable wings or engines—is ours! (Here we have answered the "how" question.)

Another very powerful technique that can be applied in computer-aided creativity is the so-called experts' judgment. The computer's memory can store experts' estimations of methods, approaches, shapes, techniques, properties, and so on. As mentioned, one of the advantages of the computer lies in its ability to collect information, knowledge, and experience from many sources. In addition, it is capable of processing this information and producing an average estimation. For instance, we may ask how to produce an opening L millimeters in length and D millimeters in diameter in a specific material. A program tailored to answer such a question would use the recommendations of a number of experts (which do not always coincide). The program would carry out a sort of "voting" procedure, finally recommending what the majority of experts would have recommended. Let us take another example. Say we have to decide what material is suitable for a static structure such as the housing of a ball bearing (where weight is not a particularly significant consideration) of which about 1000

Table 8-2.
Matrix Describing the Set of Entities

	T_1	T_2		
S_1	0	0	0	
S_2	0	1	1	
S_3	1	0	2	decimal numbers
S_4	1	1	3	

units a year will be produced. Most engineers would choose cast iron. This represents the kind of problem, but more complicated in nature, that can be solved by a computer.

To illustrate the next avenue of thinking formalization, we use a historical example. Thomas Young (1773–1829), an outstanding scientist in his day, is famous for his exposition in 1807 of a mechanical constant known as Young's modulus. This constant is used in the well-known equation describing the elasticity of material:

$$\sigma = \varepsilon E \tag{11}$$

where

σ = the stress developed in the material under tensile force
ε = dimensionless elongation, which is defined as the ratio between the elongated pattern and its initial length
E = Young's modulus

We do not know exactly how Young carried out his experiments, but he would have had to invoke the following type of procedure. He would have prepared identical shapes from different materials, and then stretched the shapes by applying increasing forces and simultaneously recording the change in the lengths of the shapes. In dividing the new length L by the original L_0, he would have calculated ε:

$$\varepsilon = L/L_0 \tag{12}$$

Then he would have built the dependence between the applied force F and ε. We assume that the area of the cross section A of the shapes did not change during the elongation, and therefore the stress σ is proportional to the applied force F:

$$\sigma = F/A \tag{13}$$

Young then would have possessed the group of dependences that enabled him to derive the following conclusion: In the range of elasticity, every material under stretching load changes its length in proportion to the applied force and is described by a specific constant or proportionality coefficient E.

Now let us imagine that groups of numbers gathered from these experiments were introduced into a computer programmed to look for analytic approximations. The computer would reveal very quickly that the best approximation is a linear one and that the proportionality coefficients for each group equal a certain constant. If we give some thought to this example, we see that the human brain can be stimulated by information collected from observation or experiments (as in the case of Thomas Young). On the other hand, the computer is not able to initiate (at least for the time being) a search since it does not possess the curiosity to analyze the numbers; however, as we see from the example of Young's modulus, it can simulate the process of analysis. In such a case, the computer operates quickly and accurately, and can estimate the reliability of the "discovered" laws. We must emphasize here that the computer has been programmed for this type of discovery. For technical purposes, we would consider it a satisfactory achievement if the computer could solve creative problems on the level of Young's law.

To enable the computer to approach creative problems, therefore, we have to feed the memory with information and certain rules to handle it. This requires a coding or language. We mentioned earlier that the creative, conceptual stage of design cannot be described in terms of mathematics, but because of the nature of the computer, cooperation with it can be built only on a mathematical basis. We thus have to find formulas, equations, and algorithms imitating the processes of technical creativity. In other words, we have to furnish the computer with rules and strategies in a form it can understand. This formalization of creativity in the field of engineering is the task of those who want to mobilize the computer's power in the search for technical concepts and innovation. Of course, we cannot expect a comprehensive computerized answer to problem solving to appear in the near future. The creation of such a program is not a routine operation, and is more of an art than a science.

Let us consider one more illustration of a possible formalization method—this time in the "how" category. Let us say the problem is to find an optimal solution for a device with definite kinematic properties, for instance, a planar mechanism providing a linear reciprocating output for a rotating input motion. For creative problems of this type, the computer's memory must first be supplied with the available relevant knowledge. (This step must be taken before the question arises, and constitutes a "library" that is continuously enriched. Thus when using it for a particular problem, one is not aware of the content of the memory.) The type of information that would be stored in the computer's memory is shown in Table 8-3:

Table 8-3

Section of Stored Information

i	B_i	Figure no.
1. Four-bar linkage		8-7
2. Cam mechanism		8-8
3. Gear transmission		8-9
4. Belt drive		8-10
5. Frictional drive		8-11
6. Crankshaft-slider mechanism		8-12
7. Noncircular wheel gear transmission		8-13
8. Rack and wheel		8-14
9. Cylindrical pneumomechanism and		
10. Cylindrical hydromechanism		8-15

i

n

Figure 8-7. Four-bar linkage (See Tables 8-3 and 8-4.)

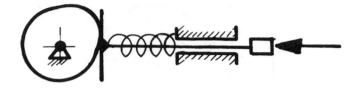

Figure 8-8. Cam mechanism (See Tables 8-3 and 8-4.)

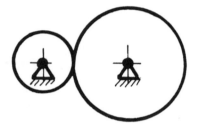

Figure 8-9. Gear transmission (See Tables 8-3 and 8-4.)

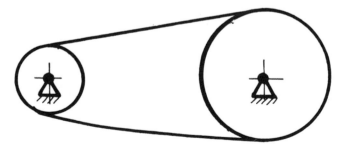

Figure 8-10. Belt drive (See Tables 8-3 and 8-4.)

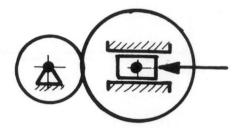

Figure 8-11. Frictional drive (See Tables 8-3 and 8-4.)

Figure 8-12. Crankshaft-slider mechanism. (See Tables 8-3 and 8-4.)

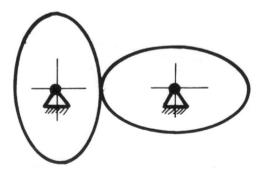

Figure 8-13. Noncircular wheel gear transmission. (See Tables 8-3 and 8-4.)

Figure 8-14. Rack and wheel (See Tables 8-3 and 8-4.)

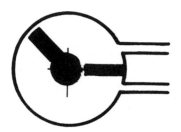

Figure 8-15. Cylindrical pneumomechanism and cylindrical hydromechanism
(See Tables 8-3 and 8-4.)

Table 8-4.
Set of Atributes Describing Subjects in Table 8-3

j   *Q*

1. *The driving link rotates*
2. *The driving link moves with an angular motion*
3. *The driving line moves with a linear motion*
4. *The driven link rotates*
5. *The driven link moves with an angular motion*
6. *The driven link moves with a linear motion*
7. *The mechanism is planar*
8. *The mechanism is spatial*
9. *Discontinuous motion*
10. *Continuous motion*
11. *Interrupted motion*
12. *Constant ratio*
13. *Periodical ratio*
14. *Nonlinear ratio*

j

k

In Table 8-3 each line represents an entity B_i *that potentially can be a sought-after solution. The proposed algorithm requires a quantitative description of each entity. For this purpose a set of properties* Q_j is introduced (Table 8-4).

We now have *n* entities described by *k* properties or attributes. Each line in Table 8-3 thus can be stored in the computer's memory by a *k*-dimensional binary vector because the simplest way of formalizing this information is to write it in the following manner:

$$\bar{B}_i(q_{i1} \cdots, q_{ij} \cdots, q_{ik}) \tag{14}$$

where

$$q_{ij} = \begin{cases} 0, \text{ when the property } Q_j \text{ does not exist} \\ \\ 1, \text{ when the property } Q_j \text{ does exist} \end{cases} \tag{15}$$

Upon organizing this information, we obtain Table 8-5.

Therefore, in the computer memory the information describing all known mechanisms appears as a matrix, a fragment of which is shown in Table 8-6.

Table 8-5.
Organization of Information from Equations (14) and (15)

	Q_1	$\cdots$	Q_j	$\cdots$	Q_k
B_1	q_{11}	$\cdots$	q_{1j}	$\cdots$	q_{1k}
$\cdots$	$\cdots$	$\cdots$	$\cdots$	$\cdots$	$\cdots$
B_i	q_{i1}	$\cdots$	q_{ij}	$\cdots$	q_{ik}
$\cdots$	$\cdots$	$\cdots$	$\cdots$	$\cdots$	$\cdots$
B_n	q_{n1}	$\cdots$	q_{nj}	$\cdots$	q_{nk}

Obviously the sought-for solution C can also be described as a binary vector in the following form.

$$\overline{C} \ (P_1, \cdots, P_j, \cdots, P_k) \tag{16}$$

And here also

$$P_j = \begin{cases} 0, \text{ when the property } Q_j \text{ is not required} \\ \\ 1, \text{ when the property } Q_j \text{ is required} \end{cases} \tag{17}$$

The algorithm must find those known and stored solutions that best fit the required conditions. What the algorithm does can be expressed as follows:

$$\overline{S} = \overline{B}_i(q_{i1}, \cdots, q_{ij}, \cdots, q_{ik}) - \overline{C}(P_1, \cdots, P_j, \cdots, P_k) = 0 \tag{18}$$

To describe equation (18) in words, we subtracted the sought-after value from each of the stored values and ordered the computer to print out only those i numbers (remember, i is the number of a line in Table 8-5 that corresponds to a specific mechanism)

Table 8-6.
Matrix Fragment

10001010010010
10000110010010
10010010010100
10010011010100
10010011010100
10000110010010
10010010010010
01000111100010
00001110001000
00001110001000

that promise complete identity of properties between the stored
and sought-for mechanism. The mechanism we are seeking can be
formally described in terms of equation (16) in the following form.

$$\overline{C} \; (P_j) = 10000110010000$$

Thus the operator obtains several different solutions for the general case. In our specific example, these solutions may be

1. Crankshaft-slider mechanism.
2. A cam and slider-follower.

Lines 2 and 6 fit this description, and from Table 8-3 we find the
"unknown" mechanism.

EXERCISES

1. Try to "invent" new machine tools imitating the creativity
process with the aid of the algorithm shown in Table 8-2 for the
following list of attributes.

T_1—the blank rotates
T_2—the blank moves linearly
T_3—the cutter rotates
T_4—the cutter moves linearly

2. Continue Table 8-3 for about another ten entries and describe them in binary form using the attributes given in Table 8-
4.
3. What mechanism will answer the sought vector $\overline{c}$ described
in the following form?

$$10010010010100$$

Describe it in words in accordance with Table 8-4.

Chapter *9*

MARKETING

We have discussed the technical aspects of the design process of new engineering-based products, machines, and devices. There is, however, a wide field of activity that is devoted to introducing the engineer's creation to the consumer. This activity is aimed at producing income for the manufacturer, not only as profit, but also to compensate the manufacturer for expenses incurred in the development of the new product and to facilitate its further improvement. At this stage salespeople rather than engineers are usually mobilized to deal with market penetration. The marketing problems involved are based on:

* The commercial situation.
* The psychological and intellectual orientation of the consumer society.
* The political climate.
* The technological level of the society.

Thus the engineers turn over the articles which they have created to salespeople for introduction to the marketplace. Obviously there must be some interaction between these two groups of workers.

THE PROBLEMS

In this section some ideas pertaining to the marketing aspects of design are considered briefly. It should be noted that, to some extent, the problem of marketing should be dealt with in the "what" and "how" solution-seeking directions. When a new product, machine, or device (a new "what") is introduced into the market, the problems differ from those that arise when a new model of an existing product (a new "how") penetrates the market.

For a product, machine, or device to be competitive, it must be characterized by one or more of the following.

* It must be cheaper—which implies lower costs of production, exploitation, and installation.
* It must be more functional—that is, be more efficient, more accurate, more reliable, safer, more productive, and so on.
* It must be more esthetic—that is, be more pleasing in form, color, texture, and so on.
* It must be more easily exploitable—that is, be more convenient to use, smaller, lighter (if desirable), and so on.

If the company is already in the market to which the new product belongs, it is, of course, in a better competitive position. Otherwise it must offer something that will surpass the merits of competitors' products to a superlative degree. From this point of view, "how" solutions are pertinent to those manufacturers already in the relevant business. Newcomers to a particular marketing branch must come out with new "whats" if they intend to penetrate the market.

It is of great importance to distinguish between inner and outer markets; that is, the volume of the market plays a significant role in decision making. This is especially true for small countries. No less important is the geographical location of the market. What is worthless in one place can be sold in another. For instance, engineers working on a chlorination device for swimming pools found an original solution for chlorination of the water. The question then arose as to whether it would be possible to apply these ideas to water chlorination in general. After a market search had been conducted, it was concluded that in some underdeveloped countries that lack central water-purification facilities, the new device could be installed in private homes to chlorinate well water for domestic consumption.

This is an example of a product finding a market because of the relatively low technical level of the country. It would be a mistake, however, to assume that any product could be sold here. Care must be taken not to attempt to introduce "overqualified" products into this type of market: the lack of service for the product, machine, or device, and the relatively low technical expertise of the users will combine to make the introduction a failure. For example, one cannot sell modern automobiles in a country with no modern roads (unfortunately such societies often purchase tanks and the like).

Thus the questions the designer must answer before a technical solution can be offered for marketing are not solely of a technical nature. A wide range of commercial and juridical considerations also must be taken into account before the decision can be made as to whether the product will succeed in the market. To this end a substantial market research effort is usually devoted to determining the place of the new product in the market. Of course, it would be preferable to have a complete picture of the market before efforts to create a new product are even initiated, but in practice it is very often the case that only after a product or solution has been created is enough information available for conducting market research.

When a market search is carried out, the time factor must always be kept in mind. To develop a machine, device, or product, time is needed. Time is also needed to investigate the market requirements, the commercial aspects, and the technical specifications. As a result of these seemingly banal facts, the engineer often is successful in creating a product, only to find that it has little or no commercial effect.

THE CONCLUSIONS

From the foregoing discussion, we can draw the following conclusions:

1. To save time market research and product development should be carried out to some extent in parallel.
2. It is sometimes better to patent a nonperfected product than not to develop it at all.

These conclusions can be illustrated by the following example. Engineers in the author's company came up with the idea of developing a device that would warn drivers when they exceeded the speed limit, and thus help ensure a safer ride. Because we realized that such an idea was too simple to be original, in parallel with the beginning of the development of the device, we began to investigate the market. We knew that the simplest technical solution would be mechanically to link the speed indicator of the warning device to the rotating parts of the car engine or transmission. Thus to increase the potential for marketing the product, we decided to avoid using mechanical connections. We felt that this approach would offer the following advantages.

1. The possibility of inventing something already invented would be less.

2. The buyer would have no problem in installing the new product (a convenience property of the product).

3. From the previous point, it follows that the general cost to the consumer would be lower.

4. The device would be more easily adaptable to different car models.

Most of the competitive devices already available on the market, and those that appeared at about the same time (about 1980), were designed to be inserted between the speedometer of the car and the flexible cable shaft. Another type of competitive device included an adapter that had to be fastened to the ignition distributor shaft. The latter had the disadvantage that the gear ratio influences the operation of the device.

Our approach led to the birth of a device—called "the speed warning bleeper"—which, although not the only one on the market, was competitive with the others, because the time factor had been taken into account during its development.

Another example was the invention of the carbon lamp in 1878–79 by Thomas Edison (1847–1931). He also designed and manufactured all the accessories required for the introduction of his lighting techniques. His invention was, however, a failure because it was based on the use of direct current. During the same period, Edison's competitor Nikola Tesla (1856–1943) invented the much more efficient polyphase alternating-current system. A power struggle ensued between Edison and Westinghouse (who bought the rights to Tesla's patent). Of course, this quarrel impeded the technical progress of both parties to a certain extent. Modern engineering history abounds with such collisions. Engineers often have to design an entirely new product rather than improve an existing article to circumvent competitors' patents. In addition, an original patent is sometimes bought, but never exercised, for commercial reasons. For example, even though the new product might not have great intrinsic value, it might affect the profit of a competitive item. In this case purchase of the rights to the new patent stops the "intruder" from penetrating the market. This is another example of marketing policy that has nothing to do with technical solution seeking. This aspect of marketing will not be discussed here. We will deal only with the creative and technical aspects of marketing problems (while keeping the political aspects in mind).

We view the first step in this direction as the market study. There are a number of examples that show that patent laws and commercial interests may prevent optimal technical solutions from penetrating the market in the best way. We will consider two of these.

The first is a well-known story. James Watt (1736–1819), the inventor of the steam engine, could not use the simple, reliable slider-crank mechanism for transmission of the reciprocating piston motion into rotation of the crank and the flywheel. This widely known (and today much used) mechanism had already been patented by somebody else. Watt created another four-bar linkage to guide the piston rod of his engine on an approximately straight path, and in 1781 he invented the sun-and-planet gear for generating the rotating motion.

The second example is taken from our own experience. Before finalizing the design of a flowmeter and commencing its manufacture, we performed a market analysis. Some of the conclusions we reached as a result of this analysis are used in the following to illustrate what a market search is all about.

It appeared that:

1. There are three main fields of application for flowmeters for low flow rates (such as the type we developed); these are, in order of preference:

    a. Medical uses.

    b. Measurement of fuel consumption.

    c. General uses in chemical and other laboratories.

2. The flowmeters already on the market designed for a flow range of about 0.2–10 cm^3 sell for about \$200–\$250, whereas the price of our device was estimated at about \$30.

3. The design concept we used for our flowmeter had certain advantages over existing competitive designs.

4. Medical applications require far higher sensitivity than we could offer (thus, despite the fact that this domain could constitute the biggest market, we had to withdraw from the medical field).

5. Flowmeters of the type under consideration must be able to sustain a certain internal pressure (about 20 atm).

This market analysis, together with a working prototype, was presented to potential manufacturers. Our offer was accepted by a modestly sized company involved in the fluid and gas-flow measuring business. The subsequent turn of events constitutes a good example of the difficulties that accompany the process of introducing a new product into the market.

The engineers of the accepting company redesigned the flowmeter so that it could be manufactured by using metal- and plastics-casting techniques (the prototype was designed to be produced by cutting). On the basis of the amount of material that was needed and the production costs involved, it was estimated that the selling price could be fixed at as little as \$25 per unit for batches of about 10,000–15,000 meters (the price being dictated by the modest market in which the company was involved). For purposes of strength (ability to withstand 20-atm inner pressure) and resistance to chemical attack by the fluids flowing through the meter, a special kind of plastic material was chosen. This material is produced by a large company in the United States and (as became evident only during negotiations with the company) can be provided only in the form of the completed article and not as the raw material. As a result costs for production of the flowmeter had to be recalculated, and the decision made under these specific circumstances was to postpone production of the device.

The conclusions we can draw from this specific example can be generalized:

1. When a product or article is redesigned so that less material is required in its manufacture or so that its weight and/or size are reduced, the new product becomes more competitive. The reason is, obviously, the lowering of its selling price as the result of the reduction in material and transportation costs. Sometimes a device must be made more sophisticated before weight and size can be reduced.

2. The potential market for a new article may be satisfactory for a medium-sized company working within a modest market, but completely unprofitable for a large company.

Let us now consider an unusual example. Company X is in the orange business, as are companies Y and Z. What can X do to compete successfully with Y and Z? (Company X enters into the "how" domain.) Make the oranges better? This would, of course, be a step in the right direction, but here the problem of agricultural selection arises: such a path takes years to complete and its outcome is certainly doubtful. Perhaps it would be worthwhile to consider peeled oranges. Perhaps a highly productive machine and process could be designed to "strip" the oranges and wrap them in attractive paper or in plastic. Perhaps the peel could be made edible—sweet or tart. Or perhaps each orange could be packed with a cheap knife for peeling it.

A different approach would entail making the oranges cheaper to the consumer. One way of reducing the price would be to cut down on transportation expenses. For instance, a change from air freight to ships would reduce the expenses considerably, but the problem then arises of how to keep the fruit fresh while being shipped. One Israeli company has found a solution to this type of problem for tomatoes. It has developed a product with an extended shelf life: the tomatoes remain unspoiled for about three months (but this again is a problem of agricultural selection). Another way to reduce the cost of transportation would be better utilization of the cargo's volume: cubic oranges would occupy less space (about 50 percent) in the hold of a ship or aircraft; or cube-shaped eggs packed in plastic sheets not only would save volume, but also would provide a solution to the problem of handling the cargo "like eggs."

As has already been discussed, to capture the market a product must be cheaper than its competitors, have at least the same quality, and serve the same comparative purposes. One of the most effective means of achieving this aim is to make the product disposable wherever possible and acceptable. It then can be mass produced, and the most effective manufacturing and processing techniques can be used. In this way costs can be reduced, as can the selling price per product unit. Three excellent examples of this type of marketing policy are as follows.

1. Single-use injection syringes and infusion containers can be produced from plastics instead of from glass and metal, since they do not have to stand up to the demands of repeated sterilization. These medical items can thus be mass produced by highly productive casting machines.

2. Many soft-drink containers are now in the form of light metal or plastic cans (instead of glass bottles). Here again, highly productive machines can be used for their manufacture. The low weight of these containers reduces transportation expenses, the fact that they are disposable reduces strength requirements, and washing problems are obviated. Costs can thus be reduced dramatically.

3. The ballpoint pen with a disposable refill is another good example of the manufacture of a cost-effective product. The demand for refills is sufficiently large to warrant completely automatic mass production and assembly of the components of the refills. In this way the expenses per refill become so low that the market is flooded with several kinds of refills produced by several companies.

Another powerful weapon that can be used to capture the market is the development of an article that is more universal than those now available and thus can replace a whole range of products. Consider the following example.

Any automatic or semiautomatic machine used in manufacturing is equipped with one or more feeders, that is, devices that automatically provide the processing units of the machine with raw materials and parts. For many years there was a large variety of feeders on the market—drum, bin, revolving plate, swinging, plunger, sweep-fork. In the 1950s, a feeder based on a new concept—vibration—appeared, and soon replaced almost all the existing types of feeders used in automatic production machines. In this way the market was increased considerably, and the chances for commercial success of the product were similarly improved. The vibrating-feeder concept (see Principle IV) is thus a shining example of the effect that can be achieved by introducing a revolutionary idea for solving a "how" type of problem. Vibrating feeders are much more universal, more flexible, and cheaper than their predecessors.

Let us now look at a different way of market penetration. Many products on the consumer market can be improved or changed so as to obtain new properties by integration of an additional part or device. This is often typical of electronic equipment, but is also true for mechanical and combination items. The creation of such adapters is a useful tool for penetrating a market. Obviously in the initial development stage these adapters belong to the "what" kind of problem.

The "speed warning bleeper" serves as an example of such an adapter. The tremendous number of cars on the roads provides a reasonable source of optimism in the prediction of the marketing fate of the device. The air compressor driven by a car's exhaust gases is another example of such an adapter-type product. Perhaps someone can design an adapter to transform a washing machine into a dishwasher.

In this book we have considered the conceptual design process from the very beginning when the question of "what" to design is first formulated, and have gone through the stages of "how" to solve the specific technical problems. We have also shown the interaction of the design process as creative thinking with the marketing issue. At this point it seems appropriate to wish the reader good luck in the creative process. Should this text prompt some useful associations and help to initiate fruitful ideas, the author will feel deep satisfaction with his endeavors.

Appendix

BIBLIOGRAPHY

1. Altshuller, H.S., *The Algorithm of an Invention* (in Russian), Moskovskij Rabochy, Moscow, 1973.
2. Hansen, R.F., *Konstruktionssystematik. Grundlagen für Eine Allgemeine Konstruktionslehre*, VEB Verlag Technik, Berlin.
3. Jewkes, J., Sawers, D., and Stillerman, R., *The Sources of Invention*, 2d ed., Norton, New York.
4. Krick, E.V., *An Introduction to Engineering and Engineering Design*, Wiley, New York, 1965.
5. Mayall, W.H. *Principles in Design*, 1st ed., Van Nostrand Reinhold, 1979.
6. Orlov, P.I., *The Basics of Design* (in Russian), Mashynostrojenie, Moscow, 1968.
7. Phal, G., and Beitz, B., *Konstruktonslehre*, Springer Verlag, Berlin, 1976.
8. Rodemacker, Wolf G., *Methodisches Konstruiren*, Springer Verlag, Berlin, 1976.
9. Hubka, V., *Theorie der Konstruktionsprocesse*, Springer Verlag, Berlin, 1976.
10. Artobolevsky, I.I., *Mechanisms in Modern Engineering Design*, 6 vols. (translated from Russian by N. Weinstein), MIR Publishers, Moscow, 1975.
11. Bellman, R. *An Introduction to Artificial Intelligence: Can a Computer Think?* Boyd & Fraser, San Francisco, 1978.
12. Rayen, D. L. *Computer-aided Kinetics for Machine Design*. Marcel Dekker, New York, 1981.

References 1–5 and 7–9 constitute excellent reading material in the field of conceptual and creative design and thinking. Reference 6 is an excellent source of the knowledge, rules, and ideas of design and of solution choices in the "how" direction (unfortunately it is available only in Russian). Reference 10 is a superlative collection of kinematic, mechanical, hydraulic, pneumatic, and electromagnetic solutions. References 11 and 12 discuss the role of the computer.

RECOMMENDED READING

The following list gives additional material on different aspects of creative thinking and conceptual design.

Archer, B., "A View of the Nature of Design Research," in *Design: Science: Method* (R. Jacques and J.A. Powell, eds.)., Westbury House, 1981.

Asimow, M., *Introduction to Design*, Prentice-Hall, Englewood Cliffs, N.J., 1966.

Bowman, W. *Graphic Communication*, Wiley, New York, 1968.

Burstall, A.F., *A History of Mechanical Engineering*, Faber & Faber, 1963, 86 pp.

Chestnut, H. *System Engineering Methods*, Wiley, New York, 1967.

Cooper, R.G., "Project New Product, Factors in New Product Success," *Europ. J. Marketing*, 14:277–292, 1980.

De Bono, E., *Teaching Thinking*, Temple Smith, London, 1976.

Faradane, J., *Information for Design. Design Method*, Buttersworth, London, 1966.

French, M.J., *Engineering Design, the Conceptual Stage*, Heinemann, London, 1971.

Glegg, G.L., *The Science of Design*, Cambridge University Press, Cambridge, England, 1973.

Gordon, W.J.J., *Synectics. The Development of Creative Capacity*, Harper & Row, New York, 1961.

Gregory, S.A., *The Design Method*, Buttersworth, London, 1966.

Gregory, S.A., "What We Know About Designing and How We Know It. Current Design Thinking", *I. Chem. E. Midlands*, 815:1–13, 1979.

Hubka, V., *Principles of Engineering Design*, Buttersworth, London, 1982.

Jones, J.C., *Design Methods, Seeds of Human Futures*, Wiley, New York, 1970.

Jones, J.C., *Design Methods*, Wiley, New York, 1980.

Jones, J.C. and Thornley, D.G., *Conference on Design Methods*, Pergamon, Oxford, 1963.

Kardos, G., in *Planning and Creating Successful Engineering Designs* (S.F. Love, ed.), Van Nostrand, New York, 1980.

Krick, E.V., *An Introduction to Engineering Methods, Concepts and Issues*, Wiley, New York, 1976.

Lenat, D.B., "An Artificial Intelligence Approach to Discovery in Mathematics as Heuristic Search," in *Knowledge-Based Systems in AI* (R. Davis and D. Lenat, eds.), McGraw-Hill, New York, 1982.

Love, F., *Planning and Creating Successful Engineering Design*, Van Nostrand Reinhold, New York, 1980.

Marples, D.L., *The Decisions of Engineering Design*, Institute of Engineering Designers, London, 1960.

Morrison, D., *Engineering Design, the Choice of Favourable Systems*, McGraw-Hill, London, 1968.

Nilson, N.J., *Principles of Artificial Intelligence*, Tioga, Palo Alto, Calif., 1980.

Osborn, A.F., *Applied Imagination*, Scribner's, New York, 1963.

Ostrofsky, B. *Design, Planning and Development Methodology*, Prentice-Hall, Englewood Cliffs, N.J., 1977.

Pugh, S., "Concept Selection—The Ability to Compete," presented at Design Policy Conference at the Royal College of Art, London, July 1982.

Pugh, S., "Concept Selection—A Method That Works," *Proceedings International Conference Engineering Design* (ICED 81), Rome, 1981, pp. 497–506.

Pugh, S., and Smith, D.G., "The Danger of Design Methodology," presented at First European Design Research Conference, Changing Design, Portsmouth Polytechnic, 1976.

Roe, P.H., Soulis, G.N., and Handa, V.K., *The Discipline of Design*, Allyn & Bacon, Boston, 1967.

Roth, K., *Konstruiren mit Konstruktion-katalogen*, Springer Verlag, Berlin, 1982.

Rzevski, G., "On the Design of a Design Methodology," in *Design: Science: Method* (R. Jacques and J.A. Powell, Eds.), Westbury House, 1981.

Vesper, K.H., *Engineers at Work: A Case Book.* Houghton Mifflin, Boston, 1975.

Wallace, K.M., "Engineering Design Research," in *Design: Science: Method* (R. Jacques and J.A. Powell, eds.), Westbury House, 1981.

Wallace, P.J., *The Techniques of Design*, Pitman, London, 1952.

Wells, G.L., "A Study of Some Process Heuristics—Current Design Thinking," *In Chem. E. Midlands*, 612:1-10, 1979.

Weinberg, M. *An Introduction to General Systems Thinking*, Wiley, New York, 1975.

INDEX